IRISH ARTS REVIEW YEARBOOK

Volume 12
1996

IRISH ARTS REVIEW LIMITED

Sponsored by Glen Dimplex

IRISH ARTS REVIEW

P.O. Box 3500, Dublin 4. Ireland

Yearbook 1996 Volume 12

Publisher : Ann Reihill

Editor : Homan Potterton
Assistant Editor : Elizabeth Mayes
Advertising : Vera Finnegan
Subscriptions : Breda Conway

Editorial Advisors

Mairead Dunlevy is Director of the Hunt Museum, Limerick on secondment from
the Arts and Industrial Division of the National Museum of Ireland
Brian Ferran is Chief Executive of the Arts Council of Northern Ireland and a practising artist
John Meagher is an architect in private practice in de Blacam and Meagher and a director of the
Irish Museum of Modern Art
Alistair Smith is Director of the Whitworth Art Gallery, Manchester and a former
Editor of Irish Arts Review
Roger Stalley is Professor of the History of Art at Trinity College, Dublin

Cover Illustration
Aloysius O'Kelly (1851-c. 1928), *Girl in a Meadow*.
Oil on canvas, 45.7 x 35.5 cm. (Private Collection)

Frontispiece
Michael Warren (b. 1950): *Wood Quay*, 1995. Dublin. Red American cedarwood on steel frame,
ht. 10m on a white Portugese limestone podium, 17m long.

British Library Cataloguing in Publication Data
A catalogue record for this book is available from the British Library
Irish Arts Review Yearbook is indexed in BHA: Bibliography of the History of Art

ISBN 0 9523876 2 X (hardback); 0 9523876 3 8 (paperback); ISSN 0791-3540

IRISH ARTS REVIEW is published annually in November.
Price: IR£35 (hardback): IR£22.50 (paperback)

Subscription prices (inclusive of postage):
IR£30 (hardback) IR£20 (paperback)
Address for subscriptions: P.O. Box 3500, Dublin 4

IRISH ARTS REVIEW receives grants from the Arts Council of Northern Ireland
the Irish Arts Council/An Chomhairle [Grant-aided by the Arts Council] and assistance from the
Cultural Relations Committee of the Irish Department of Foreign Affairs

IRISH ARTS REVIEW is published for Ann Reihill by Irish Arts Review Limited, PO Box 3500, Dublin 4, Ireland
© *Irish Arts Review Limited 1995*

Designed by John Power
Typeset by Pat Brennan
Printed in Northern Ireland by Nicholson & Bass

IRISH

BOOK

CONTENTS
IRISH ARTS REVIEW YEARBOOK 1996 : VOL 12

CONTENTS

IRISH ARTS REVIEW YEARBOOK 1996 : VOL 12

FOREWORD

BY
THE EXECUTIVE CHAIRMAN OF GLEN DIMPLEX
SPONSORS OF IRISH ARTS REVIEW YEARBOOK 1996

Once again we are delighted to support the Irish Arts Review. This edition, the twelfth, follows on from the inspiration of past editions and provides a distinctive and wide ranging view of the arts. It celebrates the best of Irish and we are proud to be associated with it.

Martin Naughton
Executive Chairman Glen Dimplex

GLEN DIMPLEX

Bank of Ireland

College Green, Dublin 2

90-00-17

Valid for

Date   1996

Pay Bearer   *One Historic Day*

in

The House of Lords

Signed   *Liam Mac Thomáis.*

1783 - 1996   1808 - 1996

Guided tour dates for House of Lords 1996

Every Tuesday
during 1996
(except Bank Holidays)

Group Bookings

Tel: 6615933, ext. 2265

Tour Times:

10.30 am to 11.15 am
11.30 am to 12.15 pm
1.45 pm to 2.30 pm

Bank of Ireland

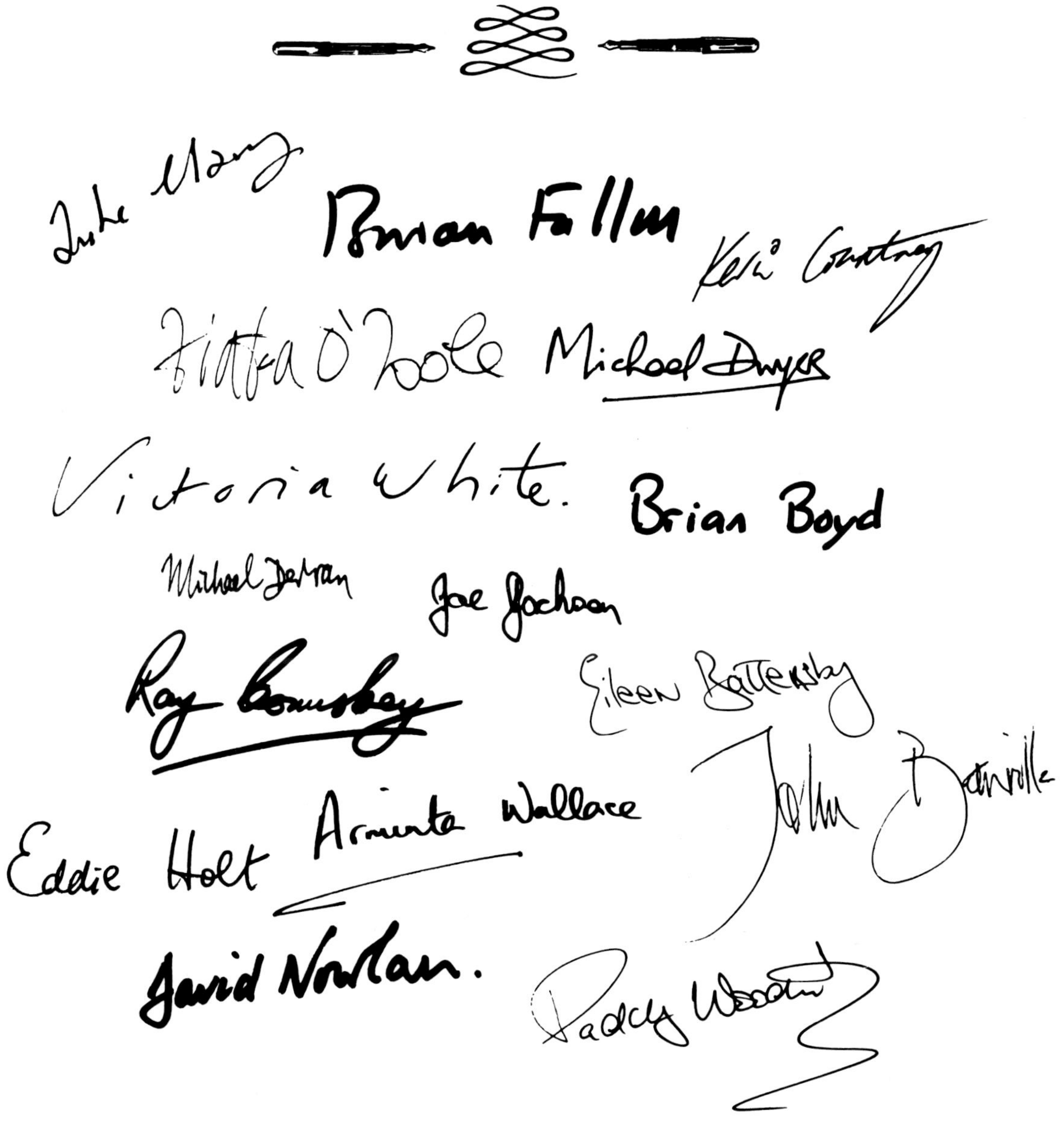

The Arts Counsel.

From the Cannes Film Festival to The Comedy Cellar.
From the Wexford Opera Festival to the Dublin Theatre Festival. The Arts,
with the experts, every day, including Sound and Vision every Friday.

THE IRISH TIMES

FOR THE TIMES WE LIVE IN

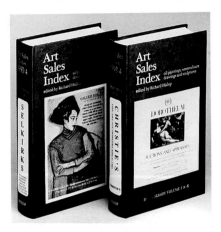

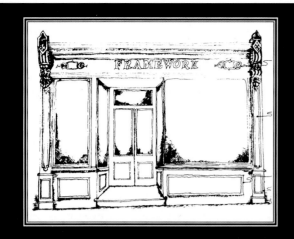
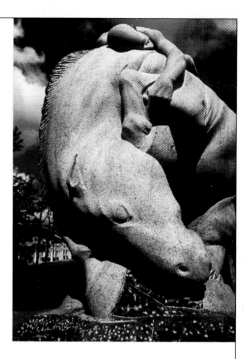

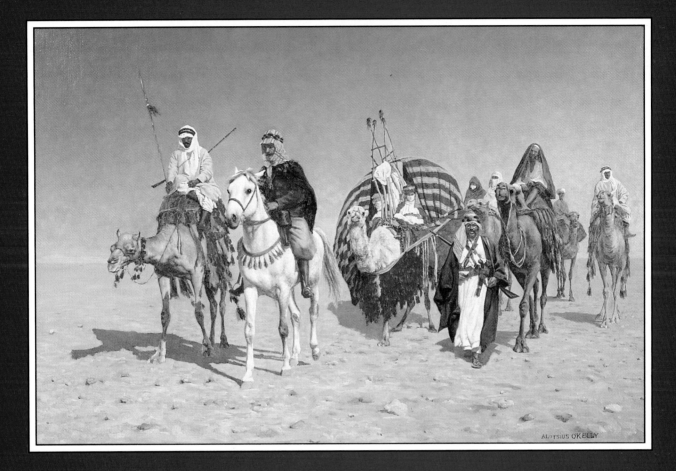

MEALY'S

THE SPECIALISTS IN IRISH COUNTRY HOUSE CLEARANCE SALES

We also specialise in the sale of fine art, antique furniture, rare books, clocks, paintings, glass, ceramics, carpets, rugs, light fittings, bronzes, garden, statuary& furniture, arms & armoury, silver etc.

We conduct regular specialised and general sales at our spacious modern auction galleries, Castlecomer, Co Kilkenny

Benjamin Williams Leader, R.A. 1831-1923 "A Welsh Stream in Summer Time" O.O.C., Signed and dated. Realised: £29,100 including premium. Sale 6th December, '94.

This superb quality Irish Georgian period mahogany Architect's Desk realised £12,300 (including premium) at our sale at Moyne Park on the 25th October, '94.

A very important Satsuma earthenware Vase by Ryozan – signed, Meiji period, with the Yasuda Co. Trade Mark, 15' realised £14,000 including premium, sold at McDonnells Part II June '94.

"The Joseph R. O'Reilly Memorial Cup – Fairyhouse Races (Ward Union Hunt), 1934" Dublin c. 1934 Realised £13,500 including premium, sold at McDonnells Part II, June '94.

A photograph from The Howard Bury Archive which contained numerous letters, journals, diaries, photographs etc. relating to the First Mount Everest Expedition which was sold at our December Book Sale realising £36,300 including premium.

Castlecomer, Co Kilkenny, Ireland
Phone No: 056-41229/41413 Fax: 056-41627

National Library of Ireland

KILDARE STREET
DUBLIN 2.

Photo: Peter Moloney
Courtesy of: Norton Associates

Telephone: +353-1-661 8811 Fax: +353-1-676 6690

The Irish Sale 1995

Sotheby's Irish Sale in London on Friday 2nd June was the most important sale
of its kind for many years and totalled £3.6 million. All sections of the sale went well with many
prices far outstripping their estimates with six lots reaching over £100,000.

Bidding, which at times was fierce, was truly international with strong interest
coming from America. The sale was well received by both sellers and buyers alike and
was extensively and favourably covered by national and international press.

Walter Frederick
Osborne, R.H.A.
(1859-1903),
The Garden Party,
signed, oil on canvas,
61cm x 46cm
(24 by 18in).
Sold for £271,000.

A carved wood mirror,
circa 1750,
attributed to John and
Francis Booker,
173cm high x 79cm wide
(5ft 8in, by 2ft 7in).
Sold for £34,500.

A Belleek 'Lipton'
flower pot
second period
(1891-1926),
26.5cm (10⅖in).
Sold for £4,255.

A George III silver
dish ring,
John Craig, Dublin,
1775,
530 grams, diameter
21.3cm (8⅜in).
Sold for £2,300.

Francis Wheatley, R.A.
(1747-1801),
*A Peasant Woman
Carrying Wood*,
signed, coloured chalks
and stump heightened
with watercolour,
42.5cm x 30cm
(16¾ by 11⅞in).
Sold for £4,830.

An interesting Irish wine
fountain and cover,
probably Cork,
circa 1800.
56.5cm (22⅛in).
Sold for £9,775.

Thomas Roberts
(1748-1778),
*A View of Slane Castle,
The Seat of Lord
Conyngham*,
oil on canvas,
40.5cm x 60cm.
(16 by 23½in).
Sold for £91,700.

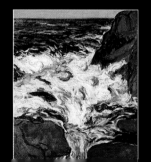

Roderic O'Conor,
R.H.A., (1860-1940),
*Maree Montante
(Rising Tide)*,
signed, oil on canvas,
65cm x 55cm
(25¾ by 21⅝in).
Sold for £111,500.

Jack Butler Yeats, R.H.A. (1871-1957),
Singing 'The Dark Rosaleen', Croke Park,
signed, oil on canvas, (18 by 24in).
Sold for £496,500.

The Irish Sale 1996

A sale of Irish paintings, watercolours, sculpture, furniture,
silver, ceramics, glass, books, maps and other works of art and antiques.

We are currently accepting entries for this important sale.
If you are interested in consigning or would like any information about the sale
please contact any of the people listed below who would be delighted to be of assistance.
Your enquiry will be treated in the strictest confidence.

Enquiries

In Northern Ireland:

William Montgomery (012477) 88666.

In Dublin:

Anne Dillon (00 353 1) 6711786.

In London:

Hugo Swire (Sale co-ordinator) (0171) 408 5484, Mark Adams (Modern British & Irish Pictures) (0171) 408 5381,
Graham Child (Furniture) (0171) 408 5347, David Moore-Gwyn (British & Irish Pictures) (0171) 408 5406,
Simon Cottle (Ceramics & Glass) (0171) 408 5133, Peter Waldron (Silver) (0171) 408 5104.

SOTHEBY'S

FOUNDED 1744

HUGH LANE MUNICIPAL GALLERY
OF MODERN ART

Charlemont House, Parnell Square North, Dublin 1.

ED AND NANCY REDDIN KIENHOLZ
"The Merry-Go-World Or Begat By Chance And The Wonder Horse Trigger" 1992 (exterior) mixed media assemblage 115 x 184 ins (diameter)

You are invited to the Castle!

KILKENNY CASTLE is one of Ireland's most magnificent historical monuments. Built for the Butler family in 1172, it's as impressive now as when the Dukes of Ormonde lorded over its lofty elegance. The Castle has been in state care since 1969 and extensive restoration work has been carried out on it by the Office of Public Works.

Today it represents a living example of a society and a way of life that no longer exists - of kings, knights, lords and ladies.

1995 saw the OPW completing the formal acquisition from the trustees of the Ormond estate of the collection of portraits and tapestries which have been on display in the Castle for many years. Their permanent display is now assured.

The Castle and grounds are open daily, so why not take up our invitation - and discover your heritage by visiting it soon!

OPW

Oifig na nOibreacha Poiblí
The Office of Public Works

Admission: Adults £3 • Senior Citizens £2 • Children/Students £1.25 • Family £7.50

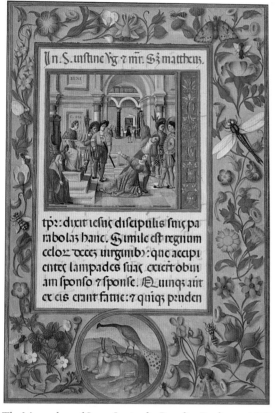

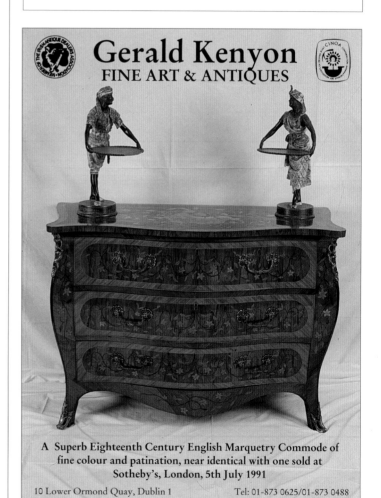

The Stag Hunt by Francis Danby A.R.A. (1793-1861)*

National
Gallery *of*
IRELAND

Merrion Square, Dublin 2
Telephone 01-661 5133 Fax 01-661 5372

Open *Monday to Saturday* 10am ~ 5.30pm
Thursday 10am ~ 8.30pm *Sunday* 2pm ~ 5pm

Restaurant and bookshop open during Gallery hours.

ADMISSION FREE

*Purchased December 1994

NATIONAL
MUSEUM
of
IRELAND

VIKING

AGE

IRELAND

ADMISSION FREE

Tuesday - Saturday 10 a.m. - 5 p.m.
Sunday 2 p.m. - 5 p.m.
Closed Mondays

KILDARE STREET, DUBLIN 2.
TEL 6777444

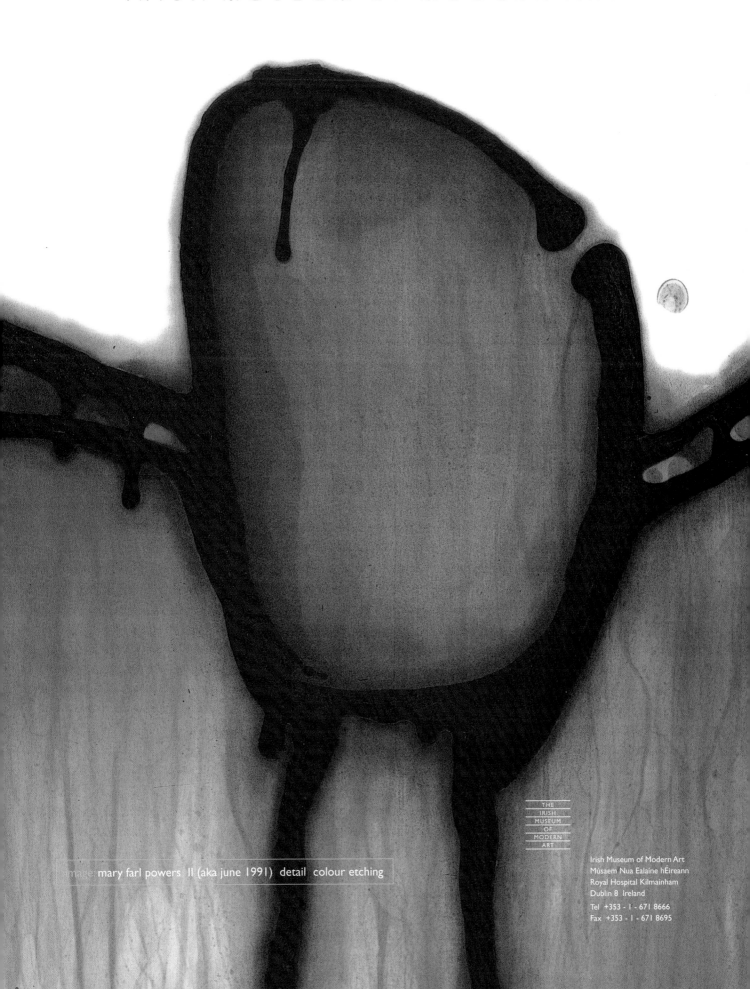

image: mary farl powers II (aka june 1991) detail colour etching

THE
IRISH
MUSEUM
OF
MODERN
ART

Irish Museum of Modern Art
Músaem Nua Ealaíne hÉireann
Royal Hospital Kilmainham
Dublin 8 Ireland
Tel +353 - 1 - 671 8666
Fax +353 - 1 - 671 8695

Sullivan Antiques

Dealers in Fine Quality Georgian and Victorian Furniture including Marble Chimney Pieces, Garden Furniture and Objet d'Art

43-44 Francis Street, Dublin 8, Ireland
Telephones: 454 1143/4539659 Mobile: 088 543399
Fax: 454 1156

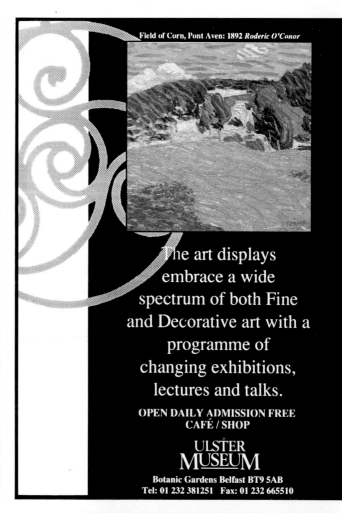

SATCH KIELY ANTIQUES

Extensive

range of 18th &

19th Century

Furniture & Objects

The Quay, Westport, County Mayo.

OPENING HOURS
2pm – 6pm Mon – Sat

Tel: 098-25775 • Fax: 098-25957

ARTISTIC LICENSE

THE OLD COACH HOUSE, DUNDALK STREET, CARLINGFORD, CO LOUTH
TEL: (042) 73745

INDIAN MAN
WATERCOLOUR BY COLUM MCEVOY
(14 x 21 INCHES)

VERONICA BOLAY
JOSEPH SLOAN
TRACEY QUINN
HAMILTON SLOAN
NEILL SPEERS
PAMELA MUSSEN
COLUM MCEVOY
BARBARA ALLEN
GERRY SHERRY
VICTOR CIREFICE
JOHN PATTERSON

ROSES (ERIN REBORN)
OIL ON CANVAS BY PAMELA MUSSEN
(27 x 19 INCHES)

PAINTINGS IN ALL MEDIA, BRONZE & WOOD SCULPTURES, RAKU POTTERY AND CERAMICS.

· FULL COLOUR CATALOGUES AND CONSULTANCY SERVICE AVAILABLE UPON REQUEST
· SPECIALIST STOCK OF LIMITED EDITION PRINTS BY LEADING IRISH ARTISTS
· EXPORT FACILITIES AND MAIL ORDER SERVICE.
OPEN SIX DAYS A WEEK, NOON – 6PM (CLOSED FRIDAYS)

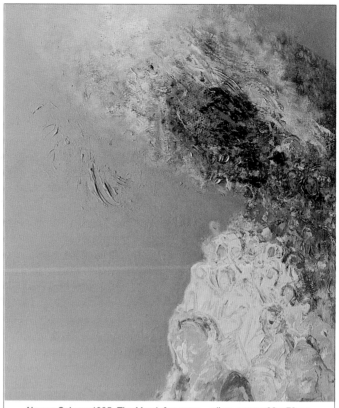

Patrick Boyle

ANTIQUE FURNITURE RESTORATION

A very rare Queen Anne bureau cabinet on stand of unusually small proportions.

Marlay Craft Courtyard

Marlay Park, Dublin 16. Tel: 01-493 6989

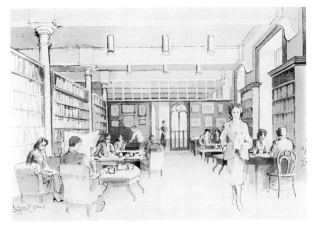

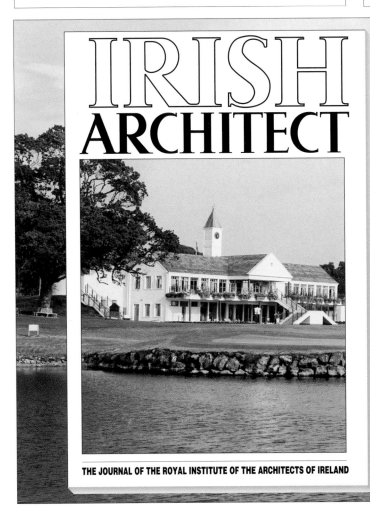

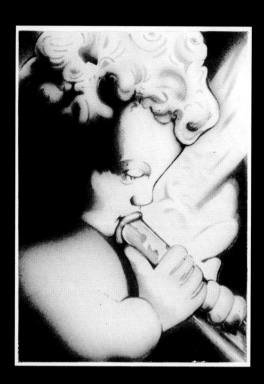

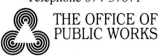

The Sculptors' Society of Ireland

The Sculptors' Society of Ireland, a thirty-two county organisation, has a pedigree reputation for the promotion of excellence in contemporary Irish sculpture. Established in 1978, the Society represents sculptors who practice in the widest range of disciplines and contexts, from the traditional materials of bronze, wood and stone to newer media such as light, sound, video and performance art.

Art Commissioning

The Society encourages professional practice and exemplary procedures in public art commissioning and welcomes enquiries from all potential commissioners.

Available for consultation on any type of sculpture commission, the Society can help those looking for the small per-sonalised gift, a major corporate work, an original site-specific garden piece or a temporary conceptual installation.

Clients have included: The Central Bank of Ireland, Waterford Regional Hospital, B&I Ferries, Kildare, Tipperary N.R. & Laois County Councils, Newry Regeneration Trust, Fermanagh District Council and numerous architects, interior design-ers and private clients.

Research

The Society has a membership of over 400 sculptors, most of whom are represented in the comprehensive slide archive which is available for viewing by appointment. Our library also holds catalogues and biographical information on many of these contemporary sculptors.

Enquiries: Aisling Prior, Executive Director, Sculptors' Society of Ireland, 119 Capel Street, Dublin 1.
Tel: 01-8722296/8722364. Fax: 01-8722364. E-mail: sculptor@iol.ie.

Board of directors: Michael Burke, Chair, Kymberly Dunne, Paul Dunne, Philip Napier, Patricia McKenna, Jane McCormick, Eilis O'Baoill, Maurice O'Connell, Eamonn O'Doherty, Niall O'Neill, reps: Eamonn Coleman, Paula Murphy, Peter McKenna, Norah Norton.

The Society, a non-profit making organisation with charitable status, is supported by both Arts Council in Ireland.

CIRCA

ART MAGAZINE

CONTEMPORARY VISUAL CULTURE IN IRELAND

Subscription Rates
(4 Issues)

INDIVIDUAL
UK £14stg
Eire £15.75IR
Europe £20stg
Overseas £30stg

INSTITUTIONS
UK £25stg
Eire £29IR
Europe £35stg
Overseas £45stg

Please make cheques payable to ...
Circa Art Magazine

Published by

67 DONEGALL PASS
BELFAST BT7 IDR
TEL (01232) 237717
FAX (01232) 237717

EDITORIAL

Museums on the Move - Sculpture Blight - New Tax Incentives for Art Collectors
Art Education in Irish Schools

After long years of agitation, the mandarins of the French Ministry of Finance have vacated their wing in the Louvre and have moved to comfortable purpose-built offices somewhere in the *banlieu*. They can park their cars outside and, by all accounts, they believe they are in heaven. As a result, the Palais du Louvre is now given over entirely to the Musée while the Forecourt (dominated by I M Pei's pyramid) and indeed most of the streets between it and the Tuileries Gardens have been surrendered to pedestrians: Paris, for both residents and tourists alike, has never been so pleasant.

Meanwhile in Dublin the opposite is taking place and what was planned (well in advance of its time) in the nineteenth century as a city-centre cultural complex is being gradually eroded by a proliferation of civil servants and government functionaries while museums are being scattered to the distant *banlieu* of Kilmainham and Arbour Hill.

Leinster House was once the seat of the Royal Dublin Society and when the Society fostered the birth of the National Gallery, the National Museum, and the Natural History Museum, they saw to it that those institutions were sited nearby where they

COLLINS BARRACKS, DUBLIN. Designed by Thomas Burgh in the first decade of the 18th century, the building is being converted at a cost of between £25 and £33 million for use by the National Museum. As it is located far from the city centre it will, like the new Museum of Modern Art at Kilmainham, be quite inaccessible for the vast majority of visitors.

were soon joined by the National College of Art. The rot started when, following 1922, the Society sold historic Leinster House - the most important townhouse in all of Dublin -to the State and when it became the Parliament House, there followed the houses of the Court: government departments unnecessarily cluttering up the centre of the city where they are neither an adornment nor a necessity. Like Topsy, they have grown and grown; but so have the cultural institutions and, as space is limited, someone has had to go. The College of Art was hived off to Thomas Street in the early 1980s and now the greater part of the National Museum is being banished to Collins Barracks where, like the new Irish Museum of Modern Art, it will be virtually inaccessible for the average visitor. (The only institution to buck the trend is the Chester Beatty Library which, having found that no one could find it in the suburbs of Ballsbridge, is moving to the central location of Dublin Castle). The Royal Hospital, Kilmainham or Collins Barracks are every bit as suitable to being government offices or parliamentary chambers as they are to being museums (for which they are not suitable at all); and had the Dail (and the civil service) been moved to either of these locations – and what an imposing parliament house either building would have made – the National Museum, the National Library, the Museum of Modern Art, the Chester Beatty, and possibly the National Archives as well, could all have been happily accomodated beside the National Gallery, in a wonderful city-centre pedestrianised zone that stretched from Merrion Square to Trinity to Grafton Street and beyond with a restored Leinster House, furnished as it would have been when the Duke of Leinster moved in in the 1740s, as its focal point.

The Duke prophesised at the time that the populace would follow him from the North Side of the city across the river to the South – and so it did. But no one need prophesy that visitors will flock to Collins Barrack or Kilmainham – because they won't.

* * *

About twenty years ago, the present writer wrote an article (in *Country Life*) called *Dublin's Vanishing Monuments*. At that time there was a vogue for blowing-up or otherwise removing public sculpture – some of it much-loved like the Crampton *Lettuce* in College Street, some of it detested like Foley's equestrian Gough in Phoenix Park – and the article lamented the loss to Irish art which this state of affairs represented.

How times change ! Now it seems that there is *too much* pub-

THE ROYAL HOSPITAL KILMAINHAM. Now the Irish Museum of Modern Art, the building would have been more appropriately used as a new seat for Dail Eireann.

lic sculpture. It is flooding on to our streets, invading our parks, disfiguring the landscaping of new roadways, making a Disneyland of our airports, and adding an element of absurdity to many of our new buildings. While some of it is certainly 'art' (see frontispiece), much of it is not; and there is a great deal that is gaudy, meaningless, kitschy, downright vulgar, and, in many cases, wildly impractical: the weather in Ireland is not appropriate for the exposure out-of-doors of iron girders – even if they are painted – in the longer term.

This situation has arisen because of something, initiated in 1988, called 'Per Cent for Art' which is Brussels-inspired, and channelled through the Department of the Environment. What this means is that 1% of the total budget for any public works scheme must be spent on art – up to a maximum of £20,000. So far about £1 million has been expended on sculpture in this way and, by now, practically every county in Ireland has been blighted as a result. The Department of the Environment is notably coy about the administration of the scheme and the Sculptors' Society of Ireland, which is funded by the Arts Councils (North and South) to promote excellence in contemporary sculpture, has attempted to step in and advise.

But something is still wrong and whether it is the Scheme, the Society, or the actual sculptors themselves, it is hard to say.

* * *

For decades, Ireland lagged behind its European neighbours in the matter of legislation favouring anything cultural. It now seems that this was just as well because, of late, several government acts have introduced measures in this respect which are much more advantageous that anything which could conceivably have been approved in earlier times. What is more they are, in their enlightenment, far in advance of similar taxation in most other countries. Tax policy in relation to heritage properties is among the kindest in Europe (see *Irish Arts Review Yearbook* 1995); and now the Finance Act 1995 (Section 176) provides for generous tax reliefs in relation to 'heritage items'.

By this is meant archaeological artefacts, archives, books, estate records, paintings or indeed any collection of cultural items or any collection in its setting. Provided that these are an 'outstanding example of the their type, pre-eminent in their class, the export of which would constitute a diminuition of the accumulated culture of Ireland' they may be donated, in lieu of tax to their full market value, to any of the national collections which is prepared to accept them. The provision applies to income, capital gains, corporation, gift or inheritance taxes. It includes arrears of tax and future liability.

That is the good news. The bad news is that the market value of any proposed heritage item must be at least £75,000. This unfortunately means that the owner, for example, of the cache of Michael Collins letters which sold recently in Dublin for £43,000 (surely a heritage item by any standard) would not be eligible to offer them to the National Library or the National Archives in lieu of tax as they were not expensive enough. Furthermore, the *total value* of all heritage items which the exchequer may accept in any one year is a paltry £500,000: at today's prices that is a single painting by Jack B Yeats.

If amended to take these restrictions into account, the new provisions will go a long way to halting, not only the export flow of heritage items which have been in Irish collections for centuries, but also the total break-up of those collections which, for decades, has been caused (in large part) by disadvantageous taxation. Perhaps even more importantly, coming at a time when a growing number of Ireland's new millionaires have been tempted into the field of collecting Irish art – with a consequent increase in the prices paid for Irish paintings – tax incentives like these are likely to encourage philanthropy on a scale (relatively speaking) that has been seen only in America in the time of Frick, Pierpont Morgan and Carnegie. The possibilities are immense. For example, living Irish writers who for long have sold their original manuscripts and papers to any American university that will buy them can now contemplate selling them in Ireland. All that is needed is a purchaser with a substantial tax demand and a willingness to present his purchase to the National Library which, when all is said and done, is where Ireland's literary heritage should be and not scattered around libraries from Texas to Tucson

*　　*　　*

'The general opinion of this year's Leaving Certificate history and appreciation of art papers was that the examiners deserved a complimentary copy of Gombrich for producing a set of papers which allowed students to demonstrate what they knew rather than faulting them for what they did not...' extolled *The Irish Times*.

Michael BURKE (b.1959): *Sister Catherine McAuley and Friend.* 1994. Bronze, 1.15m high. (Mercy Convent, Baggot Street, Dublin). The group is an affront not only to the memory of McAuley, who founded the Sisters of Mercy, but also to the architectural integrity of Baggot Street.

But surely the examiners already own a copy of Gombrich – as indeed will most teachers of the history of art – and the notion that they might need a second copy underlines just how unsatisfactory is the teaching of the art history in Irish secondary schools. Gombrich's classic, *The Story of Art*, covers everything from 'Prehistoric and Primitive' to the 'First Half of the Twentieth Century' and that, precisely, is what the Leaving Certificate syllabus requires teachers and students to cover – all of it in about one hour a week (in most schools). As the majority of those who teach art history have no training in the subject, no wonder Gombrich is popular.

Art in schools means a combination of practical art and history of art. It is taught by teachers trained in art colleges who, for the most part (understandably) regard the history element as an encumbrance. (A further absurdity is that history of art graduates are not usually allowed to teach art history as they have no Fine Art training !) Of necessity, given the very wide syllabus, teaching must be reduced to lists of artists, dates, a few major works, and potted comments and when it comes to the exam, that is a lottery: if a student strikes lucky, the right question will turn up but each year many knowledgeable students must be disappointed. Any student who expects to see an illustration of an actual work of art on the exam paper will be disappointed: there are none. This is in contrast to other subjects – Geography, History, even English – where the exam papers are full of illustrative material.

The scope of the art history syllabus ought to be drastically reduced, perhaps by offering a number of optional subjects – Italian Renaissance, Baroque, Impressionism or Portraiture, Landscape, Abstract art – which would allow students and teachers alike to study texts which are more interesting than the potted histories they currently attempt to memorise. Much greater emphasis needs to be placed on the visual whereby the analytical and observational powers of students would be developed and a better relationship between the two aspects of the subject – practical art and art history – ought to be fostered. After all, the study of English combines both a training in writing and an appreciation of literature.

And what is to be done with Gombrich ? Well, he did also write *Art and Illusion* and if that title could be substituted for *The Story of Art* (and its like), that would at least be progress.

A DIARY OF THE ART YEAR IN IRELAND

Gerard DILLON, *Tea Break*. Labour in Art, IMMA.

■ In association with the centenary of the Irish Congress of Trade Unions, the **Irish Museum of Modern Art** presented *Labour in Art*, a comprehensive exhibition, which explored the representation of labour in the fine arts in the previous century. Among the forty artists, **William Conor's** (1881-1968) fifteen works were noteworthy, depicting Belfast workers not as noble heroes, as was usual then, but in the actual process of work.

Katherine BEUG, *The Thought Before Song*. Page from the artist's sketchbook. Crawford Gallery, Cork.

■ **Katherine Beug's** paintings and lithographs were on exhibition in the **Crawford Gallery, Cork**, during May

Elizabeth Mayes
chronicles noteworthy art exhibitions and events from May 1994 to June 1995

and June. The artist, who is also a poet, came to Cork from New Jersey over twenty-five years ago, and a major element of this exhibition is *'Thought Before Song'*, an 'artist's book' of her poems which were, unusually, preceded by her drawings. A handsome catalogue accompanied the exhibition, which travelled on to the **Project** in Dublin and then to **The Butler Gallery,** Kilkenny. Relations between poem and image have been similarly explored in *The Great Book of Ireland* (1992), in Seamus Heaney and Felim Egan's *Squarings* (1993) and, to a certain extent by Paul Durcan's National Gallery collections of poems.

■ In May the **Crawford** also showed innovative acrylics by **Deirdre Meaney**, done in west Cork and the south of France, as well as award-winning architectural design projects from the **Architectural Association of Ireland.**

■ **Strokestown House**, Co Roscommon, former home of the Pakenham-Mahon family, was restored and opened to the public in 1987. In May President Mary Robinson opened a new museum devoted to the Famine which displays to striking effect the extraordinary collection of Famine documents from the Mahon family archive together with a haunting video and inventive soundtrack. Restoration work on the old walled garden is also in hand.

■ At the **Ulster Museum** in Belfast Queen's University Department of Architecture held an exhibition of the work of the 1993 RIBA Gold Medallist **Giancarlo de Carlo**. The work of twenty important printmakers in Ulster, including **Sophie Aghajanian** and **Terry Gravett,** was shown at Flowerfield in Portstewart. **Malcolm Bennett's** land-

GLASSHOUSES, c. 1845. National Botanic Gardens, restored by OPW.

■ Restoration of **Richard Turner's** finest achievement, the curvilinear mid-1840s glasshouses at the National Botanic Gardens in Glasnevin, is well advanced. One of the Office of Public Works' most impressive projects, the work is supervised by architect **Ciaran O'Connor**, with **Michael Carroll** and **Ove Arup** and is to cost over £4million.

scapes of Ulster were shown at the **Kenny Gallery** in Galway. In Lisburn, at Harmony Hill Arts Centre, **Jasper McKinney** showed new bronzes, which Gavin Weston, writing in the *Sunday Times*, found were small and icon-like, with an unsettling feeling of piety.

■ The Shannon-based GE Capital Aviation services gave £100,000 to the **Hunt Museum** in Limerick . The Old Custom House in Limerick is being refurbished as a museum to house the collection

■ In London, Colnaghi's held a retrospective of **Derek Hill's** paintings, accompanied by an illustrated catalogue while the William Jackson Gallery showed work by **Barrie Cooke, David Crone, William Crozier, Felim Egan** and **Eilis O'Connell**.

■ Large decorative abstracts of 'Modern Nature' in sumi ink and acrylic by Dublin artist **Fionnuala Ni Chiosain** were on exhibition in the **Kerlin** Gallery, Dublin. New work by Ballinglen Arts Fellow 1992, **Eamon Colman**, competent abstracts in vivid colours from New York to Little Rock, Arkansas, were displayed in the **Rubicon Gallery**, Dublin.

The artist Paul FUNGE at Eigse, Carlow.

■ Works on paper by **Jane O'Malley**, lyrical and direct, many inspired by exotic locations, were shown at **Taylor Galleries,** Dublin. Flower paintings by **Robert Janz**, some integrated with text, were beautifully presented at the **Green on Red Gallery**.

Peter TURNERELLI (1774-1839), *John, Earl of Ossory.* Cynthia O'Connor Gallery.

■ Also in Dublin, **Cynthia O'Connor** Galleries and **Jorgensen Fine Art** showed interesting *Recent Acquisitions* while the **Solomon Gallery** showed paintings of Vermont by Dublin-born **Mary Burke**. A light installation by young Limerick artist **Andrew Kearney** attracted interest at the **Douglas Hyde Gallery**.

■ Eigse **Arts Festival in Carlow**, now in its fifteenth year, has grown. Among the varied exhibitions grouped in the Eigse Centre, a former convent which is the Festival headquarters, pottery, woodturning and sculpture were featured, as well as paintings by **Elizabeth Cope, Terry Corcoran, John Shinnors** and **Oliver Comerford. Vivienne Roche's** bell-themed metal sculptures were on show, and solo exhibitions were also given to Scottish painter **Barbara Rae**, whose work was so popular at Jorgensen Fine Art a year ago, and Welsh artist

Peter Prendergast.

Brian Fallon applauded the exhibition of the work of **Frank O'Meara**, who was born in Carlow in 1853, and, after a life devoted to plein-air painting in France, came home to die of malaria in 1888: 'O'Meara is the first real figure in the Celtic Twilight, pre-dating Yeats' early volume *The Wind in the Reeds* by several years'

JUNE 1994

■ Fifty-three European Masterpieces from the **National Gallery of Ireland**, including works by Titian, Velasquez, Rubens, Poussin, van Dyck and Goya, were exhibited in Canberra at the National Gallery of Australia on 24 June. The exhibition later moved to the Art Gallery of South Australia, Adelaide.

■ At **European Fine Arts** in Lower Merrion Street, an exhibition of Old Master paintings, drawings and prints included a fine sepia brush drawing by Tiepolo (1727-1804) and a French wooden sculpture of St John the Baptist c. 1550.

■ The Minister for the Arts, Culture and the Gaeltacht announced that the **Chester Beatty Library** is to move from its premises in Shrewsbury Road to the eighteenth-century Clock Tower in Dublin Castle. The cost of the transfer of the collection of oriental and Middle Eastern artefacts and manuscripts will be about £5.5 million and will be provided by the Exchequer and from National Plan cultural funds. Refurbishment of the Clock Tower and installation is expected to take three years.

■ After 'extensive consultation and subsequent consideration', the **Arts Council of Northern Ireland** issued *To the Millenium: a draft strategy for the arts in Northern Ireland*, a blueprint for the development of the arts over the next six years. Three colloquia in provincial towns were arranged and observations and criticisms were invited.

A Diary of the Art Year in Ireland
June 1994

■ The *Royal Institute of Architects of Ireland* exhibited their regional awards 1994 in the Architecture Centre in Merrion Square. Fourteen buildings from all over Ireland won RIAI Triennial Awards, including four new visitor centres – Ceide Fields, Co Mayo; Dunquin, Co Kerry (both OPW projects); Navan Fort, Co Armagh (McAdam Design) and Ballincollig Gunpowder Mills, Co Cork (De Paor O'Neill). *Scott Tallon Walker* won an award for the UCD Biotechnology Building; *Murray O'Laoire* for their extension to Leo Laboratories, Crumlin and *Burke-Kennedy Doyle* for the 'humane and user-friendly' Hospice in Raheny. *De Blacam* and *Meagher* won for the restoration of Black's Pharmacy, Monaghan and *Peter Rogers* for a creche in Wilton Place, Dublin. In Athlone, *MV Cullinan* won for ' … a simple and appropriate residential quarter of two and three-storey terrace houses on a curved street carved out of an existing derelict area'. The clean lines and form and detailing of the exterior of Dungannon

Leisure Centre helped win an award for *Kennedy Fitzgerald & Associates,* while 'the low profile form of Ballybunion Golf Club, with its Wrightian roofs, overhangs and terraces, merging with the site won an award for *Reg Chandler & Partners.*

■ Three Irish artists were invited to take part in the Sao Paulo Biennial in Brazil. Painter *Ciaran Lennon,* sculptor *Philip Napier* and *Alice Maher,* who works in both media.

■ In Cork in June – *Images of Seamus Heaney* by *Louis Le Brocquy* in the Crawford; *Walter Verling, Liam Treacy* and *James English* in Lavitts Quay; *Brian Bourke* in West Cork Arts Centre, Skibbereen and Ulster artist *Michael Hogg's* installation of mirrors and lights at the Triskel. A new gallery, Penn Castle, was opened in Shanagarry, Co Cork by potter *Stephen Pearce;* the opening exhibition was a retrospective of work by his godfather *Patrick Scott* whose first one-man show was in 1944. His unique gold-leaf paintings were

■ *Terence de Vere White,* novelist, man of letters, collector and vice-chairman of the National Gallery of Ireland, died on 18 June, aged 82. As a member of the Board of the Gate Theatre, the Arts Council, the Friends of the National Collections, and many other bodies, de Vere White made a distinguished contribution to the cultural life of Dublin over many decades.

simultaneously on exhibition in June in the *Taylor Galleries,* Dublin.

■ The Tenth Annual *Sculpture in Context* exhibition of monumental works in magnificent surroundings took place in Fernhill Gardens, Sandyford, Dublin. A full colour catalogue documenting this decade of Irish sculpture was published to celebrate the anniversary.

■ Mixed media works by Sligo artist *Brenda Friel* were exhibited at the Arts Council while the ACNI's Belfast gallery was the venue for drawings by Liverpool artist *Mark Skinner.*

■ Oil paintings from the Blessington studio of *Trevor Geoghegan,* who teaches at NCAD, were shown at The *Kenny Gallery,* Galway.

■ Work by *Graham Gingles* was exhibited at the *Butler Gallery,* Kilkenny. On Achill Island, work by six resident artists, including *Malcolm Clark* and *Camille Souter,* was shown in Dooagh.

Patrick SCOTT, *Burnt Landscape,* 1963. Penn Castle Gallery, Shanagarry, Cork.

A Diary of the Art Year in Ireland
June-July 1994

■ In Dublin, The *Kennedy Gallery* showed delightful watercolours of landscapes by *James Flack*, the Armagh artist now working in Athy, and of orchids and poppies by *Bernadette McLeavey*.

■ Paintings and sculpture by *Felim Egan* at the *Kerlin,* Minimalist in style, showed 'perfect taste, a rare quality in Irish art'(Fallon). Egan recently won the premier UNESCO award for the arts and first prize at EVA 1994.

■ Irish artist *Sophie Shaw-Smith*, now living and working in Nepal, had her first one-woman exhibition, full of' inner harmony, peace and happiness of mind', at the *Solomon Gallery*, Dublin. The artist's husband, *Romio Shrestha*, is a Thanka painter and runs a school for this ancient art near Katmandu; his work was exhibited at the same time at the *Wyvern* Gallery, where *Peter Pearson* also celebrated Temple Bar buildings in oils and wallhangings.

■ The striking 25ft *Wounded King* sculpture which captured so much attention in Temple Bar in 1993 was by *Ronan Halpin* and *Paki Smith*. Halpin's work on a smaller scale was on show in the *Rubicon Gallery,* together with his drawings.

■ In Belfast, in addition to the retrospective exhibition from IMMA, *Patrick Swift* 1927-83, at the *Ulster Museum*, it was a lively month for young contemporary artists. At *One Oxford Street*, Belfast Young Contemporaries exhibition was, to the disappointment of *Sunday Times* critic Gavin Weston, 'all neatly pinned to the wall'. While applauding the gallery for publicising 'the wealth of talent on Belfast's doorstep' and for organising generous awards to *Nicola Robinson* and to *Noel Murphy* for their paintings, he felt that three-dimensional works and film, video, installation and performance should have been included. *Queen Street Studios* marked their tenth anniversary with a multi-venue exhibition, a 'glitzy

book' and a series of events on the theme of 'Issues and Art', involving about fifty artists, including *Michael Minnis*, 1994 NI recipient of the PS1 award to New York. At the *Fenderesky Gallery*, in homage to the Marxist philosopher *Lukacs*, twenty-four artists were issued with identical small mahogany blocks and asked to create a single work in accordance with his aesthetic ideals; interesting, but not entirely successful as an exhibition. Forty artists in a wide variety of disciplines were also invited by Catalyst Arts to 'make instantaneous response to' Wilmont House, a former nursing home in the Dixon Park; the results challenged our assumptions about art.

JULY 1994

Burren College of Art.

■ The *Burren College of Art* at Ballyvaughan, Co Clare was opened by President Robinson. Located in the

Henry HEALY (1909-1982) *Four Courts*. The Art of the State, Dublin Castle.

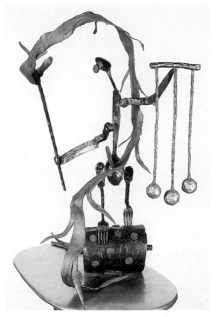

Bill WOODROW, *In Awe of the Pawnbroker*. Model Arts Centre, Sligo.

courtyard of a restored sixteenth-century castle, the purpose--built college offers courses in painting, drawing, photography, writing, poetry and sculpture in a delightful setting.

■ At the Model Arts Centre in Sligo an exhibition of sculptures by *Bill Woodrow* was opened by Barrie Cooke.

■ A new gallery, *Africa Calls*, was opened in Temple Bar to introduce contemporary 'Shona' sculpture from Zimbabwe to Irish viewers.

■ *The Art of the State*, works of art which usually grace the offices and public spaces in accommodation provided by the Office of Public Works, was exhibited in Dublin Castle. This is the fourth annual touring exhibition of selections from the 2,000 works in the State Collection, and was something of a memorial to major Irish talent of the twentieth century. In addition to *Yeats, Leech, MacGonigal, Jack Hanlon, Norah McGuinness* and *Henry Healy, Patrick Collins* (d.1994) was remembered, together with young Irish artists of great potential: *Rob Smith* (1947-90); *Mary Farl Powers* (1948-92) and *Niccolo Caracciolo* (1941-89).

A Diary of the Art Year in Ireland
July–August 1994

Two significant exhibitions at the **Irish Museum of Modern Art** impressed spectators greatly. The Spanish sculptor **Juan Munoz** (b.1953) showed figurative sculpture, including an ambitious new work specially created for the courtyard, which formed contemporary tableaux of dark drama. Drawings by the French artist **Andre Masson** (1896-1987), including some of his famous automatic drawings, were from a key period in his career,1925-65, when he was withdrawing from Surrealism in 1929, and responding as an artist to the Spanish Civil War, the Second World War and the fall of France.

The 5th Iontas *Small Works Exhibition* took place at **Sligo Art Gallery**, and toured subsequently to the RHA Gallagher Gallery.

Michael MULCAHY at the Hugh Lane Gallery.

The artist, **Michael Mulcahy**, born in Cork in 1952, recently spent a year studying Buddhist philosophy in a monastery in South Korea, where he was given the name Do-Gong, which means 'empty island, clear sky'. The Do-Gong series of paintings arising from this sojourn and its rigorous mental training attracted much appreciative attention in the **Hugh Lane Gallery**.

Zita REIHILL, *Where's John?* (detail) Iontas, Sligo Art Gallery.

Sean Scully, Dublin-born, but living and working in New York, exhibited at the **Butler Gallery**, Kilkenny Castle. With its individual consecutive spaces, this was a particularly suitable setting for Scully's huge, disciplined and deeply-coloured oils, completed between 1988 and 1994.

The **Galway Arts Festival** was ' a sunburst of activity', presenting two weeks of enormously varied events; among the many interesting exhibitions were works by **Sarah Walker, John Behan, Patrick Graham, Sean Cotter** and **Cormac Boydell**.

At the **Hugh Lane Gallery** a series of sculpture workshops for the disabled and visually impaired began with an introduction to the gallery's own permanent sculpture collection, aided by the Braille labels and Braille handbook recently introduced there. The Hugh Lane is the first Irish gallery to provide such facilities and to allow the use of guide dogs.

The **Crafts Council Gallery** in Dublin charmed viewers once more with their Gardens exhibition and displayed the work of artists and craft workers to advantage. Meandering through the vine-decked pergola, round terracotta planters, ceramic decorative features, wrought-iron screens and garden furniture of distinction, it became apparent that the visitor had also passed from sunlight into night, for one came upon a moon-dial, a chair for moon-gazing, and finally , in a marble courtyard, a spectacular greeny-blue moonlit glass fountain by **Salah Kawala**.

AUGUST 1994

The £4million restoration of the very fine Georgian **Kilkenny College** as Kilkenny County Hall provoked criticism from Frank McDonald of *The Irish Times*. He approved, however, of the equally costly restoration by the Office of Public Works of **Kilkenny Castle**.

In Cork, American **James Turrell's** light installations caused a stir. Turrell, a former psychologist, whose first love is aviation, is artist-in-residence at the Old Yacht Club, Cobh, and exhibited at the Butler Gallery in Kilkenny last year. His works were to be experienced in both the National Sculpture Factory and in the Crawford Gallery.

Events at the **Hugh Lane Gallery**, Dublin, in August included a fascinating series of lectures by contemporary Irish artists, all of whom are represented in the gallery's first full-colour catalogue of the permanent collection : **T P Flanagan, Michael Mulcahy, Dorothy Cross, Felim Egan, Michael Warren, Michael Cullen, Brian Maguire** and **Ciaran Lennon**. A 'Peace Mandala' was also completed at the gallery by **Romio Shrestha**, the Buddhist Thanka painter from Nepal, who is married to Irish artist **Sophie Shaw-Smith**.

'Best of the summer shows', according to Mebh Ruane, was in the **Kerlin Gallery**, 'a temple of good taste' and 'one of the trendiest contemporary galleries'. **Brian Maguire's** *Homage to Hubert*

Kathy PRENDERGAST, *Two Hundred Words for Lonely*. Kerlin Gallery.

Butler was singled out for praise, as was **Kathy Prendergast's** tiny pillow inscribed with *Two Hundred Words for Lonely*.

■ Critics and Curators exhibited art works at Warren's Boathouse Gallery, Castletownshend, Co Cork, but Alannah Hopkin thought them 'a conventional, unadventurous crew': **Peter Murray** (Cork), **Paul O'Reilly** (Limerick), **Brian Ferran** (ACNI) – 'modish compositions featuring primitive heads'. She thought the Critics marginally better – **Aidan Dunne** (*Sunday Tribune*), **William Packer** (FT), **Celia Lyttleton** (*Tatler*) and **William Feaver** (*Observer*). **Giles Auty** (*Spectator*) came out top.

■ At the **Kenny Gallery** in Galway, August exhibitions were of paintings by **Kenneth Webb** and porcelain by **Vivienne Foley**, whose popular textured glazed pieces are more often seen at Designyard in Dublin.

■ Hilary Pyle has been appointed Curator of the Yeats Room planned for the **National Gallery of Ireland**. This is to be a centre displaying not only the NGI's magnificent collection of the paintings and drawings of **Jack B Yeats**, but also works by his father, **John Butler Yeats**, and material about his

brother, the poet, **William Butler Yeats**, and W. B.'s daughter, the artist, **Anne Yeats**.

■ An exhibition and lecture on the work of the Italian architect **Giancarlo de Carlo**, winner of the RIBA Gold Medal for his work on urban renewal, were arranged by the Royal Institute of the Architects of Ireland at the Architecture Centre of Ireland.

■ Derry artist **Willie Doherty**, well-known for his video and photographic installations of 'the Troubles' in Northern Ireland, was shortlisted for the £20,000 Turner Prize.

■ At the **RHA Gallagher Gallery**, works by the distinguished English artist, **Anthony Wishaw** RA, were on tour from the Barbican Centre, London. Calligraphy and mixed media art by **Denis Brown** was also on show, part one of an exhibition which continued at the **Hallward Gallery**, Merrion Square.

■ At the **Rubicon Gallery**, Ted Hickey, recently retired from the Ulster Museum, curated *Generation*, which showed work by living and dead artists related to one another, such as **Jack B** and **Anne Yeats** (uncle and niece), **Pauline Bewick** and **Poppy Melia** (mother and daughter), **Gerda Fromel** and **Killian Schurmann** (mother and son).

■ **Kilkenny Arts Week** offered an unprecedented 120 exhibitions, as well as a feast of classical music. In the Butler Gallery at the Castle, there were drawings by the English artist, Richard

Sioban PIERCY, *Fear of Being Alone*. Screen print. Kilkenny Arts Week.

9

Wilson, for his installation projects, while upstairs the American conceptualist feminist artist, Barbara Broughel, had created two medieval-style beds from ideas developed when she was artist-in-residence at a Carthusian monastery in Switzerland. In Butler House, Australian artist Ruth Johnstone exhibited an installation of large wood-cuts on paper and there was also an exhibition of painting and sculpture by Sydney Harpley, Francis Tansey, Paula Minchin and Joseph Sloane. Prints by Sioban Piercy and Declan Holloway were exhibited in Kilkenny School of Music.

Gerard McGANN, *Children in the Snow*. Solomon Gallery.

■ *Gerard McGann*, born in Dublin in 1968, presented his first exhibition at the *Solomon Gallery*, representational oils of restraint and sensibility, romantic in feeling.

Tony O'MALLEY, *Landscape with Figure, Clare Island, 1960.* Crawford Gallery, Cork.

■ At the *Crawford* a *Tony O'Malley* retrospective selected by Vera Ryan.

Last year he celebrated his 80th birthday, was elected a Saoi, the highest honour in Aosdana, and in July 1994 was given an honorary doctorate by Trinity College, Dublin.

SEPTEMBER 1994

■ The *Irish Museum of Modern Art*, now three years old, marked this important stage in its development with *From Beyond the Pale: Artists at the Edge of Consensus*, a season of major interrelated exhibitions, artists' projects and residencies which explored issues of identity and diversity. The core exhibition, *From Picasso to Koons*, demonstrated how Picasso contributed to the break with the Renaissance pictorial tradition of perspective based on a single viewpoint, and included exhibits to challenge one's perception of art such as *Marcel Duchamp's* urinal, *Koons'* vacuum cleaners and spray 'paintings' and works by *Warhol* and *Beuys*. Juxtaposed with this was an

Willie DOHERTY, *Border Incident*, 1994. IMMA Collection. From *Beyond the Pale*.

exhibition in association with the National Museum of Ireland of Sheela-na-Gigs, pre-Renaissance sculptures of the female. Also featured was *Archive*, a stocktaking by *Nigel Rolfe* after twenty-five years as a performance artist addressing socio-political issues. Rolfe, born in 1950, lives and works in Dublin; he performed *The Spear Thrower* at IMMA and was also showing *Field of Dreams* at the *Green on Red Gallery*. The series also included exhibitions of *American Paintings of the Eighties*; painted 'waterfalls' by *Pat Steir*, both inside, in dazzlingly painted rooms, and outside in the trees; video work by *Fran Hegarty*,

■ The *Pantheon Gallery* in Dawson Street won praise for its *Ben Stack* exhibition of delicate watercolours by an Irish artist based in Sydney.

sculpture by *Kiki Smith*, *Louise Bourgeois, Dorothy Cross* – a saddle with upturned cows' udders – and *Alice Maher*; photoworks by *Willie Doherty* and *Yasamusa Morimura* – a striking Arcimboldo-style *Mother Judith II* – and installations by *Miriam Cahn* and *Beverly Semmes*. The status of art object was further challenged by soundworks

SHELLA-NA-GIG. *Medieval female display figure from the National Museum of Ireland. From Beyond the Pale at IMMA.*

and Audio Artists Radio Transmissions, a licensed radio transmission. And then there were those billboards ... *Les Levine's* four billboard works on show at forty sites around Dublin consisted of photo images which he took in Ulster in the 1970s overlaid with huge lettering – *Kill God, Blame God* and so on. Levine argued not against God but against horrific acts carried out in his name, but this message failed to get through, and controversy ensued in pubs, drawingrooms and radio talkhours, to be assuaged only by Director Declan McGonagle's letter to the paper and the removal of the offending billboards.

A DIARY OF THE ART YEAR IN IRELAND
SEPTEMBER 1994

■ The September exhibition in the **Douglas Hyde Gallery** was *The Lark in the Morning* by Mullingar-born artist **Patrick Graham**. 'Crude, bold, aggressive statements of tragedy', Graham's work is 'grand in scale, muted in colour range and full of human passion and violent imagery'. Writing in the accompanying catalogue, Peter Murray, Director of the Crawford Gallery, Cork, where the exhibition appeared from November 1994 until the end of January 1995, found Graham's paintings, 'an age away from the tradition of William Orpen and Sean Keating, of which his teachers thought he would be the torch-bearer'.

Patrick GRAHAM, *The Lark in the Morning I.*
Douglas Hyde Gallery.

■ The **Hugh Lane Municipal Gallery** featured the work of four Irish, three Spanish and three French artists in *A Kaleidoscopic Pilgrimage*. The result of a project conceived by the Tyrone Guthrie Centre at Annaghmakerrig, the exhibition explored the theme of migration and transmigration between Ireland, Catalonia and Southern France. The Irish artists were **Rachel Brown, Marie Foley, Micky Donnelly** and **Alice Maher**, and the exhibition went on tour to Annaghmakerrig, to the Orchard Gallery in Derry as well as to Toulouse, Barcelona and other French and Spanish venues.

■ Prints on the theme of animals – even minotaurs and squid – by twenty-nine printmakers from the **Graphic Studio Workshop** in Green Street East, Dublin, were exhibited at the **Kilcock Art Gallery** in Co Kildare.

■ A rare exhibition of the work of **Anne Yeats** was in the **Taylor Galleries**, Dublin, in which she showed her diversity and her absorbing interest in texture and pattern. See *Irish Arts Review* vol. 10 (1994), pp.117-121.

■ Sligo Arts Festival featured **Tom Carr, Charles Cullen, T P Flanagan, F E McWilliam, Neil Shawcross** and **Charles Tyrrell** at an exhibition in the Model Arts Centre.

■ **Paul Muldoon's** poem *Incantata: in memory of Mary Farl Powers (1949-92)* forms the text of a book which includes eleven prints by artists , such as **Patrick Pye, Patrick Hickey, Brian Bourke** and **Carmel Benson**, who were specially associated with her in her work as founder and Director of the Graphic Studio Workshop and Gallery. It was launched by Seamus Heaney at the Gallery in September; the poem is included in Paul Muldoon's new collection *The Annals of Chile*.

■ **The Arts Council of Northern Ireland's** touring exhibition of contemporary craftwork in ceramics, fabric, glass and jewellery featured the work of young craftspeople who had attended an intensive three-month course in Denmark to assist them in setting up business in Northern Ireland.

■ The largest wooden sculpture in these islands was put in place outside the new Civic Offices of Dublin Corporation at Wood Quay (See frontispiece). The ten metre high cedarwood structure inspired by the Viking longboat is by **Michael Warren**, whose work is also in IMMA. Opinion is divided about the new phase of the Civic Offices, a £14million project designed by **Scott Tallon Walker**.

■ At the Philadelphia Art Alliance, seventy-five examples of the finest Irish crafts were on show, together with an exhibition on *The Artist in Rural Ireland: Images of North Mayo*. This initiative by the **Crafts Council of Ireland** included work by silversmith **Kevin O'Dwyer**,

Barrie Cooke, *Bonnien*, 1964. Kerlin Gallery.

■ A retrospective exhibition of works on paper by **Barrie Cooke** (1955-94) selected by the artist himself from a period of over forty years was on show at the **Kerlin Gallery**. An exploration in various media of his recurrent and interrelated themes of landscape, water, animals, bone, nude, knot and pollution, the works, most of which had never been seen before, had also toured to Belfast, Sligo and Limerick.

ceramics by **Cormac Boydell**, textiles by **Karen Fleming** and **Janet Ledsham**, jewellery by **Fiona Mulholland** and **Derek McGarry**, and woodturning by **Ciaran Forbes** and **Liam O'Neill**.

Ros HARVEY, *Donegal Seas and Skies*. Kennedy Gallery.

■ September exhibitions included paintings by Donegal artist **Ros Harvey** at the **Kennedy Gallery** and, at the **Gorry Gallery**, delightfully coloured paintings of interiors by **James O'Halloran**.

James O'HALLORAN, *Drawing-Room*. Gorry Gallery.

■ In Galway, a seventeenth-century merchant's house has been restored by the Office of Public Works and the Heritage Council at a cost of £300,000 to become **Design Concourse Ireland**, a 'one-stop shop' to display the best of Irish design and manufacture. Also in Galway, the Galway Arts Centre held *The Fibre Show*, showing work by four young artists – **Catherine Harper, Des Dillon, Nicola Henley** and **Tim Johnson** – in both man-made and natural fibrous materials, including wood and peat-bog.

■ Arnott's Portrait Award, established in 1985, attracted more than 70 artists in an open submission exhibition. The open award of £2000 went to **James Hanley** for an expressive portrait of Eithne Hanley; the over-35 award of £1000 went to **Michael O'Dea**; subsidiary awards were won by **Betty Dowling, Martin Wedge, Tom McGuirk, Geraldine O'Neill, Robert Patrick Cragg** and **Lorraine Cooke**.

■ The Victor Treacy Award Show, now in its fourth year, took place in the **Butler Gallery** at Kilkenny Castle. The Judge was Aidan Dunne; his choice from the selectors' nominations of 12 artists under 30 was Kildare painter **Rebecca Peart**.

■ **Noirin Mooney**, who has been living and painting in the Burren for decades, exhibited Burren landscapes at The **Kenny Gallery** in Galway. There were exhibitions by two interesting woman artists at the Model Arts Centre in Sligo: **Katherine Beug's** abstract canvases and new paintings by **Janet Pierce**.

■ The Gulbenkian/Norwich Union Awards for Museums and Galleries in Ireland, now in their third year, were presented by the Minister for Arts, Culture and the Gaeltacht, Michael D Higgins, to the following: £2,000 to the **Ulster Folk and Transport Museum**, Cultra, Co Down, for 'The Irish Railway Collection', for high-quality display and friendly and accessible interpretation; £2,000 and a specially commissioned sculpture by John Behan to **The Famine Museum, Strokestown**, Co Roscommon, for telling the story of the great Irish Famine of 150 years ago with courage and originality. A special award of £500 went to the **Foynes Flying Boat Museum**, Co Limerick, for its 'atmospheric, enthusiastic and humorous presentation' of wartime events. **Fermanagh County Museum**, Enniskillen, Co Fermanagh, were worthy winners of two awards, Best Visitor Care and Best

Martin GALE, *End of August*. RHA Banquet Exhibition.

Museum Education Project – the nine judges were especially enthusiastic about this museum's high standards.

■ At the **RHA Gallagher Gallery** the *5th Annual Banquet Exhibition* was the largest ever, featuring the work of Academy members alongside that of their invited guests — in all 362 works, representational and abstract, in a variety of media. **Carey Clarke** PRHA had invited Portadown figurative artist, **John Long**; **T P Flanagan** RHA PPRUA invited **Deborah Brown**, whose bronze gates were inspired by Mahler;

Michael O'DEA ARHA, *From the Studio II*. RHA Banquet Exhibition and Arnott's Portrait Award.

A DIARY OF THE ART YEAR IN IRELAND
OCTOBER 1994

Eithne Carr ARHA invited *Philip Moss*, winner of an Arnott's Portrait Award and the 1994 Irish Antique Dealers' Award; the choice of *Melanie Le Brocquy* ARHA was *Jane O'Malley; Barbara Warren* RHA showed oils of Howth fishing scenes beside *Julian Campbell's* views of Cobh and three stylish Gold Paintings by *Patrick Scott* HRHA hung beside *Corban Walker's* Structural Drawings. The Earl of Gowrie, chairman of the English Arts Council, addressed the Annual Gala Dinner and a new RHA gold medal for lifelong contribution to art was presented for the first time. Sponsored by KMPG Stokes Kennedy Crowley and specially designed by *Thomas Ryan* PPRHA, it was presented to *Lady Beit*, widow of the late *Sir Alfred Beit*.

■ The restoration of the eighteenth-century headquarters of the National Youth Federation at *20 Lower Dominick Street* in Dublin's north inner city was launched by the *Irish Georgian Society*. The house, which is of outstanding architectural merit, was built by the architect and stuccodore, *Robert West*, in 1755, and contains remarkable interior Rococo stuccowork. Funds were contributed by the Georgian Society's American members, by the Federation, by the Bath Preservation Trust and £10,000 from an opera held in Dublin in 1992. The first stage of the restoration involved the removal of the aluminium-framed windows.

■ The *Gorry Gallery* in Dublin held a particularly good exhibition of eighteenth, nineteenth and twentieth century Irish paintings, which included fine landscapes by *George Barret, William Ashford* (see *Irish Arts Review 1995*, pp. 119-130), *Patrick Vincent Duffy* and *Jeremiah Hodges Mulcahy*. A lively '*Self-Portrait*' by *Leo Whelan* was sold, as were two charming Osborne oils.

■ *Jorgensen Fine Art* in Dublin was the venue for an Irish/Hungarian/Italian watercolour exhibition organised by the European Institute of Watercolours,

which was founded in Brussels in 1987. The Irish element consisted of work by, among others, *Carey Clarke, Kay Doyle, T P Flanagan, Arthur Gibney, Brett McEntagart, Nancy Larchet, James Nolan* and *Liam O'Herlihy*.

John BEHAN, *Icarus*. Hallward Gallery.

■ A first solo show for *Anne-Marie Keaveney*, an NCAD graduate whose work is in several public and private collections in Ireland and abroad, was in the *Guinness Gallery*, Foxrock. New work by the sculptor *John Behan* was in the *Hallward Gallery*. Paintings by Limerick Art School graduate *Anne Ryan* were on show at the Arts Council and *Patrick Viale* showed delightful still-lives and landscapes redolent of Italy at *The Gerald Davis Gallery* in Capel Street.

■ The *Kerlin Gallery* moved from their Dawson Street premises to a new space on two floors in Anne's Lane (South Anne Street), 'custom designed to be anonymous, allowing paintings and sculpture to acquire their full potency'. The architect was *John Pawson*, whose projects include the Waddington Gallery, London, and the PPOW Gallery, New York, and the opening exhibition was a series of characteristically geometric paintings by the Korean born artist *Chung Eun-Mo*. Her recent *Parallel Windows* installation was a success at IMMA.

■ The *Kennedy Gallery* held two exhibitions in October: Dublin artist *Philippa Bayliss*, well-known for opera design in Ireland and for her restoration work in Castletown House, showed paintings inspired by the garden she created, and the exhibition of paintings by the picture restorer *Matthew Moss* coincided with the launch of his new book, *Caring for Old Master Paintings*, which is reviewed in this issue.

■ To mark the retirement of *Patrick Hickey* as Director of the Graphic Studio, and to highlight his long and illustrious career as graphic designer, painter, printmaker and architect, the Architectural Graduates Association (NUI) organised

■ *Eithne Jordan,* who was awarded first prize in this year's *Limerick EV+A* by adjudicator Jan Hoet, had a successful show in the Rubicon Gallery. Mebh Ruane in *The Sunday Times* praised her lustrous and sensuous figure studies which 'reveal an artist who has firmly hit her stride'. The artist is the subject of *Works 16 – Eithne Jordan*, one of a series of well-illustrated and well-designed Gandon Edition books which have become essential reference works on contemporary Irish art; priced at only £3.99, the other titles in this latest set are *Tony O'Malley, Gwen O'Dowd* and *Charles Tyrrell*.

A DIARY OF THE ART YEAR IN IRELAND
OCTOBER–NOVEMBER 1994

an exhibition of Early Prints by Hickey at the RIAI Architecture Centre, Merrion Square, at which the artist also gave a public lecture.

■ Installation artist **Annabel Koenig** and composer **Donal Hurley** presented *Ice to Water, Water to Words*, in the artist's own two-up, two-down house in Stoneybatter, a setting which felt appropriately both secure and claustrophobic. The four-part installation featured sculptural elements, beginning with a suspended doll made of ice, and explored attitudes to power, change and domestic violence.

■ Bronze sculpture, light, delicate, even fragile-looking, by young Dublin sculptor **Linda Brunker** was on exhibition at the **Solomon Gallery**; her skilled craftsmanship created fluid airy forms based on imagery of feathers, leaves and seaweed.

■ Bright and spontaneous landscapes of Kinsale and Kerry by **Louise McKeon**, on show at the Yello Gallery, Kinsale, Co Cork, showed the influence of her sojourn in Japan in their delicacy of

■ Among the museums short-listed for the Gulbenkian/Norwich Union awards was the Ulster-American Folk Park, Omagh, Co Tyrone, for their exhibition 'Immigrants' and for visitor care. This museum has recently dismantled a Catholic Mass House of 1768, donated by the parish of Tullyallen, near Dungannon, Co Tyrone, and re-constructed it in the Park.

TULLYALLEN MASS HOUSE. Restoration project at the Ulster American Folk Park.

detail, while **Ursula Murray**, an 'female abstract formalist' and artist-in-residence at the **Belltable Arts Centre** in Limerick, showed work displaying her confident sense of colour.

NOVEMBER 1994

■ The *Temple Bar Gallery and Studios* (illustrated in Frank McDonald's article in this issue), which has fostered contemporary visual arts in the Cultural Quarter since 1983, was launched in November after major renovations costing £1.4 million. Architect Valerie Mulvin of **McCullough Mulvin** and Gallery Director Ruairi O Cuiv developed a spacious, stylish complex, with innovative use of light, featuring a new ground level gallery and thirty fully serviced studios for artists. Opening night featured work by international artists **Julian Schnabel** and **George Baselitz** from a prestigious Irish private collection, and, in their studios, work from **Stephen Walsh, Margaret Tuffy, Patrick Hall, Robert Armstrong** and others.

■ Awards for the 1994 *Best Arts Sponsors of the Year* were presented by President Mary Robinson. Cothú – the Business Council for the Arts – had commissioned sculptures by Cormac Boydell as trophies and the winners were Boyne Valley Honey Company for its sponsorship of the National Library of Ireland and in particular for the publication of *Treasures of the National Library* (reviewed in this issue). Glen Dimplex was highly commended for its IMMA Glen Dimplex Artists' Award. Best First-Time Sponsor was DHL International Ireland for the DHL Art Lift Award which sponsors four visual artists annually, enabling them to participate in overseas exhibitions. Guinness & Mahon, who sponsored the Caravaggio Exhibition at the NGI were highly commended. Siemens Nixdorf Information Systems and John Player & Sons also won trophies and a Special Award went to ESB for its sponsorship of Number Twenty Nine Lower Fitzwilliam Street

and its long established commitment to the arts in Ireland.

A new Cothú/Ernst & Young Award was won by the Butler Gallery in Kilkenny for its effective and imaginative use of sponsorship by Maguire removals, Stena Sealink and Victor Treacy International.

Siobhan CUFFE, *Floating in an Anaesthetic*. From Siolru, centenary exhibition of the National Maternity Hospital.

■ The National Maternity Hospital in Holles Street celebrated its centenary with a number of events, including the commissioning of eight site-specific works for the Hospital: **Angela Forte** wove a tapestry, **Pauline Cummins** presented a video, **Aileen Mac Keogh** said it with flowers, **Rita Duffy** linked images with the Belfast Maternity Hospital and the names and dates of a hundred babies born in the NMH over the century are displayed throughout the hospital by **Aine Nic Giolla Coda**. Paintings and sculptures by 142 major Irish artists on the theme of birth and regeneration were exhibited in the **RHA Gallagher Gallery** under the title Siolru, and are recorded in a handsome colour catalogue.

■ The Turner Prize of £20,000 was awarded to **Antony Gormley**, whose exhibition of striking figure sculpture at IMMA in April 1994 was one of the shows on which the jury based their decision.

Gormley's grandfather emigrated to England from Derry and the sculptor was brought up in the Roman Catholic faith, attending a Benedictine boarding school before graduating from Trinity College, Cambridge. The other short-listed artists included **Willie Doherty** from Derry.

A DIARY OF THE ART YEAR IN IRELAND
NOVEMBER 1994

■ An exhibition of 75 oil paintings by *Henri Hayden* (1883-1970) was opened by President Robinson at the *Hugh Lane Municipal Gallery*. Hayden, who worked in France, developed his affection for Ireland when he befriended *Samuel Beckett* in 1942; he had a solo exhibition in 1952 in the Victor Waddington Gallery in Dublin. The opening was attended by Beckett's nephew.

■ *The Watercolours of Ireland: works on paper in pencil, pastel and paint c.1600-1914* by Anne Crookshank and the Knight of Glin, reviewed in this issue, won the 1994 prize of the Conféderation Internationale des Négociants en Oeuvres d'Art. The annual prize of $10,000 went to the publishers, Barrie & Jenkins, and the book was nominated by the Irish Antique Dealers' Association which is a member of CINOA.

■ Contemporary furniture in Irish hardwoods by Belfast-born *Michael Bell* was shown in the Guinness Hopstore, together with rugs and wall hangings by *Fiona Gilboy* and *Denis Kenny*.

Sean SCULLY, *Tabarca*, 1994. Kerlin Gallery.

■ *Sean Scully*, the Dublin-born abstract expressionist artist, now based in New York, who was short-listed for the 1993 Turner Prize, delivered the Hugh Lane Memorial Lecture at the Hugh Lane Municipal Gallery. On exhibition at the Gallery for the first time was the artist's powerful painting *Sanda*, which was purchased in 1994 with funds from the Tokyo Shimbun which borrowed seven works from the Hugh Lane Gallery's French collection for a touring exhibition. A simultaneous exhibition at the new *Kerlin Gallery* represented the full range of Scully's art practice including woodcuts (1992), etchings (1993) and recent watercolours, pastels and paintings. The series of etchings accompanying the thirteen poems in Joyce's *Pomes Penyeach* (1927) were available in their limited editions.

Terence GAYER, *Shorelines*. Water Colour Society.

■ The *Water Colour Society*, founded in 1870, held its 140th Exhibition in the Royal Hibernian Academy Gallagher Gallery. *Wanda Ryan-Smolin* writes: 'While the exhibition of more than 250 works was, on the whole, rather staid and unadventurous, there were many memorable and worthy individual works. *Terence O'Connell's Calm Before the Storm, Lake Derravaragh* and his *Woodpigeon* were captivating for their extraordinary clarity and precision and *Valerie Moffy Empey's Coolbeg, Co Wicklow* and *Winter Trees* illustrated a refreshingly individual approach. Among the more modern semi-abstract works were *Terence Gayer's* prismatic pattern paintings of land and sea and *Max Maccabe's* very appealing fish paintings. *Patricia Jorgensen's Gull's Wing* and *Study of Crabs and Rocks* stood out, not only as accomplished works but also for their stylistic divergence from the main body of the exhibition as did *Marc Raynaud's Parisian views*. Representative of the traditional watercolour aesthetic were *Tom Ryan's* works which included a very fine study of a bridge over the Grand Canal near Maynooth reminiscent of some of the best nineteenth-century examples of the genre. *Wendy Walsh's* superb flower paintings also come into this category with her miniature-like *Cuphea ignes* and *Cuphea lanceolata* painted on vellum being particularly evocative of the eighteenth/nineteenth-century heyday of botanical illustration. The exhibition also embraced a small but noteworthy number of works in the aligned medium of printmaking, including *Gerald Davis's Dream Mouse* and *Tangai* monoprints and *William Carron's* etching *The Bent Tree*'.

■ The *Gorry Gallery* featured attractive works by two women artists in November: recent oil paintings done in Ireland by Chicago painter *Amy Berenz* (born 1964) and a delightful collection of watercolours by *Helen Colvill* (born 1856) who lived and worked in Howth, county Dublin, until her death in 1953.

1 5

A pupil of Rose Barton, Helen Colvill was a committee member of the Water Colour Society and exhibited regularly there for more than 60 years.

Rowan GILLESPIE, *The Dreamers*. Solomon Gallery.

■ Dublin exhibitions included a major sculpture exhibition by *Rowan Gillespie* at the *Solomon Gallery*, and at the *Green on Red Gallery* new works by Dublin artists *Simon Reilly* and *Mary Fitzgerald*. *Sharon O'Malley* showed recent paintings at the *Hallward Gallery* and the *Graphic Studio Gallery* had new prints by *Valerie Hannan* and *James*

O'Nolan. *John Shinnors* at the *Taylor Galleries* showed paintings of such maturity that Brian Fallon concluded they were good enough to add to any Irish public collection.

■ The *Crawford Municipal Gallery* in Cork celebrated their new acquisitions which included paintings by historic Cork artists *Nathaniel Grogan, James O'Mahony* and others; contemporary Irish work included a portrait of poet *John Montague* by *Barrie Cooke*, who had a recent retrospective in the Kerlin Gallery, work by *Felim Egan* and *Katherine Beug*, and stained glass by *James Scanlon*, sponsored by the Friends of the Crawford. Other benefactors included the Friends of the National Collections, the Elizabeth and Alfred Bendiner Foundation and Bruce Arnold, who presented a watercolour by Mainie Jellett.

■ Other exhibitions in the Crawford in November were paintings by *Bernadette Kiely*, *The Lark in the Morning*, *Patrick Graham's* striking canvases from the Douglas Hyde Gallery and work by three members of the National Sculpture Factory in Cork – a large metal and stained glass piece by *Maud Cotter*, ceramic panels by *Hugh Lorigan* and sculpture, influenced by archaeology, by *Ben Reilly*.

DECEMBER 1994

TABLE BY DUFF/TISDALL. From the Castlethorn showhouse

■ *Irish by Design* was an interesting innovation by Castlethorn, the developers of the former Carysfort site in Blackrock. They invited designers David

Averill, Duff/Tisdall, Peter Johnson and Gerry Brouder to create showhouse interiors resulting in an admirable showcase of the best of Irish craft and design.

■ The *National Museum of Ireland* exhibited late nineteenth-century glass, mainly Dublin-made articles from the glassworks of *Thomas* and *Richard Pugh*, with emphasis on the decorative designs of *Franz Tieze*, a Bohemian engraver who settled in Dublin. (See *Irish Arts Review* 1995, Vol.11, pp.185-88). The exhibition, from the Museum's extensive glass holdings, was assembled by Mary Boydell, who also wrote the accompanying well-illustrated catalogue. Commenting in the Foreword on the interesting decorative motifs, John

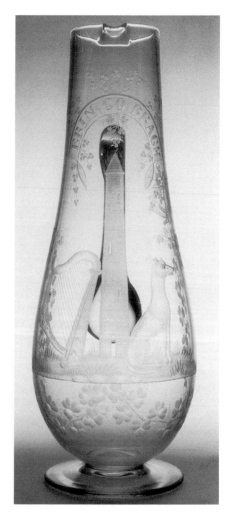

GLASS JUG, *probably by Pugh*, c. 1880/90, engraved by Tieze. National Museum of Ireland.

Teahan, Keeper of the NMI Art and Industrial Division, noted that both the fern and the deer featured on Killarney furniture from even earlier in the nineteenth-century.

■ On the shortlist for the IMMA Glen Dimplex Artists' Award 1995 were: **Dorothy Cross**, born in Cork in 1959, whose sculptures of cow hide and found and fabricated objects explore the power relationship between women and men; **Elizabeth Magill**, born in 1959, who grew up in Northern Ireland, and who endeavours in her paintings to deal with the undifferentiated images and paradoxes to which we are constantly exposed; **Andrew Kearney**, born in Limerick in 1961, who was nominated for his recent light and sound installation in the Douglas Hyde Gallery which explored boundaries between interior and exterior space; and video installation artist **Willie Doherty**, born in 1959, who lives and works in Derry, which has been the subject of his work since the 1980s. The IMMA Glen Dimplex Award, which is now in its second year, marks, with a prize of £15,000,' a significant level of achievement or development in the work and practices of exhibiting artists'. It is open to Irish artists and non-Irish artists who have exhibited in Ireland.

■ The uniquely humorous approach of **John Kindness** to subjects of political and cultural identity showed to advantage in a new series of panels in the traditional medium of lime fresco at the

Michael COLEMAN, *Hoey's Court II*, 1994. RHA Gallagher Gallery.

■ **Michael Coleman's** *Hoey's Court Paintings* (so called after the artist's studio near the birthplace of Jonathan Swift) were striking new abstract works, with a bold urban tone, specially created for the spacious **RHA Gallagher Gallery**.

Kerlin Gallery. The architectural frieze conjured up the artist's boyhood in the Belfast of the 1950s while knowing references to future and past events teased the viewer. The exhibition was in collaboration with the Ulster Museum.

■ The final exhibition in the **Irish Museum of Modern Art's** season of works and projects by contemporary artists, *From Beyond the Pale*, opened in December. *Selected Works Part II* comprised work by 13 artists including the community-assisted sculpture of **John Ahearn**, installations by V**ong**

Phaophanit, **Philip Napier**, **Alice Maher** and **Louise Bourgeois** and works by **Kathy Prendergast, Maud Sulter** and a living installation by **Maurice O'Connell**. The Artists' Work programme at IMMA produced evidence of pioneering work by the influential multimedia American artist **Joan Jonas**, including slide projections, memorabilia and video of her performance inspired by **Seamus Heaney's** *Sweeney Astray*.

■ The respected bronze sculptor, **Shane McDonnell**, son of the well-known sculptor, **Irene Broe**, and grandson of sculptor, **Leo Broe**, died tragically at the age of 33. He had exhibited in the Taylor Galleries and Kilcock Gallery and his huge 'Chestnut' at the Fernhill Garden group show had aroused great interest.

■ Delightful oils and acrylics of the landscape of Provence, where she now lives and works, were exhibited by Dublin artist **Caroline Forbes** at the **Gorry Gallery**.

■ The first exhibition held at the new **Temple Bar Gallery and Studios** since its inauguration in November 1994 was Tyrone artist **Roxy Walsh's** installation 'RSVP' which filled the gallery space with minute and delicate images, deliberately simple, drawn from childhood memories, nursery rhymes, fairy tales and songs.

■ Limerick artist **Michael Canning** exhibited at the Arts Council works composed of not only paint and canvas but also muslin, envelopes, rose petals, wheat, oil and carnations, among other material, which created a wistful, nostalgic atmosphere.

■ Christmas group exhibitions in the galleries and 'affordable picture auctions' presented attractive opportunities for gift shopping in December; the **Kennedy Gallery** featured a good selection including **James Flack, Thomas Ryan** RHA, **Philippa Bayliss** and **Bernadette Madden** while the **Butler Gallery** in the Castle in Kilkenny had a range of work from artists living and working in the

Early in the morning in our house there was a cigarette that moved around in the dark, it was my father getting ready to go to work.

John KINDNESS, *Belfast Fresco*, 1994. Kerlin Gallery with Ulster Museum.

A Diary of the Art Year in Ireland
December 1994 – January 1995

area, among them *Jane O'Malley, Marie Foley, Elizabeth Cope* and *Raimie Leahy*. *Barry McGloin* was among the artists in the *Kilcock Art Gallery* show.

■ The *Oireachtas Art Exhibition*, often the subject of heated views, took place in the Guinness Hopstore. *Kate Robinson* writes:

'The *Oireachtas* was first held in 1905, part of a cultural overview at a time when we were becoming aware of our distinctive characteristics in both the arts and crafts. The show maintained such remarkable dullness that many artists did not even bother to submit. In 1994 all changed. A new Selection Committee seemed to accept the

Veronica BOLAY, *Deanamh i Arezzo*. Pastel. Oireachtas Art Exhibition, Guinness Hopstore.

challenge to alter this perception and a collection more in keeping with modern Irish trends was presented.

Young people were encouraged for adventurous work. The sculpture *Deireadh Fomhair*, meticulously carved in wood by *Richard Lawton Jr* received the Cast Ltd Prize, while *Mary Bridget McGinty's* imaginative use of Celtic motifs merited the Waterford Glass Prize. Perhaps it was too obvious to give the major award, *Bonn an Uachtarain de hIde*, to the great, soaked colourscape by *William Crozier*, but it certainly dominated the show.'

■ *Cork Arts Society Gallery* had a solo exhibition of work by *Angie Shanahan*; Cork Ceramic Artists held their 12th Christmas exhibition in the Crawford Gallery and at the *Triskel Gallery* in Cork

Desmond Dillon showed multi-media tapestries inspired by his six-month stay in Cill Realaigh, south Kerry, *Catherine Lynch* showed 16 large and accomplished abstract oils and *Denis Siou Spillane* had a wide selection of paintings with an unusual approach to Celtic imagery.

■ In Belfast, the Chief Executive of the Arts Council of Northern Ireland, Brian Ferran, launched the *Basil Blackshaw* calendar. Also at *The Gallery in Dublin Road* was an exhibition of *Works on Paper* by a diverse group of artists who at one time or another shared Queen Street Studios, Belfast, the first large artist initiated workspace in Belfast. A collaboration involving video, objects, sound, by *Lorraine Burrell* and *Elaine Thompson* at the Crescent Arts Centre, Belfast addressed the ongoing debate of anonymity versus individuality. The Ulster Museum showed paintings by three of Ulster's 19th century watercolourists: *Andrew Nicholl, James Moore* and *Samuel McCloy*, and the Eakin Gallery Belfast showed watercolours by one of Northern Ireland's most popular and enduring artists, *Tom Carr*, who was born in 1909 and lives and works in Belfast.

Basil BLACKSHAW, *Portrait of Brian Friel* (detail) Arts Council Touring Exhibition and Calendar.

Shane CULLEN, *170 Parnell Street, Dublin*, 1995. Venice Biennale.

■ It was announced that at the Venice Biennale 1995, the largest and most prestigious exhibition of contemporary art, directed this year by Jean Clair, Director of the Picasso Museum, Paris, Ireland was to be represented by *Shane Cullen* from Co Longford, whose mixed-media work investigates political values, and Dublin artist *Kathy Prendergast*, who uses the image of the human body to map out a landscape of personal identity. After a break of twenty years, Ireland was represented in 1993 by *Willie Doherty* and *Dorothy Cross*.

■ The Office of Public Works bought the Ormonde collection of nine tapestries and more than seventy paintings; they have been in *Kilkenny Castle* since the seventeenth century, and are to remain there permanently. The paintings, which trace the history of the Ormonde family, are on display in the Long Gallery of the Castle, built in the 1860s to house them, and restored in 1970, when the State took over Kilkenny Castle.

■ A major retrospective of *John Behan's* sculpture over the past thirty years was held in the *RHA Gallagher Gallery*. Dubliner Behan now works in the west of Ireland and Galway Arts Centre showed a 'mini retrospective' in the summer of 1994. Behan works almost exclusively in metal; his first bronze bull was sold in 1969 to the playwright *Brian Friel*, and this powerful Irish iconic image still finds a place in his work.

■ An integral part of the interior decor of the new O'Reilly Hall at University College Dublin is a set of ten paintings, specially commissioned and selected by

Ciaran LENNON, *Scotoma I/V*, 1992-93. Hugh Lane Gallery.

■ Scandinavian exhibitions in January were at the RIAI Architecture Centre, of the work of the Danish architect and designer **Arne Jacobsen** (1902-71), famous for his interpretation of international modernism and at the Crafts Council Gallery of Crafts in Wood from Finland.

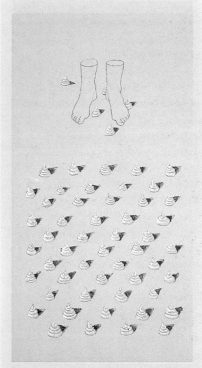

Alice MAHER, *The Little Shits*, 1994. Douglas Hyde Gallery.

the architect Dr Ronnie Tallon of Scott Tallon Walker. The paintings, all 11.5 x 5.5 ft and set flush with the panelling, are by **Mary Fitzgerald, Anne Madden, Michael Coleman, Patrick Scott, Felim Egan, Ciaran Lennon, Charles Tyrrell, Cecily Brennan, Richard Gorman** and **Barrie Cooke.**

Letitia HAMILTON, RHA, *Flowers in a Blue Jar.* Jorgensen Fine Art.

■ **Jorgensen Fine Art** presented Flower Paintings in their recently extended gallery in Dublin. A charming display of this long established still life genre featured work by more than twenty artists, including **Letitia Hamilton** RHA, **Sarah Purser** RHA, **Grace Henry** HRHA and **James Sinton Sleator** PRHA.

■ At the **Hugh Lane Municipal Gallery of Modern Art,** the distinguished art critic Dorothy Walker launched Ciaran Lennon's *Body Fold Light: The Scotoma group* book and nationwide tour of the Scotoma Group paintings. The limited edition book, which includes four original lithographs by the artist with essays by Joseph Masheck and Alison Ainley, is a 'visual' essay on the evolution of the three monumental oil-paintings made by Lennon between 1992 and 1993, one of which, *Scotoma I/V*, has recently been acquired by the Hugh Lane Gallery.

■ The path through **Anne Madden's** garden to her studio in the south of France was the motif in her exhibition in the **Kerlin Gallery.** These recent diptychs, richly coloured and expressive, seemed to explore the metaphor of darkness leading to light.

■ Two Irish artists, **Margaret Fitzgibbon** and **Colette Nolan**, spent six months in Poland last summer and their creative response to their experiences there was documented in a variety of media and shown in the **Crawford Gallery, Cork**.

■ Ceramics by Sligo potter **Elizabeth Caffrey**, on view at the Arts Council, evoked her concerns for the fading culture of the Aran Islanders.

■ **Alice Maher**, born in Tipperary, now living and working in Dublin, exhibited in the **Douglas Hyde Gallery**. The show, called *'familiar'*, comprised several large canvases, each interrelating with a sculptural object, and was memorable for its imagery of 'the little girl', interwoven with the evocative use of flax as a medium, as well as the curiously disturbing child's dress made of bees. Some of these works were shown at the Sao Paulo Biennale in October 1994, and the artist's installation, *Keep*, was simultaneously on show in *Beyond the Pale* at IMMA. A concurrent exhibition of her drawings at the **Green on Red Gallery** attracted much praise.

A DIARY OF THE ART YEAR IN IRELAND
FEBRUARY 1995

■ *The Arts Council* published its radical *Three-Year Plan*, the predominating theme of which was to allow more people more opportunities to participate in the arts. To fund the proposals, public spending on the arts would need to increase from £13million in 1994 to £26 million in 1997.

■ The *Irish Georgian Society* organised a successful conference in Dublin Castle on conserving Irish towns .
Jeremy Williams reports:
'The IGS Conference brought together the two wings of the conservation movement: the politicians, planners and architects articulating strategic utopias on the one hand, and the unpaid curators of Dublin's treasures salvaged from a century's apathy and neglect on the other. There was no shortage of eloquence, the standards being set by the Taoiseach, John Bruton, speaking perceptively about great houses and feelingly about the vernacular: his own farm buildings which, if he were a good farmer he would have pulled down long ago. He then accepted the Fitzwilliam Estate papers from Lord Pembroke. These had been gathering dust for years in a Wiltshire county library until the Knight of Glin negotiated their return to Ireland. Jim Barrett, the new City Architect, remarked that it is only very recently that any Irish architecture later than medieval has become politically correct, but the absence from the conference of Dublin Corporation, the Heritage Council, UNESCO, any European conservation body or any county manager (apart from Maurice Moloney speaking for Cork), indicated that he might have been premature in his judgement. Temple Bar Properties (who might have sponsored the conference to improve their image) were represented in the audience by a Dutch girl student who appeared unaware of their defective forensic treatment of St Michael and St John's Gothic Rococo church. The opening addresses were given by Joan O'Connor, President of the RIAI, and Liz MacManus, Minister of State for Housing. Christopher Southgate, Arthur Gibney and Jane Fenlon spoke as experts specialising in old buildings; Edward McParland, Christine Casey and David Griffin spoke as historians; Desmond Hodges on the relevance of planners. The most specific speakers were Nigel Green on pavements and Frederick O'Dwyer on the plight of the Irish sash window as opposed to the less subtle English version. How many of his audience knew the difference beforehand? The vital role of the educator was revealed by Brian Pfeiffer, Keeper of New England Antiquities in Boston, Christopher Woodward, Curator of the Buildings of Bath Museum (brilliantly displayed in a redundant church) and Dana Arnold of the Georgian Group who all showed that aesthetic infallibility is only tolerable to philistines if prescribed with charm.
The two best speeches: Liverpool conservation officer Mary King, who recorded how an inner city sector known as Canning Town, destroying itself through arson and gang warfare, has been transformed into a spa as elegant as Cheltenham, due to local housing associations working with an effective minister (Heseltine). Alas, too late for Dublin to save Summerhill. Dawson Stelfox recorded the work of HEARTH which restores ordinary Ulster's historic architecture as homes for ordinary people, exploding the myth that conservation is merely an aimable pastime for the privileged and a far cry from old buildings being retained merely to provide a context for great monuments, as previously proposed.'

■ *The Earl of Pembroke*, successor in title to Strongbow, leader of the Norman invasion in 1169, returned to the *National Archives* the records of his family's estate management in Ireland. The papers include estate maps, drawings of houses and streets, some of very fine quality, title deeds, rent rolls and leases dating from medieval times to the 20th century. The Pembroke Estate, widely regarded as a model of good management, developed much of Dublin's southside Georgian core, including Fitzwilliam Square and, in the nineteenth century, Ballsbridge.

Martin MULLIN. Brenda Kroos Gallery, Cleveland, Ohio.

■ *The Fuller Building Paintings*, work from 1993/94 by New York-based Irish artist *Martin Mullin*, were shown at the Brenda Kroos Gallery in Cleveland, Ohio (February-April). Mullin created the works in the space previously occupied by the celebrated Pierre Matisse Gallery in the Fuller Building on 57th Street, New York.

A Diary of the Art Year in Ireland
February 1995

■ The Architectural Association of Ireland's tenth annual awards attracted 50 valid entries for assessment: the Downes Bronze Medal went to **Derek Tynan** for **The Printworks** (see p 178) and there were a further six awards and 14 Special Mentions. Among the Award winners were **De Blacam and Meagher's** New Library for the RTC, Cork (*left*) with a striking curved brick wall that will delineate a new 'quad'; **Grafton Architects (Shelley McNamara & Yvonne Farrell)** for a house in **Doolin, Co Clare** (*top*) a mid-sized farmhouse – 'the planning requirement was for a strictly traditional elevation to the main road'; the same architects with **Joe O'Donovan** of **Roughan O'Donovan** for a road bridge at **Bray, Co Wicklow** (*below right*), an award that widened the scope of what architecture is about; and **Peter and Mary Doyle** for a new school at **Cashel** (*bottom left*) where simple materials – natural blockwork and open steel trusses (dictated by the budget) –were used to create and effective community-orientated space.

A Diary of the Art Year in Ireland
February–March 1995

■ A touring exhibition, *Irish Art 1770-1990*, from the **Crawford Gallery** in Cork opened there, showing work by **James Barry, Walter Osborne, Sean Keating, Jack B Yeats** and **William Orpen**, as well as specially acquired works by **Alice Maher, Willie Doherty** and **Alanna O'Kelly**, among others. Other venues for the tour are Washington DC, New York, Philadelphia, Washington and Indiana.

Dorothy CROSS. DHL Airlift Award Winner 1995.

■ The international air express carrier, DHL, has established the DHL Art Lift Award to encourage emerging Irish visual artists to further their careers by participating in international exhibitions. Presented four times a year, the award allows artists to transport original works of art to worldwide destinations, and the first winner of 1995 was **Dorothy Cross**, who plans to bring a selection of her work to the PPOW Gallery in New York, selectors from which saw her preserved cow udder sculptures at the Venice Biennale. Winners who benefited from Art Lift awards in 1994 were **Mary Lohan**, whose paintings went to Italy, **Ian Joyce** and **Oona Hyland**, whose sculpture of fourteen derelict pianos went to three centres in Spain, **David Godbold**, whose new paintings went to Australia and **Sarah Iremonger**, who brought an exhibition to Chicago.

.■ The **Rubicon Gallery** showed a preview of its artists for the year to come. Artists invited to submit one work as an indication of future shows included **Aidan Linehan, Michael Kane and Margaret Morrison** as well as newcomers **Hazel Walker, Maud Cotter** and **Tom Fitzgerald.**

■ A first exhibition in Ireland for British artist **John Lessore,** who now lives in France, took place at the **Solomon Gallery**, while **Robert Armstrong's** paintings at the **Hallward Gallery** were fresh and vibrant in colour, nature-based in subject.

■ At the **Ormond Gallery** in Dublin, graphic artist **David Quinn** showed ink sketches, while the **Green on Red gallery** celebrated the 80th birthday of **Terry Frost**, one of the leading members of the St Ives group of artists.

MARCH 1995

Geraldine HONE, *Summer Landscape, West Cork.* Guinness Gallery, Foxrock.

■ Contemporary Irish art showing at the Dublin galleries in March included: **Paddy Moloney's** ceramic sculptures at the **Hallward;** Dublin artist **Gwen O'Dowd's** Grand Canyon paintings at the **Kerlin;** paintings by **Deirdre Meany** and **Geraldine Hone** at the **Guinness Gallery;** paintings and drawings by 'surgeon, singer and artist', **Thomas Wilson** at the **Kennedy Gallery**; watercolours of Dublin by Armagh-born **James Flack** and, at the new **Temple Bar Gallery** and Studio, a collection of objects and statements

by young Dublin artist **Maurice O'Connell** entitled *Sick and Tired of Being Sick and Tired.*

Lochlann QUINN, Deputy Chairman, Glen Dimplex; the Minister for the Arts, Culture and the Gaeltacht, Michael D HIGGINS TD; winning artist Willie DOHERTY. IMMA.

■ The 1995 IMMA/Glen Dimplex Artists Award was announced at the Irish Museum of Modern Art. In presenting the award to **Willie Doherty** for his new video/audio work on Northern Ireland, Minister Michael D Higgins also looked forward to *L'Imaginaire Irlandais* in 1996, when contemporary Irish culture is to be introduced to the French public; works by selected Irish artists will be shown in Paris and regional venues.

Patrick HENNESSY, *Young Man in a Chinese Blue Silk Robe.* Frederick Gallery.

■ In South Frederick Street, Dublin, the **Frederick Gallery's** opening show included paintings by **Daniel O'Neill, Louis Le Brocquy, May Guinness** and **Evie Hone.**

■ The contemporary arts festival **EV+A** took place in **Limerick**. *Kate Robinson* writes: 'The 19th open submissions exhibition was adjudicated by Maria de Corral, former Director of the Reina Sofia Museum, Madrid who declared herself well pleased with submissions and impressed with "the abundance of women among the youngest artists". Her immediate response was that "painting is still an important medium of expression for Irish artists...it is more classical". Among the largest paintings shown at the City Hall **Margaret Tuffy's** triptych, *Scenes from the Desert* dominated one end, its dark interior querying the brilliant lights of the wings. *Shaman's Horse XXXVII* by **Danny McCarthy**, a sculpture of twigs, showed such restraint in its modelling as to be the essence of art with nearby the good company of the innovative pieces by **Michael Canning,** Open Award Winner. *I want a New Life* was a sensuous and exciting reconstruction of landscape created in lichens, mosses, silicone and board. **Robert Janz's** *Tá Am Fós* titled in Irish and English, was a caustic, but restrained comment on hope, an installation built with nails and text. Twice-previous winner **Tom Fitzgerald** was also here with his discriminating structure, *The Politics of Being*. Some were shocked in this same room by **Sharon Kelly's** video *Drawing Breath* in which the realities of illness were resolutely faced.

Two photographs based on stones were by **Carmel Cleary** (and not every artist

was permitted two entries), one a delightfully smooth buttock-shaped haunch, sitting among stones, as though on a beach.

Much use was made by women of dresses of one kind or another: **Margo McNulty's** etchings *Guna 1 and 2* recalled the child who wore them; **Joyce Duffy's** *Sugar and Spice* – a parody of Degas' little *Dancer?* Delicate froths of garments became hardy adjuncts to the female character

Robert JANZ, *Tá Am Fós* E V + A , Limerick

in **Jennifer Kotter's** photographs of *Hardware*, outer garments of varied design became still more delicate in **Cliona Harmey's** exquisite photograms: this was also an Open Award Winner. The terrible destructiveness of modern living to the individual's sense of identity was shown in **Jim Fleming's** video installation with text, *Home: Identity in Turmoil* which attempts to explore the 'fundamental constituents of identity'. Two monitors faced each other, featuring the same person, one speaking about home, belonging and place, the other about homelessness. So much was new, so much was daring, so much was inventive, the whole brilliant effort succeeded in giving a good over-all view of the work now being done.'

Carmel CLEARY, *Untitled.* E V + A , Limerick

■ The death took place at her home in Howth on 23rd March of *Mrs Gertrude Hunt*, co-founder, with her husband *John*, of the **Hunt Collection** of art and antiques which is to be displayed in the refurbished Custom House, Limerick, from next spring.

APRIL 1995

■ **Sean Shanahan**, born in Dublin in 1960, and currently living and working in Como, Italy, exhibited new works in the **Kerlin Gallery**. The exhibition was organised in conjunction with the Orchard Gallery, Derry, and was accompanied by a fully illustrated catalogue. Shanahan is one of 17 artists chosen to represent Ireland in **L'Imaginaire Irlandais** in Paris in 1996.

■ At the Triskel in Cork, **Rockscapes** by **Frieda Meaney** were exhibited and the Belltable in Limerick had Paintings and Drawings by **Samuel Walsh**.

■ At IMMA, paintings and drawings by the distinguished British artist, **Rita Donagh**, reflected her continuing preoccupation with the political future of Northern Ireland. She expressed her ideas in maps, grids and aerial views, and the exhibition included a found image of the Downing Street Declaration of 1993.

■ Oil paintings by **Patrick Viale**, reflecting his fascination with rich colour and the atmosphere of Liguria in north-west Italy, the land of his forefathers, were on show at the **Brock Gallery**, Blackrock.

■ Amsterdam-based **Ansuya Blom's** surrealist work was at the **Douglas Hyde** and **IMMA** showed unusual sculptures by **Janine Antoni**, some of them literally licked and lathered into shape.

■ A new gallery 'promoting the best in contemporary Irish art' opened in Dundalk: **Tristann's Gallery** showed the work of 22 artists from Ireland, North and South, on the theme of Peace, and two international painters too.

A Diary of the Art Year in Ireland
April 1995

■ The 165th Annual Exhibition of the *Royal Hibernian Academy* featured more than 500 works. *Hilary Pyle* writes: 'The RHA must be used to its anachronistic role, which is out of line with the best of contemporary Irish art. Paradoxically it has modernised sufficiently to find it unnecessary to require

The Artist MELANIE LE BROCQUY, HRHA, with her bronze *From the Past* at the RHA.

the standards for which the Academy, and all the notion of *academia*, were set up. Yet as always, and perhaps more than ever this year, it fails to uplift or agonise, and surely those are the functions it may still be able to fulfil. Even at a second viewing, where one can discover previously unnoticed works among the five hundred on view, the whole show retains an insistent sameness.

This is not to deny that there is quality; and there are individuals who continue to satisfy. *John Kelly* is an example. Never attempting anything vast, and seldom venturing into colour, even in monochrome his mystic heads – now shadowed by their alter egos – are intriguing. *Barry Castle*, who won the James Adam award for overall performance, is another individualist, who adds a new look at the Temptation to her store of symbolist subjects. There is a memorable *Recollection of Ibiza* by *Barbara Warren*, an artist of deceptive depth; and *Maria Simmonds-Gooding*'s *A Place of Habitation* – the ephemeral abode found at the bend of a graphite track which is traced on a background of white fresco – would be commanding

had it ot been hidden in a corner at the bottom of a stair. (There may have been some esoteric reason for such a hanging!). Another notable piece was likewise diminished – a delightful group of minute wildebeest by *Michael Keane* seen galloping on a lowly pedestal. As with *Imogen Stuart*'s pitchpine *Scholar and the Blackbird*, the Braille label (which is admirable for sculpture) was rendered unusable – in the latter case it was attached to the floor. *Benedict Tutty*'s pair of singers were well placed, though, expressing in their simple terracotta forms an astonishing degree of spiritual transportation; *Conor Fallon*'s *Crow* and his horse heads were splendid in craft and conception. There was a small tribute to the late *Simon Coleman,* taking the form of an early work of the 1940s and 50s. *Ploughing* is full of life. *Tony O'Malley*'s work was of an early period too, three small gouaches of 1966, admirable in themselves, but stifled by suave frames. *Victor Richardson* has been jolted out of his pointillist harmony into something more punchy in his *Interior with Oranges*, and *Richard Kingston*'s *Seasons of the Maple Tree*, a four-part study, is a small masterpiece.

The best portraits were by *David Hone* and *Carey Clarke*, and there was the expected *James Nolan* self-portrait. Among slightly less conventional landscapes, those *Dorothy Smith, Denise Ferran, Fiona Joyce and Louise Wall* are worth mentioning, and there was a series of refreshing views on a tiny scale by *Tom O'Toole, Bernie Masterson, Margaret O'Sullivan* (these of Allihies), *Mike Fitzharris,* and *Mary Burke.*

The non-traditionalists like *Mary Burke* did not appear out of place, but seemed curiously restrained: *Sam Walsh,* working his abstracts in colour, *Michael O'Dea* holding back the Indians charging *Up Clanbrassil Street*, and *Mary Lohan*, bringing Barga, in Italy, and Port, in Donegal, close together, in tone if not in mood. At least they were there.'

Ruth O'DONNELL. *Untitled Monoprint.* Graphic Studio gallery.

■ The Graphic Studio Gallery's first exhibition of 1995 was of new prints featuring landscapes, still-life and garden scenes by three artists – *Niall Naessens*, winner of the First Prize at the Iontas Exhibition in Sligo in 1993, and selected to represent Ireland at the 1995 Ljubljana Bienniale; *Jean Bardon*, whose interest in etching developed in Amsterdam; and Galway-born *Ruth O'Donnell*, for whom monoprints are the preferred medium.

Sarah WALKER, *Beara Bog Cut.* Hallward Gallery.

■ Other Dublin exhibitions in April were: *Roy Petley's* delicate watercolours at Jorgensen Fine Art; *Sarah Walker's* Bog Rhythm paintings and *James Hanley's* oils at the Hallward Gallery; *Eddie Cahill's* prison paintings at the Project Arts Centre; *Michael Dempsey's* figurative paintings at the Temple Bar Gallery; *Tony McGrath's* old Dublin montages at the Wyvern and *Gertrude Degenhardt's* evocations of women in music at the Goethe Institut.

A DIARY OF THE ART YEAR IN IRELAND
MAY–JUNE 1995

Rebecca PEART, *Untitled*. Kilcock Art Gallery.

■ The1994 winner of the Victor Treacy Award for emerging Irish artists was the young abstract painter, *Rebecca Peart*, and her work was exhibited in May in the *Kilcock Art Gallery*, county Kildare, together with *Fergal Flanagan's* more traditional landscapes.

Patrick HICKEY, *Still Life with Bog Cotton*. Graphic Studio Gallery.

■ Recent prints by Ireland's best-known print-maker and co-founder in 1962 of the Graphic Studio, *Patrick Hickey*, were on show at the *Graphic Studio Gallery*. In the accompanying colour catalogue, artist Cliodna Cussen wrote that 'his fruit and flower studies are complete evocations of plant rhythm, just as his beautiful bank notes of the early 1970s evoke the inherent rhythm of Irish lettering'.

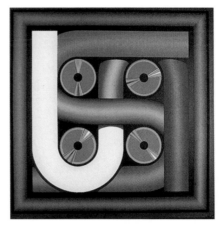

Francis TANSEY, *Processing*. Solomon Gallery.

■ May exhibitions in the *Solomon Gallery* were of new paintings by the Dublin-born Director of the Butler Gallery, *Francis Tansey*, who also works in Santa Monica, California, and of recent abstracts by *Nevill Johnson*, in which S Brian Kennedy detected ' great assurance' and 'a new dawn, free from angst.'

■ Delightful designs by two Dublin artists – *Kay Doyle*, President of the Water Colour Society, and *Deirdre Thompson* – were selected for UNICEF's best-selling greeting cards in 1995.

Kay DOYLE, *The Pink Dress*. UNICEF greeting card.

■ As part of the Sesquicentennial Celebrations, **Queen's University, Belfast,** marked its 150 years with an exhibition of the best of its art collection in the Ulster Museum. Rarely seen in public, the collection includes university portraits by well-known British painters, Philip de Laszlo, Ruskin Spear and Sir James Gunn, and more than 200 landscapes and genre paintings; among the Irish artists represented are **William Conor, Paul Henry, Humbert Craig, Frank McKelvey, Sir John Lavery** and **F E McWilliam.**

■ New paintings by *Patrick Hall*, on exhibition at the Douglas Hyde Gallery, were described by its Director, John Hutchinson, as 'awkward … his pungent subject-matter, which embraces the forbidden, the fanciful, and the inchoate, can be sulphurous'.

Stanhope FORBES (1857-1948), *The Fish Sale on a Cornish Beach*. At the Impressionism exhibition at the Hugh Lane Gallery.

■ The *Hugh Lane Municipal Gallery* filled its space with a beautiful loan exhibition *Impressionism in Britain and Ireland*.

■ The popular summer arts festival, Eigse Carlow, featured *Hughie O'Donoghue*, English-born but of Irish origin, whose paintings attracted much favourable attention at Kilkenny Arts Week in 1991. There was also a large exhibition of work by Irish contemporary artists, and an open submission exhibition, chosen by *Trevor Geoghegan*.

Bea ORPEN (1913-80) *Shelly Beach, Mombasa.* At the Droichead Arts Centre

■ In county Louth, **Artistic License**, the gallery in the Old Coach House in Carlingford, held a joint exhibition of two artists, both from Rostrevor in county Down – **Pamela Mussen** and **Colm McEvoy** – while a Retrospective Exhibition of the work of **Bea Orpen** HRHA, catalogued by Hilary Pyle, took place in the **Droichead Arts Centre** in Drogheda. In the **Orchard Gallery** in Derry, recent work by **Sean Shanahan** was on show.

Richard GORMAN, *Untitled 1995.* Kerlin Gallery.

■ New paintings by the gestural abstractionist **Richard Gorman** displaying a significant shift in approach and emphasis, were shown at the **Kerlin Gallery** prior to exhibition at the Orchard Gallery, Derry and the Butler Gallery.

■ Regional Awards for 1995 were presented by the Royal Institute of the Architects of Ireland. **Peter** and **Mary Doyle** won for Cashel second-level school, and, also in the Southern Region, the 'Ecohouse' in Cork, with its 'great visual appeal', and the only award in the 'Under £20,000' category in any region, was a winner for **Paul Leech**, Gaia Associates. The Famine Museum at Strokestown by **Orna Hanly** impressed the judges, and, also in county Roscommon, one of two restoration awards went to **Shaffrey Associates** for King House in Boyle. The other restoration award went to the **Office of Public Works** for the Glasshouses in Dublin's Botanic Gardens, while three Temple Bar buildings also won: Spranger's Yard apartments and shops, for **Burke Kennedy Doyle** and Partners; The Printworks, also 'mixed-use', for **Group 91** and another 'ecohouse', **Murray O'Laoire Associates'** richly detailed

Green Building. **Noel Dowley** won two awards – for Dublin Airport Car Park and for Ashbourne Community School.

■ **Kathy Prendergast**, representing Ireland (with **Shane Cullen**) at the Venice Bienniale, won the prestigious *Premio Duemila*, the prize for a young artist (under forty).

■ Two new galleries opened in June. In Belfast, the Art Gallery on the Dublin Road sponsored by the Arts Council of Northern Ireland moved to a refurbished venue on Ormeau Avenue and changed its name to the **Ormeau Baths Gallery**. Director Noreen O'Hare announced that the move to James Watt's Victorian public baths, which held their Last Swim in 1988, would help establish Belfast as a truly European city with a thriving artistic community. In Cork, the new gallery of **Cork Arts Society** in Fr. Mathew Street, had an opening exhibition selected by **John Behan**, RHA.

George Victor DU NOYER, *Monavullagh Mountain, Co Waterford,* Detail from a field sheet, 1850, Geological Survey of Ireland. At the National Gallery of Ireland.

■ At the National Gallery of Ireland, an exhibition of the drawings of **George Victor Du Noyer** (1817-69) was arranged to celebrate the sesquicentennial of the Geological Survey of Ireland.

■ 'A flagship exhibition' of the best of all its collections opened at the **Chester Beatty Library** in Dublin.

THE QUEST FOR SIR EDWARD LOVETT PEARCE

Maurice Craig *recalls his personal odyssey over a period of half a century in pursuit of Ireland's first Palladian architect*

I am going to set down the history of my dealings with Sir Edward Lovett Pearce because they are a little unusual in some ways and may be of interest to others.

When I was writing my Dublin book in 1946 to 1949, Pearce was a very sketchy and insubstantial figure. Almost all that was known about him was to be found in Tom Sadleir's article in the Kildare *Journal* for July 1927. Gilbert's *Parliament House Dublin*, an 1896 reprint, expanded and illustrated, from his *History* of forty years earlier, recorded Pearce's appointment as architect for the Parliament House in 1727, encomia from both Houses in 1729 and 1731, and his death in 1733, and very little else. But it did record a malicious rumour, from as far back as 1736, to the effect that the design was really by the German, Richard Castle or Cassels. This, though largely disregarded at the time and later, persisted, as such things do, and was to cause some mischief when revived in our own century.

Sadleir was a fusty old antiquary with little visual sense. I knew him: an amiable old gentleman, a barrister by profession, a herald by reversion, and at the last a librarian by necessity. With his genealogical bent he was able to establish exactly who Pearce was, whom he married, and whom his daughters married. But, as we shall see later, he completely missed the most significant genealogical trick of all. He had the sense to follow up the trail through Pearce's connection with the Allens

1. GLOSTER, Shinrone, Co Offaly. *View across the upper hall from the North Corridor to the South Corridor.* The house was built for Trevor Lloyd, one of Pearce's cousins. The general conception is very Pearcean and sophisticated, the detailed execution less so.

missed the documentary connection with Drumcondra House and, of course, all the instances where the drawing itself was the only evidence of identity, including Cashel Palace which he had himself illustrated elsewhere.

Pearce, then, was in 1949 an unsatisfactory animal: a surprisingly young architect with one major building, and little else, to his credit, who died young. Such people do exist. One has only to think of Harvey Lonsdale Elmes or, had he not lived to his full span, Sir Giles Gilbert Scott, or indeed Benjamin Woodward. But one would sooner not have to rely on such, especially when there is sniping from the neighbouring island, as there was.

I finished the text of my Dublin book in 1949, and in that year appeared Con Curran's two chapters in the *Bank of Ireland* history, about the building as parliament house and as bank, too late to affect what I had written. Curran, like Sadleir, invoked the Elton Hall drawings. But it seems that the limitations of travel in wartime prevented him from actually travelling to England to look at them. There is no evidence that he did any more than ask for photographic copies of all the drawings known to be of the Parliament House, and perhaps for a few more with obvious Italian references. I never questioned him on this point, because by the time it became interesting to me I was out of the country, and when I returned in 1970 it would have been unkind to rub it in. At all events, he gave

of Stillorgan, and to look at the large collection of drawings (Figs. 3-7) which had by then found their way to Elton Hall in England, where lived (and still live) the Proby family, heirs of the Allens. So Sadleir added to the Pearce canon the plans for the remodelling of Stillorgan House, and the actual remodelling of its garden, including the still extant obelisk. He also noted Pearce's (long-vanished) Aungier Street Theatre, and his canal concerns; but that was all. Nor did he look very hard at the Elton Hall drawings. If a drawing had a note on the face of it saying it was of such and such a building, Sadleir noted it, but not if the inscription was on the back, and not if there was no inscription. So he

no indication of having looked any more closely at the Elton Hall drawings than Sadleir had done. But he spent a good deal of space in demolishing the canard of Castle's authorship. By a curious irony of fate, he points to the career of Vanbrugh as affording parallels to Pearce's, while happily quite ignorant of how close to the buried bodies he was himself standing. He even mentions the name of Sir Dudley Carleton ...

Nobody at the time, not I, not even Summerson, made as much as should have been made of the primacy of the Parliament House as the earliest building in Europe or the world to be erected for the express purpose of housing a bicameral legislature, or drew attention to the originality of its plan. What Summerson did do was to insinuate, verbally and in print, that the design must have been slipped to Pearce under the counter by some prominent member of the Burlington circle, perhaps Burlington himself, and must have been, like all good things in Ireland, of English origin. Pearce was dismissed as a 'front-man', an aristocratic place-holder with, perhaps, a gift for administration (which would explain why the Lords and Commons were so pleased at how he had got on with the work).

2. GLOSTER. Archway with obelisks in the garden. It is designed in the Vanbrugh (therefore also Pearce) manner.

In resisting this view I was motivated not only by patriotism but by a genuine doubt of the soundness of the hypothesis. It was at about this time (1947) that the Belgium scholar F Masai sought to re-allocate the credit for 'la miniature dite Irlandaise ' – to wit, the books of Kells and Durrow.

In about 1959 or so I had occasion to make an official inspection of a building belonging to Sir Richard Proby, not far from Elton Hall. I took the opportunity to ask Sir Richard if I might have a look at the collection of drawings, and he very readily agreed. Even a casual inspection revealed that there was much more to them than had met the eyes of Sadleir or Curran or indeed anyone else. And besides the large album in which the two hundred and fifty or so drawings had been mounted, there were the two smaller albums of drawings, of Stillorgan and the Richmond 'palace' respectively. I made some hasty notes and returned to London in a state of high excitement. Whether it was on this occasion or later that I had the misfortune to lean on the glass of one of the display-cases in the Elton library and break it, I cannot now remember. This might have been an inauspicious omen. It embarrassed me greatly, but Sir Richard made light of it.

I told John Harris, then of the RIBA Library, what I had seen, and we decided to ask permission to return together, in our own time, to have a closer look. So great were John Harris's powers of persuasion that we were allowed to bring the collection back to the RIBA Library where we could

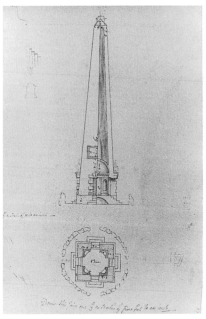

3. STILLORGAN HOUSE, Co Dublin. *Drawing by Pearce for the Obelisk.* (Elton Hall Collection). The Obelisk was designed to surmount the mausoleum of Lady Allen.

examine it at leisure.

The first fruits of this were the identification of more drawings connected with Castletown, an elevation of Drumcondra House (an easy one, this), an unlettered elevation of Cashel Palace, and, as a result of a piece of detective work of which I remain, I hope pardonably, proud, of a plan of Bellamont Forest. At one blow, so to speak, Pearce's *oeuvre* had been expanded by a factor of at least four. I wrote to Eric Dorman O'Gowan, the owner of Bellamont, asking him to be good enough to verify the dimensions of his house, and they tallied with those of the drawings. Did this mean, he asked me, that I had discovered who was the architect of his house? and with great satisfaction I was able to reply, yes, it did.

I cannot now remember the exact order of the next two revelations, nor does it much matter. Both were brought to light by John Harris. The name 'Arthur' occurred in a note on one of the Pearce drawings, and John remembered that he had seen the name in Vanbrugh's correspondence edited by Geoffrey Webb. When the two were compared it was evident that 'Arthur' (a by no means common name in the early eighteenth century) had been some kind of clerk or assistant to both Vanbrugh and Pearce. This helped to buttress the hypothesis I had begun to form – a hypothesis forced on me by the nature and composition of the collection – that the Vanbrugh drawings had passed to the Proby family by way of ownership by Pearce. But the full implications of this were still hidden from us.

The other revelation was that an elderly Austrian lady, a truly talpine figure, an indefatigable burrower in archives and a devoted student of Vanbrugh called Susi Lang, had noticed that the copy of the 1601 edition of Palladio in the RIBA Library, which contained copious notes which had optimistically (and typically) been assumed to be by Inigo Jones (but were now known not to be), had been annotated by someone else whose handwriting she had seen in the Archivio di Stato in Florence. That somebody else, she said, in a phrase uncannily reminiscent of one used by

Mahaffy half a century earlier, was 'A man called Pearce.' Comparison with the Elton drawings confirmed that it was indeed our man.

It was at this point, I think, that the devilish notion entered my head that I would give a lecture in Dublin and that the subject would be announced as 'Conolly and Pearce'. It would not be, as doubtless most of the audience would expect, about 1916, but about the Speaker and his architect in 1727 or so. I am sorry now, in a way, that I did not carry this off. As a contribution to 'revisionist history' it would have been quite something.

To resume: we now had a situation in which Pearce was clearly seen to have been a real architect, who had travelled and studied in Italy, and had a number of known and distinguished buildings to his credit, including a large unexecuted project for no less a person than King George II.

There could, at this stage, have been an awkward problem of professional etiquette. John Harris and I were keen to exhibit Pearce 'in the round' in the light of these discoveries, and this could not be done without the Elton Hall drawings. But Howard Colvin had, we learnt without surprise, been there before us, knew all about the Vanbrugh drawings, and had of course first claim on them. At that stage, at least, their significance for the biography of Pearce was not apparent to him. But this problem was to solve itself very neatly in due course.

One Sunday afternoon I was idly poring, not for the first time, over Sadleir's article, when I noticed that the name of Sir Dudley Carleton was familiar in another context. But what context? I remembered 'Arthur'. I was seized with a wild excitement. Could it be? I turned to Colvin's *Dictionary*. It was. Sir Dudley Carleton was Vanbrugh's grandfather and also the grandfather of General Edward Pearce, my man's father. So Pearce's father and Vanbrugh were first cousins. (Two of the Carleton daughters had in fact married Vanbrugh brothers). A great many things fell into place. I was so excited that I rang up John Summerson straight away. The news was greeted with a low whistle and some such remark as 'That does put a fresh complexion on things, doesn't?'

John Harris and I were deep in the study of the Elton drawings, in the RIBA, during our lunch-hours. He was also deeply involved with Sir William Chambers, on whom his book was to come out eight or nine years later. He took to addressing me as 'Sir Edward' and I him as 'Sir William' and we

4. STILLORGAN HOUSE. *Drawing by Pearce for the rock-work base of the Obelisk.* (Stillorgan Album, Elton Hall Collection). The rock-work formed the base of the Obelisk and was intended as a mausoleum for Lady Allen. The whole was inspired by Bernini's fountain in the Piazza Navona, Rome.

have kept up this piece of foolery ever since. Summerson, in the meantime, was, perforce, revising his views on the Parliament House, and gradually incorporated the necessary revisions in successive editions of his big Pelican book.

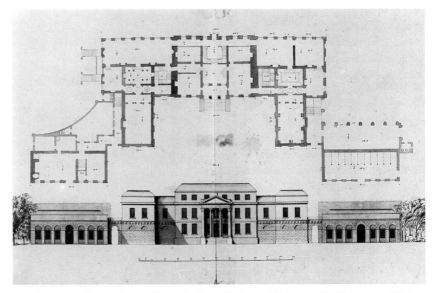

5. STILLORGAN HOUSE. *Plan and elevation by Pearce.* (Stillorgan Album, Elton Hall Collection). This is Pearce's scheme for the palladianisation of the old house (with the thick walls). The scheme was never carried out, and the house disappeared long ago.

About this time I was asked by Mark Girouard to write up Bellamont for *Country Life,* and Desmond Fitz-Gerald, the Knight of Glin, who was working on the Irish Palladians and in particular on Richard Castle, fed me some very useful observations on the family connections of Pearce. I knew already that Carters of No 9 Henrietta Street and Rathnally, Co Meath were his cousins, but Desmond pointed out that so were the Cootes of Bellamont and the Lloyds of Gloster, Co Offaly, a house which I already knew, and that some of the garden features at Gloster were startlingly close to Vanbrugh. This made me look at the house itself rather more closely. Even more significantly, he had actually read those letters in Florence which Susi Lang had noticed and Ilaria Toesca had seen while investigating Alessandro Galilei and his insular involvement, and had found further pointers towards Pearce's connection with Speaker Conolly, and that of both Galilei and Pearce with Castletown. Pearce was beginning to broaden out as a figure with a well-defined context.

I do not know exactly when the most extraordinary event of the whole business took place. I heard about it only at second-hand. It seems that a lady who worked in the Bank of Ireland happened to notice a piece of paper blowing about on the pavement in College Green just outside the old Parliament House itself. She picked it up, and it turned out to be a testimonial written by Pearce, commending Richard Castle to the nobility and gentry as an architect who had worked under him (Pearce) and could be employed with confidence. The lady passed on this document to Curran, who made a partial transcript of it, after which it disappeared from view, to surface again in the National Library, where it now safely remains.

The problem of Howard Colvin's claim on the Vanbrugh drawings was satisfactorily resolved when Sir Richard Proby was elected to the Roxburghe Club. It may here be necessary to explain that the Roxburghe Club, founded in 1812

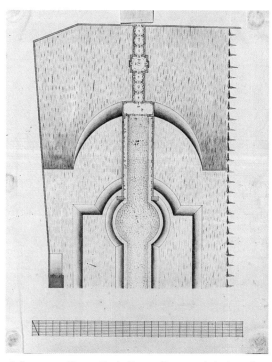

6. STILLORGAN HOUSE. *Plan by Pearce of his proposals for the garden.* (Stillorgan Album, Elton Hall Collection). Some of Pearce's garden layout was carried out and in part survives.

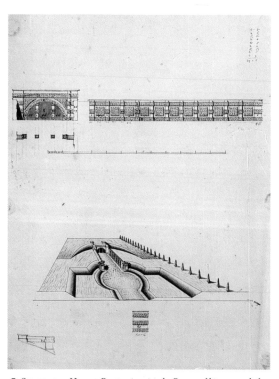

7. STILLORGAN HOUSE. *Perspective view by Pearce of his proposals for the garden.* (Stillorgan Album, Elton Hall Collection). Part of the retaining-walls of the sunken central avenue still survives, and so does the grotto, except for its frontispiece. As executed it consists of alternating domed and cross-vaulted compartments, thus more closely resembling two other of Pearce's attributed buildings Summerhill, Co Meath and North Audley Street, London.

after the auction of the Duke of Roxburghe's library, is a small society of markedly patrician complexion. Its members are mainly owners of large houses and libraries, with a sprinkling of scholars and bibliophiles of similar social attainments. A member, on election, is expected to publish, at his own expense, a book based on a notable manuscript or similar treasure in his possession, illustrated of course, and edited with a commentary either by the owner himself, if competent to do so, or by a scholar or scholars on his behalf.

Sir Richard invited Howard and me to do this for the Elton drawings. It was a wonderful opportunity. But in some ways it was not ideal. Vanbrugh, as Howard was not slow to remind me, was a much more important architect than Pearce. On the other hand Pearce, in an Irish context, was very important indeed, and the publication of these drawings would do a great deal more for Pearce's reputation than it could possibly do for Vanbrugh's. For Vanbrugh it would be a kind of *de luxe* footnote; but for Pearce it would be a substantive presentation to the world. On this basis we were able to agree to give them equal space.

To devote a Roxburghe volume to a collection of architectural drawings would be a departure; but it was agreed by our betters that it would be appropriate and could go ahead. For me there were drawbacks as well as advantages. The member was allowed to print the forty or so copies for his fellow-members, plus a certain number for presentation to libraries, and a few, a very few, to be sold through Quaritch's at an inevitably high price. Such a limited circulation was, for me, far from ideal. As against that, a substantial number of the key drawings would be reproduced in collotype, and this, together with the splendours of rag paper, Clarendon Press typography, buckram and half-morocco, was impossible to resist. I contemplated, at the time, doing an article, perhaps in *Country Life,* in which Pearce would be given a wider circulation, and I actually started writing it. But, whether through laziness or my usual reluctance to cover the same ground twice, I dropped it.

I need not have worried. In quite a short time that small section of the public who took an interest in such things had heard about the rise in Pearcean stock. In 1965 the Knight of Glin published 'New Light on Castletown' in the Irish Georgian Society's *Bulletin,* and in 1969 he, John Cornforth and I published a full-dress three-part article on Castletown in *Country Life,* which remains the fullest treatment of the house in print anywhere. Oddly enough, the propositions put in that article have been less widely taken up than those in the more out-of-the-way Roxburghe publication.

I was just in time to visit the by then derelict house in Stillorgan, where Pearce had lived, and to verify that, though it was quite possibly an early eighteenth-century house, it had been remodelled out of all recognition, before it was swept away to accommodate the four-lane bypass. Rathnally near Trim, still extant, looked, also, like a much altered early house, but the owner was away and we did not get inside it. We had better luck with the Stillorgan garden, on the edge of which Pearce's house had stood. I had noticed in Ball's *History of County Dublin* a smudgy little photograph captioned 'Grotto at Stillorgan': featureless yet suggestive. Was it the entrance to Pearce's grotto? The area was not covered with new houses, but it would be worth going to have a look. Judge of our excitement when, peering over a garden fence, we saw in the distance a row of cylindrical objects spaced out like the ventilators of a chain of subterranean vaults. And that is exactly what they were. Complete except for its columnar frontispiece now replaced by a lean-to in corrugated iron, there was the grotto, doing service for the grow-

8. GAULSTOWN, Castlepollard, Co Westmeath. This house is not to be confused with the greater (Rochfort) Gaulstown in the same county. Rowan and Casey (*The Buildings of Ireland*) suggest that this little house, of the Lill family, may be by Pearce, and they may well be right.

ing of mushrooms. More than that, substantial parts of Pearce's retaining-walls, flanking the sunken avenue leading to it, were still there, as on his drawing, brick panels and all.

The shape of the grotto, as built, turned out to have a bearing on the attribution of the saloon at No 12 North Audley Street, London, and on a discovery later made by David Griffin in the plan of Summerhill, Co Meath.

9. CUBA COURT, Banagher, Co Offaly. Photographed in 1957. The house is said to have been built by a family called Fraser. At the time this photograph was taken, the house had already been unroofed and despoiled but more recent demolitions have left, alas, almost nothing standing. The doorcase with inversely tapering pilasters derives from Michelangelo via King's Weston, which is of course by Vanbrugh, Pearce's cousin and mentor.

The Quest for Sir Edward Lovett Pearce

I am not one of those who always have a drawerful of small projects ready to be worked up into an article when one is called for. I don't know why this should be so; but it is. So when a request comes, for example to contribute to a *festschrift,* I am at a loss to know what to do. Fortunately for me, fate has always thrown in my way, just in time, a document embodying a subject of manageable size. So, when John Cornforth told me about a Pearce item in the library at Chatsworth it served very well as the basis of a contribution to a special number of the *Ulster Journal of Archaeology* (Vol xxxiii, 1970) in honour of my old mentors, Oliver Davies and Estyn Evans.

It served also to cast a little light on Pearce's relations with Burlington. It was a letter from Pearce – not to Burlington himself but to someone in his circle – about Stafford's unfinished and abandoned palace at Jigginstown outside Naas. Evidently Burlington had heard that Jigginstown was reputed to be by Inigo Jones.

There was nothing unusual in this. Almost anything of interest in this line was, for a couple of centuries at least, hopefully fathered on to Jones. (We remember the business of the RIBA's 1601 Palladio). In 1901 there even appeared a book, a handsome folio by Inigo Triggs and H Tanner, entitled *Some Works of Inigo Jones,* which I possess, illustrating a dozen buildings which are not by Jones at all, and omitting several for which, in the light of modern scholarship, a convincing attribution can be made.

Pearce was not taken in. It was clear to him that Jones had nothing to do with Jigginstown. His own response was a curious mixture of carelessness and punctilio. With his letter he sent four drawings which made it clear that, though he had measured carefully a few parts of the building, with detail carefully recorded, his examination of the rest had been perfunctory. It is easy to see why. Two of the drawings were elevational views in which hardly anything is to be seen but the jungle of vegetation which then obscured it. Pearce had used a ladder and a tape, but for the overall survey he had relied on memory and conjecture.

Some years later the sharp eye of Rolf Loeber spotted that a

10. WOODLANDS, formerly Clinshogh, Santry, Co Dublin. The house was built for the Rev John Jackson in about 1730. The ground-plan with its vaulted corridor strongly suggests Pearce, and so does the massing. The doorcase is a later alteration.

drawing in the Elton collection (No 8), lettered 'Smokingstown', which I had tried hard but failed to identify, was in fact Jigginstown. This made me feel very foolish; but I suppose you, or rather I, cannot win them all. The next development was in a quite different direction.

The affair of the Viceregal Ball began by being a typical Pearcean recognition scene, but turned out to have a twist in the tale. We all knew that Mrs Delany, then Mrs Pendarves, went in November 1731 to a ball given by the Duke of Dorset in Dublin Castle, and that the room in which it took place 'was ordered by Capt. Pierce, finely adorned with paintings and obelisks.' So what could be more satisfactory then the unearthing by the Knight of Glin of a painting belonging to a member of the Sackville (Dorset) family showing just such a ball, with obelisks and paintings as described? Better still, a few years later, some of the painted hangings were found, rolled up in an attic, at Knole.

But then along comes Freddie O'Dwyer with some good reasons to suggest that the ball in the painting took place not in 1731 but twenty years later, during the second viceroyalty of the same Duke, by which time Pearce had been long dead. Anagnoresis and peripeteia: all very Aristotelian. Except that it remains possible that the decorations were taken out and dusted off to be re-used when they were twenty years old, in which case they may be Pearce's after all.

Sir Edward, meanwhile, was preparing an ambush in another part of the forest. This time it was for Eddie McParland. There was – there is – among the Elton drawings one which had puzzled me very much: No 39. Howard Colvin thought it was probably by Vanbrugh. I was not so sure. It was a plan of an irregular but more or less T-shaped building with three staircases and a passage through the middle which should have reminded me of Woodlands, Santry, a house I had my eye on for some time past, and indeed also of the Stillorgan grotto. Our entry on it was non-committal and we did not illustrate it. We called it 'a house', which was a serious oversight.

Far away, in London, John Harris was poring for the

umpteenth time over the volumes of the old Georgian Society, where, in volume iv, of 1912, there is a photograph of the long-demolished Deanery of Christchurch. He wrote to Eddie asking, in effect, whether the Deanery could be by Pearce. Eddie had spotted, what should have been obvious, that the Elton plan was for three houses, not one. To cut a long story short, he was able to show conclusively, from contemporary documents, that the three houses, with a common entrance, had been designed and built by Pearce for the Dean and Chapter between 1731 and 1733. The result appears, most gracefully and with an air of Euclidian elegance, in my *festschrift*.

So much for the certainties. Whether to place Summerhill among the certainties is, perhaps, still a moot point. I had always been, and still am, inclined to discount the shaky attribution to Castle and give it mainly to Pearce. The indications – for I cannot go so far as to call them *proofs* – are mainly of a rather technical nature and the key figure in their identification is David Griffin. But I am morally certain that Pearce was the architect.

There remain many areas of uncertainty. Chief among these is that we still do not know when or where he was born. Neither on the Irish side nor on the English has a parish register entry come to light. The probabilities point, as they have always pointed, to his having been born in about 1699, so that he would have died at the age of about thirty-four. But it is unsatisfactory not to be sure. Not long ago someone came up with the information that a military commission had been bought in his name in 1708. This caused considerable consternation, and efforts were made to juggle the chronology about to see whether it could be made to fit. Or had he, perhaps, a cousin of the same name, remembering that both his father and his uncle were generals? In the end we comforted ourselves with the idea that it had been bought for him rather as places at select schools are, or used to be, bought, or at least reserved, years in advance.

The remaining uncertainties are the buildings which he may,

11. WARDTOWN, otherwise Ballymacward, near Ballyshannon, Co Donegal. The house belonged to the Foliott family. Now ruined, Wardtown was very similar to Arch Hall (Fig. 12) with the Vanbrughian feature of cylindrical towers and semi-circular projections.

or may not, have designed. As with Inigo Jones, as with Wren, as with Robert Adam, the temptation is strong to father any building of quality with the right date on to the favoured name. This is a dangerous procedure because it can all too easily degenerate into a circular argument. This building is so good that it can only be by Pearce. Why do we think so? Because we do not know of another architect of the time good enough to give it to. And why do we not know of such an architect? Because we have already given so many good buildings to Pearce and have not tried hard enough to find another candidate.

What about the buildings which he may have designed but which were carried out by someone else after his death? And what about those where he may have roughed out the main design but not been present on site to supervise the execution? And all manner of possible combinations of similar circumstances? It still seems overwhelmingly probable, from the evidence of silence alone, that there were no other architects about in the Ireland of 1730 with accomplishments comparable to Pearce's.

The list of candidates for buildings in some way connected to Pearce is quite long. Here is my version of it:

Trinity College, the Printing House; Dublin Castle, the North range; Dublin Castle, the South-East range; Royal Hospital Kilmainham, the Garden House; Gloster, Co Offaly; Arch Hall, Co Meath; Wardstown, Co Donegal; King House, Boyle, Co Roscommon; Gaulstown, Co Westmeath; Lismore, Crossdoney, Co Cavan; Cuba Court, Co Offaly; Woodlands, Co Dublin; Desart Court, Co Kilkenny; Seafield, Co Dublin; Rathfarnham, the Palliser House (Loreto Convent); Dublin, La Touche's Bank, Castle Street; Downpatrick, the Southwell almshouse and schools; London, No 12 North Audley Street (in part).

The probability is that between two-thirds and three-quarters of these have an authentic Pearce connection, and that documentary proof will, sooner or later, come to light in the case of a few of them. Five of them are country houses which are in ruin or no longer exist. Not all the attributions are mine: some are

THE QUEST FOR SIR EDWARD LOVETT PEARCE

12. ARCH HALL, Wilkinstown, Co Meath. Arch Hall is credited as the home of a family called Garnet of whom nothing seems to be known. The arch on the axis, which gives Arch Hall its name, is similar in feeling to that at Gloster.

grounded in similarity of style or plan, others in connections of another kind.

To judge by his form to date, it seems likely that Sir Edward will spring some more surprises on us. Who will be the favoured recipient of further revelations it is impossible to predict. But revelations there will, surely, be.

DR MAURICE CRAIG's books include The Volunteer Earl *(London 1948),* Dublin 1660-1860 *(Dublin 1952),* Irish Bookbinding, 1600-1800 *(London 1954),* The Personality of Leinster *(Dublin 1961),* Classic Irish Houses of the Middle Size *(London 1976),* The Architecture of Ireland *(London and Dublin 1982),* The Elephant and the Polish Question *(Dublin 1990).*

AUTHENTICATED WORKS BY SIR EDWARD LOVETT PEARCE IN IRELAND:
The Parliament House, Dublin.
Nos 9 and 10 Henrietta Street, Dublin.
Christchurch Deanery, Fishamble Street (demolished).
The Theatre, Aungier Street (demolished).
Stillorgan, Co Dublin, Obelisk and garden works including grotto.
Drumcondra House, Co Dublin, S front etc.
Castletown, Co Kildare, entrance hall and other interiors; colonnades and wings almost certainly.
Bellamont Forest, Co Cavan.
Cashel Palace, Co Tipperary.
Crom, Co Fermanagh, temple on island (probably unexecuted)
Loughgall, Co Armagh, market house (probably unexecuted)

LESS THAN COMPLETELY AUTHENTICATED:-
Summerhill, Co Meath

WORK IN OR FOR ENGLAND:-
Shadwell Park, Norfolk (*Country Life,* 2 July, 1964).
Heydon Hall, Norfolk (possible additions).

Ashley Park Surrey, documented additions (John Harris in *Decantations,* ed. Agnes Bernelle, 1992).
12 North Audley Street, London, the saloon (highly probable).
Palace or large house for King George II at Richmond, Surrey, (unexecuted).

BIBLIOGRAPHY OF PUBLISHED WRITINGS DEALING WITH PEARCE:
Sir John Gilbert, *Parliament House, Dublin* (Dublin & London, 1896).
Thomas Ulick Sadleir, 'Sir Edward Lovett Pearce', *Journal of the County Kildare Archaeological Society,* Vol. X, No. 5, (1927).
Constantine P Curran, 'The Architecture of the Bank' [i.e. the Parliament House] in F G Hall, *The Bank of Ireland* (Dublin & Oxford, 1948).
Desmond Fitz-Gerald, 'Richard Castle, a synopsis', *Irish Georgian Society Bulletin,* Vol. VII, No. 1 Jan-Mar, 1964.
Ilaria Toesca, 'Alessandro Galilei in Inghilterra' in *English Miscellany,* - ed. Mario Praz, (Rome, 1952).
Howard Colvin and Maurice Craig, *Architectural Drawings in the Library of Elton Hall by Sir John Vanbrugh and Sir Edward Lovett Pearce,* (Oxford, 1964).
Maurice Craig, 'Bellamont Forest, Co Cavan', *Country Life,* 21 and 28 May, 1964.
Desmond Fitz-Gerald, Knight of Glin, 'New Light on Castletown', *Irish Georgian Society Bulletin,* Vol. VIII, 1 Jan-March, 1965.
Maurice Craig and Desmond Fitz-Gerald, 'Castletown, Co Kildare', *Country Life,* 27 March and April 3, 1969.
Anne Crookshank and Desmond Fitz-Gerald, *Irish Portraits 1660-1860* (p.37) n.p. Paul Mellon Foundation, 1969.
Maurice Craig, 'New Light on Jigginstown', *Ulster Journal of Archaeology,* 1970 III, 33. Reprinted in *Journal of the Co Kildare Archaeological Society, Vol. XV,* No. 1, 1971.
Maurice Craig, 'Sir Edward Lovett Pearce', *Irish Georgian Society Bulletin,* Vol. XXVII 1-2 Jan-June 1974.
Edward McParland, 'Edward Lovett Pearce and the Deanery of Christ Church Dublin' in *Decantations,* ed. Agnes Bernelle, (Dublin, 1992).
Frederick O'Dwyer, 'The Ballroom at Dublin Castle', *Decantations* (as preceding entry) 1992.
Howard Colvin, *Biographical Dictionary of British Architects,* (London, 1978).

IRISH GOLDSMITHS' WORK OF THE LATER MIDDLE AGES

Raghnall Ó Floinn *examines some rare surviving treasures of Medieval Ireland*

Any consideration of Irish goldsmiths' work of the later middle ages must take into account the problems of attribution and place of manufacture.[1] Because of the absence of any early Irish silver marks an Irish origin can only be proven by examining the small number of surviving inscriptions on objects which sometimes give the craftsman's name or by examining the style of particular pieces. Throughout the later middle ages a high proportion of luxury goods, such as jewellery and silver plate for the table and altar, must have been imported. A recent study of medieval jewellery from Ireland has shown that many of the types and decoration of finger rings, brooches and pectoral crosses can often be paralleled in England and Scotland.[2] It must be said, however, that jewellery of the same type is found across northern Europe, from France to Scandinavia so that one must not assume that influences necessarily came always from Britain. Indeed, recent work has identified a small number of gold and silver artefacts of the twelfth century which are imports from the Rhineland.[3]

Surviving examples of Irish medieval goldsmiths' work are rare. Given the nature of the raw materials used, the majority would have been melted down or recycled. Natural disasters also contributed to the loss of valuable items as, for example, in July 1461 when the east window of Christ Church Cathedral, Dublin was blown in by a storm 'and the falling stones broke many chests containing jewels, relics, ornaments and vestments of the altar ... By a miracle the Staff of Jesus, though the chest in which it was kept and other relics therein was destroyed, was found uninjured lying above the stones.'[4] The effects of the Reformation confiscations were devastating and included the destruction of many works of art including, in 1541, the public burning in Dublin of the aforementioned Staff of Jesus – a relic of St Patrick which was the most venerated relic in Ireland and a prized possession of Christ Church Cathedral. The wars of the sixteenth and seventeenth

1. The SHRINE OF THE STOWE MISSAL. Copper alloy covered with parcel gilt silver with niello inlay, enamel, rock crystal, and glass, 18.7cm high. c.1360/70. (National Museum of Ireland). An inscription in Irish records that the Shrine was redecorated by the goldsmith Domhnall O Tolari for the King of Ormond. The engraving technique of the figures is very similar to that on the contemporary Shrine of St Patrick's Tooth which may well be by the same hand.

centuries took their toll also. The devastation was so great that not a single example of pre-Reformation panel painting, stained glass or church vestments of certain Irish manufacture survives.

What little we know of the organisation of the craft of the goldsmith in late medieval Ireland suggests that it was based mainly in towns and commissions came largely from wealthy lay and ecclesiastical patrons. Royal charters gave towns the right to set up guilds and a guild organisation was already in existence in Dublin by the close of the twelfth century. At this time also, goldsmiths are recorded as being admitted to the Dublin Gild Merchant and all have Anglo-Norman names; the list includes two which are certainly of English origin: William of Shrewsbury and Godard of London. Later, in the thirteenth century, the inclusion of one Maurice of Connacht indicates that craftsmen from other parts of Ireland were being admitted.[5] By the early sixteenth century – and perhaps from a much earlier date – the goldsmiths' quarter in Dublin was located in St Werburgh's parish.[6] In the fifteenth century, Irish goldsmiths are found practising their trade in other towns and a few of them are identified by name – John O'Bardan in Drogheda[7] and Thomas O'Carryd who made the magnificent mitre and crozier for Conor O'Dea, Bishop of Limerick in 1418, who was probably based in Limerick.[8] Some were sufficiently wealthy to be able to grant lands to the church. In 1200 Walter the goldsmith granted land in the western suburbs of Dublin to the Hospital of St. John the Baptist.[9]

In that part of the country outside Anglo-Norman control, artisans – including goldsmiths, carpenters, masons and scribes – were regarded, as in pre-Norman times, as members of the professional learned classes, equal in rank with lawyers, historians and poets. These crafts were often hereditary. We can tell this from the death notices of a number of craftsmen which are recorded in the *Annals of Ulster*. In 1425 and 1443, respectively,

2. The LIMERICK CROZIER. (Detail of the head). Silver, gilt silver, enamel and pearls. 198cm high overall, 60cm high (the crook). Dated 1418. (Collection The Bishop of Limerick). The scene depicted is the pelican nourishing its young with its own blood as an image of the self-sacrifice of Christ.

the deaths of Eogan and Solomon Ua Diarmata are noted. Both are described as *saer* – a term which can mean either a carpenter or a mason. Another family of artisans were the Uí Chiarmaic of Fermanagh, the deaths of two members of which, Augustin and Mathghamain, are recorded in 1431 and 1533. The O'Dowgans, who were the bishop's carpenters at Raphoe, Co Donegal,[10] were also masons and the family name appears on the foundation stone of St Mary's Augustinian Priory at Devenish, Co Fermanagh[11] and on a memorial stone bearing a mason's mallet and chisel at Clonca, Co Donegal.[12]

Such families of craftsmen were also to be found in the towns. Members of the O'Tunney family, who specialised in the production of effigial tombs throughout the sixteenth century, were traditionally supposed to have had workshops at Callan, Co Kilkenny and signed examples of their work are known from some eight separate locations in counties Kilkenny and Tipperary.[13] Some Irish craftsmen travelled abroad: members of the Irish families of Ua Brolcháin and Ua Cuinn worked as master masons at Iona and Oronsay Priory in western Scotland in the late fifteenth century.[14]

Information on goldsmiths is less forthcoming but the names of William and Christopher Cornell, armourers, are recorded as residing in the parish of St Werburgh's in Dublin in the latter half of the fifteenth century.[15] The goldsmith William Cornell, who made the gilt silver Lislaghtin Cross (Fig. 4) for an O'Connor chief in 1479, may well have been a member of this Dublin family. Some goldsmiths seem to have worked for particular patrons or worked in particular parts of the country. The *Annals of Ulster* record the death in 1479 of Matthew Ua Maelruanaigh who is described as the *ollamh* in metalwork to the Maguires of Fermanagh and a skilled goldsmith (*sai orcerda*) and in 1491 the death took place of one Tadhg Ua Siriden who was described as the best goldsmith in Leath Chuinn (i.e. the northern half of Ireland). A decorated ceremonial goblet belonging to the Maguires, dated 1493 and made by an unnamed craftsman, is preserved today at Dunvegan Castle on the isle of Skye (Fig 6). Its unusual form is derived from the four-sided wooden drinking cup or mether which was peculiar to Ireland in the later middle ages. The wooden goblet was covered in gilt silver fittings and, according to its inscription, it was commissioned by Catherine O'Neill, wife of the Maguire chieftain, John, and

3. The LIMERICK CROZIER. (Detail of the crook). Silver, gilt silver, enamel, and pearls. 198cm high overall, 60cm high (the crook). Dated 1418. (Collection The Bishop of Limerick). The scene depicted is the Annunciation. The crozier was made for Conor O'Dea, Bishop of Limerick in 1418 and is probably the work of the goldsmith, Thomas O'Carryd, whose name appears on a jewelled mitre made for the same patron.

bears the date 1493. The only other secular piece of metalwork to have survived the medieval period is associated with another great Irish family. This is the Kavanagh 'Charter' Horn, preserved at Borris, Co Carlow since late medieval times (Fig. 10). It was so called because it symbolised the MacMurrough-Kavanagh family's claim to the kingship of Leinster.[16] In its present state it consists of a carved elephant ivory tusk held in a brass stand. These late mounts mask the presence of earlier mountings indicating that it was a valued heirloom. The craftsman Tigernanus O Lavan, whose name is inscribed on the rim, may well have been belonged to a family of hereditary artisans of the Kavanaghs as the name is found in north county Wexford, an area at the heart of the Kavanagh's kingdom.[17] Another product of Kavanagh patronage is the now sadly mutilated Shrine of the Book of Moling commissioned by Art MacMurrough Kavanagh in 1402.[18]

The unique churchwarden's accounts for St Werburgh's in Dublin offer us a glimpse of the modest wealth of an urban parish church. In 1511 the church plate consisted of a cross,

censer, pax, bust (probably a head reliquary) and four chalices, all of gilt silver. The accounts also list repairs to the plate, the purchase and repair of books and vestments as well as work done on the fabric of the building.[19]

One of the few surviving pieces of goldsmith's work from a town is the gilt silver crozier which, along with a matching jewelled mitre, was made in 1418 for Conor O'Dea, Bishop of Limerick (Figs 2, 3). The mitre bears the signature of the goldsmith Thomas O'Carryd, who may also have made the crozier. In the crook of the crozier is an Annunciation scene and immedi-

4. (*Overleaf, left*) PROCESSIONAL CROSS (Detail). Gilt silver, 62.7cm high. Made in 1479 for the Franciscan Friary of Lislaghtin, Co Kerry. (National Museum of Ireland). The maker of this cross in the International Gothic style was William Cornell who may well have been one of a family of armourers who lived in St Werburgh's parish, Dublin.

5. (*Overleaf, right*) The SHRINE OF ST PATRICK'S TOOTH. (Detail of the figure of a bishop). Parcel gilt, gold and silver filigree, niello inlay, rock crystal and glass 27.5cm high. c.1350. (National Museum of Ireland) A Latin inscription records that the shrine was made for Thomas de Bermingham, Lord of Athenry.

6. The DUNVEGAN CUP. Wood covered with parcel gilt silver mounts, 26.5cm high. Dated on the rim 1493. (Dunvegan Castle, Isle of Skye). An inscription on the rim records that this ceremonial goblet was commissioned by Catherine O'Neill, wife of the Maguire of Fermanagh: its unusual form is derived from the four-sided wooden drinking cup or mether which was peculiar to Ireland in the later middle ages.

ately below this is shown the pelican nourishing or reviving its young with its own blood – a symbol of the self-sacrifice of Christ derived from legends contained in medieval bestiaries. The crozier is adorned with cast figures and architectural elements soldered to silver plates which comprise the shaft and crook. The latter in turn contain smaller panels of gilt silver with engraved designs of flowers inlaid with translucent enamel and set with pearls. The inscription which names the patron is in *champlevé* red and blue enamel.

Much of the metal work which survives consists of additions or repairs to earlier reliquaries of Irish saints which were preserved in the hands of successive generations of hereditary keepers who were often descended from the administrators of church property. One of the finest is a shrine known as the Domhnach Airgid (Fig. 7). Originally made around 800 AD to contain relics given by St Patrick to Macartan, patron saint of Clones, Co Monaghan, it was completely remodelled around 1350 for the abbot of Clones, John O'Carbri. It is decorated with cast and gilt silver plaques bearing figures of saints and apostles. The relief casting of the Domhnach Airgid shrine is unusual. The work also bears the name of the craftsman who made it, John O'Bardan, and it was probably made in Drogheda where a goldsmith of the same name is known to have lived.

Occasionally the hand of the same craftsman can be seen on more than one piece, as in the case of panels on the Shrine of St Patrick's Tooth and the Shrine of the Stowe Missal (Figs. 5, 1). Both date to around 1350 and were made for patrons at Athenry, Co Galway and Lorrha, Co Tipperary which are situated only some fifty kilometres apart. The techniques employed on both are very similar. In particular, both carry panels of parcel gilt sheet silver engraved with human figures against a rock-traced background and the engraved lines are emphasised by a niello inlay. One of the principal differences between the two objects is that the inscription on the Athenry reliquary is in Latin while that on the Lorrha shrine is in Irish, probably reflecting the different backgrounds – Anglo-Irish and Irish – of the patrons, respectively Thomas de Bermingham, Lord of Athenry and Philip O'Kennedy, King of Ormond.

The principal face of the Shrine of St Patrick's Tooth contains a series of figures which are executed in *repoussé* from existing dies (Fig. 8). Such stamped work is common on Irish metalwork of the period and in some cases the die

7. The DOMHNACH AIRGID SHRINE. Cast and silver gilt, niello, enamel and rock crystal, 23cm long. c.1350. (National Museum of Ireland). Originally made about 800AD to contain relics given by St Patrick to Macartan, patron saint of Clones, the shrine was completely remodelled about 1350, probably by a craftsman in Drogheda.

patterns are repeated on the same face either as a border (usually of confronted animals) or even on the principal face. An example of this is the Shrine of St Caillin, a book shrine preserved at Fenagh, Co Leitrim (Fig. 9). Here a pattern of three figures under niches occurs four times. A cache of dies belonging to a goldsmith was found in the last century at Lough Fea, Co Monaghan[20] and included dies for border panels similar to those found on objects such as the Shrine of St Patrick's Hand,[21] the Cathach and the Shrine of St Patrick's Tooth (Fig. 8).

Another feature of Irish goldsmiths' work of the period is the sparing use of precious or semi-precious stones. This could be simply due to the fact that few of the surviving pieces come from the larger towns where such raw materials were more readily available. However, it could also be a reflection of the relatively modest revenue-generating potential of the Irish economy in the later middle ages where architectural projects, whether parish churches, abbeys or cathedrals, were on a more modest scale than their equivalents elsewhere in north western Europe.[22]

The surviving corpus of metalwork of the later medieval period from Ireland is very limited and, with the exception of some repre-

sentations of jewellery on tomb sculpture, there are no contemporary pictorial sources to show the types of object produced by Irish goldsmiths. Written evidence in the form of wills, inventories and port and guild records, along with finds from archeological excavations, offer the best hope of resolving questions such as how the craft was organised, what raw materials, manufacturing techniques and tools were being used and what kinds of objects were produced. One can only wonder, for example, what the 'gold square with four pearls and a gold clasp with white enamel and a gold lock', willed by John Chever of Dublin to his daughter Jenet in 1474, actually looked like.[23]

RAGHNALL Ó FLOINN is Assistant Keeper in the Irish Antiquities Division in the National Museum of Ireland and author of Irish Shrines and Reliquaries of the Middle Ages *(Dublin 1994).*

8. (*Overleaf*) The SHRINE OF ST PATRICK'S TOOTH. Parcel gilt, gold and silver filigree, niello inlay, rock crystal and glass 27.5cm high. c.1350. (National Museum of Ireland). The figures on either side and below the Crucifixion are executed in response and represent the national saints Brigid, Patrick and Colmcille as well as St Benan, a local saint.

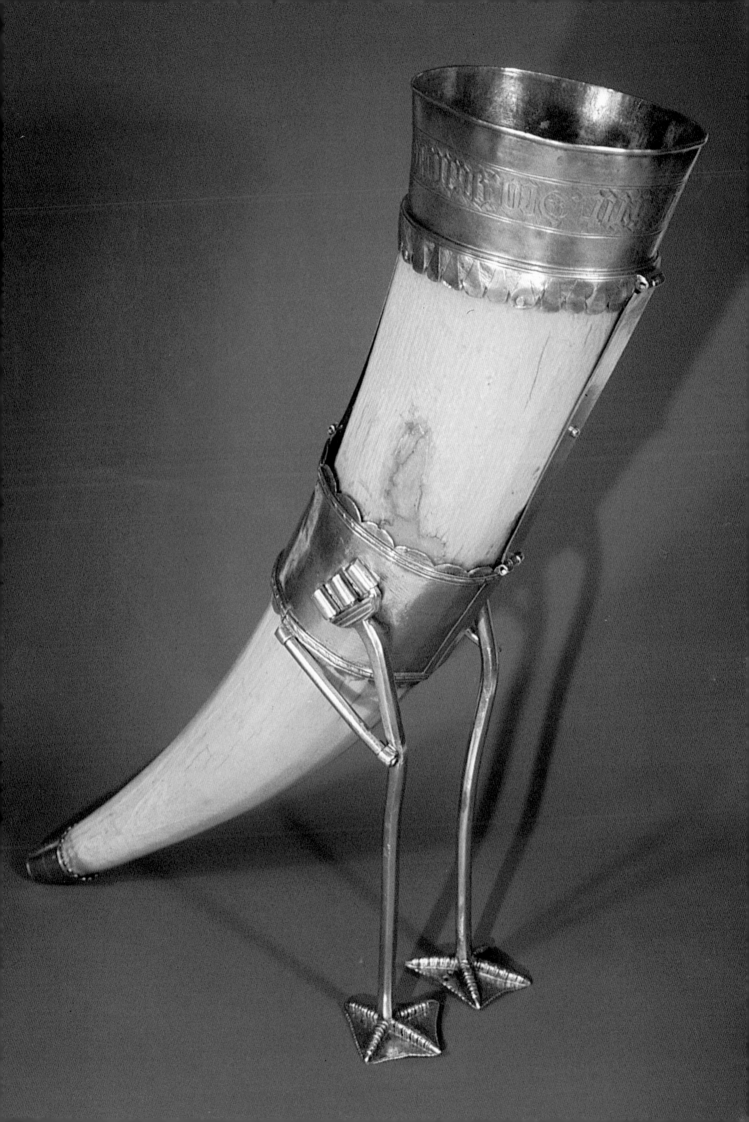

9. The SHRINE OF ST CAILLIN. Gold, copper alloy, silver, niello inlay, rock crystal and glass, 27.5cm long. Dated 1536. (National Museum of Ireland). The Shrine comes from Fenagh, Co Leitrim. The repeated stamped panels are typical of goldsmiths' work of the end of the medieval period.

10. *(Previous page)* The KAVANAGH 'CHARTER' HORN. Carved ivory elephant tusk with brass mounts of the fifteenth century. 42cm high. (National Museum of Ireland). Inscribed on the rim with the name of the craftsman, Tigernanus O Lavan. The horn symbolised the MacMurrough-Kavanagh family's claim to the Kingship of Leinster.

1. There is no published survey of the subject. The best photographic coverage is still the two volume survey *Christian Art in Ancient Ireland,* Vol. 1, edited by A Mahr, Dublin 1932 and Vol II, edited by J Raftery, Dublin 1941.

2. J Cherry, 'Medieval Jewellery from Ireland: A Preliminary Survey' in G Mac Niocaill and P F Wallace (eds) *Keimelia – Studies in Medieval Archaeology and History in Memory of Tom Delaney,* Galway 1988, pp.143-159.

3. R Ó Floinn, 'Innovation and conservatism in Irish metalwork of the Romanesque period', in C Karkov, M Ryan and R Farrell (eds), *The Insular Tradition,* New York 1995 (American Early Medieval Studies 2).

4. H J Lawlor, 'A Calendar of the Liber Niger and Liber Albus of Christ Church, Dublin', *Proceedings of the Royal Irish Academy,* 27C (1908-9), pp.1-93, at p.56.

5. H F Berry, 'The Goldsmiths' Company of Dublin', *Journal of the Royal Society of Antiquaries of Ireland,* 31, (1901), pp.119-33 at pp.119-20.

6. H F Twiss, 'Some ancient deeds of the parish of St Werburgh, Dublin. 1243-1676', *Proceedings of the Royal Irish Academy,* 35C, (1918-20), pp.282-315 at pp.292-313.

7. W G H Quigley and E F D Roberts, (eds.) *Registrum Iohannis Mey,* Belfast 1972, p.52.

8. J Hunt, *The Limerick Mitre and Crozier,* Dublin (no date), p.10.

9. E St John Brooks, *Register of the Hospital of St John The Baptist,* Dublin 1936, pp.113-14.

10. K Nicholls, 'Gaelic society and economy in the high middle ages' in A Cosgrove (ed) *A New History of Ireland II Medieval Ireland 1169-1534,* Oxford 1987, pp.397-438 at p.418.

11. J E McKenna, *Devenish (Lough Erne): Its History, Antiquities and Traditions,* Dublin and Enniskillen, 1931, p.72.

12. R A S Macalister, *Corpus Inscriptionum Insularum Celticarum,* Vol.II, Dublin 1949, p.116.

13. J Hunt, 'Rory O'Tunney and the Ossory Tomb sculptures', *Journal of the Royal Society of Antiquaries of Ireland,* 80, (1950), pp.22-28.

14. K A Steer and J W M Bannerman, *Late Medieval Monumental Sculpture in the West Highlands,* Edinburgh 1977, pp.105-09 and 119-21.

15. H F Twiss, 'Some ancient deeds of the parish of St Werburgh, Dublin 1243-1676', *Proceedings of the Royal Irish Academy,* 35C, (1918-20), pp.282-315 at pp.288-90 and

304-07.

16. R Ó Floinn, 'The Kavanagh "Charter" Horn', in D Ó Corráin (ed), *Aspects of Antiquity: Essays in Honour of M J O'Kelly,* Cork 1981, pp.268-78.

17. E St John Brooks, *Knights' Fees in Counties Wexford, Carlow and Kilkenny,* Dublin 1950, pp.132-33.

18. J Raftery, *Christian Art in Ancient Ireland,* Vol.II, Dublin 1941, p.164 and pl.122.

19. J L Robinson, 'Churchwardens' accounts, 1484-1600, St Werburgh's Church, Dublin', *Journal of the Royal Society of Antiquaries of Ireland,* 44, (1914), pp.132-142 at pp.139-40.

20. E P Shirley, *The History of the County of Monaghan,* London, 1879, p.170.

21. C Bourke, 'The Shrine of St Patrick's Hand', *Irish Arts Review,* Vol.4, no.3, (1987), pp.25-27.

22 R A Stalley, *Architecture and Sculpture in Ireland 1150-1350,* Dublin and London, 1971, p.16.

23. H F Berry, (ed), *Register of Wills and Inventories of the Diocese of Dublin in the time of Archbishops Tregury and Walton 1457-1483,* Dublin 1898, (Royal Society of Antiquaries of Ireland Extra Vol., 1896-98).

TOURISM AND INDUSTRY
KILLARNEY AND ITS FURNITURE

Brian Austen

*provides a definitive
account of some distinctive
Irish woodwork*

Centres of tourism provide markets for souvenirs and may develop distinctive manufactures to meet this need. As early as the first half of the seventeenth century the town of Spa, now in Belgium, was offering such wares and this was soon followed by Tunbridge Wells in Kent where wooden goods, initially produced in London, were a feature. Subsequent centres of western tourism to develop local woodworking industries included Brighton, Sorrento, Madeira, the Black Forest region of Germany and Jerusalem.[1] Killarney attracted visitors because of its lakes and mountains but by the mid-nineteenth century they were not the only attractions featured in guide books. One book of 1853 advised that 'of the arbutus wood a variety of toys are made at Killarney, for which there is a considerable sale to visitors anxious to retain some palpable reminiscence of the beautiful lakes'. At that date five establishments existed in the town offering wares manufactured from arbutus, yew and bog oak, the largest of which employed 'during the whole year fifteen or sixteen hands'.[2]

Killarney attracted tourists from the mid-eighteenth century and guide books were published simultaneously in London and Dublin in 1776. It was in September of that year that Arthur Young arrived in

1. DESK AND CABINET by James Egan. 1861. 115cm high, 84cm wide, 59cm deep. (National Museum of Ireland). Veneered in arbutus, holly and other woods. The doors, bearing the coat-of-arms of the United Kingdom enclose five long drawers depicting on their fronts Muckross Abbey, Aghadoe, Ross Castle, Innisfallen and Dunloe Castle; the hinged top to the desk covers six small drawers. The desk was presented to Queen Victoria during her visit to Killarney in 1861.

as 'too fatiguing and long'. For the visitor from Britain it was worse. The railway eventually provided a solution but it was not until July 1853 that Killarney was connected. From 1841, however, British visitors could utilise the Great Western Railway to Bristol, steam ship to Cork and coach or car onwards. By 1849 the Great Southern & Western Railway had reached Mallow and a six hour journey by road covered the forty and a quarter miles onward to Killarney.[4] The second inhibiting factor was the town of Killarney itself which initially contrasted greatly with the delights of the surrounding scenery. Its lack of cleanliness and facilities appalled visitors. Young in 1776 described the inns as 'miserable and the lodgings little better,' a traveller of 1804 described 'the new inn' as 'dirty and uncomfortable' and as late as 1834 Inglis could declare the town 'biggish, populous, noisy and not very pretty'. Standards were, however, improving from the 1820s and a guide of 1822 mentioned 'three tolerable inns' and a 'public reading room'. Lewis in 1837 commented on 'two commodious and respectable inns for the reception of the numerous visitors to the lakes' and additionally 'several lodging houses'. Two subscription reading rooms existed, one of which had a billiard room

Killarney at the start of an extensive Irish tour. He spent several days in the area and declared 'the lakes that I have seen can scarcely be said to have a rival'. Later travellers were equally loud in their praise of the region's scenic charms. Leitch Ritchie, writing in 1838, praised the variety of scenery for 'within the circuit of a moderate day's walk, almost every possible variety of the wild, the majestic, the beautiful, the picturesque' could be found and 'these beauties are ... of the first class'.[3] Two factors, however, inhibited visitors. The first was the inaccessibility. The journey from the Irish capital of nearly 190 miles was described

attached. It was this growing tourist trade that was to promote the local manufacture of woodwares.[5]

The first mention of the manufacture of woodwares at Killarney is in 1837. Lewis noted 'a variety of useful and ornamental articles are made from the arbutus tree, and sold to strangers visiting the lakes'. The raw material was readily at hand as the slopes of the hills surrounding the lakes were thickly clothed in woods. The arbutus (*arbutus unedo*), also known as the strawberry tree, is a tree shrub of Mediterranean origin, which flourished in the mild and damp climate of South-West Ireland,

2. DAVENPORT. c.1860. 69cm wide, 103cm high, 64cm deep. (Private collection). Veneered in arbutus, holly and other woods, inlaid with sprays of arbutus and ferns, the desk lid with a view of Muckross Abbey. The doors of the cabinet enclose five drawers.

3. TABLE c.1870. 73cm high, 55cm wide. (Private collection). Veneered in arbutus, holly and other woods inlaid with shamrock trails and fern sprays, the hinged top with a view of Muckross Abbey sits above a removable, sectioned and lidded tray with a well beneath.

in some cases reaching seven feet in circumference. Also in the woodlands elm, ash, holly and yew were to be found growing abundantly. Timbers, long immersed in waterlogged ground, such as bog oak and bog yew were also utilised for the souvenir trade. Both woods were close-grained, carved well and took 'a fine polish' while the 'inky blackness' of bog oak and the resemblance of bog yew to rosewood were attractive.[6] The date when manufacture commenced is uncertain but initial production may have been small carved objects of bog oak or yew. The earliest claim to manufacture at Killarney is that of Jeremiah O'Connor who, when advertising his 'Arbutus and Irish Bog Oak Factory' in 1858, claimed to be the original maker, 'Established 1825'.[7] Another early maker of bog oak was Dennis Connell. His success in selling 'his work to the visitors as souvenirs of the locality' led him to seek a wider market by moving to Dublin about

4. DAVENPORT . c.1870. 106.7cm high 86.4cm wide, 73.7cm deep. (Muckross House, Killarney). Veneered in arbutus, holly and other woods with bog-oak pillar supports. The lid inlaid with a view of Killarney House and ferns (outside) and a harp and shamrock trails (inside); the doors inlaid with views of Muckross Abbey and Ross Castle enclose four drawers.

1845. The trade in bog oak was certainly centred in Dublin and may well have developed there first. Publicity was given to the timber when in 1821 Patrick M'Guirk presented a carved walking stick to George IV on his visit to the city. By 1834 he was conducting a flourishing bog oak manufactory at 1 George's Hill.[8] Great publicity was afforded for the material by the display of a suite of furniture carved with Irish emblems made by Arthur Jones, Son & Co. of Stephen's Green at the Great Exhibition in Hyde Park, London in 1851 and the Dublin Exhibition of 1853. By 1870 there were no fewer than seventeen bog oak ornament manufacturers and dealers in Dublin.[9] The trade continued actively at Killarney as well, with most makers producing such objects. Most of the manufactures were of small objects such as brooches, bracelets, necklaces and ear rings and motifs emblematic of Irish culture and history in general rather than

5. BOOK STAND. Attributable to Henry Hollamby, Tunbridge Wells.c.1870. 28cm high, 36cm wide. (Muckross House, Killarney). The stand is veneered in rosewood and decorated with Tunbridge Ware tessellated mosaic panels depicting Muckross Abbey and Ross Castle with a mosaic border of roses.

6. GAMES TABLE by John O'Donoghue. 1929. 77cm wide, 45cm deep. (Muckross House, Killarney). Veneered in arbutus, holly, and other woods, the double swivel top depicts Muckross Abbey with a border of arbutus trails and on the under surface provision for backgammon, chess and cribbage, the frieze of the table with oak and ivy trails.

7. SOUVENIR WARES. Late nineteenth-early twentieth century. The desk, 34cm wide, 26.5cm deep; book rack, 37cm wide; book, 17.5 x 12.5cm; box 16 x 6cm. (Muckross House, Killarney). Veneered in arbutus inlaid and decorated variously with views of Muckross Abbey, Ross Castle and arbutus and shamrock sprays and trails.

8. (*Opposite*) CENTRE TABLE. c. 1860. Oval 130 x 100 cm, the top. (Muckross House, Killarney). Veneered in arbutus, holly, and other woods, inlaid with oak leaves and ferns. The border with views of Killarney House, Ross Castle, Inishfallen, Glena, Old Weir Bridge, Derrycunnihy, Muckross Abbey, and Muckross House.

9. CENTRE TABLE. c.1850. 134cm diameter. (Private collection). Yew, the top and base veneered in triangular segments, hinged top, stamped on the base *Killarney*. This Killarney table is unusual in that it lacks any inlay.

10. DAVENPORT: *Detail of the hinged desktop* (Fig 2). A view of Muckross Abbey flanked by fern sprays, the borders with sprays of acanthus showing the flowers and berries.

specific to Killarney were used. However, a brooch in the Ulster Museum depicts Muckross Abbey wreathed in ferns and a casket presented to Queen Victoria on her visit to Killarney in 1861 depicted in its carving Killarney House, Glena Cottage, Innisfallen, Muckross Abbey, Ross Castle, Dunloe Castle, Weir Bridge and Aghadoe 'Church'. Production at Killarney of bog oak and bog yew objects was to continue with three manufacturers still active in 1894, one of whom was making exclusively bog wood wares. At late as 1930 a guide book could comment that 'some of the shops make a great display of articles manufactured from bog oak and the wood of the arbutus, and these, together with lace made here, are favourite souvenirs of a visit to Killarney'.[10]

The use of arbutus wood, which was to become central to the appeal of Killarney woodwares, may well have commenced soon after the exploitation of bog oak. It was mentioned in 1837 as one of the woods used and by 1846 *Slater's Directory* provided a separate listing for 'arbutus manufacturers & dealers' of which three were listed. The manufacture of arbutus wood items appears to have been confined in the main to Killarney though the wares were also being retailed in Dublin in 1851 by Dennis Connell of 26 Nassau Street and Cornelius Goggin of 13 Nassau Street.[11] At first the arbutus goods may have been carved and turned items in the same tradition as those of bog oak, and 'toys' aimed at the tourists were always a large feature in the trade. A guide book of 1850 mentions 'card cases, needle-boxes, paper cutters, silk winders' as characteristic wares on sale. Puzzle boxes were mentioned in 1853 and snuff boxes and rings in a 1856 directory. Dennis Connell of Dublin in 1851 displayed at the London Exhibition book ends, chessboards and card cases of Killarney arbutus. Many of these were ideal for hawking round the hotels and places likely to be frequented by tourists by the arbutus ladies with their baskets of wares.[12] Small impulse purchases by tourists were, however, seasonal and makers sought larger rewards and a less seasonal trade from the manufacture of substantial and decorative items of furniture. This was aimed at the more discerning patron, including the Irish nobility and gentry, and was of a quality and sophistication which allowed its inclusion in national and

11. CABINET. 119cm high, 89cm wide, 79cm deep. (Irish Georgian Society). Veneered in arbutus, holly and other woods with bog-oak pillars carved with shamrock trails. The top inlaid with a view of Glena Cottage, the doors with views of Ross Castle and Muckross Abbey enclose four drawers inlaid with oak and rose trails; one side inlaid with a harp and round tower, the other with an eagle.

international exhibitions. The skills required to produce substantial items of furniture were different from those employed by 'toy' manufacturers. There was no long-standing woodworking tradition in the Killarney area. Directories of the 1820s fail to record any turners, toy or furniture makers and only carpenters feature. Where did the expertise required to establish furniture making in the town come from? No evidence has yet come to light. Cork was the nearest centre of furniture making and was not unfamiliar with decorative wood inlays. A 'shamrock table' employing thirteen varieties of rare Irish timber, including yew and bog oak, was shown by John Fletcher of Patrick Street at the Irish National Exhibition in 1852 and in the following year at the New York Exhibition. At the Crystal Palace Exhibition in London in 1851, Fletcher had been awarded a prize for his 'Gladiatorial Table'.[13] By the mid-nineteenth century the making of large pieces of furniture was already established at Killarney with a guide of 1850 listing 'tables, writing-desks, workboxes' as items of production. James Egan six years later advertised the availability of 'Loo, Oval, Card, Sofa, Chess, Office, Work and other Tables, Davenport Cabinets, Chiffoniers, Chess Boards, Work Boxes, Dressing Cases, Writing Boxes &c &c.'

A distinctive style of marquetry was adopted to decorate these arbutus wares ranging from small toys to substantial items of furniture. Marquetry and inlay featured local views of which the most common was a depiction of Muckross Abbey (correctly Friary) from the east end. This view appears to have been derived from a woodcut in *Ireland: its Scenery, Character &c* (1841) by Mr and Mrs S C Hall. Where, on smaller items, only one view is shown it is invariably of Muckross. Other fairly common views are of Glena Cottage and Ross Castle, both near the lake shore. For the drawer fronts of cabinets or the tops of large tables, where an extended range of views were required, those of Innisfallen, Aghadoe, Dunloe Castle, Killarney House and others were utilised. The ferns that grew abundantly in the area provided further motifs as did the mountain eagles and deer. Wreaths and trails of shamrock, rose and thistle are found on mid-nineteenth century items, symbolising the union of Great Britain and Ireland, but are significantly absent from later items.

Arbutus sprays, trails of shamrock alone and Irish harps are also featured in inlays. High quality furniture lacking this inlay was also produced, probably for local demand. At least some of these pieces were stamped KILLARNEY to identify their origin, something unnecessary with marquetry furniture (Fig. 9). Bog oak and Killarney arbutus toys and boxes are known, embellished with Irish diamonds (iron pyrites) and inscriptions such as 'Killarney Lakes'.[14]

The best known of the Killarney manufacturers was James Egan though, as was common, he did not identify his products by label or stamp. His business was possibly established in 1844 in Main Street and was certainly trading soon after. By 1850 the factory was producing both arbutus and bog oak articles and was described as the principal establishment for such wares. He relied on aggressive pricing to attract custom claiming in 1858 a twenty per cent discount over his rivals. His advertising cautioned visitors to avoid hawkers and it is possible that he relied on direct marketing rather than wholesaling. He was also determined to attract the custom of the affluent by the quality of the furniture that he produced which he showed at the major exhibitions, London in 1851 and 1862, Cork in 1852 and Dublin in 1853 and 1865, receiving a number of prize awards.[15] He took full advantage of the royal visits of 1858 and 1861. On the first evening of the Prince of Wales' visit in 1858 he was able to display his wares to the royal visitor who purchased a 'small but elegantly finished chess-board and some other small but elegantly finished articles.' This royal patron subsequently purchased a table, a replica of which Egan displayed in his showroom. For Queen Victoria's visit three years later he was commissioned by Lord Castlerosse to make a fine inlaid arbutus cabinet and desk and a casket of bog oak. The cabinet and desk are in the collection of the National Museum of Ireland. Other patrons of James Egan included the Earl of Clarendon, the Earl of Lanesborough, the Earl of Kenmare, the Earl of Eglinton, Viscount Hill and Lord Headley. The Earl of Eglinton purchased a 'ladies' work table with work box, writing stand and book stand, formed from the pillar of the table, the whole elaborately inlaid with 157,000 pieces' which

12. CABINET. c.1850. 153cm high. 100cm wide (National Museum of Ireland). Veneered in arbutus, holly, and other woods. Four drawers inlaid with shamrock trails and views of Muckross Abbey, Glena Cottage, Ross Castle, and Innisfallen enclosed by doors; the doors of the upper cabinet inlaid with views of Muckross Abbey and Glena Cottage with shamrock and oak trails.

he displayed under his own name at the 1853 Dublin Exhibition. Egan's business continued into the 1870s but by 1870 his attention may have been diverted in another direction as he was by then the proprietor of the Innisfallen Lake Hotel.[16]

James Egan's main competitor was Jeremiah O'Connor whose business antedated that of his rival if his claim to have started in 1825 is accepted. His manufactory was in Main Street 'near opposite the church' and by 1858 he had additional premises in Main Street opposite the Kenmare Arms. He manufactured both arbutus and bog oak articles and stamped some pieces of furniture 'J O'Connor Arbutus & Bog Oak Manufacturer Killarney'. He exhibited at the London (1851), Cork (1852) and Dublin (1853) Exhibitions and as late as 1882 was showing 'Inlaid Arbutus and Carved Bog Oak Work' at the Exhibition of Irish Arts and Manufactures at the Rotunda, Dublin. At the time of the Prince of Wales' visit in 1858 he was able to offer a varied and substantial stock which included 'Tables, Devonposts (sic), Cabinets, Sugar and Tea Stores, Chess-boards, Work Boxes, Writing Desks, Envelope Boxes, Glove Boxes, Book Stands, Ink Stands, Card Stands, Card Boxes, Card Cases &c. &c.' From his stock the Prince 'made some large and select purchases'. Additional attractions displayed on the floor above the manufactory included live mountain eagles, a wild deer's head and 'other ornaments characteristic of Killarney'. The last record of the business was in 1886 when it was listed merely as a 'bog oak warehouse'.[17]

Another substantial manufacturer in the mid-nineteenth century was Jeremiah Crimmin. The factory may well have originated in the business operated by the early 1840s by a Mrs Neate, a widow, and her daughters, which traded from a small shop opposite the Kenmare Arms in Main Street close to the business of Jeremiah O'Connor. An 1846 guide recommended readers to patronise this business as 'a fairer price is asked there than at other shops'. By 1850 Mrs Neate had moved to Dublin and the business was being carried on by her daughter, by then Mrs Crimmin. From this date there was a close connection with Cornelius Goggin of 13 Nassau Street, Dublin, a bog oak carver and at times the business traded as Goggin & Crimmin. The

TOURISM AND INDUSTRY: KILLARNEY AND ITS FURNITURE

Dublin business stocked arbutus wares which were amongst the exhibits that Goggin showed at the 1853 New York Exhibition for which a bronze medal was awarded. The Prince of Wales visited Crimmin's factory during his stay in Killarney in 1858 and made some purchases. Goggin & Crimmin's advertisement in that year emphasised the patronage of Queen Victoria, the Prince of Wales and other royal and noble patrons and medals won at Dublin (1853), New York (1854) and Paris (1855), but much of this business may have been due to the Dublin part of the enterprise. Crimmin displayed under his own name at the Paris International Exhibition of 1862 showing 'Fancy cabinet articles in bog oak &c'. Trading in Killarney must have ceased soon after this date though Cornelius Goggin and later Jeremiah Goggin continued to trade in Dublin in bog oak and spar wares in the early twentieth century.[18]

It was in the period when the manufacture of arbutus furniture and souvenir wares were at their height that competitive wares aimed at the same market were imported to Killarney. These were made by a manufacturer at Tunbridge Wells, a spa centre famous for its souvenir woodwares. The maker was Henry Hollamby who traded at various addresses in Tunbridge Wells from 1845 until the closure of his business in 1891.[19] Although he produced for local sale, he also wholesaled his manufactures on an extensive scale. Using a tessellated mosaic marquetry technique, fundamentally different to the inlay and pyrography used by Killarney makers, he developed a range of depictions of buildings. These included places close to Tunbridge Wells and East Sussex but also in other parts of Britain. As far as Ireland was concerned only Killarney attracted Hollamby's attention. Veneers were manufactured depicting Muckross Abbey, Ross Castle and Glena Cottage. These were in some cases sold as veneers to makers at Killarney to be incorporated in their boxes. They are, however, more frequently found on Tunbridge Wells-made items, book stands, tea caddies, playing card boxes and workboxes usually veneered in rosewood, a timber unknown in Killarney-manufactured items. Hollamby also used his mosaic veneers to spell out the names of resort centres and small boxes are known inscribed 'Lakes of Killarney'. When these items were

first marketed is difficult to ascertain, but they are likely to have been in manufacture by the 1850s. The Muckross block was certainly in production by 1862 and a visitor to Hollamby's works in 1882 noted both this and the Ross Castle one amongst the views on offer.[20] Subsequent to 1891 Hollamby's business passed to Boyce, Brown & Kemp and production at Tunbridge Wells continued until 1927 when the last manufacturer, The Tunbridge Wells Manufacturing Company ceased trading. Some of Hollamby's pictorial veneers continued in use until this date but no evidence has been seen of the Killarney views this late.

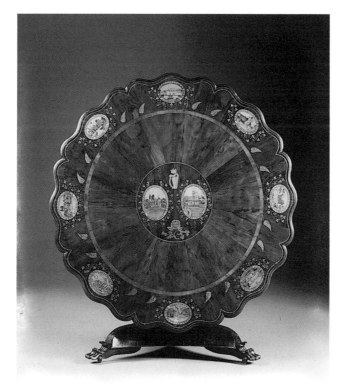

13. CENTRE TABLE. c.1860. 148cm diameter. (Private collection). Veneered in arbutus, holly and other woods, the centre inlaid with a crowned Irish harp, views of Muckross Abbey and Glena Cottage with shamrock trail borders and, beneath, the combined thistle, rose and shamrock motif. The table border with views of Killarney House, Ross Castle, Innisfallen, Glena Cottage, Old Weir Bridge, Derrycunnihy, Muckross Abbey and Muckross House.

Like the Killarney makers, Hollamby relied on engravings as the source of his designs for local views.[21] There may be a further connection between the Tunbridge and Killarney woodware trades. Mosaic marquetry techniques capable of providing pictorial veneers come into use at Tunbridge Wells from the mid 1830s. This poses the possibility that the Killarney industry was at least influenced by that of Tunbridge Wells. Certainly by the 1850s parallels are being drawn.[22] Tunbridge Wells did not produce extensive ranges of furniture, small work, writing and games tables being the largest items manufactured, but the ranges of smaller desks, boxes and souvenirs follow very similar lines.

By the 1880s the arbutus industry was in decline in Killarney but its demise was not to come until many decades later. The decline in furniture manufacture appears to have been part of a general trend in Southern Ireland due to competition from outside suppliers, notably from Britain. Under-capitalisation, lack of design innovation and an inflexible work force unwilling to change from piece work rates were other factors suggested for the decline in the Cork furniture industry. However, James Coakley displayed arbutus furniture at the Cork Industrial Exhibition of 1883 as did James French, a newly established maker in the Gap of Dunloe whose exhibits consisted of an inlaid cabinet and card table. Bog oak wares were seen to have a more healthy future than furniture production provided they featured 'the four modern symbols of Irish nationalism' and avoided subjects such as 'Paddy and his Pig' which perpetuated prejudice.[23] There is evidence to suggest that in some cases Killarney makers began to place a stronger emphasis on bog oak than arbutus wares. Jeremiah O'Connor's business in 1886 was listed as a 'bog oak warehouse' while James Coakley in the 1890s and into the next decade was described as a 'bog oak manufacturer'. Guide books in this period significantly fail to mention the 'arbutus factories'.[24]

The decline of the woodworking industry was of concern to the Earl of Kenmare, the largest local landowner. In 1895 he provided a house in which a school of arts and crafts was set up. A master was engaged from London and equipment included a lathe and a circular saw. The Countess of Kenmare encouraged Anton Lang, a carver from Oberammergau, to move to Killarney to teach his trade and he stayed for ten months. Drawing and woodcarving classes were formed. By 1897 twelve men and boys were said to be in employment by the day and twenty attended evening classes. The school, however, appears to have veered away from the traditional products of the town. Its manufactures were marketed

14. WHATNOT. c.1860. 82cm high, 52 cm wide. (Private Collection). veneered in arbutus and holly, the upper tier inlaid with fern sprays and edged with shamrock trails which also feature on the lower tier and base where the shamrock is combined with a thistle and the rose.

under the name 'The Killarney Furniture Industries' and at the St Louis World's Fair in 1914 the exhibits included a 'carved oak bedstead, two chairs and a settle' together with gilt candlesticks and sconces, fire screens and mirrors.[25] Some of the furniture produced was in the Arts and Crafts tradition.[25]

The focus for arbutus furniture production transferred from the town to the Gap of Dunloe about six miles distant. The reason for this move is unclear. James French was already located there in 1883 and he continued in business until at least 1905 and probably much later. His trade as recorded as 'arbutus and bog oak manufacturer' and he followed the tradition of producing large items of furniture. A visitor in 1901 was shown a large 'escritoire' destined to be shipped to New Zealand. In that year the sole buildings at this spot were described as a 'red shuttered shop' in which French traded and 'a wooden police hut'. A guide of c1930 still referred to the building as 'French's (or Arbutus) Cottage'. In Killarney town as late as 1905 there were two bog oak manufacturers, one referring to himself as 'bog oak and arbutus carver', but manufacture was soon to be replaced

by mere retailing, the articles possibly coming from the Gap of Dunloe.

The period of World War I and the troubled years that immediately followed were not best calculated to a prosperous tourist industry but trade had revived by the early 1930s. Guide books of this period, however, directed souvenir-seeking visitors to the Presentation Convent where lace had been produced since early in the century and where the workrooms were open to the public. By 1929 arbutus production in the Gap of Dunloe had passed to John Kiernan. In his employ at that date was John Donoghue, a skilled inlayer who had entered the trade about 1906 and was first cousin to his employer. In that year a fine games table was produced for Fr Walsh, a curate in Tuogh at a cost of £60. This is now in the collection of the Centre for Kerry Folk-life and History at Muckross House. The business was still active in 1946 and by then was employing also John Peter and Eleanor Kiernan, son and daughter of the proprietor. Furniture production ceased in that year, it being too time-consuming to be profitable. A folding card table, the top inlaid with local views, which sold for £60 was said to have taken five months to produce. In 1952 a fire destroyed the workshop and stock and the business never recovered from this setback though production of some smaller items such as boxes, trays and portable desks continued until the mid 1950s. By then the elderly John Kiernan had died and Eleanor had married and moved to England. In more than a century of production there had been little design innovation. The inlaid views, especially that of Muckross Abbey, continued as the main theme until the end of production and sprays and trails of foliage continued to be used for borders. Holly, sycamore and arbutus remained the timbers in favour throughout. Today only the products of the industry and the ruined workshop and cottage in the Gap of Dunloe remain to remind us of a once flourishing craft.[26]

BRIAN AUSTEN *is author of* Tunbridge Ware and Related European Decorative Woodwares, *(1989) (London, revised edition, 1995).*

TOURISM AND INDUSTRY: KILLARNEY AND ITS FURNITURE

1. Brian Austen, *Tunbridge Ware and Related European Decorative Woodwares*, London, 1989.
2. S C Hall, *Handbook for Ireland – The South and Killarney*, London 1853, p.64.
3. Arthur Young, 'A Tour of Ireland', in John Pinkerton, *A General Collection of … Voyages and Travels*, Vol 3, London, 1809, p.847; Leitch Ritchie, *Ireland Picturesque and Romantic*, London, 1838, p.250.
4. E Churton (publisher), *A Familiar and Accurate Hand-Book from London to the Lakes of Killarney*, London, 1846, p.6; James Fraser, *Hand Book for the Lakes of Killarney*, London, 1849; *The Times*, 2 Dec., 1853.
5. Young, *op cit*, p.847; Anon., *Journal of a Tour of Ireland … performed in August 1804*, London, 1806, p.29; Henry D Inglis, *A Journey throughout Ireland during … 1834*, London, 5th edn, 1834, p.125; G N Wright, *A Guide to the Lakes of Killarney*, London, 1822, p.6; Samuel Lewis, *A Topographical Dictionary of Ireland*, London, 1837, Vol II, p.127.
6. Anon., *A Tourist's Picturesque Guide to Killarney and Cork*, London, 1872, pp.68-69. See also N Irons, 'Irish Bog Oak Carving', *Irish Arts Review*, Vol. 4, no.2 (1987), pp.55-63.
7. Anon., *Killarney – The Prince of Wales' Visit*, London, 1858.
8. Henry Parkinson & Peter Lund Simmons, *The Illustrated Record and Descriptive Catalogue of the Dublin International Exhibition of 1865*, Dublin, 1866, p.303; Pettigrew and Oulton's, *The Dublin Directory*, Dublin, 1834.
9. Arthur J Jones, Son & Co., *Description of a Suite of Sculptured Decorative Furniture Illustrative of Irish History and Antiquities*, Dublin, 1853; *Slater's Directory of Ireland*, 1870-71.
10. Jeanne Sheehy, *The Rediscovery of Ireland's Past: The Celtic Revival*, London, 1980, pp.86-87; *The Tralee Chronicle and Killarney Echo*, 27 Aug, 1861; *Royal National Directory*

of Ireland, 1894; Ward Lock & Co. (publishers), *Killarney and the South West of Ireland*, London, c1930, p.86.
11. Anon., *Picturesque Guide to the Lakes of Killarney*, Dublin, 1851, advertisements; *Official Descriptive and Illustrated Catalogue of the Great Exhibition*, London, 1851, Vol 2, p.675.
12. Hall, *op cit.*, p.64; A.R.B., *Lake Lore*, Dublin, 1853, p.11; *Slater's Royal National Commercial Directory of Ireland*, 1856.
13. Pigot & Co's, *City of Dublin and Hibernian Provincial Directory*, London 1824, 1826-27; John Francis Maguire, *The Industrial Movement in Ireland as Illustrated by the National Exhibition of 1852*, Dublin, 1854, p.80; *Science and Mechanism: Illustrated by Examples in the New York Exhibition 1853-54*, New York, 1854, Class XXVI.
14. Hall, *op. cit.*, p.64; *Slater's Royal National Commercial Directory of Ireland*, 1856, advertisement of James Egan.
15. Michael Norton, 'Muckross Abbey Furniture', *Country Life*, Vol. CXVIII, no.3053, 21 July 1955, p.154; *Slater's National Commercial Directory of Ireland*, 1846; C Hall, *A Week at Killarney*, London, 1850, p.120; *Killarney – The Prince of Wales' Visit*, 1858 advertisement; *The International Exhibition of 1862 – Illustrated Catalogue of the Industrial Department – British Division*, Vol II, London, 1862, p.11; *Dublin Industrial Exhibition of Arts & Manufactures 1865*, Dublin, 2nd edn, 1865, p.28.
16. *Killarney – The Prince of Wales' Visit*, 1858, p.7, advertisement; *The Tralee Chronicle*, 27 Aug 1861; *Irish International Exhibition of 1853 – A Detailed Catalogue of its Contents*, Dublin, 1854, p.412; *Slater's Royal National Commercial Directory of Ireland*, 1870, advertisement.
17. *Killarney – The Prince of Wales' Visit*, 1858, p.9, advertisement; *Catalogue of the Exhibition of Irish Arts and Manufactures*, Dublin, 1882, p.42; *Guy's Directory of the Province of*

Munster, Cork, 1886.
18. Anon., *A Familiar and Accurate Hand-Book from London to the Lakes of Killarney*, London, 1846, p.27; C Hall, *A Week at Killarney*, London, 1850, p.121; *Picturesque Guide to the Lakes of Killarney*, Dublin, 1851, advertisement of Cornelius Goggin; *Killarney – The Prince of Wales' Visit*, 1858, p.9, advertisement; *The International Exhibition of 1862 – Illustrated Catalogue of the Industrial Department – British Division*, Vol II, London, 1862, p.6; *Thom's Directory*, Dublin, 1867; *Report of Executive Committee, Awards of Jurors, Cork Industrial Exhibition – 1883*, Cork, 1886, p.421.
19. Austen, *op. cit.*, pp.146-48; 192-93.
20. Henry W Wolff, *Sussex Industries*, Brighton, and 1883, p.51.
21. Austen, *op. cit.*, pp.120-27.
22. *Slater's Royal National Commercial Directory of Ireland*, 1856.
23. *Cork Industrial Exhibition, Report of Executive Committee, Awards of Jurors*, Cork, 1886, pp.256, 226, 417.
24. *Guy's Directory of Munster*, Cork, 1886, 1893; *Royal National Directory*, 1894; *Kelly's Directory*, 1905; Ward Lock & Co., (publishers), *Descriptive and Pictorial Guide to the Killarney Lakes*, London, 1896.
25. *Journal and Proceedings of the Arts and Crafts Society of Ireland*, Dublin, 1897, pp.175, 177; *Irish Industrial Exhibition, World Fair St Louis*, Dublin, 1914, p.42; Norton, *op. cit.*, p.154.
26. *Cork Industrial Exhibition, 1883, op. cit.*, p.417; *Kelly's Directory of Ireland*, 1905; Bella Sidney Woolf & Thomas Julian Goodlake, *Killarney and Round About*, Dublin, 1901, p.21; Ward Lock & Co. (publishers); *Killarney and the South West of Ireland*, London, c.1930, p.86; Norton, *op. cit.*, pp.152-54; *The Irish Press*, Dublin, Vol XVI, No.170, 18 July 1946.

APPENDIX

KILLARNEY ARBUTUS WARE MANUFACTURERS AND RETAILERS

Only specialist retailers of arbutus wares are indicated here. Many more retail outlets sold such wares in addition to other trades. No local directories exist and general trade directories of Ireland are sparse, especially for the twentieth century. The dates here may therefore not reflect the full span of a firm's operation.

M= Manufacturers   R= Retailers

COAKLEY, James (M)
From 1894 listed only as bog oak manufacturer
4, Main St, 1858-1905

CONNELL, Denis (M)
Worked at Killarney c.1830-45, subsequently sold arbutus wares at Dublin
10 Nassau St, Dublin (1846)
13 & 26, Nassau St, Dublin (1851-53)

CONNELL (widow) (R?)
Killarney 1853

CRIMMIN, Jeremiah (M)
In partnership part of this period with Cornelius Goggin. Surname also spelt Cremmin
Main St, Killarney c1852-62

DALY, John (R)
Main St, Killarney 1870

EGAN, James (M)
New St, 1844-70 Killarney
8 Main St, Killarney (1846)
5 Main St, Killarney (1870)

EAGER, Edward (R)
Arbutus dealer
Main St, Killarney 1856

FRENCH, James (M)
Gap House, Gap of Dunloe, Killarney c1883-1925

GOGGIN, Cornelius (M)
Manufacturer of bog oak wares and partner of Crimmin in the 1850s. May have operated in the Killarney area before 1850. Sold arbutus wares in Dublin.
10, Nassau St Dublin (1850)
13 Nassau St, Dublin (1851)
75 Grafton St, Dublin (1870-83)

GOGGIN, Jeremiah (R)
Bog oak manufacturer & dealer in fancy goods
74 Grafton St, Dublin 1855-1901
Wood Quay, 1902-06

HUDSON, John (R)
Photographer & wholesale publisher of views of Irish scenery
Main St Killarney 1870

KIERNAN, John (M)
Arbutus Cottage, Gap of Dunloe, Killarney c1925-55

M'CARTHY, Justin (M)
Displayed furniture at the Cork Exhibition (1852)
Killarney 1852

NEATE (widow) (M)
Husband may have manufactured pre-

vious to 1841. Moved to Dublin and daughter married Jeremiah Crimmin
Opposite the Kenmare Arms, Killarney 1841-c52

O'CONNELL, Daniel (M)
Arbutus and bog oak carver
New St, Killarney 1886-93

O'CONNELLY, John (R)
Arbutus dealer
Main St, Killarney 1846-47

O'CONNOR, Jeremiah (M)
Described in 1886 as a bog oak warehouse
Corner Shop opposite the church, Main St, Killarney.c1835-86 Also (1858) additional premises opposite the Kenmare Arms, Main St, Killarney.

ADOLESCENT ARCHITECTURE AND AFTER
THE FORMATIVE YEARS OF TIMOTHY HEVEY (1846-78)

Seán O'Reilly

investigates a rare scrapbook which casts light on a little-known Irish Victorian architect

Charles Eastlake, writing in his *History of the Gothic Revival* in 1872, points out that 'a young designer is subject to a variety of impressions from various sources'.[1] In the case of most architects it is rarely possible to be more precise on this point beyond a cursory acknowledgement of a young man's eclectic predilections or the noting of prodigious talents. An opportunity for a more detailed consideration of an architect's earliest interests has been provided by the recovery by Prof Alistair Rowan of a scrap-book, created by a young Irish architect, Timothy Hevey (1846-1878), containing material relating to the first years of Hevey's studies. The designs included in the scrap-book, together with those published by Hevey in the journal for which he then worked, *The Dublin Builder,* afterwards *The Irish Builder,* allow for an unusual personal insight into Hevey's early interests.

Hevey, though not especially well known today, distinguished himself as one of the more incisive Irish architects in an age when Ireland's architecture was at its most progressive. His early death, aged thirty-two, as his practice began to flourish, has obscured his contemporary significance. Hevey's small but distinguished body of work, together with his participation in many important local events, confirm his position as one of the most important architects of his day in Ulster's Catholic circles.[2] The award to Hevey of the commission for the gates for the new Catholic cemetery on the Falls Road in 1870 – in political terms one of the most sensitive issues of the day – is an indication of the esteem in which the architect was held as early as the first year of his private practice,[3] while his church of St Joseph on Prince's Dock in Belfast (1877-1880), built after Hevey's death by his former partner, Mortimer H Thomson, is an intriguing essay on the theme of a modern Catholic church architecture.

Hevey was born about 1846, the second surviving son of Timothy and Martha Hevey of Belfast.[4] His father was a builder-architect who later established himself as a landlord in Ballyhill, near Carrickfergus in Co Antrim. The young Hevey, presumably with his brother John, was educated in St Malachy's College in Belfast.[5] His first experience of architecture was probably gained in the context of his father's business but he took his articles in the firm of Boyd and Batt, a small but not inconsequential practice established in Belfast and Derry about 1862 by John Boyd and William Batt.[6] Their practice was wide ranging in style and building type, though not particularly extensive.[7]

Hevey's earliest surviving drawings date from September 1865, when he was about nineteen years old. These represent his abilities at the time of his departure from Boyd and Batt. His 'Sketch for an Architect's Office' (Fig.1) is typical of his manner at this time. Dated September 1865, it is a project which must have originated in Hevey's immediate experiences working in his employer's offices. Essentially pictorial in nature, it is a perspective study in pen and ink with sharply defined forms, precise contours, and crisp details, all somewhat obscured by a liberal use of hatching.

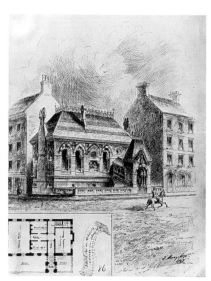

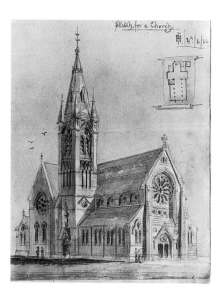

1. Timothy HEVEY (1846-78): *Sketch for an Architect's Office.* Dated 1865. (Irish Architectural Archive). Drawn when the architect was nineteen years old, the design is inspired by the Italianate style of Deane and Woodward's Museum Building in Trinity College, Dublin.

2. Timothy HEVEY: *Design for a Church.* Dated October 1865 (Irish Architectural Archive). The architect's first design for a church. The influence on the design of contemporary ecclesiastical architects in England, such as William Burges and George E Street, is obvious.

3. Timothy HEVEY: *Sketch for a Church.* Dated June 1866. (Irish Architectural Archive). Early in 1866, Hevey joined the architectural practice of Pugin & Ashlin whose style is echoed in many of the details of this design.

ADOLESCENT ARCHITECTURE AND AFTER
THE FORMATIVE YEARS OF TIMOTHY HEVEY (1846-78)

Hevey's general inspiration is clear. He pays direct homage to the ornate and colourful Italianate style promulgated by the Irish firm of Deane and Woodward. Their Museum Building in Trinity College Dublin, of 1853, designed under the influence of the writings of John Ruskin, is a watershed in the history of architecture in these islands (see *Irish Arts Review*, Vol 11 1995, pp. 149-54), while its themes – a polyglot style dominated by Italian sources, polychromatic effects, and a sympathy for materials allied with a concern for craftsmanship – outlined the concerns of more than two generations of architects.

In Hevey's own projected offices the broad and low mass, loosely symmetrical and heavily sculpted, the round arches and the expressive fenestration are all firmly rooted in the Museum Building. His *tour-de-force* of the bridge over the area, though undoubtedly impractical, is striking in effect, and may have been suggested by the internal entrance staircase leading directly to the first floor which Woodward used with particular effect at Clontra, Co Dublin.[8] Its presence on the exterior is very much in the vein of the extravagant entrances provided in more experimental designs of the late 1850s, such as Henry and Sidney Goodwin's proposal for the Chelsea Vestry Hall of 1858.[9]

Hevey's first church project post-dates the designs for offices by one month and, while comparable in style, emulates architects with more specifically ecclesiastical interests (Fig.2).[10] Robustly proportioned, profusely ornamented, and with thick walls of suitably solid construction, it captures a mood inspired by the English High Victorian master William Burges, while the two-tiered tower is a dramatic arrangement probably derived from a proposal for St Dionis, Blackchurch, London, by Burges's compatriot George Street, and published in the *Ecclesiologist* in 1860.[11] However, Hevey imposes the formal devices characteristic of the late 1850s and 1860s onto what is in essence a traditional early Victorian church composition characterised by the distinct articulation of its separate elements, notably the nave and chancel, the north porch and asymmetrical tower. The porch captures best the peculiarities of the whole. Carried on monolithic columns of suitably stubby proportions, it sits unhappily as a *leitmotif* of a modern mood tacked on to an out-moded scheme.

Sources for Hevey's first drawing style are equally eclectic. The draughtsmanship of contemporary architects would have proved attractive to the young architect, not least the fluid

4. Timothy HEVEY: *Sketch for a Cathedral Church.* Dated October 1866. (Irish Architectural Archive). This is one of the two projected schemes by Hevey for a cathedral which draws together themes from both Burges and from Pugin & Ashlin.

styles of George Street, whose *Gothic Architecture in Spain* was known to Hevey.[12] The work of the Rev Narcissus Batt, a relative of William, may also have been an important influence on the young man.[13] Batt was a talented amateur artist with a taste for the Gothic while his ability to create atmospheric compositions of ancient buildings would have impressed itself on an aspiring medievalist.

Between December 1865 and May 1866 Hevey joined the firm of Pugin and Ashlin,[14] an established practice consisting of AWN Pugin's son Edward, working in England, and George Coppinger Ashlin as his Irish partner. Together the partnership created some of Ireland's finest Victorian churches. Hevey's association with the firm, represented by his illustration of their church at Arless, Co Laois, for *The Dublin Builder*,[15] began in December 1865, just two months after his own design for a church discussed above. Under the influence of his new employers Hevey's work changed radically. Determined not least by the economic dictates of their Catholic patrons, Pugin and Ashlin's architecture explored the potential of severe, compressed, and often plain geometric masses, rather than the textured surfaces of the richly carved and ornamented forms which had attracted Hevey's attention previously.

Hevey's manner as it develops under the impact of Pugin and Ashlin is represented neatly by his 'Sketch for a Church' of June 1866 (Fig.3). It is fashioned after Pugin and Ashlin's larger churches, with five bays to the aisles, transepts and a tower. Hevey's sources are explicit with the west front, for example, being appropriated from the Dominican church at Tralee, even to the detail of the aisle windows. The slim advancing buttresses, the quatrefoil clerestory lights, the limited tracery and restricted polychromy also originate with Pugin and Ashlin.

When Hevey departs from the firm's usual pattern for church designs problems arise, indicating his inability, as yet, to accommodate his own interests with more familiar forms. His arrangement of the chancel revives a distinctly *retardataire* pattern, particularly in its unusually extensive length. The type, though popular in the 1840s was unsatisfactory in the 1860s: formally, because of its lack of compressed tension in the design and practically, because of its obstruction of the view of the altar. The location of the tower in the western return of the north transept is not old-fashioned but it is less orthodox. Pugin and Ashlin's towers are

Adolescent Architecture and After
The Formative Years of Timothy Hevey (1846-78)

usually, though by no means always, set to the west end of an aisle. In Hevey's arrangement the obtrusion of the tower into the space of the church itself is awkward, and its supporting wall obstructs the internal space with no compensating advantages.

The style of Pugin and Ashlin, though naturally dominant, is not Hevey's only source of inspiration over these early years. Hevey's designs for a cathedral dating to the latter half of 1866 (Fig.4) indicate a continuing interest in the work of William Burges, notably through his St Fin Barre's Cathedral in Cork of 1863. This building is the complete realisation of Burges's ambitions, originating in the 1850s, to create 'a fully-fledged thirteenth century French Cathedral, complete with aisles, towers, spires and sculpture'.[16] It is not surprising then that Hevey should explore this epitome of High Victorian ecclesiastical Gothic. Following St Fin Barre's, Hevey's variation has a crossing-tower and eastern chevet to his Latin cross plan, but he bows to his employers by simplifying the massing through the omission of the western towers and adopting details which reflect Pugin at Tralee rather than Notre Dame de Paris. Similarly Burges's historically informed composition is developed into a more compressed mass by eliminating the projecting ambulatory at Cork and instead emphasising the tall buttresses between the windows – an arrangement perhaps inspired by Street's submission for the Crimean Memorial church of 1856 but also one popular with Pugin and Ashlin.

Hevey's work at this time was not wholly derivative. Late in 1866 the architect, then only twenty years of age, developed two projects which represented his exploration of more personal sources, a design for a belfry (Fig.5), and a house for the Catholic businessman Daniel McDevitt in Glenties, Co Donegal (Fig.6).[17] The belfry was derived from the lantern of the old Cathedral in Salamanca, Spain. Though Hevey's design was based on the illustration provided by George Street in his *Gothic Architecture in Spain*,[18] his particular interest may have been suggested by a more personal association with the city, perhaps by contacts deriving from the extensive Catholic links with the city created through the Irish college there. For example, from 1862 to 1864 Fr Jeremiah McAuley, the architect-priest of St Peter's in Belfast and a figure who moved in the same circles as Hevey,[19] completed his religious study at Salamanca.[20]

Hevey's design, dated October 1866, is certainly a more ordinary composition than its medieval inspiration. The original

5. Timothy HEVEY: *Sketch for a Belfry*. Dated October 1866 (Irish Architectural Archive). The drawing is based on an illustration of the Lantern of Salamanca Cathedral from George Street's *Gothic Architecture in Spain* which was published in 1865.

two-tiered structure is reduced to one storey, while the round arches of the original become pointed, gables are eliminated and the distinctive stumpy caps to the corner towers are stretched into more familiar proportions. In general Hevey imposes onto his source the formal rationale of a French Gothic composition, retaining only the low spire and the circular tourelles – these last being consistent with the unexecuted tower of Pugin and Ashlin's Dominican church in Tralee.[21] However if the modification of Hevey's Iberian model betrays the more general Francophile mood of the period, the design as a whole is progressive for in the 1870s the lantern at Salamanca became an especially popular source for architects.[22]

The new house for Daniel McDevitt is Hevey's earliest complete architectural commission.[23] Hevey's proposal, published in *The Dublin Builder* in November 1866, is a composition of youthful exuberance somewhat coarsened by a jarring variety of scales and a composition of masses which aspires to muscularity but attains only awkwardness. The treatment of the tower is of greatest interest. The abrupt conjunction of the tower and the porch in the re-entrant angle, an arrangement which had appeared in Hevey's first church project, recalls not only the work of Street and William Butterfield in the previous decade, but such contemporary designs as John L Pearson's Christ Church, Appleton-le-Moors, Yorkshire, of 1863-66,[24] in addition to anticipating Hevey's future concerns.[25]

With Hevey's growing confidence the forms of Pugin and Ashlin come to dominate his outlook. This character appears in Hevey's last major church project before entering into private practice, his 'Sketch for an east end' published in *The Irish Builder* in 1868 (Fig.7).[26] Hevey takes full advantage of the tight, eastern massing of Pugin and Ashlin's churches. The saddle-back tower, for which he prepared a more detailed study, is a good example of its type. Here lancets rise on each face above a plain set-back with a steep saddle-back roof replete with angels, crockets, ridge finials and early tracery. Yet the source is less medieval than modern, in this case E W Pugin's proposed church at Wolverhampton which Hevey had illustrated in *The Dublin Builder*.[27]

Over these years Hevey's architectural draughtsmanship ranges between the soft-pencil and watercolour wash, popular with Pugin and Ashlin, and a heavier, more solid style, looking to his earlier studies, and represented by his scheme for a cathe-

ADOLESCENT ARCHITECTURE AND AFTER
THE FORMATIVE YEARS OF TIMOTHY HEVEY (1846-78)

dral. A figure who may have played a role of particular importance in Hevey's style over the 1860s – and who may have influenced Narcissus Batt's own drawings[28] – was the Rev John Louis Petit.[29] Petit's picturesque and popular architectural illustrations were especially influential in the 1840s and 1850s while the graphic nature of his drawings, with short strokes, solid and hatched,[30] is a precursor of Hevey's more summary sketching style. Petit may have had a more personal significance to Hevey through his illustrated paper on Irish medieval architecture delivered to the Royal Institute of British Architects on 23 March 1863.[31] The paper, though more a review for the architect than a history for the antiquarian, provided a coherent body of information on Irish medieval architecture which might have impressed a young Irish architect.

In 1869 the partnership of Pugin and Ashlin was dissolved and Hevey returned to his native Belfast to establish his own private practice there. Taking advantage of the increasingly important programme of church building in the north, especially that in Belfast under the energetic leadership of the Catholic Bishop of Down and Connor, Dr Patrick Dorrian, Hevey quickly established his name. However, during his first years there the interests which had engaged him prior to his encounter with Pugin and Ashlin were hardly evident. The for-

7. Timothy HEVEY: *Sketch for an East End.* Dated 1868. (*The Irish Builder,* 1 April 1868). This was Hevey's last major church project while working with Pugin & Ashlin and demonstrates clearly their influence on his style.

mal clarity of Deane and Woodward's Museum Building in Trinity and their fusion of grandeur and narrative richness, found also in Burges' work, was largely subsumed in the pervasive influence of Pugin and Ashlin's practice. One of his first successes after his return to Belfast, the church of St Mary at Leitrim, Co Down, is an eloquent statement, admirably composed and especially well preserved, but one wholly in the spirit of Pugin and Ashlin. It is only after some three years that Hevey gained sufficient confidence to explore again the interests of his early years.

The Hibernian Bank in Letterkenny, Co Donegal, of 1874, was among the first of Hevey's buildings to manifest clearly the architect's return to the inspiration of his adolescent years (Fig.8). Hevey, adopting features of the round-arched style of the Museum Building, designed a regular two-storey block in stone with grouped windows and entrances surmounted by balconies with its low proportions exaggerated by the shallow hipped roof, projecting frieze and horizontal strings. A general context for the manner was provided by the bank itself, which had adopted round arches, described as 'Italian Gothic', in its Dublin branch of 1871, designed by William G Murray.[32] Despite the smaller scale of Hevey's design he added impact by returning to the Trinity Museum Building, and imposing an aggressive symmetry which pays no heed to

6. Timothy HEVEY: *Design for a Residence for Daniel McDevitt, Glenties, Co Donegal.* Dated October 1866. (*The Dublin Builder,* 15 November 1866). This was the architect's earliest commission and the design is characterised by a jarring variety of scales and somewhat awkward composition of masses.

8. Timothy HEVEY: *Design for the new Hibernian Bank, Letterkenny, Co Donegal.* 1874. (*The Irish Builder,* 15 May 1871). In this design, Hevey derives inspiration, as he had done in his early years, from Deane & Woodward's Museum Building.

the internal planning of the bank. The clear massing, fenestral variety, projecting balconies and decorative carving of the earlier building are all revived but now transformed through the smaller scale, richer colour and stylised detail characteristic of the 1870s.

Hevey's first architectural designs confirm his innate sense of the character of High Victorian architecture, especially his appreciation of robust massing derived from the progressive architects working in the 1850s. The development of his work indicates how such a natural disposition might only gradually re-assert itself in a mature expression. The more robust features of his earliest style appear only occasionally during his experience of the lighter and more practical style of Pugin and Ashlin and are subsumed until the arrival of a suitable opportunity for their further exploration. Significantly the opportunity for such a specific revival of adolescent interests, the Letterkenny bank,

appears in a secular context, one largely foreign to the experiences gained in Dublin. However in his contemporary churches, notably in St Patrick's, Donegall Street, Hevey revives some of the more distinctive features of his earliest interests. Here such details are more fully absorbed and more subtly expressed, making them more suitable as a subject of study in their own right.

DR SEAN O'REILLY has lectured and written widely on Irish architecture, post-1700. For the past decade he has worked with the Irish Architectural Archive and is at present lecturing in Trinity College Dublin.

ACKNOWLEDGEMENTS
I would like to thank Professor Alistair Rowan for permission to reproduce the illustrations from the scrap-book. Professor Rowan has also provided important advice in the preparation of the article. I would also like to acknowledge the assistance of the Irish Architectural Archive and its staff in my research and to thank the archive for permission to reproduce the photographs and illustrations.

1. Charles L Eastlake, *A History of the Gothic Revival*, London, 1872, (Reprinted with an introduction by J Mordaunt Crook, Surrey, 1970), p.317.
2. For which see the author's unpublished thesis 'Timothy Hevey (1846-1878) – an episode in Irish High Victorian architecture', University College, Dublin, 1994.
3. For a general discussion see Ambrose McCauley, *Patrick Dorrian, Bishop of Down and Connor, 1865-85*, Dublin, 1987, p.152 *et seq.*
4. The date of Hevey's birth is based on the obituary in the *Ulster Examiner and Northern Star* (UENS), which gives his age as thirty-two, 'Death of Mr Timothy Hevey', UENS, 31 December 1878, p.3, c.3). The obituary appearing in *The Irish Builder* (IB) in 1879 gives his age as thirty-three ('The Late T Hevey, Architect', IB, vol.21, no.457, 1 January 1879, p.4).
5. 'Death of Mr Timothy Hevey', *loc cit.* The death of Hevey's brother is recorded in 'Deaths', *Belfast Newsletter*, 11 September 1874, p.1, c.1. I am indebted to Dr Eamonn Phoenix of St Malachy's for providing me with information on the college and for assisting me in my research there.
6. See the Irish Architectural Archive (IAA), IAA Index of Irish Architects; Boyd, John, BOY011; Boyd & Best, BOY015; Batt, William (2), BAT009. See also IAA, Alfred Jones Biographical Index: B127, Boyd, John, and B50, Batt, William.
7. The IAA Index of Irish Architects (Boyd & Batt, BOY015) lists only ten works by the partnership between 1862 and 1865.
8. See Eve Blau, *Ruskinian Gothic. The architecture of Deane and Woodward 1845-1861*. Princeton and Guildford, pp.122-25, and plate 123, and Frederick O'Dwyer & Jeremy Williams, "Benjamin Woodward", in Tom Kennedy, *Victorian Dublin*, Dublin, 1980, p.60.
9. 'A Design for the Proposed Vestry Hall for Chelsea', *The Builder*, vol.16, no.828, 8 December 1858.
10. 'Design for a Church', *The Dublin Builder* (DB), vol.8, no.146, 15 January 1866, Hevey's inscription on his own copy, 'My First', indicates its position within his ecclesiastical work

(Scrap-book, p.157, item 209).
11. 'Design for rebuilding Church of S Dionis, Blackchurch, London', *The Ecclesiologist (E)*, vol.XIX, no.CXXXVII, April 1860, p.88.
12. George E Street, *Some Account of Gothic Architecture in Spain*, London, 1865. Hevey's interest in this volume is discussed below.
13. I am indebted to Ann Martha Rowan for drawing my attention to this figure through her research on the figure of William Batt. The work of Narcissus Batt is reviewed in Martyn Anglesea, 'Sketches of a Victorian Vicar; Narcissus Batt, 1824(?)-98', *Ulster Genealogical and Historical Guide Newsletter*, vol.1, no.9, 1983, pp.282-89.
14. For an introduction to the work of the partnership see especially Frederick O'Dwyer, 'A Victorian Partnership – the architecture of Pugin and Ashlin', in *150 Years of Architecture in Ireland, The Royal Institute of the Architects of Ireland, 1839-1989*, Dublin, 1989, and sources cited there.
15. 'Church of the Sacred Heart at Arles', *(DB)*, vol.7, no.142, 15 December 1865.
16. J Mordaunt Crook, *William Burges and the High Victorian Dream*, London, 1981, pp.195-96.
17. Hevey did complete one architectural project at this time – the new stone porch for the local church, now demolished, a competent, even strong design.
18. George E Street, *Some Account of Gothic Architecture in Spain*, London, 1865, plate x, and reproduced in *The Builder*, 'Gothic Architecture in Spain, Fig.1, Salamanca Old Cathedral. Exterior of Lantern', B, Vol.23, No.1153, 11 March 1865, p.172.
19. Hevey provided designs for tabernacles to St Peter's about 1870.
20. James O'Laverty, *An Historical account of the Diocese of Down and Connor, Ancient and Modern*, Dublin, 1878-1895, vol.2, p.428.
21. 'New Dominican Church, Tralee', *DB*, vol.8, no.153, 1 May 1866, p.112.
22. Hevey's scheme has more than just a flavour of the 1870s. The advanced nature of the design is confirmed in the interest taken in the same source by the foremost American architect of the day, H H Richardson, giving real perspective to Hevey's interest in the tower.

The Spanish tower, the inspiration for 'a most influential Richardsonian borrowing', was 'only taken … (by Richardson) as a model in that spring of 1874', appearing most notably in is design for the central tower at Trinity church, Boston. (See Henry Russell Hitchcock, 'Ruskin and American Architecture', in John Summerson, ed., *Concerning Architecture – Essays on Architectural Writers and Writing presented to Nikolaus Pevsner*, London, 1968, p.196, n.1). The Spanish lantern was used again in his submission for the new Cathedral at Albany, New York State (Sarah Crewe ed., *Visionary Spires*, London, 1986, p.88).
23. 'Residence, The Glenties, Co Donegal', *DB*, vol.8, no.166, 15 November 1866.
24. David Lloyd, 'John Loughborough Pearson: noble seriousness' in Jane Fawcett, ed., *Seven Victorian Architects*, London, 1976, pp.66-83, esp. pp.70-71 and Fig.65.
25. For example a comparable insertion of a tower into a corner appears in Hevey's seminary at Violet Hill, Newry, begun in 1874.
26. 'Sketch for an east end by T Hevey, Dublin, 1868', IB, vol.10, no.199, 1 April 1868.
27. 'New Catholic Church, Wolverhampton, E Welby Pugin Arch.'. DB, vol.8, no.163, 1 October 1866.
28. As a resident in England, and a traveller in the manner of Petit, Batt probably would have been aware of Petit's work.
29. Petit's influence on the High Victorian style is referred to in Stefan Muthesius, *The High Victorian Movement in Architecture*, London and Boston, 1972, pp.17-18.
30. Muthesius' description of Petit's style as 'short pen-strokes of even breadth' (*op. cit.*, p.18) is an over-simplification but a good starting point.
31. The Rev J L Petit, 'On the Abbeys of Ireland, with illustrations', *Papers read at The Royal Institute of British Architects, Session 1862-63*, London, 1863, pp.190-208.
32. 'The Hibernian Bank, College Green', IB, vol.13, no.272, 15 May 1871, p.134.

IRISH PORTRAITS IN THE
ETON COLLEGE LEAVING COLLECTION

Marie Davis

introduces a group of privileged Irishmen

'Education led to a number of Irishmen going to England at some time in their lives. During the last half of the eighteenth century over 250 Irish boys went to either Eton College or Harrow, the Etonians outnumbering the Harrovians by almost three to one.'[1]

Thus the Irish historian, R B McDowell, drew attention to the fashion amongst Irish Ascendancy parents of sending their children to be educated in England.

Records of Irish pupils attending Eton College go back to at least the early seventeenth century when Conn O'Neill, second son of Hugh O'Neill, Earl of Tyrone, was taken to England by order of James I and sent as a pupil to the College in June 1615, remaining there until August 1622. Another Irish boy, Terence O'Brien, is also recorded as an Eton pupil at that time.[2] Robert and Francis Boyle, sons of the Earl of Cork, were sent to Eton in 1635 and attended for three years.[3]

Occasionally political upheaval in Ireland, such as the countrywide disturbances during the 1790s, influenced parents in deciding upon an overseas education for their children. In the case of Eton, a strong pattern of Irish family adherence to the College can be seen by inspection of surviving school lists and registers. Dynasties are obvious: six Tighes are recorded as pupils between 1753 and 1775; five members of the Wellesley family between 1771 and 1789; six of the King family of Rockingham between 1781 and 1789, three brothers entering together in 1781; three La Touche sons between 1788 and 1811 and four Beresfords entered between 1789 and 1826.

A fortunate result of this educational migration has been the inclusion of Irish sitters amongst the collection of Eton College Leaving Portraits commissioned between 1754 and 1843. These little-known portraits, numbering about two hundred in all, of which approximately seventeen depict Irish[4] boys, illustrate an aspect of the culture of Ascendancy Ireland and are also representative of the tradition of English portraiture.[5]

The custom of Eton boys donating a leaving portrait is believed to owe its origin to the practice, first recorded in the seventeenth century, whereby the poorly paid Head Masters presented books,

1. George ROMNEY (1734-1802): *Richard Colley Wellesley, later 1st Marquess Wellesley (1760-1841)*. Oil on canvas, 81 x 69cm. (Eton College). The portrait was painted over a period of six years between 1781-87: the sitter was the older brother of the Duke of Wellington.

2. George ROMNEY: *The Hon George King, later 3rd Earl of Kingston (1771-1839)*. Oil on canvas, 76 x 64cm. (Eton College). Painted in 1788 when the sitter, who was seventeen at the time, sat to Romney on four occasions; he wears an Oxford undergraduate's gown.

3. George ROMNEY: *William Tighe (1766-1816)*. Oil on canvas, 76 x 64cm. (Eton College). This is one of two portraits of the sitter which the artist painted over fourteen sittings between 1785-87: the second portrait hung at the family home in Co Wicklow.

4. William BEECHEY (1753-1839): *Henry de la Poer Beresford, Earl of Tyrone (1772-1826)*. Oil on canvas, 76 x 61cm. (Eton College). Painted about 1790, the sitter was the son of the Marquess of Waterford.

'to all the young gentlemen who took leave of them handsomely'.[6] This implied a monetary gift of £10-£15 being slipped discreetly on to the Head Master's desk by the departing pupil.

Dr Edward Barnard, a particularly successful Etonian Head Master (1754-65) who raised the educational standards of the College and cultivated wealthy parents, conceived the idea of requesting a portrait from certain chosen departing boys, supposedly in lieu of a leaving fee. However, records indicate that the practice of 'leaving money' continued, in addition to the portrait gift.[7] The portraits were commissioned as a result of collaboration between the current Head Master and the boy's parents, the instigator being the Head Master who selected the sitter from amongst the boys in their final year at Eton. Foremost artists, including several academicians, were commissioned by the boys' parents. Romney, Lawrence, Hoppner, Northcote, Beechy and Shee were chosen to paint the Irish sitters. Occasionally boys sat while still at the College but it was more usual for a portrait to be painted immediately after the boy's final departure from Eton. The portraits were then presented as gifts to the Head Master. He and his successors subsequently bequeathed the paintings to the Provost's Lodge at Eton and so

was formed the Leaving Portrait Collection which is still intact today. Some of the portraits hang in the Lodge, others are now dispersed throughout the College.

The choice of sitters rested with the headmaster and in Dr Barnard's case it appears that aristocratic background and wealth were necessary requirements; parental ability to pay was essential and would ensure that leading artists would be commissioned. Intellectual ability and outstanding personal qualities were additional assets sought in the chosen donors. Young men who seemed destined to have successful careers were also likely choices. During his headship Dr Barnard did not request leaving portraits from any Irish pupils although sons of a number of titled and wealthy Irish families were then Eton pupils. Fourteen pupils with Irish addresses are listed in the College registers for the period 1754-1765, including such well known names as Perceval, Offaly, Aylmer, Brabazon, Luttrell, Bingham, Monck and Luke Gardiner.[8] It was not until 1781, under headmaster Dr Jonathan Davies (1773-92) that Richard Colley Wellesley (1760-1842), eldest son of the 1st Earl of Mornington, was to become the first Irish sitter, painted by Romney. Surprisingly his younger brother, Arthur Wellesley (1769-1852) later Duke of Wellington, was not

5. Philip JEAN (Fl. 1795): *The Hon Charles O'Neill, later Viscount O'Neill (1779-1841)*. Oil on canvas, 61 x 51cm. (Eton College). Painted in 1795 when the sitter was sixteen: he is shown with the short powdered hair that was not uncommon among the older boys.

6. John HOPPNER (1758-1810): *The Hon Dupré Alexander, later 2nd Earl of Caledon (1777-1839)*. Oil on canvas, 76 x 64cm. (Eton College). Painted during his final year at the school, in 1796, the portrait was exhibited at the Royal Academy the same year. In later life the sitter was the first Governor of the Cape of Good Hope.

asked for a leaving portrait. This may have been due to his widowed mother's straightened financial circumstances at that time which forced her to remove this son from Eton in 1783 and send him to a military academy in Angers, in France. However, in the general portrait collection at Eton, there are two portraits of the Duke, by Lawrence, donated later by admirers.

Seventeen leaving portraits were presented by Irish boys to successive headmasters between 1781 and 1842 (see Figs 1-8). Of the seventeen sitters, twelve were titled and the remainder were sons of substantial landed gentry who were, in most cases, Members of Parliament.

The leaving portraits, all in oil on canvas, are mostly half lengths, though some are three quarters, varying in size from 61cm x 51cm to 91cm x 76cm. The sitters, then aged between sixteen and twenty, are seated formally posed against a dark background though occasionally there is a hint of a distant landscape. The young men are dressed in the fashionable clothes of the period wearing coats, sometimes of velvet, over stocks or frilled shirts. (At Eton, uniform was worn only by the younger pupils). The Duke of Leinster (Fig. 8) painted by Northcote two years after leaving Eton, is depicted wearing a nobleman's gown, this being

his academical vestment as a student at Christ Church Oxford. Hair styles vary from the formal powdered wig, to long loose hair and short hair, which in some cases was powdered (see Figs 1, 4 & 5). Although most leaving portraits were painted following departure from Eton it was a common practice during the eighteenth century for many of the older boys to powder their hair while at the College. School accounts for an Irish pupil at Eton from 1790 to 1796, John Trant of Dunkettle, Co Cork, reveal that he owned two powdering gowns supplied during the school year.[9]

The number of sittings and, in two cases, the cost of the three Romney leaving portraits are recorded, those of Richard Colley Wellesley, George King and William Tighe. For his large three-quarter portrait, Richard Colley Wellesley (Fig. 1) appears to have sat to Romney over a period from 1781 to 1787; as Lord Wellesley on seven occasions in 1781; twice as Lord Mornington in 1784 and one further sitting in 1787. No details of cost are given.

The Hon. George King (1771-1839) (Fig. 2), eldest son of 2nd Earl of Kingston, one of the richest landowners in Ireland, sat four times to Romney in 1788. For this leaving portrait his father paid 12 guineas (half-price). The seventeen year old boy is depicted full face wearing an Oxford undergraduate's gown

7. John HOPPNER: *Robert La Touche (1783-1844)*. Oil on canvas, 76 x 64cm. (Eton College). The sitter, whose family came from Harristown, Co Kildare, was just sixteen at the time the portrait was painted.

8. James NORTHCOTE (1746-1831): *Augustus Frederick Fitzgerald, 3rd Duke of Leinster (1791-1874)*. Oil on canvas, 76 x 64cm. (Eton College). Painted about 1809, the sitter is shown as an Oxford undergraduate in a nobleman's gown.

over a dark coat. Fourteen sittings between 1785 and 1787 were required for the two three-quarter portraits which Romney painted of William Tighe (1766-1816), son of William Tighe MP of Rosanna, Co Wicklow (Fig. 3). Twenty guineas was charged for the first and twenty-five guineas for the second, which was subsequently hung at Rosanna. The young William Tighe was apparently regarded as one of a fashionable group when at Eton according to a writer in the *Pall Mall Magazine* in 1901.[10] She refers to his portrait as one of the 'best examples among a crowd of fashionables', and describes him as 'Mr Tighe, in a coat of bleu mourant'. Tighe's reputation for fashion is reinforced from statements in contemporary letters written by his cousin, John Bligh, Viscount Clifton, to his father the Earl of Darnley. Bligh, a fellow Etonian, writes of him in 1781 as wearing 'a vast military [hat]' and 'Tighe's clothes are scarlet lapelled and lined with green silk'.[11]

Between 1790 and 1809 a further six portraits of Irish boys were commissioned at the request of four Head Masters. Henry de La Poer Beresford, Earl of Tyrone (1772-1826), son of the 1st Marquess of Waterford, was painted by Sir William Beechey R A, (1753-1839) c.1790. He appears framed in an oval, in a half-

length portrait, and is shown with long, powdered hair (Fig. 4). In 1795, the Hon Charles O'Neill (1779-1841), son of the 1st Viscount O'Neill, painted by Philip Jean, is also depicted with powdered hair, but in this portrait the sitter's hair is short (Fig. 5).

Two leaving portraits were painted by John Hoppner R A, (1758-1810). In his final year at Eton in 1796, Dupré Alexander (1777-1839), only son of Viscount (later Earl) Caledon sat to him and in the same year the portrait of the almost childlike nineteen-year old was exhibited at the Royal Academy (Fig. 6).

By contrast Robert La Touche (1783-1844), only son of John La Touche of Harristown, Co Kildare, as painted by Hoppner when he was sixteen, looks to be a mature young man. In this portrait, the subject's short curly hair and style of dress are indicative of Lawrence's influence on Hoppner (Fig. 7).

James Lonsdale (1777-1839) painted Arthur Sandys Trumbell Hill, 3rd Marquess of Downshire (1788-1845) in 1805, in a half-length portrait which shows a short-haired, fashionably dressed young man, wearing a dark coat with high fur collar. Augustus Frederick Fitzgerald, 3rd Duke of Leinster (1791-1874) was painted by James Northcote R A, c.1809. It can be seen from this portrait that the sitter was then an

Oxford undergraduate; he is wearing his academic dress of nobleman's gown (Fig. 8).

In all seventeen portraits of Irish Etonians had been painted by 1843; details of the remaining nine are listed in the appendix (below). The tradition of presenting Leaving Portraits as such came to an end in 1834, with the retirement as Head Master of Dr Keate, but some oils and several chalk-drawn portraits were donated during the 1840s and 1850s. In 1867 the status of Eton Head Masters was raised by a Commission which abolished entry and leaving payments.

Six of the young men featured in the foregoing eight portraits went up to Oxford on leaving Eton: five to Christ Church and one to Exeter College. Subsequently five of the number became Members of Parliament: William Tighe, Robert La Touche, Richard Wellesley, George King and Dupré Alexander. The remaining three managed their estates and entered public life at county level. Ultimately the most distinguished of the group were Dupré Alexander and Richard Colley Wellesley. The former, as Earl of Caledon, became the first Governor of the Cape of Good Hope, while the latter, as Earl of Mornington (later created Marquis Wellesley and Knight of the Garter), held many high political offices, including Governor-General of India 1797-1805, and was twice Lord Lieutenant of Ireland 1821-28, and 1833/34. A friend and benefactor of Eton College, to which he sent his two illegitimate sons, Richard and Gerald, he died in 1842.

Painted at a time when English portraiture was at its height, the Irish leaving portraits in Eton College 'in origin, in subject, in historic interest and in artistic excellence... form a unique collection'.[12]

MARIE DAVIS completed her master's thesis on Childhood in 18th Century Ireland *at Trinity College Dublin.*

IN ADDITION TO THE PORTRAITS ILLUSTRATED, THE FOLLOWING IRISH SITTERS ARE REPRESENTED IN THE ETON COLLEGE COLLECTION
Details of the portraits are taken from L Cust, *Eton College Portraits*, London, 1910.

1. Hugh Montgomery (1779-1838), eldest son of Hugh Montgomery of Castle Hume, Greyabbey, Co. Down. — c 1797, 76 x 64 — Sir Martin Archer Shee, P.R.A.

2. Richard Wellesley (1787-1831), son of Richard, Marquess Wellesley. — c.1805, 91 x 71 — Sir Thomas Lawrence, P.R.A.

3. Hon. Frederick Stewart (1805-1872), only son of Charles William, Baron Stewart, afterwards Marquess of Londonderry. — c.1820, 76 x 64 — Artist unknown

4. Hon. Hayes St. Leger (1818-1887), only son of Hayes, 3rd Viscount Doneraile. — c.1837, 76 x 64 — Artist unknown

5. Henry Francis Seymour Moore (1825-1892), only son of Lord Henry Moore, later 3rd Marquess of Drogheda. — c.1842, 91 x 76 — J Barker

6. Ulick Canning de Burgh (1827-1867), Viscount Dunkellin, eldest son of Ulick John, 1st Marquess of Clanricarde. — c.1843, 76 x 64 — Artist unknown

7. John Butler-Clarke (1813-1856), eldest son of Hon. Charles Howard Butler-Clarke of Castlecomer. — c.1830, 74 x 61 — Artist unknown

8. Francis Charles Needham, Viscount Newry, eldest son of Francis Jack, Viscount Newry and Mourne. — c.1860, 69 x 53 — James Rannie Swinton

9. Arthur Sandys Trumbell Hill (1788-1845), 3rd Marquess of Downshire — 1805, 76 x 64 — James Lonsdale

The following portraits are of sitters who held titles of Irish creation but were not resident in Ireland

George Broderick, 4th Viscount Midleton, (1754-1863), eldest son of George, 3rd Viscount Midleton. — 1773, 91 x 76 — David Martin

Charles William Fitzwilliam, Viscount Milton (1786-1857), only son of William, 4th Earl of Fitzwilliam. — c.1803, 91 x 76 — John Hoppner, R.A.

Charles William Fitzwilliam, Viscount Milton (1786-1857), only son of William, 4th Earl of Fitzwilliam. — 1804, 91 x 76 — Thomas Phillips, R.A.

1. R B McDowell, *Ireland in the Age of Imperialism and Revolution 1760-1801*, London 1979, p.143.
2. T W Moody, 'The School bills of Conn O'Neill at Eton 1615-22.' *Irish Historical Studies* 2 (1940-41), p.180. Conn O'Neill was an ancestor of Charles O'Neill (1779-1841) whose leaving portrait painted by Philip Jean is reproduced in Fig. 5.
3. H Maxwell-Lyte, *History of Eton College 1440-1910*, London, 1911, p.221.
4. Some difficulty arises in defining the 'Irishness' of some sitters. George Broderick, 4th Viscount Midleton, whose antecedents were undoubtedly Irish and whose Irish estate of over 6000 acres in Co Cork brought in an income three times that of his English lands, was born in England and spent much of his time there and Charles William Fitzwilliam, holding the Irish titles, Viscount Milton and later 5th Earl Fitzwilliam, and notwithstanding his ownership of 92,000 acres in Ireland and an Irish seat at Coolattin Park, Co Wicklow probably should be excluded. [see Appendix]
5. The Leaving Portraits have only been exhibited outside the College publicly on two occasions. Fifty-two were exhibited at the Tate Gallery in April and May 1951 and forty-nine were exhibited in the Dulwich Picture Gallery, 18 July – 20 October 1991. There are catalogues for both exhibitions, *Eton Leaving Portraits*, Tate, 1951, and *Leaving Portraits from Eton College*, Dulwich, 1991.
6. *Eton Leaving Portraits, op.cit.*, p.4.
7. 'Barnard's account book records a list of "presents" from parents ranging from a couple of guineas to £50, P Quarrie, *Eton Leaving Portraits Catalogue*, Dulwich, 1991, p.7.
8. R A Austen-Leigh, ed., *The Eton College Register 1678-1790*, 2 vols, Eton, 1927.
9. 'April 1st 1794. To a flannel powdering gown, 13s, 1d.'; 'April 1st, 1794. To a cotton powdering gown, £1 2s 9d.' National Library of Ireland MS no.1603.
10. B W Cornish, (wife of a Vice-Provost of Eton), 'Portraits and Prints at Eton', *The Pall Mall Magazine*, XXI, (1900) p.513.
11. PRONI T 2851/24 (*Darnley Papers*) The clothes described above were to be worn at a Royal visit by George III to Eton.
12. *Tate Catalogue*, (1951) *op. cit.*, p.4.

William Sadler's views of Killua Castle, Co Westmeath

1. KILLUA CASTLE: *the Entrance Front and Side Elevation.* c.1864. The gothicisation of the original eighteenth-century castle, carried out in the 1820s and 1830s, is attributed to James Shiel.

Killua Castle (Fig 1) situated in what has been described as 'one of Ireland's most romantic landscaped demesnes'[1] can perhaps be best appreciated in a rare series of early nineteenth-century views by William Sadler II.

The castle, which is now in ruins, is situated beside the village of Clonmellon in Co Westmeath and was the seat of the Chapman family. Originally from Leicestershire, the Chapmans were cousins of Sir Walter Raleigh and through his patronage received land in Kerry where they first settled in Ireland. At a later date Benjamin Chapman I received land in Westmeath from Oliver Cromwell (land which had been confiscated from the Knights Hospitallers of St. John). Benjamin's grandson, Benjamin III, who was a barrister and an MP, inherited the estate in 1779 and was created a baronet in 1782. It was during his time that the old family home, St Lucy's, was pulled down and Killua Castle built in its stead. On his death in 1810 the title and estate went to his brother, Sir Thomas Chapman, under whom further extensive

Wanda Ryan-Smolin

describes the genesis of a Romantic Irish demesne

changes were made. It appears more than probable that Sadler's views of Killua were commissioned by Sir Thomas, though the exact date is difficult to establish as the works are, typically, neither signed nor dated. The question of dating the paintings is an interesting one as it focuses attention on Sadler's *oeuvre* in general and the place of these paintings within it. Curiously, given the proliferation of the artist's work on the Dublin market over the years, little attention has been given to the chronology of his production. It has, however, been noted that the overall standard of his work is very uneven and that this in part may be explained by works which are attributed to him being perhaps the work of a factory or possibly by his son William III.[2] Despite this problem of attribution there are sufficient works extant which are documented as being by Sadler to permit some assumptions regarding his development as a painter.

William Sadler II (c.1782-1839)[3] was the son of an historical and portrait painter of the same name who had come to Dublin

2. William SADLER II (c.1782-1839): *A View of Killua from across the lake*. Oil on canvas, 53 x 79cm. (Private Collection). The house in the painting is the one that was built about 1784 and gothicised in the 1820s and 1830s.

from England at an early age. He lived in Dublin and is known for his numerous small views of the city and its surroundings which he often executed on mahogany panels. These included straightforward topographical views such as *A View of the Four Courts*, (National Gallery of Ireland) or *A View of The Provost's House* (NGI) (both closely based on Malton views) or, more commonly, topical views of a newsworthy type such as *The Burning of Holms Emporium*. Equally, he did many copies of Dutch seventeenth-century landscapes and views of various parts of the country which, like his Dublin paintings, often had an historical or topical slant such as *The French in Killala Bay*, *The Search for Michael Dwyer*, *A Revenue Raid* or *The Stag Hunt at Killarney*. Among these and other works traditionally attributed to Sadler there is, quite apart from the question of quality, a clear division between them in terms of style and general mood which ranges from the calm and contemplative to the excited and at times almost frenzied. The explanation for this is surely a stylistic one connected with Sadler's artistic development over the years. Thus the calmer, more classically inspired works, to which the Killua views belong, can be identified as early works, while the many lively, emotionally charged Romantic style works can be

categorised as later works. An example of Sadler's later dramatic style is *The Burning of Holms Emporium* (NGI) which presumably can be identified as *The Burning of the Arcade in College Green* mentioned by Strickland as having been sold (along with the entire of his last year's production) in 1838 under instruction from Sadler by C Bennett, auctioneer. Also sold at that time were *An Eruption of Mount Vesuvius*, *The Burning of the Royal Exchange* and *The Wreck of the Killarney*, all highly charged emotional subjects typical of the Romantic era.

Notwithstanding a certain characteristic naiveté in the handling of the compositions, Sadler's three views of Killua stand out as particularly fine examples his work making it altogether easier to believe the suggestion that James Arthur O'Connor received his first and only lessons from Sadler.[4] An unusual, though not entirely unique, feature of the three paintings is the comparatively large format and canvas medium. The principal view is of *Killua from Across the Lake* (Fig.2) which includes two figures and a boat at the shore of the lake in the foreground. Beyond the lake between the trees a carriage is glimpsed approaching the house on its garden front. The house, which can be clearly discerned, is the one which was built around

3. William SADLER II: *A View of the Lake from Killua Castle.* Oil on canvas 57 x 79cm approx. (Private Collection). The gothic ruins in the distance are in the family graveyard of the Chapman family of Killua.

4. William SADLER II: *The Park at Killua.* Oil on canvas, 53 x 79cm (approx). (Private Collection). This is the view from the entrance front of the Castle with the spire of Clonmellon Church in the distance (left).

William Sadler's views of Killua Castle, Co Westmeath

1784[5] to replace an older house on the site; but Sadler does not show any of the Neogothic alterations which began with the building of a large round tower in 1821. Further towers were added later and the whole house was eventually transformed into a castle by the addition of battlements and by refacing it with random ashlar stone. This remodelling has been attributed on stylistic grounds to James Shiel who is known to have worked at relatively nearby Tullynally Castle in the early 1840s and also at Killeen Castle and Dunsany Castle where he was responsible for the design of the gothic style library and the dining room.

In *The Lake from Killua* (Fig.3) the ruined church in the Chapman family graveyard is prominently visible on a hill beyond the lake while in the middle distance to the left of the painting are the Gothic ruins in the shrubbery. These sham ruins, which are still partially intact today, were built with stone brought from the abbey of Multyfarnham by Sir Benjamin Chapman in 1800 and form an entrance to that part of the garden in which the holy well of St Lucy is situated. The lake was originally a small round natural lake which was first enlarged in the 1790s and

5. MAP OF KILLUA. Detail from William Larkin's *Survey of the County of Westmeath* (London 1808). The map shows St Lucy's, as Killua was originally called, the Chapman graveyard, and the lake before its enlargement in 1812 when two small islands were also created.

then further increased in 1812 and 1818. Sadly it has now reverted to its original insignificant size (Fig. 5).

The third painting, *The Park at Killua* (Fig. 4) is of the broad open vista from the entrance front of the house. In the foreground two elegant figures walk along the serpentine approach to Killua from the village of Clonmellon which is indicated by its church spire just visible in the far distance.

Judging by the inclusion of the shrubbery ruins of 1800 and the considerable size of the lake in Sadler's paintings, it is clear that the set must post-date at least the 1812 enlargement of the lake and possibly even that of 1818. But they could not be later than 1821 when the first tower was added to the house. This period corresponds with the recorded dates for Sadler's first contributions to Dublin exhibitions which were between 1809 and 1814 and in 1819. Also significant is the exclusion of the obelisk dedicated to the memory of Sir Walter Raleigh. This is one of the most important features of the demesne and would not have been left out of the views for any reason other than that it had not yet been built. For although it bears an inscription with a date of 1810, the year of Sir Thomas Chapman's succession to the

6. THE WALTER RALEIGH OBELISK AT KILLUA. Dated 1810, the year of Sir Thomas Chapman's baronetcy, the obelisk was not erected until 1834.

7. KILLUA CASTLE: *the Garden Front and Side Elevation*. This recent photograph shows the Castle in its present condition: it had remained intact until stripped of its fittings in 1944.

WILLIAM SADLER'S VIEWS OF KILLUA CASTLE, CO WESTMEATH

8. CLONMELLON LODGE, Killua. As part of the gothicisation programme of the 1820s the Lodge was transformed into a triple-towered Gothic folly. It has been restored in recent years by the author.

9. THE GOTHIC LODGE, Killua. Now derelict, this gate-lodge was built around 1828.

Baronetcy, it was not in fact erected until 1834 (Fig. 6).

Sadler's views of Killua are particularly valuable from an historical point of view as they highlight and illustrate the genesis of what was a most eloquent essay in landscaping in the Romantic style spanning several generations. Looking at the demesne today we find the castellated house roofless but with its Gothic exterior still standing and the last remnants of its eighteenth century interior and its fine plaster work crumbling away (Fig. 7). Around the perimeter of the demesne are dotted five gate lodges the earliest of which is the Palladian-style Temple Lodge of 1804-07. Also built at this time, but transformed into a triple-towered Gothic folly in around 1828, is the Clonmellon Lodge (Fig. 8), which was built to match the new exterior of the castle, as was the equally eye-catching Gothic Lodge[6] (Fig. 9). Both the Temple and Clonmellon Lodges have been saved from oblivion and vandals in recent years and restored but the even more fanciful Gothic Lodge, which is a lodge-gate in the most literal sense of the word, has been completely neglected. Other structures rapidly deteriorating are the eighteenth-century ice-house with its corbelled brick interior, the Walter Raleigh Obelisk, the earlier Lord Nelson Obelisk (1806-07), a subterranean passage and a number of sham ruins which are scattered in and around the former demesne while the pleasure gardens,

labyrinth and woods have long ago disappeared without trace.

An interesting postscript to the history of Killua is that if fate and the social mores of the Edwardian period had not intervened it could have been the home of the suitably romantic figure 'Lawrence of Arabia'. When the 5th Baronet, Sir Benjamin Chapman, died childless in 1914 the title and estate went to his first cousin, Thomas Robert Chapman of nearby Southill in Delvin. Sir Thomas had, however, by this time left Ireland and his wife and four daughters and was living in England under the assumed name of Lawrence with Sarah Junner, the former nurse to his daughters. By Sarah he had five sons including T E Lawrence, later the legendary Lawrence of Arabia. But as all of Sir Thomas' sons were illegitimate none could inherit Killua or the title which became extinct when he died in 1919. Killua went to a cousin, General Fetherstonhaugh, and subsequently to a succession of owners, one of whom held a sale of its fittings in 1944. The castle's final destruction came shortly afterwards when the roof was removed and its lead sold to a firm of builders' providers in Dublin.

WANDA RYAN-SMOLIN, formerly on the staff of the National Gallery of Ireland, is author of King's Inn Portraits, (Dublin 1992).

1. Maurice Craig and the Knight of Glin, *Ireland Observed*, Dublin and Cork, 1970, p.70-71.
2. Anne Crookshank and the Knight of Glin, *The Painters of Ireland, c.1660-1920*, London 1978, p.191.
3. Walter Strickland, *Dictionary of Irish Artists*, Dublin & London, 1913, Vol. II, pp.317-18.
4. *Ibid.*
5. For confirmation of this and other dates of buildings and structures at Killua see the copy of 'Lady Chapman's notes on Killua' (the original of which was at one time in the possession of Eugene Sheridan who purchased Killua in 1931) in the Irish Architectural Archive.
6. Two further lodges were built on the Kells road approaches to the castle in 1855 and 1856 and these, though less interesting architecturally, have been in continuous occupation ever since.

KATHLEEN COX
AN IRISH POTTER OF THE THIRTIES

Peter Lamb *traces the short-lived career of a talented and unusual artist*

Twenty years ago, I began collecting modern Irish pottery and quickly discovered it was a rather rare commodity. Less than half a dozen potters worked in Ireland between the 1880s and 1920 (not counting Belleek and its off-shoots) and they were equally scarce in the 1920s and 30s. Although efforts had been made to stimulate pottery manufacture by the Department of Agriculture & Technical Instruction at the turn of the century, and investigations into Irish pottery clays had been made, nothing much happened until the late 1920s when the Carrigaline pottery was established in Co Cork.

At about the same time, a small group of students emerged from the Metropolitan School of Art in Dublin. Two of them opened pottery workshops. The group who had overlapped in the School from 1926-29 included Kathleen Cox, (Fig. 6), a star pupil of Oliver Sheppard, who won the Taylor Prize three times and who opened her pottery studio in 1929. The others were Stella Rayner from Clontarf, who became Kathleen's assistant, and Edel Dill-Williams who had a pottery studio in Dun Laoghaire in the grounds of Knapton House throughout most of the 1930s. Kathleen specialised in figures, the other two in tableware.

Kathleen Cox was born on 2 July 1904 at Wo Sung, China, the eldest daughter of Dr R H Cox, the Port Health Officer at Shanghai, one of the Cox family of Dundalk. Kathleen spent the first seven years of her life in China which made a deep and lasting impression on her, not only visually but culturally.

In 1911, the family returned to live in Ireland, settling in Howth in an old house with a big garden called Hawthornden. Kathleen grew up in idyllic surroundings; her father, who was also an amateur geologist, modelled in clay and spent his retirement inventing useful things including a periscope which was used by the Navy during World War I.

Kathleen was educated at Alexandra College – she did not do

1. Hilda ROBERTS (1901-82): *'Strange Spirit'. Kathleen Cox in her studio.* Oil on canvas, 60 x 50cm. Signed. (Private collection). Cox opened her studio in Schoolhouse Lane, off Molesworth Street, Dublin in 1929 and worked there until 1935 when she abruptly gave up pottery and smashed all her moulds.

well at exams and her father decided to enter her, at the age of seventeen, in the Metropolitan School of Art. There she remained from 1921 until 1929, proving to be an excellent student under the Master of Sculpture, Oliver Sheppard. She won the Taylor Prize for the first time in 1925 with a sculpture entitled *Adam* and again in 1926 and 1927 with *An Excavator* and *A Dancer*. She visited Paris for a few months in 1929 with the £50 she had won as a prize for her work. Oliver Sheppard was clearly the major influence on her artistic development.

There was another side to her, however. Her talents as an artist were matched by psychic and spiritual gifts, commented on by many of her contemporaries, and ultimately the development of these gifts became the main priority of her life. She was highly independent and detached herself from the belief system she was born into, developing a new one of her own, which included a belief in the universal soul, the great spirit present in all things. When she subsequently met some theosophists she found her views coincided almost exactly with theirs and she joined their ranks and frequently spoke at their meetings. She also became a vegetarian early in life.

It was when she was in Paris that she had an extraordinary visionary experience that was to be inspirational throughout her life. It happened unexpectedly in the street and took the form of a moment of divine enlightenment in which she simultaneously knew herself to be both the centre of, and at one with, the entire universe. Like others who have had the mystical experience, she became a person who radiated love and goodness in the world, and this had a profound effect on her work.

Following this, she came under the influence of Rev Will Hayes, a former journalist who came from England to live in Dublin between 1929 and 1933. He lectured extensively on comparative religion and founded the Order of the Great Companions, a group dedicated to the promotion of world

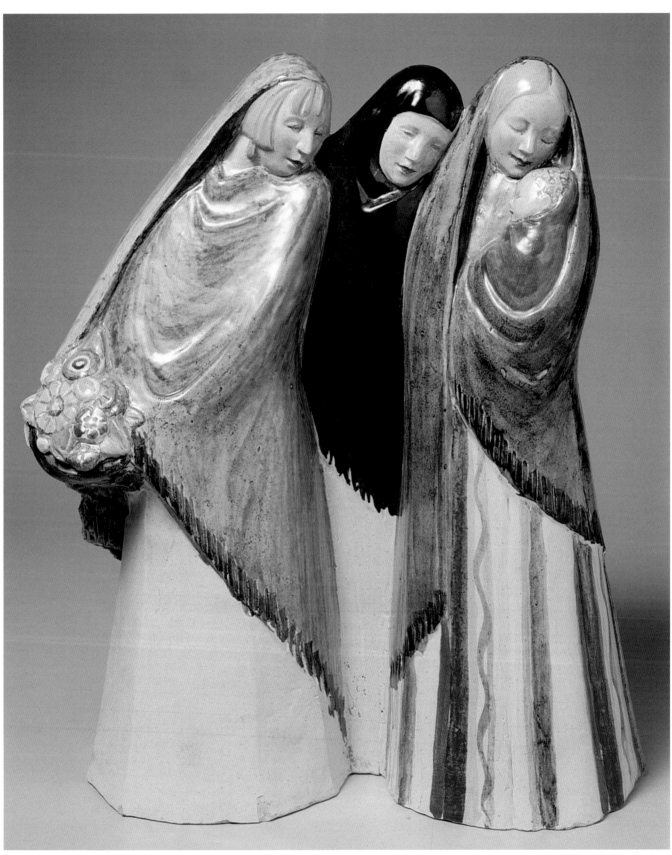

2. Kathleen Cox (1904-72): *The Seed.* 29cm high. 1932 (Private collection). For her more popular designs, Cox was influenced by the type of figure groups produced at the time by the Doulton Burslem factory.

brotherhood. She absorbed the influence of mystical writers and drew inspiration from the illustrations of William Blake and Kahlil Gibran. Many of her friends said she seemed to be on another plane but she had a strong practical streak and a good sense of humour which helped her to keep her feet on the ground. By the time she left college she had developed both her artistic skill and her spiritual outlook to a point where she was ready to begin work.

She opened her pottery studio at No 7 Schoolhouse Lane, off Molesworth Street in Dublin. There she also lived in an apartment furnished with deck chairs and decorated in her idiosyncratic way: the curtains were orange (the colour of life) painted with flames (to represent the life force). Outside her door hung her sign (Fig. 18), a wooden board also painted orange with her logo painted in gold. The logo represented a vase and a naked woman (both

3. Dermod O'BRIEN (1865-1945): *Still-life*. Oil on canvas, 60 x 35cm. (Private collection). The pottery bowl in the foreground, left, was made by Kathleen Cox in 1930 and must have been acquired by Dermod O'Brien as it features in several of his paintings.

vessels) from which stream golden flames symbolising the creative energy of the life force shaping and forming the pot and the woman.

Womanhood is the major theme in Kathleen's work: woman as mother, as worker, and as spiritual being. Many of her women are shown with closed eyes lifting their heads up to the light or deep in some private and ecstatic reverie, others are full of the wonder of new life as are her many Madonnas with their children, others abandon themselves to the great forces of nature, wind and water, or contemplate her beauties; all seem to have an intense inner life. Judging from the portraits that exist of Kathleen she was just such a woman herself (Fig 1).

She was joined in the studio by her college friend, Stella (Estelle) Rayner, Kathleen making mainly figures but also occasional cups, saucers, plates and bowls, and Stella making tableware and occasionally

4. Kathleen Cox: *Bowl*. 6.5cm high. 1930. (Private collection). This is the bowl which was acquired by the painter Dermod O'Brien who used it as a prop in several of his still-lifes. Most of Cox's work is in the form of figures although she occasionally made cups, saucers, plates and bowls.

5. Kathleen Cox: *The Lavender Man*. 27cm high. 1932. (Private collection). By this stage Cox had decided to produce some pieces that were more commercial and she modelled this figure on a well-known Dublin character of the time.

KATHLEEN COX: AN IRISH POTTER OF THE THIRTIES

terracotta buttons. They experimented with clay from Howth but it lacked plasticity and they resorted to Wenger's clay imported from London. They fired their ware in a small electric kiln (see photograph in *The Daily Sketch*, 18 February 1933), the first of its kind in Ireland, and despite the fact that elements kept breaking, they persevered with it right through to the close of their potting careers at the end of 1935, a period of about six years in all.

Among the first pieces produced are a *Madonna and Child* plaque (Fig. 10) in which the Madonna with out-turned, raised hands, gazes in rapture at her baby. Another dated piece from 1929 is the *Portrait Mask of Norris Davidson* (Fig. 7), a friend and neighbour whose film

6. Kathleen COX. *Photograph taken in her studio, c.1930.*

Suicide starred Mary Manning. Norris commissioned a poster from Kathleen for this film and also a bird bath in the form of St Francis with up-turned hands.

The following year, 1930, she exhibited at the Royal Hibernian Academy for the first time. Her superb *Portrait Mask of Brigid O'Brien* (Fig. 9) was priced £2. Brigid had been a fellow student under Oliver Sheppard and was a daughter of Dermod O'Brien, the painter. Dermod must have acquired a little bowl (Fig. 4) that she made that year as it became a familiar prop in his paintings, turning up frequently in the foreground of his flower pieces (Fig. 3). That year, she also exhibited a pair of *Madonna and Child* bookends (Fig. 8).

In 1931, she exhibited again at the RHA and also held an

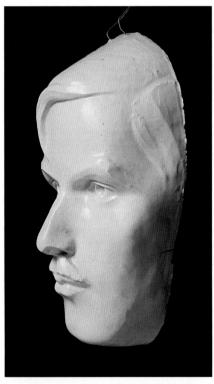

7. Kathleen COX: *Portrait mask of Norris Davidson.* 23cm high. 1929. (Private collection). This is one of Cox's early portrait masks, a form which was relatively unusual for a potter. The film director Norris Davidson was a friend and neighbour of Cox's.

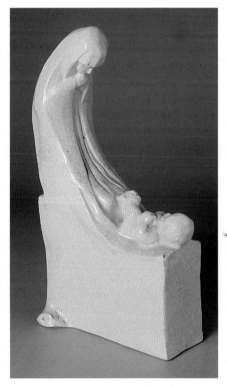

8. Kathleen COX: *Bookend in the form of a Madonna and Child.* 20.75cm high. 1930. (Private collection). Cox exhibited a pair of these bookends at the RHA in 1930.

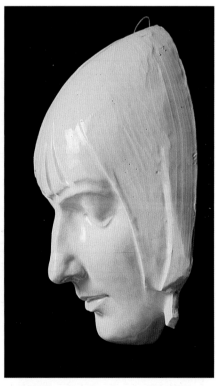

9. Kathleen COX: *Portrait mask of Brigid O'Brien.* 21.5cm high. 1930. (Private collection). Cox exhibited this piece at the RHA in 1930 where it was priced at £2: the subject was the daughter of the painter Dermod O'Brien.

10. Kathleen Cox: *Plaque with the Madonna and Child.* 35.5cm high. Dated 1929. (Private collection). This is one of the first pieces produced by Cox after opening her Dublin studio in 1929. At first she experimented with the use of clay from Howth but later imported Wenger's clay from London.

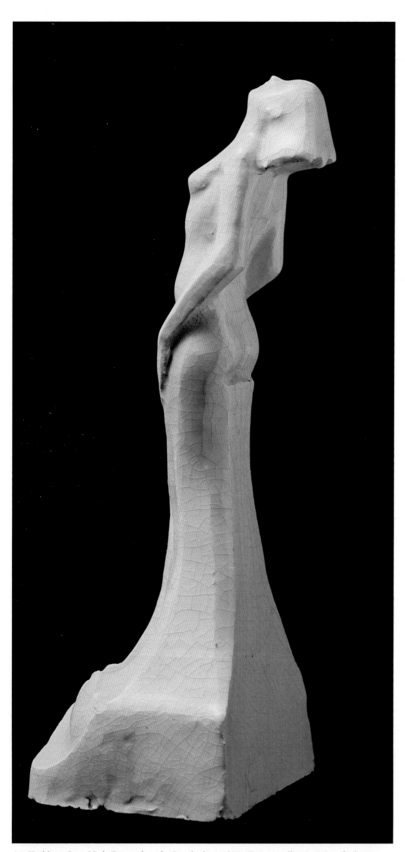

11. Kathleen Cox: *Nude Figure of a girl.* 17cm high. c. 1931. (Private collection). It is fairly certain that the pose of the girl with head thrown back was inspired by an Augustus John drawing, *Nirvana*, in the Tate Gallery, London, a postcard of which was among Cox's possessions.

exhibition at her studio in Schoolhouse Lane. Included was her figure *A Woman Carrying Something*, (a mysterious burden hidden beneath the woman's shawl) (Fig. 17). She issued this piece in various colourways. Her editions of each piece were limited to six. From this period also comes a small nude figure of a girl with head thrown back basking in light (Fig. 11), clearly inspired by Augustus John's *Nirvana* in the Tate Gallery of

12. Postcard of *Nirvana* by Augustus JOHN (1878-1961). This Tate Gallery postcard was among the potter's possessions.

which Kathleen possessed a postcard reproduction (Fig. 12).

By 1932, Kathleen was finding it difficult to keep going financially making purely 'Art' pieces. She decided to do a commercial line as well and made a number of figures based on the style of Leslie Carradine of the Doulton Burslem factory. These included an *Old Woman Selling from a Barrow*, and

13. Kathleen Cox: *Bookends in the form of male nudes.* 26cm high. 1932-33. (Private collection). This extraordinary design is inspired by a story of a drowned girl whose spirit in the form of a bird sits on the young man's shoulder.

14. Kathleen Cox: *Bookends in the form of a Sea Woman.* 18cm high. 1932-33. (Private collection). These bookends are among the most beautiful of all Cox's designs with the naiad-like figure rising from the waves.

15. Kathleen COX: *Plaque – The Barge Woman*. 25cm high. 1932-33. (Private collection). One of Cox's last pieces.

16. Kathleen COX: *The Fruit-Seller*. 19.5cm high. 1932-33. (Private collection). The somewhat angular treatment of the drapery in this figure marks a new development in Cox's style.

17. Kathleen COX: *A Woman Carrying Something*. 24cm high. 1931. (Private collection). This was Cox's own title for the figure which she made in both plain white and in colour.

the charming figure *The Lavender Man* (Fig. 5), modelled on Michael Clifford, a well known Dublin character, who sold his wares from a tray, on buses and street corners. He was a native of Genoa and was recorded by other Dublin artists, including Harry Kernoff.

The Seed (Fig. 2), a group of three women in shawls admiring a baby, was also shown in 1932, as was the seated nude girl, *Eternity* of which she made a special inscribed copy for Sarah Purser.

In the 1932/33 period she produced the male nude bookends, (Fig. 13), depicting the story of a drowned girl whose spirit in the form of a bird sits on a young man's shoulder and whispers in his ear. Also the extraordinary *Sea Woman* (Fig. 14) bookends in which woman, horse and waves seem to blend together in ecstatic union. The lovely contemplative *Fruit Seller* (Fig. 16) and the serene *Barge Woman* (Fig. 15) are from this period. The latest dated piece to come to light is a *Portrait Bust of Maureen O'Brien* (sister of Brigid) inscribed 'Jan, 1934'. In 1934 she also made an art-deco teaset with a sign of the zodiac painted on each cup. The current whereabouts of this teaset is unknown.

During the mid-1930s Kathleen gradually stopped making pottery, the end being brought about by a combination of factors. She felt trapped in an ivory tower and, as an artist, unable to influence society or change the world. In the face of the rise of Nazism in Germany and the looming World War II this sense of futility increased. She also came to feel very strongly that pottery should be useful and not merely ornamental. Her visit to the Chinese Exhibition in London in 1935 confirmed this. She returned to Dublin and smashed all her moulds and closed down the pottery and, from then on, avoided talking about her work.

L S Gogan, a former Keeper of the Art Industry Division of the National Museum of Ireland described her (in a letter to the author) as 'a somewhat fugitive genius' whose work was 'surprisingly sophisticated' who 'in normal circumstances ought to have become the founder of quite a factory.'

In 1937, she married and moved to London. She spent the war years with her husband, a conscientious objector, running a farm at Meopham, Kent, next door to her old friend and mentor, Will Hayes. In 1950, she returned to London to raise her two daughters. She wrote and illustrated a book for children called *A Story of Stories* (published 1970 by Volturna Press) about the great religions of the world. She travelled to North Africa where she was accepted to their hearts by the native people. A photograph of her published with an interview by Jill Tweedie in 1971 shows an extraordinarily open, joyful face.

She died in London in 1972.

PETER LAMB is a collector and connoisseur of twentieth-century Irish decorative arts.

ACKNOWLEDGEMENTS
I am grateful to all the people who have helped me with information about Kathleen Cox; I am particularly thankful to Stella Rayner, Alan Palmer and Grania Balfour for their assistance in writing this article.

18. Kathleen COX: *Studio signboard.* House-paint on wood, 100cm high. (Private collection). The orange of her studio sign represented the colour of life; the woman with a pot surrounded by flames symbolised the creative energy of the life force.

ALOYSIUS O'KELLY IN BRITTANY

The Breton subject-matter of many of the artist's pictures is examined by **Julian Campbell**

Among the paintings by Aloysius O'Kelly which have come to light in recent years, many have been of Breton subjects. Viewers have often been puzzled at the variety of styles attaching to these works. This is compounded by the different dates given for O'Kelly's birth, and the artist's indication in later exhibition catalogues that he was American-born.[1] The fact is that there were two distinct Breton periods in his career: the first at Pont-Aven in the late 1870s, when he was in his twenties; the second, at Concarneau thirty years later. This article will consider briefly O'Kelly's Breton oeuvre, attempting a precise dating of pictures and identification of locations, and relating him to his contemporaries.

O'Kelly had studied at the Ecole des Beaux Arts in Paris. He entered Gérôme's atelier on 7 October 1874.[2] His address was at 4 Rue St. Sulpice, near to the Ecole. Gérôme was a successful academic and Orientalist, who had opened his studio in 1863; in 1874 he had just returned from a trip to the Middle East. Two of his French students, Abram and Dagnan Bouveret, were later to

2. (Above) Aloysius O'KELLY (1851-c.1928): *The Ferry, Concarneau.* Oil on canvas, 73.5 x 93cm. Signed c.1906. (Private Collection). O'Kelly features the ferry point at the end of the walled town (Ville Close), Concarneau, and the Passage Lanriec opposite. Probably set at evening, O'Kelly's figure subjects of the early-twentieth century have a liveliness of outline, while his harbour scenes at Concarneau show a new-found impressionism.

1. (Opposite) Aloysius O'KELLY: *Old Couple at the Door of an Inn.* Oil on canvas, 48 x 38cm. Signed. c.1876-77. (Private Collection). Probably one of O'Kelly's earliest outdoor subjects, and painted at Pont-Aven in the late 1870s.

work in Brittany. Gérôme had a reputation for being tolerant to American students, amongst whom in this period were Thomas Eakins, Alden Weir and Alexander Harrison. British students included William Stott and William Bartlett. Of most significance to O'Kelly would have been the arrival in the atelier

William Lippincott. French students included Caillebotte and, later, Toulouse-Lautrec. Bonnat was a successful portraitist, with an admiration for Velasquez. O'Kelly also had great respect for his assistant, Gabriel Ferrier.[5] From these teachers, O'Kelly would have received an academic training, a strength of figure drawing, and perhaps an interest in Oriental subjects. But of equal importance was the fact that in summer time many of Gérôme's and Bonnat's students (including all those mentioned above) gravitated towards Brittany.

3. Aloysius O'KELLY: *Breton Woman Cleaning Bowls.* Oil on canvas, 63.5 x 53.5cm. Signed and dated 1909. (Private Collection). Although painted at Concarneau in 1909, the subject recalls the 'Dutch'-style interiors popular amongst artists at Pont-Aven in the 1860s and 1870s.

O'Kelly may have first arrived at Pont-Aven in summer 1876, the same time as another Irish-born artist, Thomas Hovenden, and shortly after Augustus Burke from Dublin. A colony of American painters, under the dominant figure of Robert Wylie, had developed over the previous decade,[6] and O'Kelly joined this community. He set about painting market and street scenes, villagers playing bowls, and landscapes.[7] *Old Couple at the Door of an Inn*[8] (Fig. 1), is probably one of his earliest Breton works, with its intense realism (particularly in the headdress and costume of the woman), the dramatic contrast of light and shadow, which was a characteristic of the outdoor scenes of the early Pont-Aven school, and the neat, forward-sloping signature. The simple decoration in the stonework is characteristic of the Pont-Aven region.[9] The composition of two figures beside an open door is remarkably close to that of Burke's *At the Chapel Door*, 1876, indicating a similar date.[10]

The Evening Pipe (Fig. 5) shows a villager with broad-rimmed hat, loose trousers and clogs, leaning over the hearth. The convincing drawing and

shortly after him of the Boston-born painter William Picknell.[3]

Probably later in the 1870s, O'Kelly studied in the private atelier of Bonnat in Montmartre, which also attracted foreigners.[4] Amongst these were Sargent, Stanhope Forbes, Walter Gay and

relaxed composition are evidence of O'Kelly's Paris training, while the costume and interior detail indicate his developing interest in rural life. O'Kelly's work also shows admiration for Courbet, the dominant influence upon the Pont-Aven School, even in the style of signature. His use of a rounded 'a' for 'Aloysius' or 'al' and the slightly backward-sloping signature, characterises this early Breton work (indeed his oeuvre up to the early 1890s).

Picknell had by this time become one of the leading figures at Pont-Aven, and his beautifully-realised landscapes made an impact upon O'Kelly.[11] Both artists painted the classic view of the harbour at Pont-Aven, with its fishing boats, waterfront and church spire, nestling in a wooded landscape. Compared to Picknell's more detailed version, dated 1879, O'Kelly's landscape (Fig. 4) has a simplicity and lightness of touch, with delicate hues placed upon a warm pink ground. The harbour was also painted by Gaston Roullet in 1878, Walter Osborne in 1883, and featured in picture postcards around 1900.[12]

Two of O'Kelly's portraits, of an old woman seated and of a girl, hung in the collection of the Pension Gloanec for many years.[13] Although the work of O'Kelly, Burke and Hovenden shows differences of emphasis, these three artists may be seen as comprising an informal Irish group at Pont-Aven, and were the first Irish 'School' in Brittany.[14] It is possible that O'Kelly made a return visit to Finistère around 1885; he painted a portrait of a Breton man (See p. 95). This was praised in the *Dublin University Review* in 1885, as 'the best work' that O'Kelly had shown at the Royal Hibernian Academy thus far.[15]

After painting variously in Connemara, England and Egypt, O'Kelly seems to have left for America in 1895.[16] Then, suddenly, he reappeared in Brittany in 1908-09,[17] perhaps as early as 1905.[18] He was now based at Concarneau, which had succeeded Pont-Aven as the most popular artists' colony. He lodged at the Hotel de France, where the Dublin-born painter W J Leech was staying in 1906.[19] O'Kelly worked intensively. His Concarneau oeuvre is diverse, and can be divided into six loose categories: interiors with figures; outdoor figure subjects; close-up portraits of fishermen or women; studies of the harbour; landscapes; and small sketches of the market. On the one hand, his interiors show a nostalgia for the indoor subjects of Hovenden and Wylie at Pont-Aven thirty

4. Aloysius O'KELLY: *View of the Harbour – Pont-Aven.* Oil on canvas, 66 x 45.7cm. Signed. c.1878. (Private Collection). O'Kelly shows the view of the harbour, le Port en Amont, and town of Pont-Aven from downstream. This view was depicted by several artists in the period and became popular in postcards about 1900.

years earlier, on the other hand, his harbour scenes are light and colourful, with a new embracing of impressionism.

The interiors show an interest in Breton domestic life, for instance, women in the kitchen, spinning wool, or sitting around the fire, at an inn or celebrating a child's christening. *Breton Woman Cleaning Bowls* (Fig. 3) 1909, has a warm, burnished tone, with a skilful rendering of still-life detail. The woman sits in relaxed pose, while light falls on her face and bonnet. In *The Christening Party*, 1908, and other interiors, the presence of a small casement window, through which the harbour at Concarneau and fishing boats can be glimpsed, has an alluring quality, unconsciously echoing Caspar Friedrich's magical painting *Woman by a Window*.[20]

Some of O'Kelly's Concarneau paintings have a strong narrative element. He had no shyness in taking on subjects with different types of figures: girls, children and old men. The decorative white bonnets of the women, with four 'lapettes', were characteristic of Concarneau; in Pont-Aven, bonnets had two 'lapettes'.[21] O'Kelly's interiors are curiously old-fashioned for their date, reminiscent even of Dutch interiors.[22] Yet it would be simplistic to say that they were painted solely for the market; there is a personal sense of enjoyment in them. Amongst his outdoor subjects, the evening scene *The Ferry* (Fig. 2) c.1906 shows the Passage Lanriec, at the end of Concarneau's walled town[23] where a ferry (now motorised) still plies across the sound. The figures have a relaxation in pose and liveliness in outline, different from the earlier Pont-Aven paintings.[24] An impressionistic influence, present in the sunny housefronts and rippling reflections, is even more evident in O'Kelly's radiant harbour scenes, notably *Harbour Scene, Concarneau*, and *Awaiting the Return, Concarneau*, with their light brush strokes, and tones of blue and pink, maroon and turquoise.[25] Similar studies of the harbour and fishing fleet were painted by many of the artists resident at Concarneau, for instance, Leech, Fromuth, Terrick Williams and Bulfield. Yet O'Kelly's paintings are amongst the most pure examples of Impressionism by an Irish artist.

O'Kelly exhibited two Breton subjects, *La Sortie* and *Devant le*

5. Aloysius O'Kelly: *The Evening Pipe*. Oil on canvas, 44.5 x 53cm. Signed. c.1877. (Private Collection). Probably painted at Pont-Aven in the late 1870s, this canvas shows O'Kelly's early interest in interiors and his skill in figure drawing.

Feu at the Paris Salon in 1908, and two, *L'auberge* and *"'Ave Maria", procession religieuse en Bretagne'* in 1909.[26] The latter, set before the Ville Close, may be one of his largest and most crowded compositions. The charming painting *Corpus Christi Procession* (AIB Collection, Dublin) may well be a study for it.

His Concarneau paintings bear a squarer, crisper signature than previously, with a capital 'A' for his Christian name.[27] His first and second Breton periods, at Pont-Aven and at Concarneau, can thus be identified by means of signature, and by the costume and location of their subject, as well as through stylistic analysis.

By December 1909, O'Kelly had returned to New York. He brought with him many of his Breton pictures. He tried to interest the Macbeth Gallery in his work, but without success.[28] However, he exhibited his Breton paintings at Moulton and Rickett's Gallery in 1912. O'Kelly was now sixty but, as Homan Potterton details (pp.91-95), life in America was not necessarily easy for the Irish artist.

DR JULIAN CAMPBELL is a tutor in History of Art at the Crawford College of Art and Design, Cork

1. Catalogues of Paris Salon, 1908-1909. O'Kelly described himself as 'né a New York (Etats Unis d'Amerique)'. The date of birth given in the registers of the Ecole des Beaux Arts, June 1851, would seem to be the most authentic. Although O'Kelly provided the month and year, he was the only student not to give the day of birth.
2. Registers of Ecole des Beaux Arts, Archives Nationales de France A.J. 52-248.
3. Registers of Ecole des Beaux Arts, *ibid*. See also H. Barbara Weinberg, *The American Pupils of Jean-Léon Gérôme*, Fort Worth, 1984.
4. See Gerald Ackerman, 'Thomas Eakins and his Parisian Masters Gérôme and Bonnat', *Gazette des Beaux Arts*, April 1969, p.235-56. Bonnat allowed foreign students to pay by the class. O'Kelly may have studied with Bonnat in the late 1870s, between visits to Brittany; certainly prior to 1882, when Bonnat became a teacher at the Ecole.
5. He listed Ferrier's and Bonnat's names in Salon catalogues for 1884, and 1908-1909. Interestingly, he did not include Gérôme's name on either occasion.
6. See Robert Sellin, *Americans in Normandy and Brittany*, catalogue of exhibition, Phoenix Art Museum, Phoenix, 1982; and Michael Jacobs, *The Good and Simple Life, Artist Colonies in Europe and America*, Oxford, 1985.
7. O'Kelly exhibited a handful of Breton subjects at the Royal Hibernian Academy, Royal Society of British Artists and Royal Academy, 1876-79. (*Street Scene, Brittany*, his first exhibit at the RHA, 1878 cat.no. 168, is not included in *Royal Hibernian Academy of Arts Index of Exhibitors 1826-1970*)
8. All pictures referred to in the text are in private collections, unless otherwise stated.
9. This old building has not been identified, but may have been in the old Rue du Abbes

Tanguy, Pont-Aven, and is characteristic of vernacular architecture in this region.
10. See Julian Campbell, *Onlookers in France, Irish Realist and Impressionist Painters*, exh. cat. Crawford Art Gallery, Cork, 1993. cat. no.7. The shadowy figure of the girl inside the doorway is later echoed by the maid on the left of O'Kelly's *Christening Party*.
11. For information on Picknell, see Sellin, *op.cit.*; and *William Lamb Picknell, 1853-1897*, by Lauren Robb and David Sellin, exh. cat., Taggart and Jorgensen Gallery, New York, 1991. Picknell also used a 'Courbet-like' signature.
12. Picknell's painting of the harbour is in Phoenix Art Museum, Phoenix; Roullet's in Musée de Pont-Aven; Osborne's in a private collection.
13. I am grateful to Mme Catherine Puget, Director of the Musée de Pont-Aven, for providing me with this information. The portraits are now in the Gloanec family collection.
14. See J. Campbell, 'Irish Artists in Brittany, 1860-1914', *Irlande et Bretagne, Vingt Siecles d'Histoire*, (ed.) Catherine Laurent and Helen Davis, Rennes, 1994, p.228-35.
15. *Un Breton de Finistère*, exhibited at RHA and Irish Artisans Exhibition, 1885; *A Vendean of Finistère, Brittany*, RA, 1886. See Julian Campbell *The Irish Impressionists*, exh. cat., National Gallery of Ireland, Dublin, 1984, cat. no. 24. The portrait exhibited in 1984 is not O'Kelly's 1885 portrait, but belongs to his later Concarneau period.
16. O'Kelly ceased exhibiting at the RHA and at British exhibitions in 1895. In going to America, O'Kelly may have been hoping to establish contact with old associates from Pont-Aven. But Hovenden died in 1895, Picknell in 1897.
17. Catalogue of Paris Salons, 1908-09.

18. His Breton painting, *The Stained Glass Window* is dated 1905. (Exhibited at Cynthia O'Connor Gallery, Dublin, July – August 1994, cat. no. 1).
19. In 1908-09, Leech was staying at the nearby Voyageurs. (Catalogues of RHA and ROI, 1906-09) For information on Leech, see Denise Ferran, 'WJ Leech's Brittany', *Irish Arts Review*, 1993, p.224-232.
20. Staatsgalerie, Berlin.
21. I am very grateful to Mme. Catherine Puget, Director of the Musée de Pont-Aven, for providing me with information on Breton regional costumes.
22. See *The Irish Impressionists, op. cit.* p. 164. For example, O'Kelly's *Spinning Wheel, Brittany*, c.1908 recalls paintings of spinners, made popular by artists such as Abram, Peel, Hagborg and Van den Anker, in the early 1880s. *The Christening Party*, 1908 bears comparison with interiors by Wylie as early as the 1860s, and with Trayer's *Marchand de crepe à Quimperlé*, 1866 (Musée des Beaux Arts, Rennes).
23. *Le Passage* was also depicted by French artist Lucien Gros.
24. See *The Ferry*, in 'Irish Paintings', Gorry Gallery, Dublin, April-May 1988, p.12. Catalogue entry by J Campbell.
25. These pictures were exhibited in *The Irish Impressionists*, 1984, cat. no. 28; and *Onlookers in France*, 1993, cat. no. 10, respectively.
26. Catalogues of Paris Salon, 1908-09.
27. All those Breton paintings exhibited in *The Irish Impressionists*, bearing this upright signature with a capital 'A', belong to O'Kelly's Concarneau period, c. 1905-09.
28. In late December, 1909, O'Kelly was writing to the Macbeth Gallery, New York, from a New York address. See *The Irish Impressionists op. cit.*, p.124.

ALOYSIUS O'KELLY AND THE ILLUSTRATED LONDON NEWS

1. Aloysius O'KELLY (1851-c.1928): *Disturbed Ireland: Before the Magistrate* (From *The Illustrated London News,* 5 February 1881, Extra Supplement). 31.5 x 47 cm. Signed: *A O'Kelly* (bottom left), *Swain* (bottom right). One of many illustrations by O'Kelly, the equivalent of modern press photographs, which accompanied articles in *The Illustrated London News* on the Irish Land War of the 1880s.

Aloysius O'Kelly,[1] the Dublin-born artist, is best remembered as a painter of genre and landscape scenes.[2] However, a lesser known but nonetheless fascinating part of O'Kelly's oeuvre is his series of illustrations for *The Illustrated London News* done in the 1880s. It is difficult to establish a definite chronology for O'Kelly's life as he travelled extensively. In the 1870s O'Kelly went to Brittany and was one of the first of a younger generation of Irish artists to paint there.[3] It is not known how long O'Kelly spent in Brittany but it is likely that he returned to London and Ireland and then visited Brittany again on further occasions. Sometime in the mid-1880s, possibly 1885, he visited Egypt and a considerable proportion of his work thereafter was inspired by his time there. He emigrated to the United States sometime before 1909 and lived in Brooklyn, New York. He painted in both New York and Maine. O'Kelly's date of death is problematic.[4] It was thought to have been 1926 or 1928 but this date has been disputed and it may be as late as 1935.

Topical illustrations made during the Land War of the 1880s are a surprising and little-known aspect of the Irish painter's oeuvre as **Margarita Cappock** *reveals*

In the early 1880s the editors of *The Illustrated London News* assigned several of their artists to cover the Irish Land War. The illustrations are the equivalent of modern-day photographs and each illustration was accompanied by an article which explained the background to the situations depicted. The scenes represented events which occurred as a result of the political upheaval in Ireland in these years. Other illustrations on nonpolitical events such as a series on the ancient Celtic monuments of Ireland (5 March, 1887) and the State visit of the Prince of Wales, Albert Victor (9 July, 1887) are also included but these are in the minority. In total approximately two hundred and sixty-six Irish illustrations featured between the years 1880 to 1889. During this time *The Illustrated London News* had artists in Mayo, Killarney, Waterford, Roscommon, Fermanagh, Youghal and Dublin. Three artists whose work featured regularly are Richard Caton Woodville, Claude Byrne and Harry Furniss. Caton Woodville[5] was an American who moved from Baltimore

Aloysius O'Kelly and The Illustrated London News

to London where he made his name as a painter of military panoramas. He began working for *The Illustrated London News* in 1875 and went as an artist to the Turkish War of 1878 and the Egyptian War of 1882. Woodville did a number of illustrations on Irish scenes in 1880. One of his best illustrations of an Irish scene is *Disturbed Ireland: A Visit from 'Rory of the Hills'* (22 January 1881). His scenes are more melodramatic than O'Kelly's. Claude Byrne,[6] an Irish illustrator from Rathmines in Dublin, contributed scenes of Irish distress to *The Illustrated London News* in 1886. He was also a painter and exhibited at the Royal Hibernian Academy in 1884. Byrne's illustrations, for example, *'Warming the Ground', A Sketch at Gweedore, Donegal* (8 May 1886) are less detailed than O'Kelly's and more sketchy.

Dublin scenes. O'Kelly presumably spent a large part of 1881 in Ireland, in particular in the West of Ireland, and made further visits in the subsequent years. That O'Kelly was also painting during this time is indicated by the fact that he exhibited four West of Ireland scenes at the Royal Hibernian Academy from 1880 to 1885.[8] In fact O'Kelly succeeded in being accepted to exhibit his painting of a West of Ireland scene, *Messe dans une chaumière de Connemara* at the Paris Salon in 1884.[9] Unfortunately this work is untraced.[10] The majority of O'Kelly's illustrations are of situations he himself witnessed in the West of Ireland. They are all of political significance with the exception of one illustration entitled *The Steerage of the Steamer Solway at Kingstown. After the Fire on Board*, 3 December 1881. O'Kelly contributes less to *The Illustrated London News* in the subsequent years with three illustrations by him in 1882, one in 1883 and two in 1886. This adds up to thirty illustrations attributable to O'Kelly in total. They vary in size with some measuring up to 31.5cm x 47cm. Nine illustrations are on double pages and these large illustrations are among his most successful.

2. Aloysius O'KELLY: *An Eviction in the West of Ireland* (from *The Illustrated London News*, 19 March 1881). 31.5 x 47 cm. Signed: *A O'Kelly* (bottom left), *W J Palmer Sc* (bottom right). O'Kelly vividly depicts the harsh realities of the time in Ireland; the despair of the evicted family is evident in the figure of the seated woman with her head in her hands.

A differentiation must be made between signed illustrations and illustrations done from a sketch by Aloysius O'Kelly. There are fifteen illustrations bearing O'Kelly's signature on the actual illustration. Out of these fifteen illustrations signed by O'Kelly ten carry an engraver's name and five do not have engravers' names on them. Most of the illustrations have two signatures: that of the artist and that of the engraver. The initials 'WQ' appear four times, W J Palmer's signature appears three times, R Taylor's twice and the name 'Swain' once. Five of O'Kelly's signed illustrations are on double pages. These are as follows:

Harry Furniss,[7] born in Wexford of English parents, worked as a Special Artist for *The Illustrated London News* in the 1880s. He tried his hand at social realism in his illustrations such as *The State of Ireland: Sketches in Galway* (21 February 1880) but he is best known as a humorous illustrator.

Between January 1881 and December 1886 *The Illustrated London News* carried a total of one hundred and forty illustrations of Irish events. O'Kelly's signature appears on an illustration for the first time on 5 February 1881. During the course of that year it would appear again another eleven times. In six instances the illustration itself is not signed by O'Kelly but the caption underneath states 'From a Sketch by our Special Artist, Mr A O'Kelly.' On seven further occasions in 1881 O'Kelly is named as the artist in the accompanying article. Indeed of the forty-seven Irish illustrations which featured during that year O'Kelly's name is associated with over half of the total. The remaining Irish illustrations for that year are for the most part

Disturbed Ireland: Before the Magistrate (5 February, 1881) (Engraver: Swain) (Fig. 1), *An Eviction in the West of Ireland* (19 March, 1881) (Engraver: W J Palmer Sc (sculpsit)) (Fig. 2); *The Land League Agitation in Ireland: A Sheriff's sale of Cattle to Pay Rent* (18 June, 1881) (no engraver's signature) (Fig. 3); *Departure of Irish Emigrants at Clifden, County Galway* (21 July, 1883) (W J Palmer Sc) (Fig. 4); *On Eviction Duty in Ireland: Sketches in Galway with the military and police forces* (9 scenes) (1 May, 1886) (Engraver: R Taylor) (Fig. 5)

O'Kelly studied with both Gérôme and Bonnat in Paris and Gérôme's influence is particularly evident in O'Kelly's signed illustrations for *The Illustrated London News*. Gérôme's standards for his students' draughtsmanship were extremely exacting and this training was obviously of great benefit to O'Kelly. The composition of each of O'Kelly's illustrations is well-balanced and his drawing of individuals and their variety of facial expressions is very accomplished. For example, in the illustration, *Disturbed*

Ireland: Before the Magistrate (5 February 1881) (signed A. O'Kelly) (Fig. 1) the grief of presumably the female relatives of the prisoner is evident from the poses of the three seated women. The faces of the women crowding the entrance are also extremely sorrowful, in particular the woman who clasps her hands together as if in prayer. They are prevented from entering the room by members of the Royal Irish Constabulary.

Some of O'Kelly's best illustrations are those in which he is portraying confrontational scenes. One such illustration is *The Land League Agitation in Ireland: A sheriff's sale of cattle to pay rent* (18 June 1881) (Fig. 3). This illustration depicts a confrontation between the tenants, members of the Land League and a landlord. If a tenant was unable to pay his rent, the landlord had the right to sell his cattle in order to raise the money owed to him. These sales were normally turbulent affairs and O'Kelly's illustration conveys this very clearly. As no auctioneer was willing to officiate, a sheriff has taken his place and stands on the cart. Members of the 'Emergency Committee' stand next to the cart. These are friends of the landlord who stand ready to buy the cattle if no buyers are forthcoming. The cattle are defended by a line of policemen who are also holding back the crowd, many of whom are armed. On the far right a detachment of dragoons stand in readiness to aid the police if a riot breaks out. The majority of the tenants would be members of the Land League, which would arrange for the cattle to be bought back again. The tenants hold banners which proclaim 'Hold the Harvest',[11] 'The Land for the People' and 'Down with Landlordism'. The arrangement of the various groups of figures is made into a convincing composition by O'Kelly.

The themes of emigration and eviction are both treated in a sympathetic and realistic way by O'Kelly. In the illustration *Departure of Irish Emigrants at Clifden, County Galway* (21 July, l883) (Fig. 4) the realities of emigration are forcefully presented. The scene is crowded with convincing detail. A priest stands by to bid farewell to the emigrants and the uncertainty and sadness of emigration is visible in the worried face of the woman with a child on her lap who is waiting to leave. Those left behind are also portrayed, such as the woman waving a handkerchief from a window. It must be remembered that at this time emigration was a final step and most of the people who emigrated never saw their families in Ireland again. In the illustration *An Eviction in the West of Ireland* (19 March 1881) (Fig. 2) another of the harsh realities of the time is portrayed. A family, who have obviously failed to pay their rent, are evicted from their thatched cottage. The family's furniture has been thrown outside the cottage and the figure of the woman seated on the wardrobe with her head in her hands is expressive of the despair of an evicted family.

In two cases, O'Kelly divides an illustration into nine small sections and each section features a particular occurrence, for example, *On Eviction Duty in Ireland: Sketches in Galway with the Military and Police Forces* (1 May 1886) (Fig. 5). This interesting illustration shows the arrival of the troops, the execution of the eviction and the end result for the family which in this case is a straw hut on the side of a mountain. Scene seven is one of great despair as the family are shown sitting on the ground in a dejected state. One also observes that the military are heavily armed. This illustration indicates that O'Kelly was skilled at drawing on a small scale as well as on a large scale.

The other fifteen illustrations attributable to Aloysius O'Kelly

3. Aloysius O'KELLY: *The Land League Agitation in Ireland: A sheriff's sale of cattle to pay rent* (From *Illustrated London News*, 18 June 1881, Extra Supplement). 31.5 x 47 cm. Signed: *A O'Kelly* (bottom left). An angry confrontation between tenants, whose cattle are about to be sold, the landlord and members of the Land League is convincingly portrayed by the artist.

4. Aloysius O'KELLY: *Departure of Irish Emigrants at Clifden. County Galway* (From *The Illustrated London News*, 21 July 1883, Extra Supplement). 31.5 x 47 cm. Signed: *A O'Kelly* (bottom right), *W J. Palmer Sc* (bottom left, centre). A sympathetic rendering, with many convincing details, of the painful reality of emigration.

5. Aloysius O'KELLY: *On Eviction Duty in Ireland: Sketches in Galway with the military and police forces* (9 scenes). (From *The Illustrated London News*, 1 May 1886). 31.5 x 47 cm. Signed: *A O'Kelly* (centre right), *R Taylor* (bottom left). Showing his skills in small-scale drawing, the artist depicts the great despair of the family evicted by the heavily-armed military forces.

ALOYSIUS O'KELLY AND THE ILLUSTRATED LONDON NEWS

are either captioned 'From a sketch by our Special Artist, Mr A O'Kelly' or described in the accompanying articles as 'a sketch furnished by Mr A O'Kelly'. It can be presumed that O'Kelly provided the sketches and accompanying notes but was not the actual illustrator. The names which appear most frequently on these sketches are F Dadd, W H Overend, Palmer, Taylor and the initials CH. It would appear that Palmer and Taylor were engravers but Dadd and Overend were artists. F Dadd's signature appears most frequently; an example of his work is provided by the illustration *The State of Ireland: Stopping a Hunt. From a Sketch by our Special Artist Mr A O'Kelly* (24 December 1881). Another illustration bearing F Dadd's signature is *The State of Ireland: Arrested under the Coercion Act – A Sketch at Roscommon*

6. Aloysius O'KELLY: *The State of Ireland: Arrested under the Coercion Act – A Sketch at Roscommon Railway Station (From a sketch by Mr A O'Kelly).* (From *The Illustrated London News*, 3 December 1881). 31.5 x 47 cm. Signed: *F Dadd* (bottom left). This illustration was accompanied by O'Kelly's own vivid account of the event which took place at 2 a.m.; the bearded man wearing a cap and looking out of the train window may well be the artist.

Railway Station (3 December 1881)(From a sketch by Aloysius O'Kelly)(Fig. 6). This illustration is particularly interesting as O'Kelly's own account of events is included in the article which accompany the illustration. The scene represented took place in Roscommon Railway Station at two o'clock in the morning. The Land League conspirators, arrested under the Coercion Act, are being put on the train for conveyance to prison. On the platform are a number of Land League sympathisers who obviously oppose this action. In this particular case O'Kelly was actually on the train travelling from Westport to Dublin and gives this first-hand account of events:

> 'I was fast asleep in the carriage when I was suddenly awakened by the screaming and yelling of a crowd on the platform. Above the din rose the frequent cry of "Hurrah for Parnell!". The night was dark, and I could see nothing till I put my head out of the

railway carriage. Then I was astonished to find the platform lined with soldiers, two deep, behind whom was the screaming mob. The people were standing on the benches and window-sills, and hanging on wherever they could get a footing They were shouting, gesticulating, and waving hats to several men who had been arrested, and who were being put into the train to be sent to Galway prison. Around the carriage door, a few privileged friends of the prisoners – who had been allowed to bid them good-bye – were pushing and struggling to get a farewell shake of the hands before the train started. Standing near them was an escort of police, ready to get into the compartment with the prisoners. It appears that these men were the leading Land Leaguers of the town of Roscommon, who had been arrested during the day, and had been lodged in the Police barracks in the town. There had been reason to suppose that unless the assistance of the military was obtained there would be an attempt to rescue the prisoners on their way to the railway station. The soldiers, therefore, by previous arrangement, marched into the town at night, just in time to conduct the prisoners to the station. No one was aware that the soldiers were coming and their little plan for a rescue was a failure. These scenes have been frequent for some time past, and every morning's paper brings the news of fresh arrests, and I have no doubt they will continue to occur for some time'.

It is quite possible that Dadd includes a portrait of O'Kelly in this illustration as in the article O'Kelly refers to himself and says that on hearing the noise he put his head out of the railway carriage to see what was going on. In the illustration a bearded man wearing a cap is looking out the window of the first class carriage of the train. O'Kelly's commentary is also included in the article accompanying his illustration *Irish Harvesters on their way to England* (28 May 1881). These accounts are extremely interesting and to a certain extent reveal O'Kelly's own opinion of the situations he was witnessing.

W H Overend[12] (1851-98), who also exhibited at the Royal Academy, did a considerable amount of work for *The Illustrated London News*. Two of his illustrations are *The State of Ireland: The Affray at Belmullet, County Mayo* (12 November 1881) and *The Irish Land League: Recreation time in Kilmainham Prison* (12 November 1881) both from sketches by Aloysius O'Kelly. The illustration of the affray at Belmullet portrays a violent conflict between the police and the peasantry. Overend's treatment of the Irish peasantry is not flattering and their faces look brutish. This is also evident in Dadd's illustrations in particular *Stopping A Hunt*. Neither Overend nor Dadd treat Irish physiognomies in as kindly a fashion as O'Kelly did. O'Kelly's peasants look noble,

ALOYSIUS O'KELLY AND THE ILLUSTRATED LONDON NEWS

for example, in the illustration *The Land League Agitation: Attack on a Process Server* (21 May 1881) and *Irish Harvesters on their way to England* (28 May 1881). A recurring motif in O'Kelly's work is his portrayal of the innocent victims of the disturbances such as poverty-stricken women dressed in shawls and generally holding babies and also elderly men and women who find themselves being evicted.

Taken together, the thirty illustrations and the accompanying articles give an interesting insight into the history of the time as seen by *The Illustrated London News*. The conflicts between the peasants and either the upper classes, the military or process servers are graphically illustrated. The articles are generally quite fair and objective and vary in length depending on the significance of the event. *The Illustrated London News* appears to be sympathetic to the dire circumstances in which many Irish people found themselves and scenes of evictions and emigration feature in the illustrations. Nevertheless, it is highly critical of the Land League and the brutality and violence committed against both the landlords who instigated the evictions and the Irish people who occupied land from which another person had been evicted.

It is clear from his illustrations for *The Illustrated London News* that O'Kelly is very sympathetic to the plight of the Irish. The faces of the peasants are noble and in the case of some of the women almost saint-like and it would appear that O'Kelly had a profound understanding of their concerns. They are portrayed as being hardworking, diligent people. It can be assumed that O'Kelly's family background and the political involvement of his brother, combined with his travels to the affected areas as an illustrator, gave him a deep insight into the political situation. It is also of importance to note that O'Kelly's paternal grandparents were from Roscommon, an area badly affected by the Great Famine of 1845 and by the threat of further famine in 1877 and the ensuing tensions between landlords and tenants.

One of the most perplexing aspects of O'Kelly's work for *The Illustrated London News* is the fact that his brother, James J O'Kelly (1845-1916) was directly involved and actually arrested for his activities in the Land League, an organisation strongly disapproved of by *The Illustrated London News*. James J O'Kelly's name appears frequently and he is featured on a number of occasions in illustrations (not by Aloysius O'Kelly) such as *Prohibited Meeting at Brookeborough, County Fermanagh: The Magistrate ordering Mr O'Kelly, M.P. out of the field* (18 December 1880) by Wallis Mackay. The question that arises is why Aloysius O'Kelly was working as an illustrator for a London publication which opposed the workings of the Land League in which his own brother was heavily involved. In addition, Julia O'Kelly,[13] Aloysius O'Kelly's sister, was also indirectly involved in the politics of the time. She was married to Charles Hopper, a brother-in-law of James Stephens (1824-1901) an important leader of the Irish Republican Brotherhood, which James J O'Kelly joined as a teenager. Charles Hopper owned a cigar shop in Henry Street, Dublin which was used as a rendezvous for members of the Irish Republican Brotherhood.

Perhaps O'Kelly worked for *The Illustrated London News* purely for financial reasons as his income as an artist was insufficient and he required a regular salary to finance his travels abroad. This supposition is reinforced by letters[14] between O'Kelly and his brother which date from 1877 and in which Aloysius states

he is 'hard up'. *The Illustrated London News* played a major part in providing constant employment for young or less successful painters.[15] O'Kelly's work as an illustrator was, nevertheless, of benefit to him as an artist. As Mason Jackson[16] points out 'the production of works in black and white, whether as engravings or drawings, is no doubt good artistic practice in the study of light and shade, and the young artist who draws on wood as a means of helping him to live while he is waiting for fame, is at the same time pursuing a useful branch of his art education.' It is also possible that through his illustrations O'Kelly hoped to highlight the Irish situation and gain the sympathy of the British reader by showing the hardships endured by the Irish peasant such as eviction, emigration and constant surveillance by the military and police. Perhaps O'Kelly's motives were a combination of these two factors.

Aloysius O'Kelly has taken his rightful place in the history of Irish painting. Hitherto, however, attention has not been drawn to his graphic work which is of considerable interest both artistically and in the context of the socio-political history of Ireland in his lifetime.

MARGARITA CAPPOCK *has an MA degree in History of Art and a Diploma in Arts Administration from University College Dublin. She has worked at the Musée D'Art Moderne de la Ville de Paris on the exhibition* Figures du Moderne – L'Expressionisme en Allemagne (1905-1914).

LIST OF ILLUSTRATIONS OF IRISH EVENTS ATTRIBUTED TO ALOYSIUS O'KELLY WHICH APPEARED IN *THE ILLUSTRATED LONDON NEWS*

1. *Disturbed Ireland: Before the Magistrate*, 5 February 1881 [Extra Supplement] 31.5 x 47cm. Signed: bottom left: *A. O'Kelly*, bottom right: *Swain*
2. *An Eviction in the West of Ireland*.19 March 1881, 31.5 x 47cm. Signed:bottom left: *A O'Kelly*, bottom right: *W J Palmer*
3. *Prisoners charged with shooting Mr. Hearn at Ballinrobe, Mayo brought before him for identification*. 26 March, 1881, 21.2cm x 29.8cm Signed: bottom left: *WJP Sc*, bottom right: *A O'Kelly*
4. *The State of Ireland: Tilling the land of an Imprisoned Land Leaguer*. 7 May, 1881. *Plate size: 21.3cm x 30.1cm.* Signed: bottom left: *A O'Kelly* bottom right: *WQ*
5. *The Irish Land League Agitation: Mr. Walter Burke serving writs on his tenants*. 14 May, 1881, 15cm x 22.5 cm Signed: bottom right: *A. O'Kelly*
6. *The Irish Land League Agitation: Attack on a Process Server*. 21 May, 1881. 27.5cm x 21.5cm. Signed: bottom left: *A. O'Kelly*, bottom right: *WQ*
7. *Irish Harvesters on their way to England*. 28 May, 1881. 15cm x 22.5cm. Signed: bottom left: *WQ* bottom right: *A. O'Kelly*
8. *The Land League Agitation in Ireland: A Sheriff's sale of cattle, to pay rent*. 18 June, 1881 [Extra Supplement]. 31.5cm x 47cm. Signed: bottom left: *A. O'Kelly*
9. *The State of Ireland: Kilmainham Jail*. July 30, 1881. 15cm x 22.3cm Signed: bottom right. *WQ* This illustration appears on the same page as illustration no. 10 which is signed by O'Kelly. In the accompanying article it says 'The scene represented by our Special Artist's second sketch...' (referring to 'Surrendering arms in a proclaimed district') so it can be deduced that O'Kelly was the illustrator of Kilmainham Jail although it is not signed by him.
10. *The State of Ireland: Surrendering arms in a proclaimed district*. 30 July, 1881. 15cm x 22.5cm. Signed: bottom left: *WQ* bottom right: *A. O'Kelly*
11. *The State of Ireland: Police Patrol challenging a suspected person*. 6 August, 1881. 27. 7cm x 21 .3cm. Signed: bottom right: *A O'Kelly*
12. *The State of Ireland: The Affray at Belmullet, County Mayo, From a Sketch by Aloysius O'Kelly*. 12 November, 1881. 27.5cm x 23.2cm. Signed: bottom left: *W H Overend*, bottom right: *W J Palmer*
13. *The Irish Land League: Recreation time in Kilmainham prison, From a sketch by A O'Kelly*. 12 November, 1881. 22.5cm x 31.5cm. Signed: bottom left: *W H Overend*

14. *The State of Ireland: Posting the Government Proclamation in Connemara.* 19 November, 1881. 22.5cm x 30.4cm. Signed: bottom left: *R & E Taylor*. The accompanying artide states: 'Our Special Artist, Mr A O'Kelly, now in the west of Ireland, contributes a sketch of a scene that he witnessed two or three weeks ago, while driving through Connemara.'

15. *Opening of the New Irish Land Court in Connaught under Police Protection. A sketch at the Claremorris Courthouse, by our Special Artist* 26 November, 1881. 15cm x 22.5cm. Signed: bottom left: *A O'Kelly*

16. *Opening of the new Irish Land Court in Connaught, Consulting the Priest: A sketch at Claremorris, County Mayo, by our Special Artist.* 26 November, 1881. 15cm x 22.5cm. Signed: bottom right: *F D.* The accompanying article states: 'Our Special Artist in the West of Ireland, Mr A O'Kelly, furnishes the Sketches engraved for this week's publication, which represent the scenes at the opening of the Western Sub-Commission of the Land Court…'.

17. *Opening of the new Irish Land Court in Connaught: A sketch at the Claremorris Court-House, County Mayo, By Our Special Artist Mr A O'Kelly.* 26 November, 1881 [Extra Supplement]. 31.5cm x 47cm. Signed: bottom left: *F Dadd*

18. *The Steerage of the Steamer Solway, at Kingstown, after the fire on board.* 3 December, 1881. 27.3cm x 21.6cm. Signed: bottom left: *R & E Taylor,* bottom right: *A O'Kelly*

19. *The State of Ireland: Arrested under the Coercion Act – A Sketch at Roscommon Railway Station, From a sketch by Mr A O'Kelly.* 3 December, 1881. *31. 5cm x 47cm.* Signed: bottom left: *F Dadd*

20. *Sketches in Ireland: by our Special Artist, Property Defence Association: Digging Potatoes at Woodgyft, County Kilkenny.* 10 December, 1881. 15cm x 22.5cm. Signed: bottom left: *CH.*The accompanying article states: 'Our Special Artist, Mr A O'Kelly, contributes two sketches; one is that of some volunteer gentlemen potato-diggers … the other is that of the Land Leaguers, on their side, putting up some wooden huts (illustration no. 21).

21. *Building a Land-League hut for the evicted tenants at Hacketstown, County Carlow.* 10 December, 1881. 15.5cm x 22.5cm. Unsigned.

22. *The State of Ireland: Dispersing a Ladies' Land League Meeting.* 24 December, 1881. 15cm x 22.5cm. Signed: bottom left: *WH O.* The accompanying artide states: 'Our Special Artist, Mr A O'Kelly, has furnished the Sketches of two scenes which he recently witnessed, characteristic of the disturbed state of Ireland – namely that of a Ladies' Land League Meeting dispersed by the police; and that of the stopping of a fox hunt.'

23. *The State of Ireland: 'Captain Moonlight: surprised by a police patrol.* 24 December, 1881. 15cm x 22.5cm Unsigned. The accompanying artide states: 'He (our Special Artist, Mr A O'Kelly) contributes also the Sketch of "Captain Moonlight".'

24. *The State of Ireland: Stopping a Hunt, From a sketch by our Special Artist, Mr A O'Kelly.* December 24, 1881. 31.5cm x 45cm. Signed: bottom right: *F Dadd.*

25. *The State of Ireland: Demonstration on Mr. Parnell's estate, Avondale, Wicklow – Friends ploughing his land. [9 scenes], From a Sketch by Our Special Artist, Mr A O'Kelly.* 7 January, 1882. 31cm x 46.3cm. Signed: bottom centre left: *Palmer Sc*

26. *The State of Ireland – From Sketches by our Special Artist. Mr A O'Kelly, Seizure of arms and ammunition in Dublin: the prisoners before the Magistrate.* January 7, 1882. 15cm x 22.5cm. Signed: bottom left: *C H,* bottom right: *FD*

27. *The prisoners in the police cell.* 7 January, 1882. 15cm x 22.5cm. Signed: bottom left: *FD,* bottom right: *R & E Taylor*

28. *Departure of Irish emigrants at Clifden, County Galway.* 21 July, 1883 [Extra Supplement]. 31.5cm x 47cm. Signed: bottom centre left: *W Palmer Sc,* bottom right: *A O'Kelly*

29. *On Eviction Duty in Ireland: Sketches in Galway with the Military and Police forces [9 scenes].* 1 May, 1886. 31.5cm x 47cm Signed: bottom left: *R Taylor,* centre right: *A O'Kelly*

30. *Distress in the West of Ireland. Waiting for relief outside the Priest's house at Kilronan, Aran Island.* May 8, 1886. 15cm x 22.5cm. Signed: bottom right: *A. O'Kelly*

ACKNOWLEDGEMENTS

I would like to express my sincere thanks to Dr Eileen Kane for her helpful comments during the original writing-up of this topic. I am grateful to Dr Julian Campbell for directing me towards bibliographical material. I also wish to thank the staff of the Picture Library at the offices of The Illustrated London News *for their courtesy and helpfulness when I visited their offices in London and for their permission to publish the illustrations in this article. This article results from a thesis presented for the degree of MA in the Department of the History of Art, University College Dublin.*

1. O'Kelly was born in Dublin in June 1851 (This birthdate is taken from the roster of Jean-Leon Gérôme's American pupils, listed in H Barbara Weinberg, *The American Pupils of Jean-Leon Gérôme*, Fort Worth 1984, n.383, p. 103).Biographical information on Aloysius O'Kelly presented here is from John Devoy's *Recollections of an Irish Rebel*, Shannon, 1969 (First Edition, New York 1929) pp.333, 334. Aloysius O'Kelly's father, John O'Kelly, kept a blacksmith and draymaking establishment in Peterson's Lane, Dublin and was the owner of the Cumberland Cottages in a small street near Westland Row railway station. John O'Kelly's parents were from Roscommon. Aloysius O'Kelly's mother was a sister of John Lawlor, a prominent Irish sculptor in London, and encouraged her sons to become artists like her brother. O'Kelly had three brothers, James, Stephen and Charles and one sister, Julia. Aloysius was the youngest son. Charles and Stephen were also artists. James became MP for Roscommon and a close friend of Charles Stewart Parnell.

2. Little is known about O'Kelly's early artistic career but presumably he began his art studies in Dublin. He went to Paris in 1874 and is listed as having enrolled at the Ecole des Beaux Arts on 7 October 1874. (Weinberg, *op cit*, p.103). His name is listed as a student in the ateliers of Jean-Leon Gérôme (1824-1904) and Leon Joseph Florentin Bonnat (1833-1922). O'Kelly was listed as a pupil of Bonnat in the catalogue of the 1884 Salon, no. 1828, 1828 p.163.

3. Julian Campbell, *The Irish Impressionists: Irish Artists in France and Belgium 1850-1914.* National Gallery of Ireland, Dublin, 1984.

4. Daniel T Mallett, *Mallett's Index of Artists: International and Biographical*, New York, 1935. Supplement. 1940. (Reprint: New York, Smith, 1948; Bath, England, 1976, Supplement, 1977) gives 1935 as O'Kelly's date of death. I am grateful to Dr Clark S Marlor, Emeritus Professor, Brooklyn, New York, for drawing my attention to this information.

5. Lewis Perry Curtis, *Apes and Angels: The Irishman in Victorian Caricature,* London, 1971, pp.84 - 86.

6. Simon Houfe, *The Dictionary of British Book Illustrators and Caricaturists, 1800-1914,* Suffolk, First Edition, 1978, Revised 1981. p.253. It is interesting to note that O'Kelly is not included in Simon Houfe's book although he in fact did substantially more work for *The Illustrated London News* than Claude Byrne.

7. *Ibid*, p.311.

8. 1880 *Feeding Hens – West of Ireland* (no. 150),1882 *Lough Fee, Connemara* (no. 335), *Lough Mask* (no. 624), 1885 *Seaweed Gatherers, Connemara* (no. 68).

9. This painting is listed as number 1828.

10. Kenneth McConkey, *A Free Spirit: Irish Art 1860-1960,* London 1990, p.22.

11. Noel Kissane, *Parnell: A Documentary History. National Library of Ireland,* Dublin 1991, p.53 states that Fanny Parnell, Charles Stewart Parnell's sister and an accomplished poet, wrote a poem called 'Hold the Harvest' which Michael Davitt regarded as 'the Marseillaise' of the Land League.

12. Bryan's *Dictionary of Painters and Engravers.* Volume IV N-R, London, 1926, pp.52-53.

13. Devoy, *op cit,* Chapter XLII on James Stephens, pp.272-79.

14. John Devoy Papers, Manuscripts Section, National Library of Ireland, letter dated 1 October 1877 from Aloysius O'Kelly, Finistère, Pont-Aven to James J O'Kelly. Aloysius writes to his brother and asks him to sell four paintings and two sketches for him as he is 'hard up'. He also says he will spend the winter in Pont-Aven as it is cheaper for him to live there.

15. Houfe, *op. cit.* p.151.

16. Houfe, *op.cit.* pp.74-75 quotes Mason Jackson, *The Pictorial Press,* London 1885, pp.356-57.

ALOYSIUS O'KELLY IN AMERICA

1. Aloysius O'KELLY (1851-C.1928). *The East River, New York.* Oil on canvas, 56 x 73.5 cm. Signed. (Sold at William Doyle Galleries, New York, 24 October 1984, lot 120). The view is looking north from Manhattan towards Queens with the Queensborough Bridge spanning the river. The Bridge was completed in 1908 and O'Kelly's picture may date from that time.

The few known details about the American career of the peripatetic Aloysius O'Kelly are contained in Mantle Fielding's *Dictionary of American Painters, Sculptors, and Engravers* first published in 1926.[1] To this Dr Julian Campbell has been able to add important information contained in letters from O'Kelly to the New York dealer, William Macbeth, in the period 1909-12.[2] Fielding's account is derived from the *Who's Who in Art* that was published approximately every other year in the *American Art Annual*[3] from Volume VI (1907-08) onwards and, as this was compiled from questionnaires sent to artists all over the United States, it is a primary source for a host of contemporary painters of the

Homan Potterton

delves into New York Census and Immigration Records in an attempt to piece together the artist's later years

period including O'Kelly.

In the 1907-08 volume (the first in which the artist is listed) O'Kelly's address is given as Concarneau, Finistère, his date of birth is given as 1850, and it is stated that he was a pupil of Bouguereau and Gérôme at the Ecole des Beaux-Arts. In the subsequent volume (VII, 1909-10) his address is 402 Clermont Avenue, Brooklyn and in the next published *Who's Who* (vol.X, 1913) this information is repeated – except that the artist Bonnat is now substituted for Bouguereau – and the additional details are given that O'Kelly's summer address is the Hotel de France, Concarneau, and that he is a member of the New York Watercolor Club. With one or two exceptions –

the summer address is dropped and, in 1915, an address c/o Snedecor Gallery, 107 West 46th Street, New York is substituted for Clermont Avenue, and his date of birth is changed to 1853 in 1919 – the entry remains the same until 1922 when O'Kelly is listed for the last time and still at Clermont Avenue.[4]

The picture conveyed by this series of biographies – arrival in New York about 1908 from Concarneau, a settled existence over fifteen years at Clermont Avenue, summers in France – is,

2. Aloysius O'KELLY: *A Stroll in the Hospital Grounds.* Oil on canvas, 56 x 73.5 cm. Signed and dated 1924. (Sold at William Doyle Galleries, New York, 2 May 1990, lot 81). The picture depicts the original Metropolitan Hospital at its former location underneath the Queensborough Bridge, New York.

however, very different from the reality of O'Kelly's life in New York as evidenced by official documents.

As Julian Campbell has conjectured elsewhere in this volume, O'Kelly is most likely to have first arrived in America in 1895. His Petition for Naturalisation, lodged with the US District Court in New York, is dated 1 July 1895 and it contains details about the artist's life. His address at this time was 164 West 20th Street, his date of birth is said to have been 15 July 1853, and he stated that he had arrived at the port of New York in May 1895. None of these facts required verification, however, and they may not be true: an examination of the passenger lists of all ships arriving in New York from Ireland in May 1895 has, for example, failed to produce any record of O'Kelly's passage. The artist was admitted a Citizen on 1 May 1901 and at this time his address was given as 463 West 163rd Street; but that may only have been a convenience as his referee – an artist called Sydney Moran who swore that he had known O'Kelly for six years – resided nearby on West 166th Street. A year earlier, at the time of the 1900 Census (on the 1st June), O'Kelly was living 'alone'

as a 'renter' at 39 West 42nd Street and on this occasion he gave his date of birth as 26 July 1861.

If his entries in *Who's Who* give the impression that subsequent to his immigration O'Kelly summered each year in France, this is not borne out by the passenger manifests of ships arriving in New York between 1897 and 1925. These are indexed and only once does O'Kelly's name appear – sailing on the *Finlandia* having embarked at London on 13 November 1915. While it is possible that he might have re-entered America on other occasions through some other port, it would seem fairly extraordinary as he was always resident in New York and at this time several ships each week sailed to New York from the ports of Ireland, England, and France.

Dr Campbell believes that O'Kelly returned to Concarneau in 1908-09 and cites as evidence the entries in the Salon catalogues of those years when the artist was an exhibitor. His belief is substantiated by the fact that O'Kelly gave the Hotel de France, Concarneau as his address in the Chicago exhibition catalogue of 1908 (see Appendix I) and also in the *Who's Who* of 1907-08. If he did actually visit France in these years – and based only on the evidence of entries in exhibition catalogues, can we really be certain? – he absolutely did not return to America via the port of New York; but he was definitely in New York in December 1909 as his letter to Macbeth confirms.

O'Kelly is said to have died in 1928 – although Margarita Cappock points out that it could have been in 1935 – and hitherto it has seemed reasonable to assume that he died in New York; but a check of the New York Department of Health's lists of deaths recorded in all five boroughs between 1925 and 1942 provides no evidence of the artist's demise. In the Catalogue of the New York Watercolor Club's exhibition for 1920-21 O'Kelly – a Member although not on this occasion an exhibitor – is listed with 'Paris, France' as his address and it would be tempting, therefore, to think that O'Kelly returned to his beloved France at the end of his life.[5] However, at the time of the 1920 New York Census, he was resident at 253 38th Street and the records of the Babcock Galleries – which succeeded and took over Snedecor[6] – show that the artist was also in New York in 1919, in 1924, and 1925. On 29 November 1919 he took delivery of one of his paintings, *Pool through the Woods*, from Babcock; on 17 December he brought in a watercolour, *Donkey Boy and*

Camel Driver (this was returned to him on 9 September 1924); and on 1 April 1925 he took delivery from Babcock of another picture, *French Fishing Port* which, the Gallery records show, had been exhibited in 1920 at Columbus, Ohio (see Appendix I).

And what of the artist's career in America? The information is, again, scant and elusive. He exhibited very intermittently (see Appendix I). He appears to have been represented by the Snedecor Gallery – 'Picture Framers and Modern Paintings' – from about 1909 until at least 1925; and he had an exhibition at Moulton & Ricketts (12 West 45th Street) in February 1912 which was subsequently shown (by the same dealers) in Chicago and Milwaukee. According to the *New York Evening Post* (10 February 1912), this consisted of 'some two dozen impressions in vivid color of the scenes of Concarneau'. He exhibited at various prestigious loan exhibitions in Boston, Chicago, and elsewhere (see Appendix I) and he had at least a modest portrait practice (see Appendix III). O'Kelly tried, in 1909, 1910, 1911, and again in 1912 to interest the most esteemed New York dealer in contemporary pictures, William Macbeth, in his paintings; but to no avail.[7] He painted, in both watercolour and oil, in and around New York and he travelled – where almost all American landscape painters of the time travelled – to Maine[8] and to New Mexico[9] to paint. Single and always living alone, he seems never to have had a studio, a fact which possibly explains why his pictures are all relatively small. Other than these few details the only testimony we have as to his American career are the pictures which he painted. These are known to us through exhibition records (see Appendix I) and by means of the canvases by him which appear regularly on the market in America today and which, for the most part, must have been painted there (Appendix II).

On balance, there are relatively few American scenes and this is remarkable and all the more so if, as seems at least possible, he did not regularly visit Europe after emigrating to the States. Throughout his later years, Brittany, Egypt, and Morocco continued to inspire him in his choice of subject matter and he seems to have cared little for the spectacular streetscapes, extraordinary viewpoints, and exhilarating light of Manhattan which provided inspiration for so many artists. For his one-man show in 1912, at least seventeen years after his arrival in New York, he chose Brittany as his theme and, of the paintings he exhibited in other exhibitions, almost all were of non-American scenes. Did O'Kelly believe that foreign subject-matter would make his works more appealing to prospective purchasers? Or was it a case that the experiences of his formative

3. Aloysius O'KELLY: *Southeast New Mexico.* Oil on canvas, 51 x 86.5 cm. Signed. (Sold by Skinner, Bolton, Mass., 20 November 1984, lot 95). It is not known when O'Kelly visited New Mexico where the expansive, barren landscape and brilliant light has attracted numerous painters to the artists' colonies of Taos and Santa Fe throughout this century.

4. Aloysius O'KELLY: *On the Sheepscott River, Maine.* Oil on panel, 25.5 x 31 cm. Signed and titled on verso. (Milmo Penny Fine Art). O'Kelly wrote to the New York dealer, William Macbeth in November 1912: 'Having just returned from Maine after a residence of five months on the Sheepscott River, I take the liberty of submitting to you what I believe to be a faithful interpretation of this Country in Autumn'.

years remained a genuine inspiration to him throughout his life? As to whether he actually returned to France as frequently as he claimed, that question too, like the date and place of his death, remains unanswered until further evidence of his American years is discovered.

HOMAN POTTERTON is Editor of Irish Arts Review Yearbook.

APPENDIX I: PAINTINGS EXHIBITED BY ALOYSIUS O'KELLY IN AMERICA
(Most references generously provided by Professor William H Gerdts)

1899: Art Institute of Chicago – *Annual Exhibition of American Painting & Sculpture*
No.233: *A Musician of the Riff Mountains, Morocco*
(O'K's address: 39 West 42 Street, New York)

1906: New York Watercolor Club
No.89: *The Ferry, Concarneau*
(O'K's address: 729 Sixth Avenue, New York)

1907: Boston Art Club
No.77: *A Camel Driver and Donkey-boy, Cairo*
No.151: *A Musician of the Riff Mountains, Morocco*
(O'K's address: 729 Sixth Avenue, New York)

1907: Corcoran Gallery, Washington – *Corcoran Biennial of Contemporary American Paintings*
No.178: *Devotion, Brittany*
(O'K's address: 729 Sixth Avenue, New York)

1908: Art Institute of Chicago – *Annual Exhibition of American Painting & Sculpture*
No.202: *By the Fireside* (See Appendix B, no.31)
No.203: *Ready for the Road*
(O'K's address: Hotel de France, Concarneau)

1909: Art Institute of Chicago – *Annual Exhibition of American Painting & Sculpture*
No.190: *Ave Maria*
(O'K's address: c/o Snedecor)

1911: Art Institute of Chicago – *Annual Exhibition of Watercolors by American Artists*
No.433: *Mosque at Ezbeck, Cairo*
(O'K's address: 402 Clermont Avenue, Brooklyn)

1916: New York Watercolor Club
No.336: *Evening on the Bronx*
(O'K's address: 402 Clermont Avenue, Brooklyn)

1917: New York Watercolor Club
No.315: *The Italian Garden, Bronx*
(O'K's address: 402 Clermont Avenue, Brooklyn)

1920: Columbus (?Ohio): place and title of exhibition unknown
French Fishing Port (18 x 26 ins)
Consigned to the exhibition on O'K's behalf by Babcock, 5 March 1920, returned 10 June 1920

APPENDIX II: PAINTINGS BY ALOYSIUS O'KELLY SOLD AT AUCTIONS IN AMERICA

1. *A Toast*
   28 x 36 ins. S & D 1908. Sotheby Parke Bernet, 12 Oct 1978, lot 51
2. *Farmyard Scene*
   15 x 18 ins. S. Christie's, 19 May 1979, lot 481
3. *Harbor Scene*
   21 x 25 ins. S. William Doyle, New York, 24 Sept 1980, lot 27.
4. *Horses pulling a Load of Seaweed*
   20 x 30 ins. S. Sotheby Parke Bernet, 13 December 1980, lot 126
5. *Sunlit Procession*
   24 x 16 ins. S. William Doyle, New York, 24 Sept 1980, lot 25
6. *A Stroll in the Hospital Grounds (The Metropolitan Hospital, Queensborough Bridge, New York)*,
   22 x 30 ins. S & D 1924. Sotheby Parke Bernet, 29 Jan 1981, lot 119; William Doyle, New York, 2 May 1990, lot 81
7. *The Lake, Van Cortlandt Park, New York*
   9 x 13 ins. Christie's East, 2 June 1983, lot 159
8. *Portrait; a Harbor Scene* (a pair)
   William Doyle, New York, 2 June 1983, lot 39
9. *Two Peasants Entering a Cottage*
   18 x 15 ins. S. Stalker, Boos (Birmingham, Michigan) 29 Oct 1983, lot 188.
10. *Woman in a Park with a Gazebo*
    11 x 8 ins. S. Milwaukee Auction Galleries, 12 Nov 1983, lot318 (ill.)
11. *Harbor Town*
    8 x 12 ins. S. Christie's East, 31 Jany 1984, lot 147

12. *Figures by a Tavern Door*
    19 x 15 ins. S. Christie's, New York, 25 May 1984, lot 250
13. *Moonlight*
    14 x 21 ins. S. Young (Portsmouth, New Hampshire), 30 June 1984, lot 170 (ill).
14. *The East River, New York*
    22 x 29 ins. S. William Doyle, New York, 24 Oct 1984, lot 120
15. *Southeast New Mexico*
    20 x 34 ins. S. Skinner (Bolton, Mass.) 20 Nov 1984, lot 95
16. *Dry Goods Sellers, Brittany*
    9 x 13 ins. S. William Doyle, New York, 26 June 1985, lot 68
17. *Boy Fishing*
    36 x 24 ins. S. Hubley (Cambridge, Mass.) 18 Feb. 1985, lot 48
18. *Confidences, Riverside Drive, New York*
    13 x 9 ins. S. Phillips, New York, 8 Aug 1985, lot 145
19. *Woman & Girl at a Fountain*
    12 x 10 ins. S. Skinner (Bolton, Mass.) 26 Feb 1986, lot 17
20. *On the Sheepscott River, Maine*
    9 x 13 ins. S. Phillips, New York, 6 June 1987, lot 429
21. *Cows Grazing in a Field*
    10 x 13 ins. S. William Doyle, New York, 16 Sept 1987, lot 68
22. *The Market at Concarneau; Autumn Landscape* (a pair)
    9 x 13 ins. S. William Doyle, New York, 16 Sept 1987, lot 67
23. *The Market at Concarneau*
    9 x 13 ins. S. William Doyle, New York, 16 Sept 1987, lot 66
24. *A Coastal Village, Brittany*
    29 x 36 ins. S. Sotheby's, 29 Oct 1987, lot 375
25. *The Market Place, Tangier*
    13 x 14 ins. S. William Doyle, New York, 16 Nov 1988, lot 25
26. *Turkeys and Geese in a Landscape* (a pair)
    Watercolor, 24 x 19 ins. S. William Doyle, New York, 8 Feb 1989, lot 75
27. *The Harbour, Concarneau*
    9 x 12 ins. William Doyle, New York, 22 Feb 1989, lot 73A
28. *Young Breton Maiden* (ill. IAR, vol. 9, p.253)
    16 x 13 ins. S. William Doyle, New York, 17 April 1991, lot 2
29. *Respite from the Midday Sun, Brittany* (ill. IAR, vol.9, p.253)
    32 x 39 ins. S. Christie's, New York, 23 May 1991, lot 246.
30. *Young Breton Maid holding a flower*
    24 x 16 ins. S. William Doyle, New York, 6 Nov 1991, lot 28
31. *By the Hearth*
    24 x 29 ins. S. William Doyle, New York, 6 Nov 1991, lot 29
32. *Reflections at Concarneau*
    17 x 22 ins. S. William Doyle, New York, 6 May 1992, lot 79
33. *Street Scene, Cairo*
    20 x 14 ins. S. Skinner (Bolton, Mass.) 11 Sept 1992, lot 201A
34. *Portrait of Clarence Hungerford Mackay & his daughter, Katherine*
    9 x 7 ins. William Doyle, New York, 6 May 1992, lot 79A,
35. *Inside the Chapel*
    36 x 29 ins. S. & D 1904. William Doyle, New York, 4 May 1994, lot 109
36. *Portrait of a man in Top-Hat and Yellow Scarf*
    18 x 14 ins. S. William Doyle, New York, 4 May 1994, lot 110
    (Previously sold, Christie's South Kensington, 3 June 1993, lot 156)
37. *Englewood Cliffs, New York*
    S. William Doyle, New York, 9 Nov 1994, lot 40

APPENDIX III: PORTRAITS BY O'KELLY IN THE AMERICAN IRISH HISTORICAL SOCIETY, NEW YORK

1. *Portrait of Governor Martin Glynn*
   Oil on board, 13 x 9.5 ins. Signed.

2. *Portrait of Senator O'Gorman*
   Oil on board 13 x 9.5 ins. Signed.

3. *Portrait of Mayor & Mrs Mitchell*
   Oil on board, 13 x 10 ins. Signed.

4. *Portrait of John Mitchell*
   Oil on board, 13 x 9.5 ins. Signed.

1. Mantle Fielding, *Dictionary of American Painters, Sculptors, and Engravers.* 2 vols. (Philadelphia, 1926; later eds. New York 1945 and 1965).

2. Julian Campbell, *The Irish Impressionists: Irish Artists in France and Belgium, 1850-1914.* exh.cat., The National Gallery of Ireland, Dublin 1984, pp.56 and 124. The seven letters date between 27 December 1909 and 16 November 1912 and are written variously from Snedecor Gallery or 402 Clermont Avenue, Brooklyn. They are in the Macbeth Archive of the Archives of American Art.

3. *American Art Annual*, (Vol 1, New York 1898-)

4. Number 402 Clermont Avenue still exists. It is a handsome red brick and brownstone row-house in what is now a Landmark neighbourhood of Brooklyn. The trouble is, that in all probability, O'Kelly never actually lived there. The 1910 New York Census lists the inhabitants of number 402 as a thirty-eight year old bank clerk, James Herbert, his wife Jeanie, and their two year old daughter, Jessie. Jeanie Herbert's mother Jane (née Young) also lived in the house and then there was a lodger; but this was a singing-teacher called Jessie Mattheson and not an Irish artist called Aloysius O'Kelly. O'Kelly was certainly in New York at the time of the 1910 Census – there are letters from him to Macbeth, both sent from the Snedecor Gallery's address, dated 27 December 1909 and 24 March 1910 – but as this Census has not been indexed it has not been possible to establish his address except to say that it is extremely unlikely that he was at Clermont Avenue. In 1915 O'Kelly returned to New York from Europe and the manifest of passengers aboard the *SS Finlandia* on which he sailed from London gives his address as with a 'nephew' at 402 Clermont Avenue. As the Herberts were still living at number 402 at the time of the 1920 Census, they must have been there in 1915 and it must have been James Herbert to whom O'Kelly was referring as a nephew. As the Census informs us that both Herberts were born in England (about 1870) and the mother-in-law was born in Scotland it seems fairly unlikely that they were related to O'Kelly although, as he used their address as a mail-drop over so many years, they had to be friends.

5. It may be noted that the Watercolor Club continued to list him, possibly unreliably, as a Member in their catalogues up to and including 1929.

6. I am indebted to Prof William H Gerdts for letting me know that Babcock succeeded Snedecor and to Ms Jeanne Baker at Babcock for searching the records for me. She has pointed out that the Snedecor records from the earlier part of the century while in existence have not been indexed and are, therefore, relatively inaccessible; but she has been able to provide me with information on the pictures by O'Kelly which passed through the Gallery in the 1920s.

7. See note 2.

8. He wrote to Macbeth on 13 November 1912, 'Having just returned from Maine after a residence of five months on the Sheepscott River...'; and for one of his pictures from that time, see Appendix II, no.20.

9. See Appendix II, no.15.

SOURCES: the New York Census returns for 1900, 1910, and 1920 are available on microfilm in New York Public Library. The New York Health Department Death Lists are also available on microfilm in the same location. The Passenger Lists for ships arriving at the Port of New York are available on microfilm in the National Archives – Northeast Region in New York; and the indices to Petitions for Naturalisation (on microfilm) and the New York District Court grants of citizenship (in manuscript) are available at the same location.

An Early Breton Painting by Aloysius O'Kelly

Dominic Penny writes:

'Labels on the reverse of a Breton painting by Aloysius O'Kelly establish the picture as a much exhibited work and provide us with documentation as to the artist's movements in the years 1885-88. The picture was exhibited at the RHA in 1885 (no.49) as *Head of a Breton of Finistère* and again in the same year (as *Un Breton de Finistère*) at the Irish Artisans Exhibition which was held at the South City Markets in Dublin.

The earliest label on the stretcher relates to either of these 1885 exhibitions and gives O'Kelly's address as 65 Bessborough Street, St George's Square, London. This was the address of his brother James and is the same address that he gave in the catalogue of the Paris Salon of 1884. A second label gives the title of the picture as *A Vendean of Finistère, Brittany* (the title used in the Royal Academy exhibition catalogue -no.17 - of 1886: a Vendean being a native of the Vendée region) and this label is inscribed 'No 7 £25' and 'No 3 £21'. O'Kelly's address on this label is Laddingford House, Yalding, Kent. The third label refers to the Irish Exhibition in London in 1888 (at Olympia, June - October) where the picture was shown as *Head of a Vendean of Finistère* and O'Kelly's address was listed as 40 Shaftebury Avenue, Piccadilly Circus W. '

Aloysius O'KELLY (1851-c.1928): *Head of Vendean of Finistère.* Oil on canvas, 61 x 51 cm. Signed *A O'Kelly.* (Milmo Penny Fine Art). The picture was described in the *Dublin University Review* (1885) as 'a truthful and careful study with, however, a slight indication on the part of the painter of too much blackening of the shadows...'

'YEATS SOUVENIRS'
CLUES TO A LOST PORTRAIT BY J B YEATS

Ruth Barton *sifts through the contents of a box of Yeats memorabilia*

The cardboard box had spent years in closets and attics, but the label was still clear: 'Yeats Souvenirs.' It was part of the inheritance which Marie (Mieze) Rosenhaupt, née Freudenthal, had left her son Hans, which had in turn passed to Hans's widow, Maureen Rosenhaupt. It contained a collection of first editions and Abbey Theatre playbills, but its unique contents were these: two pencil portraits by John Butler Yeats (one of W B Yeats, the other almost certainly of Marie Freudenthal), correspondence to Marie Freudenthal from John Butler Yeats, Lily and Elizabeth C (Lollie) Yeats, and an autograph book with short pieces by William Butler Yeats, A E (George Russell), Padraic Colum and many actors and actresses of the Abbey Theatre. The letters refer frequently to a portrait that John Butler Yeats painted of Marie Freudenthal in 1905, but, to date, Mrs Rosenhaupt has been unable to find any leads concerning the portrait's present whereabouts or what may have happened to it.

Marie Freudenthal, daughter of Jacob Freudenthal, professor of philosophy at Breslau, probably met Lily and Lollie Yeats when they visited Germany early in the 1900s. In the spring of 1905, Miss Freudenthal stayed for almost two months with the Yeats family in Dublin. While she was there, John Butler Yeats started painting her portrait. In the autograph book, Alfred K Moe, American Consul, has sketched John Butler Yeats painting the portrait of Freudenthal. The sketch is dated 17 June '05, and in the sketch the portrait appears almost finished. On a blank page facing Moe's sketch, in Marie Freudenthal Rosenhaupt's handwriting, is this inscription:

Alfred K Moe (Amerik-Konsul (?) in Dubln) zeichnet John B Yeats, den Vater des Dichters W B Yeats, während er Frl. Freudenthal porträtiert. Dies Porträt wurde als 'Lady in Blue' in Dublin ausgestellt u. dann Frl. Fr. geschenkt. Sie wird es nach Amerika mitbringen. (Alfred K Moe (American Consul? in Dublin), draws John B Yeats, father of the poet W B Yeats, while he paints the portrait of Fraulein Freudenthal. This portrait was exhibited in Dublin as 'Lady in Blue,' then presented to Frl. Fr. She will bring it with her to America.)

Maureen Rosenhaupt believes that the note regarding the portrait could not have been added to the autograph book until shortly before World War II when Marie Freudenthal and her husband left Nazi Germany. At no time before that had they considered emigrating from Germany to America. William Murphy, author of *Prodigal Father: The Life of John Butler Yeats (1839-1922)*, says that some of the correspondence of Lily Yeats indicates that Marie Freudenthal and her husband Heinrich Rosenhaupt's coming as refugees from Germany 'aroused Lily's ire against Hitler and all he stood for.' So far as Mrs Rosenhaupt has been able to determine, the note in the autograph book is the last thing her family knows about the portrait.

The two longest letters in the souvenir box give information about the portrait. On March 7, 1906, Lily wrote a chatty letter to Marie in which she comments: 'Your portrait has gone to the Dublin Academy and when it comes away I will see that it is sent off to you.' In a letter dated 21 March 1906, Lily wrote:

1. John Butler YEATS (1839-1922): *Pencil sketch of W B Yeats*, (Rosenhaupt Collection). Signed by W B Yeats and dated May 1905. Inscribed: *The poet talking to Fraulein Freudenthal.* Marie Freudenthal, who had probably met Lily and Lollie Yeats when they visited Germany in the early 1900s, stayed with the Yeats family in Dublin in the spring of 1905.

2. John Butler YEATS: *Pencil sketch of a young woman, probably Marie Freudenthal.* Signed and dated May 1905. (Rosenhaupt Collection). Marie Freudenthal's collection of Yeats memorabilia, which dates from her visit to Dublin in 1905, was bequeathed to her son, Hans, whose widow has shared it with the author.

3. John Butler YEATS: *Autograph letter with a pen and ink sketch of his portrait of Marie Freudenthal.* Dated 28 October 1906, (Rosenhaupt Collection). This sketch records the now lost oil portrait which at the time this letter was written was still unfinished. After being exhibited at the RHA in 1906, it was sent to the sitter and was probably taken by her to America shortly before the second World War.

'Yeats Souvenirs': Clues to a Lost Portrait by J B Yeats

The two longest letters in the souvenir box give information about the portrait. On March 7, 1906, Lily wrote a chatty letter to Marie in which she comments: 'Your portrait has gone to the Dublin Academy and when it comes away I will see that it is sent off to you.' In a letter dated 21 March 1906, Lily wrote: 'Your portrait looks very well in the academy I hear, it only opened on Monday.' J B Yeats was not through with the portrait, however. In a long letter dated 28 October 1906, he urges Marie to return to Dublin:

> Except that I have tried to finish the shoulders of the dress I have not done anything to your portrait – of course without (sic) I do not dare to touch the face. Now I would like very much to finish it and send it to you – [pen sketch of the portrait] and to enable me to do this properly you ought to come back here and stay a few weeks. I of course would like this very much even if there was no portrait in question, and Lily tells me to tell you that she would like greatly to see you here again.[5]

Later he return to the portrait: 'I have been doing a lot of portraits and am very much improved in power of painting. My first few touches will transform your portrait as if I was a magician.' Nothing in the correspondence suggests that Marie Freudenthal did return to Dublin, but the note across the page from Moe's sketch of J B Yeats shows that she did receive the portrait.

The Rosenhaupt collection contains a number of pieces printed by the Dun Emer Press – bookmarks, invitations, postcards. Several present art by Jack B Yeats: an invitation to a private showing of 'Sketches of Life in the West of Ireland,' (scene showing a man on a wagon moving along beach), a bookmark for John Quinn, and a postcard of a young man on crutches, bearing the handwritten quotation: 'For the World's more full of sorrow / Than you can understand.' It is signed W B Yeats.

Certainly Marie Freudenthal's souvenirs indicate a busy time while she was in Dublin. She kept playbills for Lady Gregory's *Kincora*, Yeats's *The King's Threshold* and for a double bill, Yeats's *The Hour Glass, A Morality* with Padraic Colum's *The Land*. Many of the entries in Freudenthal's autograph book were made by the actors, and the passages they put in the book are often variations on something in one of the plays. Padraic Colum wrote out his 'Woman of the Roads' from *Wild Earth*, and G W Russell (AE) wrote out and illustrated his 'Winds of Angus.' W B Yeats wrote a slight adaptation from 'To

4. Alfred K Moe: *Pencil sketch of J B Yeats painting Marie Freudenthal's portrait.* Signed and dated *17 June 05.* From an autograph book. (Rosenhaupt Collection). Moe was the American Consul in Dublin.

a Rose upon the Rood of Time:' 'To find in foolish things that live a day / Eternal Beauty wandering on her way.' Appropriately enough, John Butler Yeats has the last entry in the autograph book: 'Great is the worth of prudence Great also the cost – therefore – carpe diem.'

DR RUTH BARTON lectures in the Department of English, Colorado College, Colorado Springs.

1. Hans Rosenhaupt was for many years president of the Woodrow Wilson Fellowship Foundation, Princeton, N.J., USA.
2. Anyone who knows anything about the portrait, especially any information about its location following World War II, should contact Professor Ruth Barton, The Colorado College, Colorado Springs, CO 80903; telephone 1 719 389 6503; Fax 1 719 289 6837.
3. John O'Grady, University College Dublin, points out that the catalogue of the 1906 Royal Hibernian Academy exhibition, lists the work as 'Portrait of Fraulein Frendenhall (sic.)' I am indebted to Professor Thomas W Ross for the translation.
4. Ltr William Murphy to Maureen Rosenhaupt, January 15, 1993.
5. I am grateful to William Murphy for his help deciphering J B Yeats's handwriting

MRS. DUNCAN'S VOCATION

Patricia Boylan *outlines the career of Ellen Duncan, friend and supporter of Hugh Lane and founder in 1907 of the United Arts Club, Dublin*

Charming. Gifted. Formidable, Kind. Indefatigable. Good-looking. These were traits attributed to Ellen Duncan (Fig. 1), wife of James Duncan, a civil servant in charge of the teachers' pensions office in Dublin Castle. None in itself would mark her from her contemporaries in the Dublin of the early 1920s; together they combined to strengthen a vocation she could not escape and a mission she faithfully served: her cause was Art.

She was born in Dublin in 1850 and was educated at Alexandra College and at the Royal Irish College of Music. She became an accomplished pianist, a connoisseur of painting and contributed articles on literature and the visual arts to magazines and newspapers. Her husband, James, was in command of all the pursuits desirable in anyone calling himself a gentleman. An impression emerges of a man who spent a great deal of time improving the shining hours in an enjoyable social round away from his undemanding job. Fortunately for Ellie, as she was known, he had not the least interest in art. She was free to indulge her genuine interest in it almost to the point of enslavement.

Their daughter, Betty (Beatrix) was born in 1893 and their son Alan, in 1895 when, at over forty years of age, their mother was riskily old.

Hugh Lane was an intimate friend. The Duncan children called him 'Uncle.' As temporary curator he had successfully managed the inauguration of a municipal gallery of modern art in 1905, in Johannesburg, and was mulling over the possibility of procuring such a gallery for Dublin when a visit to Paris shocked him into action. He saw an exhibition of Impressionists at the Durand Ruel Galleries and realised that no gallery could call itself modern without example of them.

By giving and begging and borrowing he got together one hundred and sixty works, hung them in the Royal Hibernian Academy and showed them to the public who received them with gratifying enthusiasm. It was in what Lady Gregory called 'that excited time' of Irish cultural renaissance and

Ellie Duncan was in the thick of it. W B Yeats organised students in the arts schools to set up fund-raising committees for the proposed gallery. President Theodore Roosevelt sent a cheque. George Bernard Shaw gave a bust of himself by the great French sculptor, Rodin. Lady Gregory roused women writers to do their bit. Countess Markievicz started a Womens' Picture League. George Russell and Douglas Hyde contributed and the Prince and Princess of Wales, on their first visit to Ireland, presented two Corots and three Constables. Ellie Duncan organised the purchase of a painting by Wilson Steer (a founder member of the new English Art Club): *A Summer Afternoon*, no. 56 in the original catalogue. She had found her métier.

Ellie had much to do. Art was part of the cultural section of the Department of Agricultural and Technical Instruction. It was evident that a special effort would have to be made to maintain the interest of artists, patrons and the public and to combat the attitude to modern art as expounded by so high an official as Col G T Plunkett, the director of the Dublin Museum. He said, 'I never hope to see a picture hung in Dublin until the artist has been dead a hundred years.'

Dublin now had a collection, but where to house it? Ellie, as art critic, contributed to *The Burlington Magazine*. She knew its editor, Roger Fry. He was a member of the New English Art Club. So was Wilson Steer whose work she admired. An Irish Arts Club? Regular meetings of enthusiasts would keep the momentum going. Events were encouraging for on 24 March 1905 the Municipal Council allowed a grant of £500 'for the maintenance of a gallery.' In June the Council authorised the hire of temporary premises in which 'these works of art can be preserved and exhibited, pending the erection of a permanent building ...' Surely a club would be a useful source of support for the acquisition of suitable premises and for a modern movement in all the arts?

Towards the end of 1906 Mrs Duncan headed a committee of eight in whose names A

1. Casimir MARKIEVICZ (1874-1932): *Portrait of Ellen Duncan (1850-1939)*. Oil on canvas, 111 x 76cm. (Private Collection). The painter, husband of the revolutionary Countess Markievicz, was one of the first members of the United Arts Club in Dublin of which Ellen Duncan was founder.

MRS. DUNCAN'S VOCATION

Circular Proposal For An Arts Club was addressed 'to all cultivated people'. The other signatories were Count Markievicz, George Russell, Dermod O'Brien, Llewellyn Meredith, T W Rolleston, Lady Shaw, and W T Strickland. A meeting was held in the Hibernian Hotel on 3 January, 1907, when eight men and five women were invited to form a committee. The men were strongly representative of the arts and included Sir Walter Armstrong RHA, Dermod O'Brien RHA, Count Markievicz, painter/playwright/actor/writer and T W Rolleston, poet/litterateur. The women were Lady Drogheda, Lady Ardilaun, Lady Shaw, Mrs Bellingham and Mrs Duncan. Excepting Ellie, they could be said to underpin the club's social aspirations. Because of her activities and friendships she had achieved the remarkable coup of bagging all the initiators of the so-called cultural renaissance for club membership; and so the United Arts Club was established in 1907 with Mrs Duncan as its founder, acknowledged to be so in a number of contemporary references.

In the meantime neither the new gallery collection nor the club had homes of their own until a house in Harcourt Street, No 17, which had once belonged to the Earls of Clonmel, was rented in 1908 and Hugh Lane began to make a gallery of it. The club found shelter at the offices of the Irish Agricultural Organisation Society at 26 Lincoln Place by grace and favour of George Russell (AE) who worked there, until rooms were rented at No. 44 St Stephen's Green in 1910 (Fig. 4).

At a meeting held on 29 June 1910, Ellie proposed and Dermod O'Brien seconded, that Sir Walter Armstrong should be elected president of the club. W B Yeats was appointed as one of five vice-presidents. That settled, Ellie had another proposal to make, that the club should hold an exhibition of Post-Impressionist works. The committee was grudging but gave permission on condition that the club should not be put to any expense, but Ellie had faith in her cause and the Exhibition opened in the Club rooms on 26 January 1911.

Thomas Bodkin recalled in his book *Hugh Lane and His Pictures* how W B Yeats wandered around the exhibition expati-

2. John Singer SARGENT (1856-1925): *Portrait of Hugh Lane.* Oil on canvas 73.7 x 61 cm. (Hugh Lane Municipal Gallery). Lane was for long a close friend of Ellen Duncan and she supported his efforts to establish a gallery of modern art in Dublin.

When Ellie goes her wandering ways
And leaves us all for London town,
The Club begins to sing her praise
And myrtle, palm, and sacred bays
They weave in garlands for her crown.
When Ellie goes her wandering ways –
Forgetful of those ancient days
When factions sought to do her down –
The Club begins to sing her praise.
Perhaps she views with some amaze
The names who care for her renown
When Ellie goes her wandering ways.
And yet she'll from her mind erase
The thought that any used to frown.
The Club begins to sing her praise
The homage that the Club conveys
Is worth perhaps a cent or brown.
When Ellie goes her wandering ways
The Club begins to sing her praise.

Villanelle *by Cruise O'Brien,*
15 December, 1922

ating on the merits of Cézanne, Gauguin, Van Gogh, Matisse, Signac and Denis. AE's dismissal of them took nearly an entire column of *The Irish Times*. 'A student of the diseases which affect old civilisations would find the Post-Impressionists an interesting pathological study ...' he wrote. 'What no person should tolerate is the art which is lifeless, which is not even debauched but is merely stupid for so the greater part of these paintings appear to me ... I except Gauguin and Denis and Signac ... I do not wish to know the names of the other exhibitors ... Incompetence can always find its brazen trumpeters.' Ellie Duncan? Hugh Lane? Brazen trumpeters?

He goes on: 'I see a man of talent, though not a master, in Gauguin ... The follower of Gauguin who truly understands the secret of the notoriety of his master will not go to New Zealand ...' Tahiti, surely? 'The St. George by Denis would make a pretty colour picture for a child's book of wonder tales. The sunlit harbour by Signac has a technical interest as well as artistic merit. It is a perfectly unemotional and cold application of science to art ... The pointillists are men of science and when science comes in at the door art flies out the window ... I cannot understand admiration of these pictures except from those ludicrous people anxious to imagine themselves in the foremost files of time.'

AE's 'ludicrous people' would certainly include Hugh Lane and Ellie Duncan. They were already well established in the 'foremost files of time' and Ellie defended their judgement in a spirited rebuttal of his attack in a letter to *The Irish Times* of 15 February 1911. She wrote that she had repeatedly been asked two questions since the opening of the exhibition: 'What defence can you offer for this method of painting?' and 'Is there anything to be said for these paintings from the point of view of art?'

She replied: 'I think that they are serious experiments made in perfectly good faith towards the rediscovery of a forgotten art ... they are careful arrangements of form and line and colour ... they are not seeking to give a correct imitation of what everyone can see with his eyes ... Why not accept their chords of pure colour, with their direct appeal to the imagination, as a fresh manifestation of the creative energy of the artist?'

Imagination, however, was in short supply and support for a municipal gallery of modern art was sluggish. The Corporation had ratified its promise of £500 a year but there was no allowance for essential services such as cleaning, heating, lighting, or staff wages. Private generosity and Hugh Lane's beneficence were stretched to the limit. The Lord Mayor, Mr John J Farrell, invited the Citizens' Committee to call a meeting at his official residence, the Mansion House, on 12 May, 1912. Mrs Duncan offered to speak for the Club if the opportunity offered.

Submissions were made by representatives of interested groups and letters from influential individuals were read to convince the sceptical that the purchase of works for the city collection was an excellent investment both commercially and culturally. Sir Walter Armstrong made the case for commerce. He wrote: 'Great as was the value of the collection (£60,000) a fortnight ago, its value has been greatly enhanced by this sale (of a Henri Rouault collection in Paris). Great enhancements of price were shown by every master included in these whose works are at present hanging in Dublin.' Augustus Birrell, the Chief Secretary, claimed that the collection had already received world wide celebrity and G B Shaw wrote that 'Sir Hugh Lane has placed in the hands of the Corporation of Dublin an instrument of culture the value of which is far beyond anything that can be expressed by figures by the City Accountant.'

In July 1912 Ellie, at the age of sixty-two, was knocked off her bicycle by a tram. Her leg was seriously injured and she was lame for the rest of her life. At the Club, Art was all but submerged by social activities but she stoically dealt with her handicap and beavered away trying to get support for a Spring exhibition of French paintings. The Duncan family had moved from Greystones to reside in the Arts Club. Ellie had undertaken certain duties of catering and domestic management. She now wanted to be relieved of them as members resented the time she spent in support of Sir Hugh Lane and the new-fangled art to the neglect of housekeeping. James took a lease on 16 Ely Place and from there Ellie kept a finger in every cultural pie the city had to offer.

She continued her elucidation of Post-Impressionist art in February 1913 in an article in *The Irish Review,* a monthly magazine of 'Irish Literature, Art and Science', written to coincide with her second exhibition of Post-Impressionists in the Club:

3. Ellen DUNCAN. A contemporary photograph. Mrs Duncan, who had organised important Post Impressionist exhibitions in Dublin in 1911 and 1913, was the first Curator of the Dublin Municipal Gallery.

'One October evening, eight years ago, a crowd of people – artists, journalists, authors, musicians ... gathered in an underground room in the Petit Palace in the Champs Elysées in Paris, for the opening of a new exhibition. The painters ... turned away from the heroic and the ideal to paint life – the life of the everyday world as they saw it ... Often they used new and strange combinations of colours, and they discarded ... all recognised rules of composition, refusing to be bound by immutable laws.

'Most of the pictures now on view in the Arts Club are by men whose work is familiar to visitors to the Salon d'Automne ... The excessive simplification beloved by some of these painters will be a stumbling block to many ...' She urged the viewer to try to understand the work and to respond to it. She described a work by Manguin as 'a large sensual, semi-recumbent figure posed on a green cushion against a flat reddish background.' She thought, a little patronisingly, that the *Petit Musicien* by Flandrin would be the most attractive to viewers in the Arts Club.

'Van Dongen, like Matisse, is one of the most daring of the innovators. His *Head of a Girl* is brilliantly executed but exaggeratedly drawn.' Harbin, Juan Gris, Marchand represented the Cubist school. Picasso showed 'a number of delicate drawings and a dainty study of a girl dancing.' Two works by the English art critic and painter, Roger Fry 'are memorable for a fine sense of design and a certain intensity of purpose.'

Ellie ended her piece with a tart reminder to 'the many people in Dublin, especially the painter-critics who regard these men as charlatans and poseurs, that Blake called Titian, Rembrandt, and Rubens "those smudgers and daubers"; Rossetti regarded the work of Fantin la Tour "as a great slovenly scrawl"; and Delacroix as "a perfect beast"; Whistler was condemned by almost all his contemporaries; the Pre-Raphaelites were condemned by the Academy and the Impressionists by the Pre-Raphaelites. But regardless of the mocking voices the artist follows the path he has chosen to tread.'

There was no mockery, however, in the pen of Mr Frank Rutter, art critic, writer, and curator of the Leeds Art Gallery when he gave credit to Ellie in a report on the state of the arts in Ireland. He wrote 'The French Impressionist movement which had left such a mark on the whole of European painting had passed, apparently without leaving a ripple upon the complacent self-satisfaction of this country. I only remember one exhibition of the works of these artists and that was the one organised by Mrs Duncan.' As Roger Fry and Frank Rutter

MRS. DUNCAN'S VOCATION

were acknowledged to be the spokesmen of the modern art movement this was credit indeed.

Many visitors to Dublin were drawn to the small Queen Anne house in Ely Place, near to the Royal Hibernian Academy, delighted to meet the occasional celebrity, eccentric, or talented native to enjoy music and conversation and a supper of tea and barm brack and to meet Ellie, now an important person having been appointed curator, the first, of Dublin's Municipal Gallery of Modern Art (Fig.3). Percy French was so sure of his welcome as to enter the house at night and to be found asleep on a sofa when the family surfaced for breakfast. He had given up engineering to become an entertainer.

His songs, comic and sentimental, were immensely popular but he took only his painting seriously. His better watercolours are now greatly valued and are prized by anyone lucky enough to own one. On 4 May, 1914, he entertained guests at a dinner in the United Arts Club to a repeat performance of a revue, *Tales from My Town*, which had played in the Abbey Theatre. *The Irish Times* reported that 'He had some amusing things to say about bridge sites and Post-Impressionist art.' The reference to 'bridge sites' and 'Post-Impressionist art' applied to public rows in which Ellie Duncan was heavily involved, over a site for the new gallery mooted by Hugh Lane and his threatened withdrawal of his gift to Dublin of thirty-nine Post-Impressionist paintings if a gallery worthy of them was not made available and soon.

4. Beatrice ELVERY (1883-1970): *The Opening Ceremony of the new premises of the United Arts Club, 7 December 1910.* In this cartoon, Ellen Duncan is shown (seated second from left) reading the *Athenaeum*, her daughter Betty is standing to the right and Beatrice Elvery is seated left. The portrait above the chimneypiece is of Dermod O'Brien by Strang.

Friends of the enterprise had put enormous efforts into raising funds for the building of a new gallery. Now they had every reason to feel hard done by for not only had Lane removed his paintings but had also abandoned the building scheme. The Citizens' Committee had the heart-breaking task of returning £11,174.6s.3d to subscribers on 14 January 1914. A far greater trial was to come, a shattering blow for Ellie in particular. Sir Hugh Lane drowned when the *SS Lusitania*, returning from America, was sunk by a German submarine on 7 May 1915.

She was one of the last people to speak to him before he left for the USA on 8 April, when they had discussed the 'Continental pictures.' In a fit of pique he had bequeathed them to the National Gallery in London but he now wished to bring them back to Dublin. He had added a codicil to his will to that effect but had failed to have it witnessed. 'We'll have great fun hanging them when I come back in the Autumn,' he had said.

The Trustees of the National Gallery in London disputed the legality of the codicil. Ellie was a chief witness in submissions made to Parliament in an effort to recover the pictures. W B Yeats, Lennox Robinson, Constance Markievicz, Lord Mayo, James Duncan and many other members of the United Arts Club, as well as of the public at large, attended meetings, addressed them, wrote to the newspapers and created a great deal of controversy but there was a war on and England was not in the mood to give in to Irish demands of any kind.

In 1918 Ellie headed a Lane Pictures Committee of Arts Club members which went in a deputation to the Lord Mayor on 2 March. Would the Lord Mayor, on behalf of the people of Ireland, request the Chief Secretary to allow a public meeting to put the case for the restoration of the French paintings to Dublin? He regretted that it would take an Act of Parliament to allow the transfer, an impossibility in wartime.

Undaunted, she herself, on the evenings of 26 and 27 March 1918, held 'a demonstration' in the Municipal Gallery of paintings lent by Lieut Col French. They included works by Charles Shannon, RHA, Charles Ricketts RHA, Alphonse Legros, Cayley Robinson, William Shackleton, and some watercolours by Sir William Orpen. And she showed for the first time the portrait of Sir Hugh Lane by John Singer Sargent RA (Fig.2), presented to Lane by public subscription in commemoration of his work in connection with the gallery.

Her glory days were ending for, with increasing unrest at home and the end of the war, James Duncan insisted on joining the exodus of those Anglo-Irish and Unionists who saw only ruin for themselves in the threat of a Republican Ireland. Ellie reluctantly joined him. She travelled back and forth from France and England to Dublin and she did have the satisfaction of living to see Hugh Lane's, and her, dream fulfilled with the opening of the Municipal Gallery of Modern Art, in the splendid Charlemont House in Parnell Square, on 19 June 1933. She was not invited to the opening ceremony. Dermod O'Brien represented the arts but he, a conservative, could scarcely be expected to applaud Mrs Duncan's enthusiasm for the aims of the moderns, as enunciated by Frank Rutter: 'simplicity, sincerity, expression.' Ellen Duncan died in Paris in 1939 aged eighty-nine.

PATRICIA BOYLAN is a scriptwriter, freelance journalist and author of All Cultivated People *(Gerrards Cross, 1988), a history of the United Arts Club.*

ACKNOWLEDGEMENTS
Thanks to Bridget Lunn, Mrs. Duncan's grand-daughter, for information and use of photographs and to the United Arts Club for photographs of cartoons by Beatrice Elvery.

A W N Pugin and St Patrick's College, Maynooth

Frederick O'Dwyer *tells of the vicissitudes encountered by the famous architect when it came to designing new extensions to Ireland's national seminary in 1845*

In the summer of 1845 the British prime minister Sir Robert Peel steered through parliament two Irish Education Acts, one of which was to provide funds for the expansion of St. Patrick's College, Maynooth, the national seminary; the other to set up the new Queen's Colleges, non-denominational universities. Under the terms of the Act the seminary was to receive, *inter alia*, the sum of £30,000 for extensions, alterations and repairs, which were to be carried out under the aegis of the Commissioners of Public Works in Ireland (generally known as the Board of Works). This reinforced the government's commitment to maintain the college (which had been set up under Act of Parliament in 1795)[1] and to increase both the annual grant and the total number of students. As if to start the project on a fresh footing, both the Board of Works chairman, Sir John Fox Burgoyne (who wanted to return to military service) and the college president Dr Montague (who was in ill health) retired days before the Act received royal assent. Montague's successor Dr Laurence Renehan was appointed on 25 June. Burgoyne resigned on 27 June but did not leave until late August.

On 30 June 1845, the day the Act came into effect, the secretary of the Maynooth trustees, Father Matthew Flanagan, wrote to Jacob Owen (Fig. 1), architect to the Board of Works seeking a consultation.[2] Owen, who could not act without official sanction, passed the letter on to the commissioners, but they were equally powerless without specific instructions from their governing department, the Treasury in London. These were not forwarded until 10 July, the Treasury's letter crossing with a (premature) letter of regret from the commissioners to Flanagan.[3] Under the terms of the Act, the Board was to be responsible for transmitting to the Treasury the plans and estimates both of the building and of the fittings and furniture, and for ensuring that there was a sufficient balance to repair the old college.

Owen was not interested in designing the Maynooth extensions and pleaded that he was already fully occupied with the proposed new convict prison (Mountjoy), and asylum for criminal lunatics (Dundrum). On 12 July, the Board of Works proposed to the Treasury and the Maynooth trustees that an Irish Roman Catholic architect be employed.[4] However, unknown to it, the

1. Artist Unknown: *Portrait of Jacob Owen (1778-1870)*. Oil on canvas. (The Royal Institute of Architects of Ireland). Owen, who was Architect to the Board of Works, was at first unwilling to provide designs for the Maynooth extensions on the grounds that he was already fully occupied with other projects. Following Pugin's 'resignation' in 1846 Owen prepared an alternative scheme for the College.

2. F Hill and J R Herbert, RA: *Portrait of A W N Pugin (1812-52)*. Oil on canvas. (British Architectural Library, RIBA, London). Pugin, who had already designed a number of churches in Ireland, was recommended to the Maynooth Trustees by his patron, the Earl of Shrewsbury, and he travelled to Ireland in July 1845 with a view to securing the commission for the proposed extensions to the College.

A W N Pugin and St Patrick's College, Maynooth

Earl of Shrewsbury, one of the leading Catholic peers, had already recommended his protégé, the English architect A W N Pugin, to the Primate, Archbishop Crolly.[5] Pugin had travelled over to Ireland on 12 July, and visited Maynooth twice (calling on the Lord Lieutenant, the Earl of Heytesbury, and meeting the Archbishop of Dublin, Dr Daniel Murray, in between visits).[6] He had returned to England on the evening of 17 July, two days *before* the Treasury formally requested Heytesbury to select an architect![7] It seems probable that Pugin's nomination had already received Peel's tacit agreement.

On 23 July, the Under-Secretary for Ireland, Edward Lucas, wrote to both the Board of Works and the Treasury informing them that the Lord Lieutenant had appointed 'Mr. Pugin for the additions and alterations at Maynooth College'. Augustus Welby Northmore Pugin, who lived at Ramsgate in Kent, was a convert to Roman Catholicism, a brilliant architect and designer, an ardent Gothic revivalist and the most influential architectural writer of the day. Aged thirty-three, he had already several Irish churches and a couple of cathedrals to his credit and was busy designing details for the architect of the new Houses of Parliament, Charles Barry.[8] Like many men of genius, Pugin could be rather dogmatic in his views and eccentric in his demeanour. His artistic success had been marred by personal misfortune; in 1844 he found himself a widower for the second time with six young children to rear.

Following his return to England on 17/18 July, Pugin wrote to Lord Shrewsbury:

> *...to all appearances, everything is arranged about Maynooth, but after the great experience I had about the uncertainty of human affairs, I shall not calculate on it until we have actually begun.*[9]

On 24 July the Board wrote to Pugin seeking an early interview, noting that 'the expense of putting the existing buildings in repair must also be borne in mind, so that before designing any work for architectural ornament an estimate for the works must be formed'. They also wrote to Flanagan, requesting a meeting with the trustees when Pugin arrived, to discuss 'the style of architecture and other matters'. However Pugin did not arrive. He had left for the continent on 26 July, travelling from Belgium up the Rhine to Switzerland and back.[10] Thus he did not reply until he returned home to Ramsgate on 19 August. He precipitantly began the Maynooth drawings a week later without the benefit of the briefing the Board of Works had wanted to give him.

The first call on the £30,000 came when the Board of Works had to proceed with repairs valued at £600 in order to make the college habitable for the autumn intake of students. The Board was asked to supply £1,200 worth of furniture and bedding for the extra students sanctioned by the Act. However, by the time Treasury approval was granted (for just £800) on 1 October, some new students were already in residence, having had to purchase their own bedding, the beds being provided from college funds.

A schedule of accommodation had been given to Pugin when he visited Maynooth in July, though as Radcliff (the Board of Works commissioner for buildings) later testily noted, this was 'before the Board of Works had been instructed to communicate with him'. Pugin arrived in Ireland in early September and was asked to attend on the Board of Works in Dublin on the 11th. The following day he travelled down to Maynooth where his sketch plans were approved by a meeting of the trustees. The damaged ink and wash axial perspective illustrated here (Fig. 3) is probably one of these drawings.[11] On the next day, Saturday 13 September, Radcliff joined him for a conference attended by all the trustees.[12] Pugin then returned to England with his designs.

At a meeting with the Chief Secretary Sir Thomas Freemantle the following week Radcliff expressed concerns about the adequacy of the £30,000, detailed in a subsequent letter. He thought the design in character with the college and considered the architectural ornament to be 'on a moderate scale.' Pugin had roughly estimated the new buildings to cost at least £20,000 with a further £5,000 for repairs and improvements. Radcliff considered this too low when compared with the cost per patient of building the English and Irish lunatic asylums (presumably the only yardstick immediately available to him). Deducting the Board's estimate of £13,580 for furniture and other contingencies would leave only £16,420 for building. It was clear from the trustees' elaborate accommodation requirements that a sufficiently capacious new building could not be erected for anything like the sum available.[13] A row developed when the Treasury censured the Board for spending £600 on repairs without submitting a detailed estimate for the expenditure of the £30,000. As the estimating was Pugin's responsibility, Ottley and Radcliff felt unfairly treated, writing to the Treasury on 3 October 1845 to complain that:

> *... the circumstance of an architect having been appointed ... whose residence is not in this country ... the first and only official interview with Mr. Pugin having taken place on 11 Sept soon after which he returned to England.*

In a further letter of 9 October, the Board told the Treasury that, having consulted Pugin, the Board had arrived at the conclusion that the £30,000 was insufficient; it wanted instructions as to whether a building should be designed in accordance with

3. A W N PUGIN (1812-52): *Axial perspective of Maynooth College.* Ink and wash. (British Architectural Library, RIBA, London). This sketch of a proposed new quadrangle is possibly one of the drawings submitted by Pugin to a meeting of the Trustees in September 1845 when his plans were approved by them.

A W N Pugin and St Patrick's College, Maynooth

the accommodation requirements or reduced to take account of the available funds, and promised to communicate with Pugin when an answer was received. In late October the Treasury agreed with a proposal to omit the furnishing of the professors' and students' rooms but refused any increase in the capital sum, asking for a plan for the appropriation of the entire £30,000.

In the meantime the Board still awaited a plan, or rather plans from Pugin.[14] The crisis occurred just as the Board received a new

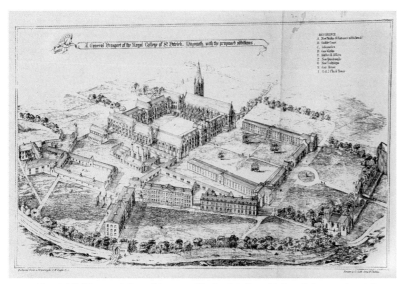

4. After A W N Pugin: *A General Prospect of the Royal College of St Patrick, Maynooth with the Proposed Additions.* Lithograph of 1845 from the Parliamentary Papers 1854-55. This illustration, which is based on a drawing by Pugin, shows his proposals for a radical re-planning of the whole campus including a new gatehouse (right) and new buildings ranged around a quadrangle.

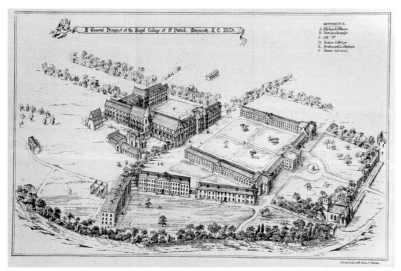

5. Anon: *A General Prospect of the Royal College of St Patrick, Maynooth, 1853.* Lithograph. This illustration shows the extent of Pugin's additions to the campus as actually built. On account of expense, Pugin's modified plans omitted the Chapel and Great Hall from the north side of the quadrangle.

chairman, Colonel Harry Jones, who was dispatched to London to ascertain the cause of the delay. A meeting took place (probably at the Senior United Service Club) on 24 October, after which three drawings and a site survey were dispatched to Dublin.[15]

There was still no estimate. The plans were returned to Pugin at his request on 5 November. A further demand for estimates was sent to him on 19 November.[16] A meeting of the Maynooth trustees took place in Dublin on 20 November at which Jones and Radcliff attended. They agreed with the trustees about the inadequacy of the funds but stated the Treasury's view that the primary objective was the accommodation of the additional students.[17] At a second meeting on 21 November the trustees set up a building committee.[18] Accounts in the press in early December claimed that the designs were to be cut back, though there is no evidence that any formal request of this nature was made to Pugin at that stage, a set of drawings still being awaited from him.[19] It was probably around this time that he wrote to Shrewsbury:

> *There are great difficulties about Maynooth; the grant is quite insufficient for the building. And it appears that the Government will neither give any more, nor consent to Dr. Crolly's proposition to take a sum from the yearly grant for its completion, so I am quite at a stand and have no idea how it will end.*[20]

The drawings were dispatched on 13 December and their receipt acknowledged six days later. Pugin estimated the cost of the new building at £57,400. The Board of Works wrote to Flanagan on 24 December seeking a meeting with the building committee to discuss reductions. Following the meeting, held in Dublin on 7 January,[21] the Board wrote to Pugin (10 January 1846) expressing its 'great surprise' at the estimate and seeking an early interview. Pugin's reply was prompt. On 15 January he wrote that he considered that there was no more nor less in his plans than what was required, and that the cost could not have been estimated until all the plans had been drawn, otherwise it would only have been guesswork. Perhaps, he continued, had he stopped in Dublin he could have been supplied with some list. If the result was unsatisfactory as regards amount, it was not his fault. He continued:

> *It is very evident that the funds are inadequate to procure even a respectable building. I have given the subject my most careful consideration and have come to the full determination not to attempt any fresh plans on a reduced scale, but to resign my appointment as architect to the work. I must either do this, or expose myself to great censure, and I prefer the former course. The Building according to the proposed reductions, will be utterly unfit for its intended purpose: the most important part of the whole, the church, is cut out and I well know, in this case, the blame would eventually fall on me.*[22]

Pugin declined remuneration, preferring the 'lesser evil of losing money and time, to the greater one of being architect of an unworthy building, for an important purpose.' He asked to be relieved of the survey (presumably of the existing buildings) and for his plans to be returned. He concluded by

104

Irish Arts Review

expressing his gratitude for the courtesy and consideration of the government in appointing him.... 'I have neither spared money nor labour, in making the designs, but I cannot effect impossibilities, and must bow to circumstances.'

For all the Board of Works's annoyance at the manner of Pugin's appointment, they sympathised with his position and wrote to the Treasury on 24 January, expressing their admiration of his plans. Acknowledging that no compensation was due to him, they recommended that he be paid £100 for his troubles. On 31 January, the Dublin architect William Deane Butler wrote to the Board seeking to replace Pugin as architect.[23] The Treasury suggested that the Board purchase Pugin's plans, but in a letter of 17 February Jones and Radcliff demurred, arguing that they were of 'no service' to them. However a cheque was subsequently sent. By this date the Lord Lieutenant and the college trustees had agreed to appoint Jacob Owen as the new architect and the Board now sought the Treasury's ratification as well as agreement to appoint a clerk of works, 'a roman catholic, of superior attainments to persons generally'. Owen's appointment would also have the advantage, they felt, of saving architect's fees. This the Treasury approved though they added that they would still favourably consider purchasing Pugin's plans if their possession 'would be attended with advantage'. In the event Pugin asked for his drawings back and these were duly returned at the end of February. By this date the workload of the Board was increasing dramatically. Not only had architects now been appointed for the three Queen's Colleges, but the Board was about to assume extensive additional duties to ameliorate the effects of the Potato Famine; a major new Act and four supplemental Acts were placed on the statute book on 5 March 1846.

The Owen plans progressed, the Board notifying Flanagan on 28 March that they would be ready the following Tuesday. The college's academic staff, headed by the Senior Dean Dr Miles

Gaffney, were unhappy at the loss of Pugin's talents. Having taken advice from a sympathetic Archbishop Murray, they wrote to each of the trustees in an effort to have Pugin reinstated, arguing that the problems might be overcome 'by hearty co-operation'. Gaffney wrote separately to Pugin on 6 April enclosing a copy of this letter and noting that he was already getting positive replies. Taking a cue perhaps from Pugin's polemical book *Contrasts*,[24] Gaffney appealed to his religious sentiment, hailing him as the man whose genius, talents and 'truly Catholic spirit were sure to leave a solemn impress of Catholicity, within and without the walls of this national establishment, which for fifty years has presented no emblem, to the eye, as of a Catholic seminary, save for the tabernacle which decorates the altar'. Gaffney continued:

> There will be a meeting of the trustees in Dublin on 22nd day of the present month, for the sole purpose of coming to a decision on the buildings. Mr. Owens [sic] will submit his plan (without a new church) on that day, but I am almost certain that the great majority of the trustees will not have any other plan than the one proposed by you last summer and approved by all. We have £30,000; let us begin with that sum, and when exhausted, Providence will not be wanting. The new church and buildings will not remain unfinished.[25]

A week later on 14 April, Flanagan reported to Renehan that he had discussed 'the embarrassing Position in which the Trustees are placed' with the Rt. Hon. David Pigott, Chief Baron of the Exchequer, who was one of the government appointed visitors.[26] Pigott had assured him that the trustees could still adopt Pugin's plans if the requisite buildings and improvements could be carried out within the budget. On Wednesday 22 April, Jones and Radcliff presented the Owen scheme to the trustees in Dublin, stating that a decision would have to be sent to the Treasury the following Monday. Clarification of details was

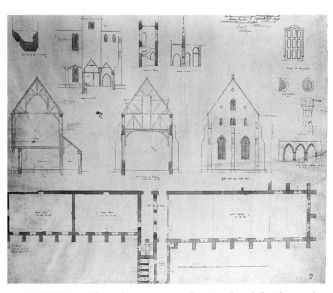

6. A W N Pugin: *The South Pane (range) with sections through the Library and Refectory of Maynooth College.* Contract Drawing no.7, dated 1846. (Maynooth College).

7. A W N Pugin: *Details of the West Pane (Range).* Contract Drawing no. 12, dated 1846. (Maynooth College).

Dublin and established in principle that by reducing the quadrangle in size and omitting the church, until funds became available, a building could be provided for the budgeted figure.[27] On 6 May Pugin met the Board of Works and agreed a scheme whereby the chapel and great hall would be deleted.[28] He wrote to Shrewsbury, apparently around this time:

> I am employed early & late now in finishing Maynooth. If your Lordship saw the roll of drawings that are going off you would be astonished. It is an enormous building, very plain, but on a grand scale, vast rooms, a refectory 120 feet long.[29]

On 5 June the Board of Works received a set of plans from Pugin which they considered would 'meet the object required'.[30] The drawings were sent to the Treasury for approval on 6 June and returned at the end of the month. Jacob Owen now dropped a bombshell. He had not, apparently, prepared the drawings for the alternative scheme himself, but had brought over his son, Thomas Ellis Owen, from Portsmouth to do so and wanted £75.3s. on account to reimburse him. The Board agreed to pay but reprimanded him: 'In future, whenever additional assistance of a similar nature may be required, the Board request that the terms upon which such is to be obtained may be stated so as to be considered before the authority is given'. Thomas Ellis Owen had performed a similar task for Charles Lanyon (his brother-in-law) in assisting in the design of Belfast Gaol in 1842[31] and one suspects that Jacob Owen had him lined up to do Mountjoy as well. This may partly explain Jacob Owen's subsequent withdrawal from the design of Mountjoy which was handed over to Major Jebb, the Surveyor-General of Prisons in England.

Thomas Ellis Owen's designs have not come to light. The earliest surviving Pugin design appears to be the axial perspective, probably dating from September 1845 (Fig. 3). A different perspective entitled 'general prospect', a more developed design for the whole college campus, probably dating from December 1845, formed the basis for the lithograph published in the Parliamentary Papers in 1854-55 (Fig. 4), to which was appended a perspective based on it, but not by Pugin, showing the college as actually built[32] (Fig. 5). In this perspective Pugin radically altered the existing campus, demolishing Stoyte House, adding a gatehouse at the College entrance, gothicising Riverstown Lodge and providing covered passages linking the various buildings; just how many of these proposed alterations were serious can only be guessed at. The new buildings in the 1845 scheme were chiefly ranged around a quadrangle, with the entrance in the form of a gatehouse. The front elevation (referred to by Pugin as the east pane, i.e. range) may well derive from his unexecuted scheme of 1841 for the rebuilding of Garendon House in Leicester, though this was castellated in style.[33] The axial perspective shows an embryonic gatehouse design with turrets like Garendon House rather than blended into the wall and roofscape as built. The proposed Maynooth chapel was to occupy a similar place to that in the Garendon composition, with its east end terminating the main elevation. Pugin's other main rooms for Maynooth were to be the great hall (behind the chapel), the dining hall (the chapel's counterpart in the south pane), and the library, set behind the dining hall, in the middle of the range. Linked to the south pane by short corridors were independent structures housing the kitchen and an oratory.[34]

The drawings submitted by Pugin in June 1846 presumably formed the basis for the contract drawings (Fig. 6-9), signed on 10 October 1846, three months after the receipt of tenders. Tracings of fourteen of these survive in the National Archives, while seven of the originals, in Pugin's own hand, survive at Maynooth. It seems clear from examination that the tracings were not personally made by Pugin. Indeed, as they exactly correspond to the surviving contract drawings, they must have been copied in Ireland where the contract drawings would have been kept.[35]

The contract, with Messrs W H Beardwood of Dublin, was for £24,037 and was to run until 1 October 1848, a date that was not met, the last two payments being made in August 1850 and February 1851. In December 1849 Beardwood was paid £1,000 on account for extras. A supplemental contract with a value of £1,963, probably for the extension of the south pane, was placed

8. A W N Pugin: *Sections and details of the East Pane (Range) of Maynooth College.* Contract Drawing no. 8, dated 1846. (Maynooth College).

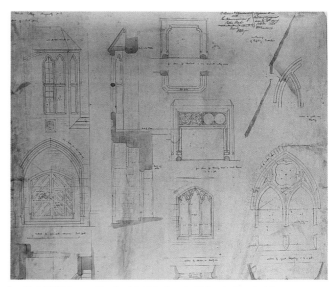

9. A W N Pugin: *Details of the East Pane including the Principal Entrance.* Contract Drawing no. 13, dated 1846. (Maynooth College).

A W N Pugin and St Patrick's College, Maynooth

with Beardwood on 1 November 1847. It was also to run to 1 October 1848, but final payment was not made until June 1850. The works were formally closed on 11 June 1853. Pugin visited Maynooth only a few times during construction; in July 1847, in May and August 1849, June 1850 and June 1851.[36] His rare appearances may have been due to his lack of enthusiasm for what he termed 'the best way of making the cheapest possible design ... not at all to be regarded as a specimen of what a pointed [ie Gothic] collegiate building ought to be'.[37] Essentially the running of the contracts was monitored by the clerk of works Richard Sharkey, employed by the Board of Works in August 1846, and by Pugin's agent Richard Pierce (1801-54), engaged two months later. Pierce, who had been acting for Pugin at the Presentation Convent, Waterford and St Peter's College, Wexford, was also to be responsible for the production of additional working drawings and details. Jacob Owen kept an eye on the job as did his own two clerks of works – his son James Higgins Owen and Frederick Villiers Clarendon (who was in charge of the renovations of the old college buildings).[38] Although Jacob Owen told a parliamentary enquiry in 1853 that, apart from certifying payments, he and his officers had 'interfered very little' (owing to Pierce's supervision), the facts suggest otherwise. Owen may have wished to disclaim responsibility for defects such as dampness which had been complained of to the committee. In February 1847, when Pugin was unable to work owing to illness, the Board had prepared drawings for his approval showing a radically revised layout requested by Renehan, which would have left the west side of the quadrangle open.[39] While this was not proceeded with, a proposal initiated around the same time by the college staff to increase the length of the south pane by fifty-two feet (submitted to the building committee on 13 March) was approved when the trustees agreed to reimburse the government. Although Pugin was asked for a revised drawing the same week, the matter was not referred to the Treasury until the following August.[40] The college had also to cover the cost of providing gutters and downpipes, excavations for deeper drains, glazing the cloisters, staining the internal woodwork and raising the height of the library staircase tower. Some essentials were totally unprovided for, the Board of Works (in their annual report for 1848) regretting the absence of heating in the students' rooms or the corridors outside them. Other economies included the omission of buttressed arcades from the ground floor of the west pane and, at the Board's request, alterations, in the size and location of joists and in internal wall thicknesses. Much of the interior planning, particularly in the east pane, was altered in execution. In 1848 the Board of Works published floor plans and an elevation of the east pane in their annual report (Fig. 10). While no north pane is shown on the plans, the

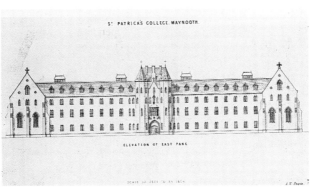

10. After A W N PUGIN: *Elevation of the East Pane (Range) of Maynooth College.* Lithograph of 1848 from the Annual Report of the Commissioners of Public Works. Note the substitution (to the right) of a gabled north-east range instead of the Chapel which the architect had originally planned.

lithographed east elevation has symmetrical gabled ranges at either end of the facade. This arrangement represents Pugin's final layout whereby it was proposed, when funds became available, to complete the east pane with a block (probably the great hall) matching the refectory. The chapel was to be moved to the centre of the north pane and placed at right angles to the quad, on a north-south axis, its narthex linking up with cloisters joining the east and west panes.[41] The west pane was to be similarly symmetrical, though it is not clear if a decision was taken to keep the great hall there or to move it to the proposed north-east pavilion. A gap on either side of the chapel was to allow free circulation of air into the quad. The west pane which had been left truncated at its north end, was to be symmetrically completed.[42]

The main contracts had concluded when Pugin's health deteriorated in early 1852. He was admitted to a private asylum in London in February and transferred to the Bethlem Hospital in June, suffering from 'mania', the supposed cause of his insanity being 'over labour and study in his profession'.[43] Moved again to a private institution, he died at his home in Ramsgate on 14 September. He had achieved much in his forty years.

It was left to Owen to report to parliament on the building in 1853. He felt it to have been 'substantially and fairly executed', though economies had meant no library fittings, window shutters, heat for the student rooms, gas light nor other essentials. Owen considered that the external walls were not thick enough though he felt that the building would dry out fully. His estimate for providing all the facilities, as envisaged by the trustees in 1845, including repairs and the addition of an infirmary, chapel and cloisters came to £32,280, additional to the £33,822 already spent.[44] These were all provided in due course, though by the time J J McCarthy's chapel was commenced in 1875 the government had ceased to be directly involved in the college buildings, a consequence of the disestablishment of the Church of Ireland in 1871. Although built on the site Pugin had originally envisaged for it, the chapel did not follow his design, the trustees wishing to avoid difficulties with Pugin's son Edward who had taken over the practice and was claiming copyright.[45] The north-west corner of the quadrangle was to remain open. While McCarthy initially proposed building the aula maxima (great hall) there, as Pugin had intended, the proposal was abandoned, a rather basically detailed hall being built away from the quad in 1891-93.

FREDERICK O'DWYER is an architect and architectural historian. He is the author of Lost Dublin (1981), and of essays on Irish public buildings and on the works of a number of Victorian architects, including Benjamin Woodward, John Skipton Mulvany and George C Ashlin.

A W N Pugin and St Patrick's College, Maynooth

1. The Board was the successor to the old Barrack Board and Board of Works, whose architect, Vincent Waldré, had supervised the building of the original college in 1795. These early buildings (now to be restored under the new Act) were extensions to an old house, the residence of John Stoyte, agent to the Duke of Leinster.

2. Jacob Owen (1778-1870), a Welshman, had come to Ireland in May 1832 at the behest of Burgoyne, for whom he had worked at the Ordnance Department in Portsmouth.

3. Letter dated 10 July 1845. Official correspondence between the British and Irish administrations was usually delivered within a day of posting. The principal source for this article is the official correspondence between the Board of Works and the Treasury in London, the government department to which they reported. Transcripts of much of the correspondence for the first few months of the project survives in triplicate and for the subsequent period in duplicate, at the following locations: (i) in a paperback minute book, with memos and a resumé of letters received and drafted at meetings of the Board, held between 12 July and 14 October 1845, now deposited in the National Archives, Dublin, OPW 37325/57/1; (ii) in a volume of transcripts of outgoing Board of Works letters, entitled *Maynooth College Letter Book No. 1* – also deposited in the National Archives, OPW 2D/60/11, continued in the Colleges Letter Book No. 2, OPW 2D/60/10, (iii) in the actual letters sent by the Board and received by the Treasury, and the draft replies to them- now deposited in the Public Record Office at Kew, T1/5132/25040. The other official sources include the Registered Papers of the Chief Secretary's Office (National Archives) and the Parliamentary Papers, specifically HC 1851 (213) L. 661, 1852-53 (599) LVII. 565 and 1854-55 (1896) XXII. 1 & 355; the latter contains the evidence and report of the royal commission of 1853-54 into the management and government of the college. Pugin's Diaries, now at the Victoria and Albert Museum, are reprinted in Alexandra Wedgwood, *A W N Pugin and the Pugin Family*, London, 1985, and hereafter cited as *Diaries*; while Jeremiah Newman in *Maynooth and Victorian Ireland*, Galway, 1983, quotes from documents in the President's Archive at Maynooth. I am grateful to Monsignor Patrick Corish, author of the official history, *Maynooth College, 1795-1995* Dublin 1995, for checking the Trustees' Minute Book on my behalf and to Monsignor Miceál Ledwith, for permission to quote from manuscript material and to reproduce drawings in the college collection. My thanks also to Penny Woods and Valerie Seymour of the college library.

4. This was the first time since its establishment in 1831 that the Board of Works had proposed engaging an independent architect in private practice for a major project. While no names were mentioned, the candidates they most likely had in mind were Patrick Byrne and John B Keane, Catholic architects whom the Board were to consider for Queen's College, Galway some months later. Byrne reputedly nominated Pugin for one of his first Irish commissions, the chapel at Loreto Convent,

Rathfarnham (1839). Keane got the Galway commission but proved a disastrous choice, failing to supervise the works and ending up in a debtors prison.

5. Letter drafted the previous day by C E Trevelyan, the assistant secretary to the Treasury.

6. This letter, recently discovered by Monsignor Corish in the Armagh Diocesan Archives, provides evidence as to the source of Pugin's nomination, hitherto generally thought to have been the Prime Minister Sir Robert Peel. It has also been suggested that the nomination came through the architect Charles Barry [Phoebe Stanton 'Welby Pugin and the Gothic Revival' (University of London PhD dissertation, 1950) and Douglas Richardson, *Gothic Revival Architecture in Ireland*, New York and London, 1983]. Dr Crolly, the Primate of All Ireland, was with Dr Murray, the archbishop of Dublin and the Earl of Fingall, both a Visitor and a Trustee of the College. There was a total of sixteen Trustees: eleven members of the hierarchy and five lay members, of whom four were peers. At an early stage in the deliberations it was proposed that the Trustees would have private rooms in the new building, where they could stay during their annual meeting. The seven Visitors, who were responsible for reporting to parliament, consisted, in 1845, of the three above-mentioned, together with the Lord Chancellor and three other senior members of the judiciary. Most of the judges were replaced by peers in 1846.

7. Pugin dined with Heytesbury on the evening of Tuesday 15 July. While in Dublin he also found time to visit St Patrick's Cathedral where he sketched some details. On the next day, 16 July, he travelled down to Rahan, Co Offaly (then Kings County) to meet Archbishop Murray at his summer residence. On 17 July he returned to Dublin via Maynooth and caught the Liverpool steamer. Pugin was almost constantly travelling during these years. His busy schedules would indicate that much of his journeying must have been done at night. Maynooth was not connected to Dublin by rail until 1847. The London to Dublin rail and steamer link via Holyhead was not completed until the opening of the Britannia Bridge in 1850.

8. Pugin's main ecclesiastical works in Ireland included churches at Barntown, Tagoat and Gorey (all in Co Wexford), convents at Gorey, Waterford and Birr and the cathedrals at Killarney (begun 1842, but halted during the Famine) and Enniscorthy (begun 1843, substantially built by 1850).

9. Quoted by Benjamin Ferrey in his memoir, *Recollections of A W N Pugin and his father Augustus Pugin*, London, 1861, pp.131-32.

10. The northern European feel of the Maynooth elevations may well have been inspired by buildings sketched during his three week sojourn, though the early axial perspective design illustrated here is less continental than the executed building.

11. This drawing, now catalogued as No. [53], is inscribed 'St Patrick's College No.' (missing), indicating that it was part of a set. It is drawn in pen with brown and grey washes. It was

presented to the RIBA Drawings Collection in 1972 by John Hardman and Company of Birmingham and is believed to be reproduced here for the first time. See Alexandra Wedgwood, *Catalogue of the Drawings Collection of the Royal Institute of British Architects—The Pugin Family*, Farnborough, 1977, p.71. The Hardman firm was extensively employed by Pugin in making ornamental metalwork and other objects. Lady Wedgwood also notes the presence of a schedule of accommodation for Maynooth and a sketch for the chapel, with ante-chapel, in one of Pugin's sketch books in the collection.

12. The dates 10 and 11 September for these meetings given in the *Diaries* as transcribed by Lady Wedgwood (n. 3 above) are incorrect. The latter date is also incorrectly cited in a letter from the Board of Works to the Treasury (see n.14 below). The Board of Works was without a chairman at this time, Burgoyne having chaired his last meeting on Maynooth on 22 August. Pugin made a note of Radcliff's address in his diary for 1845.

13. The schedule of accommodation required by the trustees included: 'A Church to hold 600 in choir, An ante chapel, two sacristries and a Bell Tower; Three Oratories and a Prayer Hall; A Library; A Great Hall for Exhibitions to hold about 700; A Great Refectory for 300, two smaller ditto.; Two Kitchens, Skulleries, a Bake House, Larder, Pantries etc.; A Large Study Hall for the Great Department, Two Smaller Studies for the Second Department; Nine Lecture Rooms, One ditto. for Experimental Philosophy; An Ambulatory and Cloister; Lodgings for the President and Vice-President; Sixty Professors Rooms, 560 Single Rooms, Board Room, Dining Room for 40, 16 Strangers Rooms for Trustees and Secretary, A Set of Rooms for the Archbishop.' Most of the additional accommodation, including 270 of the single rooms and six of the lecture halls, was to be provided in the new building which was also to have a stable court and offices annexed. The trustees originally wanted two new infirmaries but agreed to enlarge the existing junior infirmary.

14. Although Pugin had been written to on 11 October, further letters were dispatched after a Board meeting on 13th ordered 'That immediate steps be taken to have the necessary Plans and Estimates prepared, and that Mr. Pugin be written to, to ascertain the state in which his work now is, and on what basis he has, or is, making his plans'.

15. This was a tracing of a site survey, with block plans of the existing buildings, prepared by James H Owen (Jacob Owen's son and clerk of works) on 12 October and sent to Pugin. The original survey drawing is in the National Archives.

16. Pugin replied on 22 November (letter now lost), but seems not to have provided any answers.

17. The trustees agreed to pay within two years the sum of £1,047 towards the cost of furniture rather than have it deducted from the shrinkng £30,000.

18. To consist of the four archbishops, one bishop and three lay members. The committee was 'to confer with the Board and Mr Pugin on all

necessary occasions and to supervise the execution of the works of the College'.

19. On 6 December *The Builder* reprinted a garbled account from *The Globe* to the effect that Pugin's plans and estimates had been forwarded to Peel by the college board with an application for an increase of the building fund. In reality neither full plans nor a proper estimate had been furnished by Pugin at this date. The article (which accurately reported the formation and membership of the building committee) also claimed that the board (of trustees) 'having no alternative, determined to call on Mr Pugin to make a corresponding reduction in his plans and estimates, in order that the sum allocated should cover all expenses'.

20. Quoted in Ferrey, n.9 above, p.132.

21. This meeting, like those held on 20/21 November, took place in the Parochial House on Marlborough Street.

22. Public Record Office, Kew: T1/5132/25040, transcript of Pugin's letter of resignation. This letter and accompanying papers, which do not appear to have been previously noticed, clarify doubts about the resignation raised by Michael Trappes-Lomax (1932) and other biographers of Pugin. According to Monsignor Corish another copy of the resignation letter was sent to the Lord Lieutenant (National Archives: CSORP 1846/ W1254).

23. The Board acknowledged Butler's letter on 6 February (incorrectly transcribed as 6 January in the letter book). Butler may have put himself forward at the suggestion of his patron the Bishop of Ossory, who was a member of the building committee. The Board subsequently commissioned Butler to design a new lunatic asylum for Sligo.

24. AWN Pugin, *Contrasts, or, A Parallel Betweeen the Noble Edifices of the Fourteenth and Fifteenth Centuries, and Similar Buildings of the Present Day; shewing the Present Decay of Taste*, Salisbury, 1836; revised ed., London, 1841.

25. Quoted in Benjamin Ferrey, n.9, p.136.

26. Newman, n.3, p.109.

27. Newman, n.3, p.110. The committee hoped to retain the 'Continuation of the Cloister' (presumably along the north side) but this was dropped also. The meetings were held in the Marlborough Street parochial house.

28. Memorandum by Flanagan in the Trustees' Minute Book.

29. Quoted in Stanton (1950), n.6 above, and reprinted in Wedgwood (1977), n.11 above, p.71.

30. As well as a reduction in size, the revisions involved a simplification of details such as the bell tower and the omission of stringcourses. Extra floors of rooms were provided over the refectory.

31. Paul Larmour, 'Sir Charles Lanyon', in *GPA Irish Arts Review Yearbook*, 1989-90, p.202.

32. *Report of the Maynooth Commission*, H C 1854-55 (1896) XXII 1. The original 'general prospect' perspective is now lost, but since the lithograph was made in Dublin under the auspices of the Board of Works, it may be synonymous with a Pugin drawing of Maynooth which hung in the office of Commissioner Samuel Roberts (probably placed there by Radcliff, his predecessor) until 1892 when it was loaned to the National Museum. A request by the Museum to make the loan permanent was acceded to in 1894, but a recent search has failed to locate it. The papers relating to the donation are in the National Archives-OPW 4420/94; information from Rena Lohan. The axial perspective, in the RIBA, and the 'general prospect' perspective are incorrectly assumed to be synonymous in Rory O'Donnell's article 'Pugin as a Church Architect', in P Atterbury and C Wainwright, *Pugin: A Gothic Passion* New Haven and London, 1994, p.288, n.111.

33. The comparison is made by Phoebe Stanton, *Pugin*, London, 1971, pp.176-78.

34. The oratory in the 1853 'as built' perspective is bogus, being substituted for the unpicturesque semi-open privies erected at this location. Other discrepancies in this perspective include the chimneys on the elevations of the east and west panes, which were never built, and the substitution of two storeys of windows for the tall double-height windows of the library.

35. Several are signed as having been 'compared' with the originals on 12 November, the names – W F Ryan and P Murray- being perhaps draughtsmen engaged for the task. The copies are numbered 1-14. Originals in Maynooth are numbers 7-10 and 12-14. The college also has a further unnumbered, but complementary, drawing (not in Pugin's hand) for the quadrangle elevation and part plan of the south pane.

36. The 1850 visit coincided with a meeting of the Trustees, to whom Pugin reported that 'the building of the new house was completed according to contract'. In July 1848 Pugin met the Under-Secretary for Ireland, T N Redington, in Dublin but seems not to have visited Maynooth. Redington, appointed in July 1846 after the fall of the Peel administration, was a friend in court – he was married to a daughter of Pugin's Wexford client J H Talbot.

37. Letter from Pugin's assistant John H[ardman] Powell (presumably addressed to Renehan in February 1847), cited by Newman, n.3, p.111. Powell also claimed that Pugin 'was only induced to undertake the present work by several of the trustees in order to make the best of a bad job and prevent a much worse building being erected … he expects that the building will be the cause of much disappointment'. Pugin's views seem to have mellowed somewhat by the time he wrote a humorous letter to Owen around the time of his final visit to the college in June 1851 (Newman, p.112). His expectation of criticism was realised in a review by the *Ecclesiologist* (April 1849), p.290: 'We pity any architect who has to contend with the difficulties which must environ him while rebuilding Maynooth; but still we had hoped Mr Pugin might have been a match for them'.

38. Pugin was not directly involved in the renovations for which parliament voted £5,728 between 1846 and 1850, thus allowing the £30,000 to be spent on the new buildings.

39. The purpose of the alteration was to improve lighting and ventilation to the rooms facing the quadrangle by moving the proposed west pane to the north side and locating the chapel and large hall 'elsewhere'. Although the subject had been previously raised by Renehan with Pugin, his approval was not forthcoming. Renehan appears to have been swayed by the then growing belief that disease was spread by stale air. In 1847 the English commissioners in lunacy effectively banned enclosed quadrangles by requiring 'free access of the air and the sun' in new buildings [H C 1847-48 (34) XXXII. Appendix E]. Pugin noted in his diary for 3 February that he was 'quite blind'. J H Powell attributed this to 'inflamation of the head' (Newman, n.3, p.111). The cause of Pugin's ailments, possibly psychosomatic, has never been satisfactorily explained, but his constitution appears to have been affected by mercury prescribed for the eye condition. Lady Wedgwood has suggested (n.3, pp.89, 94), that Pugin destroyed his diaries for 1843 and 1846 because these were emotionally unhappy years for him. In 1846 his efforts to find a wife and mother for his six children ended in an acrimonious broken engagement. He finally remarried in 1848 and had a further two children.

40. This drawing, initialled by Pugin and dated 1847, is now in the National Archives.

41. The chapel was to be built on the site of the old senior infirmary, seen in the 'general prospect' perspectives. The proposed rearrangement, representing Pugin's final intentions, was conveyed by Jacob Owen in a writtten memorandum, dated 26 January 1854, to the Royal Commission (n.3 above).

42. Following a serious fire in the west pane in 1878, all plans to extend it were abandoned, part of the insurance proceeds being used to tidy up the unfinished gable end; information from Monsignor Corish.

43. Bethlem Hospital clinical report quoted in Patricia Spencer-Silver, *Pugin's Builder, The Life and Work of George Myers*, Hull, 1993, p.75.

44. Of the £33,822, the trustees had contributed £3,796, according to the Board of Works. However, in his evidence to the Royal Commission, the bursar gave the college's contribution as £5,097.

45. Ambrose Macaulay, *Dr Russell of Maynooth*, London, 1983, p.298. Pugin's practice was continued after his death by eighteen-year old Edward, who worked over his father's design for the chapel but lost out to McCarthy for further college work. McCarthy had been briefly A W N Pugin's Irish agent in 1851-52. Within months of raising the copyright claim Edward too was dead. For Edward Welby Pugin's Irish work see Frederick O'Dwyer, 'A Victorian Partnership- The Architecture of Pugin & Ashlin', in John Graby (ed.), *150 Years of Architecture in Ireland*, Dublin, 1989, pp.54-62. For the chapel (1875-91) and the completion of the tower and spire by William Hague (1896-1902) see Jeanne Sheehy, *J J McCarthy and the Gothic Revival in Ireland*, Belfast, 1977, pp.60-61.

THE IRISH HARP ON GLASS

Barra Boydell *reports how the changing image of the national symbol in the eighteenth and nineteenth centuries may be used in the dating of glass*

The harp has been used as a national symbol of Ireland since medieval times,[1] appearing in a wide range of contexts from public buildings and official documents to coins and artifacts including glass, pottery, textiles and jewellery. It was frequently engraved on glass during the eighteenth and nineteenth centuries and the form in which it was depicted changed considerably. These changes provide important evidence for the dating of glass, including the identification of fakes or later copies of earlier glass.

It was the harp's introduction on Henry VIII's Anglo-Irish coinage in 1534 which firmly established it as a widely recognised national symbol.[2] On Tudor coinage the harp faced towards the right, but when it was incorporated into the royal arms by James I of England in 1603 it was reversed to fit into the lower left quadrant of the arms. The harp on coins followed suit, and since that time the harp as the official symbol of Ireland has always faced left.[3]

A harp with a semi-naked, draped, winged, female figure, possibly representing 'Hibernia', became the standard emblem of Ireland under British rule, and this 'winged-maiden' harp was exclusively used during the eighteenth century.[4]

The Irish harp first appears on glass in Williamite contexts of the mid- to later eighteenth century, where it is typically found on cordial and toasting (or 'firing') glasses with a classical bust of King William on one side of the bowl, and the motto, 'The Immortal Memory', with a crowned, winged-maiden harp on the other side.[5] (Fig.1). In particular, attention can be drawn to the exuberant spirals and swirls with which the base of the winged figure and the tips of her wings are joined to the ends of the soundbox: these have little connection with the strong, solid construction of a real harp but closely parallel harps appearing on contemporary Irish coins (also in combination with a classical bust of the monarch).

The rising tide of patriotic and nationalist sentiments towards the end of the eighteenth century brings with it a marked change in the ways in which the

1. Williamite FIRING GLASS, c1770-1800. (Ulster Museum). The earliest appearance of the Irish harp on glass is on mid to late eighteenth-century Williamite glasses. This form of 'winged-maiden' harp with Imperial crown is typical of the period

harp is depicted, this change being reflected on Irish glass. The first changes to be noted are not in the harp itself but in its associated symbols: previously, as on Williamite glasses of the type noted above, the harp most commonly appears as a symbol of Ireland under British rule, surmounted by an English (or 'Imperial') crown (distinguished by its curved arches). During the 1780s the growing sense of Ireland's independent identity is manifested in Volunteer flags and banners which show the harp surmounted by an 'Irish crown' (without the arches), a form of crown which was to reappear throughout the nineteenth century.[6] Sometimes the crown is even replaced by a stylized crown of shamrocks, a clear reflection of the growth of patriotic feelings: a winged-maiden harp surmounted by a crown of shamrocks occurs on a number of Irish decanters and other glass of late-eighteenth century type.[7] (Fig. 2) The engraving on these pieces demonstrates a notable degree of similarity in design and execution and can confidently be attributed to the same hand. The figure has a small, rounded head on a long neck and the body is represented by breasts below which two swags form the greater part of the forepillar of the harp. A curl, ending in a spiral, connects with the bottom of the (basically triangular) soundbox . The figure's wing forms the neck of the harp, the top of which is prolonged into an S-shaped curve meeting the top of the soundbox.

In view of the later close association of the winged-maiden harp with British rule in Ireland, it is important to note that it is this form of harp which occurs in late eighteenth- and early nineteenth-century patriotic and nationalist contexts, as described above. It is the absence of the Imperial crown which marks the significant change: winged-maiden harps (without Imperial crowns) occur on decanters with the motto of the Society of United Irishmen, *Erin Go Bragh* (spelling can vary, and this motto continued to be used throughout the nineteenth century), with the English translation of the same (Ireland For Ever), and with inscriptions representing

2. *(Opposite)* DECANTER, late eighteenth-century, probably Waterford. (National Museum of Ireland). The winged-maiden harp, of eighteenth-century type, is highly stylised and the Imperial crown has been replaced by a crown of shamrocks reflecting the rise of patriotic movements in the late eighteenth century.

opposition to the Act of Union (1801). A decanter is illustrated with the inscription 'Repeal of the Union' and a winged-maiden harp on which the tip of the wing meets the top of the (triangular) soundbox directly, without decorative scrolling. (Fig. 3) The soundbox is decorated with three stars, an expression in glass engraver's terms of similar decorations appearing, for example, on harps on contemporary coins and on Edward Smyth's carvings on the Custom House, Dublin (c1783).

Harps occur on a number of supposedly late eighteenth-century 'Volunteer' glasses, a group which has been shown to consist largely (if not entirely) of late nineteenth- or early twenti-eth -century fakes. The iconography of the Irish harp on glasses of this group frequently supports these findings. As noted above, the winged-maiden harp was the form used by patriotic groups until at least a decade after the period of the Volunteers (1779-93): plain harps (ie not of winged-maiden type) are not found in independent contexts of confirmed eighteenth-century date. Thus the occurrence of plain harps on supposedly eighteenth-century 'Volunteer' glasses points to later engraving, if not to fakes.[8] A 'Volunteer' glass inscribed 'Dublin Volunteers Pro Patria' illustrates this point clearly: it has a plain harp (surmounted by an 'Irish' crown) whose forepillar has at its midpoint a large scrolled ornament. (Fig 4) The overall design of this harp, including the unusual forepillar, the decoration on the soundbox and the the shape of the neck, is similar to harps engraved on glass by Franz Tieze, the noted Bohemian-born engraver who came to Dublin in 1865, dying there in 1932. (See Figs. 8, 9) It is evident that this glass, or certainly the crowned harp, was engraved not in the late eighteenth but about a century later.

Winged-maiden harps do also occur on 'Volunteer' glasses.

That this is not, however, evidence in itself of an eighteenth-century date is demonstrated by a pair of decanters, each with a crowned winged-maiden harp and inscribed 'Success to the Waterford Volunteers 1782', which Francis has shown to have been engraved by Franz Tieze.[9] Sometimes winged-maiden harps betray a later date in details of the harp itself: a glass with the Volunteer inscription 'Pro Patria' (Fig. 5) has a harp whose soundbox recalls those engraved by Tieze (cf.Fig. 8), while the base of the winged figure is connected to the soundbox by a cornucopia-like device also occurring on engraved Pugh glass.[10]

Between the period immediately following the Act of Union and the second half of the century the Irish harp appears rarely, if at all, on glass. The reasons for this can be found both in the glass trade and in political developments: in the early nineteenth century heavily cut glass largely replaced the earlier engraved style of decoration in which the harp had featured, while the Irish glass industry itself declined following the heavy taxation introduced on glass in 1825. The Act of Union had also reduced the opportunities for depicting the harp on its own, since the country now formed part of the United Kingdom and it was not until the resurgence of nationalism under Daniel O'Connell that the harp again began more widely to symbolize nationalist sentiments. Thomas Davis and the Young Ireland group provided a major stimulus through their newspaper *The Nation* (from 1842) for the adoption of subjects and symbols from Ireland's past, while the Dublin Exhibition of 1853 enabled the greater public to see a selection of early Irish harps for the first time.[11]

By the time the Pugh glass factory was producing glass engraved by Tieze and other Bohemians who came to Dublin in the mid 1860s, harps (as well as round towers and other symbols

3. DECANTER, c1801. (Detail). (Private Collection). Engraved with the inscription *Repeal of the Union* and a winged-maiden harp. Even in nationalistic or patriotic contexts such as the movement to repeal the Act of Union of 1801, the Irish harp continued into the early nineteenth century to be depicted in the 'winged-maiden' form, although the absence of the crown demonstrates the desire for independence from Britain.

4. GLASS inscribed *Dublin Volunteers Pro Patria.* (Detail). (Private Collection). The form of the harp on this supposedly late-eighteenth century 'Volunteer' glass shows that this glass must have been engraved by Tieze or a contemporary. (*Cf.* Figs. 8, 9).

5. GLASS inscribed *Pro Patria*. (Detail). (National Museum of Ireland). Although this 'Volunteer' glass is engraved with a crowned winged-maiden harp ostensibly of eighteenth-century type, the form and decoration of the harp suggests that it was engraved in the later nineteenth century. (Cf. Fig. 8).

6. THE TRINITY COLLEGE (or 'Brian Boru') Harp. 14th/15th cent? (Trinity College Dublin). During the nineteenth century this harp became widely familiar through illustrations, paintings and public exhibition. It provided the model for the majority of depictions of the Irish harp. Many decorative details on harps engraved on glass in the later nineteenth century can be traced back to the Trinity College harp.

7. WATER JUG, probably by Pugh, Dublin c1880/90. (Detail). (Private Collection). The Irish harp, together with a round tower, wolfhound, shamrocks, and the inscription 'Erin Go Bragh', occurs on many pieces of late nineteenth century Pugh glass. The harp in this example is not realistic. The lozenge decoration on the soundbox derives from the Trinity College harp.

of Ireland's past) were widely current as symbols of the general revival of nationalism. Depictions of the harp were now based on early Irish harps, though most often clearly at second or third hand. Until a revival of interest in playing the instrument arose in the twentieth century, there was little if any opportunity for artists to see the Irish harp actually played.[12]

A significant number of engraved Pugh glasses include Irish harps. Some of these glasses are signed by Tieze, while drawings of harps also occur in his sketch book.[13] Early Irish harps consist of three distinct parts: a rectangular-sectioned soundbox expanding towards its base, an S-shaped neck, and a curved forepillar. The Trinity College harp (fourteenth/fifteenth century?) (Fig. 6) is richly decorated with geometric designs, with zoomorphic carving on the forepillar, and with settings for precious stones. While most harps on Pugh glass clearly derive ultimately from this instrument, individual features may be approached with a degree of artistic licence which is paral-

8. TUMBLER, probably by Pugh, Dublin, 1883. (Poor Clare Convent, Kenmare). Engraved by Franz Tieze with a harp, shamrocks and the inscription *Mother. Abbss.* (sic) *Poor. Clares. Convent. Klnmare (sic)* and on the other side *From the Cork Exhibition 1883.* Loosely based on the Trinity College harp, this is a typical Irish harp as engraved on later nineteenth century glass. Note the decorated rectangular soundbox, the neck engraved with fine zig-zags and ending in a spiral, and the curved forepillar with a prominent decorative projection.

leled by harps depicted in other media at the same period.[14] The least realistic form of harp is that in which the soundbox and neck form one continuous, curved piece, and the neck and forepillar may also be joined. The base of the forepillar may also end in a curve or spiral. A jug engraved with a harp displaying all of these features, together with round tower, wolfhound and the motto 'Erin Go Bragh', is illustrated (Fig. 7).

Most often, however, harps on Pugh glass have the correct tripartite construction. The soundbox may be decorated with groups of circles or other shapes, sometimes forming a cross shape (Fig. 8), but more often the decoration takes the form of lozenges or criss-cross lines (derived from the decoration on the Trinity College harp) (Figs. 7, 9). Although the general shape of the necks do not vary significantly, the details of decoration do: they may be plain or decorated, most often with a zig-zag line (Fig. 8), less often with longitudinal lines (Fig. 9). Above the forepillar the neck ends in one of three types of finial: most commonly an upward curve or spiral (Fig. 8); sometimes a rounded bun-shaped finial; or a cut-off end, sometimes enlarged into a rectangular or inverted-shield shape, a form which bears the closest relationship to the Trinity College harp (Fig. 9). The forepillar can range from the realistic to the wildly exaggerated, but in most cases there is some form of decoration. At its simplest this consists of a thickening of the middle of the curve into a protruding point or decoration, a feature which can be very pronounced (Fig. 8).[15] Finely cut lines sometimes run the length of the forepillar or adorn the inside edge (Fig. 9). The base of the forepillar typically joins the middle of the soundbox towards its base (Figs. 8, 9), but in a few cases it improbably meets the bottom back edge of the sound box. The yet more unreal cases of the forepillar ending in a curve or spiral touching the soundbox have been mentioned above. These Irish harps on Pugh glass of the later nineteenth century demonstrate a pattern common to contemporary depic-

9. LARGE GOBLET (one of a pair), probably by Pugh, c. 1880/90. (Detail). (National Museum of Ireland). Engraved by Tieze with the inscription *Erin Go Bragh*, an Irish harp and other national symbols. The neck on this harp has a cut-off end enlarged into an inverted-shield shape based on the Trinity College harp (Fig. 6). The longditudinal lines decorating the neck also occur on other harps engraved on Pugh glass.

tions of the harp in other media: an often exuberant degree of artistic licence reflecting the fact that these harps were not modelled on first-hand observation of actual examples, but on other harps which the engravers would have seen on buildings, monuments, ornaments, and in printed sources.

After the Pugh glass works closed in 1890 the manufacture of flint glass in Ireland ended, and with it the Irish harp effectively disappeared from glass until its reappearance in mass-produced souvenir and other glass in the twentieth century.

DR BARRA BOYDELL is a lecturer in the Dept. of Music, Maynooth College (National University of Ireland) and is a council member of the Glass Society of Ireland. He has published widely on the history of musical instruments and of music in Ireland.

ACKNOWLEDGEMENTS

I would like to thank the National Museum of Ireland, the Ulster Museum, the Poor Clare Convent, Kenmare, and the various private collectors (who wish to remain anonymous) who in the course of preparing this article have kindly allowed me to examine and to illustrate their glass. A special thanks is due to Mary Boydell for making available her extensive knowledge and photographic records of Irish glass, and to Catherine McIvor and the staff of the National Museum of Ireland for their help and cooperation.

1. It is first recorded in the 13th century. See S. M. Collins, 'Some English, Scottish, Welsh and Irish Arms in Medieval Continental Rolls', *The Antiquaries Journal*, XXI (1941), pp.208-09, Pl.XLIb.
2. See Michael Dolley, 'The Harp on Anglo-Irish Coins – A Preliminary Exposition', *Numismatic Society of Ireland. Occasional Papers No. 10* (Dublin 1970).
3. When the harp was registered as Guinness's trademark in 1862 it was made to face to the right. In other respects the Guinness harp is virtually the same as the official harp of the modern Irish state being, like it, modelled on the Trinity College (or 'Brian Boru') harp.
4. Dolley's suggestion (as note 2) that this figure was initially a male satyr, only later becoming female, is difficult to uphold.
5. The authenticity of Williamite and Volunteer glass has been questioned by Peter Francis ('Franz Tieze (1842-1932) and the re-invention of history on glass', *Burlington Magazine*, cxxxvi no. 1094 (May 1994), pp.291-302). While the iconography of the harp supports Francis's theories in relation to Volunteer glass (see below), this is not the case with Williamite glass.

6. G.A.Hayes-McCoy, *A History of Irish Flags from Earliest Times* Dublin, 1979, 89f; F. Glenn Thompson, 'The Flags and Uniforms of the Irish Volunteers & Yeomanry', *Bulletin of the Irish Georgian Society* XXXIII (1990).
7. Apart from the decanter in the National Museum of Ireland (illustrated), four others are in private collections. A double bottle with similar decoration is illustrated in Dudley Westropp, *Irish Glass* (rev.edn, ed. Mary Boydell, Dublin, 1978), pl. XL.
8. Francis (as note 5, 294-5) has shown that the engraving on many 'Volunteer' glasses is copied directly from Volunteer medals, themselves now recognised to be for the most part later fakes. Some of these medals include anachronistic harps (for example on all the Volunteer medals with harps illustrated in Hayes-McCoy (as note 6), p.90.)
9. Francis (as note 5), 291, Fig. 32.
10. Two claret jugs (nos. 37 & 78) illustrated in *Reflections: Dublin Engraved Glass in the Late Nineteenth Century* (Exhibition Catalogue, National Museum of Ireland, 1994), pp.16, 39.
11. *Official Catalogue of the Great Industrial Exhibition 1853* (4th edn., Dublin 1853), pp.142-146, 155.

12. Significantly the only Pugh glass engraved with somebody actually playing a harp shows a full-sized concert harp, not an Irish harp, despite the association with shamrocks on the same glass which might suggest that an Irish harp was intended. Illustrated in Catriona MacLeod, *Glass by Thomas and Richard Pugh in the National Museum of Ireland*, (Dublin 1983), Pl. XV.
13. MacLeod (as note 12), Pl. XLI.
14. I am grateful to Mr Miroslav Havel, former chief designer at Waterford Glass, for explaining that much of the variety in the design of harps and their decoration would reflect the technical abilities of the individual engravers. Finer details could only have been achieved by the most experienced engravers, while others would have engraved less decorated harps of simpler and often less realistic form.
15. One of the most exaggerated forms of decoration on a forepillar occurs on the harp on the 'Parnell' jug in the National Museum of Ireland (No. 13-1960). Illustrated in MacLeod (as note 12), Pl. XIXb.

A MASTER CRAFTSMAN: CAREY CLARKE, PRHA

It is said of Poussin, after his brief period of patronage at the court of Louis XIII, that he became disturbed and unhappy. He had been recalled from Rome by the King to a post as leading painter at court. There he came under the notice of Cardinal Richelieu, was given a pension, and housed for life in a residence in the gardens of the Tuileries. But he could not take the jealousies; he could not understand the intrigue. And so he departed once more for Rome, the world's best city. And there he lived out the rest of his life; and the events with which it was measured amounted to nothing more startling than the list of the works he painted. Happy Poussin!

For Carey Clarke, one would wish the same self-imposed fate: that his life would be measured, in the end, by the

The artist Carey Clarke PRHA

Bruce Arnold
assesses the work of the President of the Royal Hibernian Academy

succession of paintings which, year by year, in an undramatic, calm, lucid and original way, delight all those who have admired him for what he does, not for what he is. He is a master craftsman. He paints with something of the exact precision of classical figures such as Poussin, with the line of Ingres, with the palette of Vermeer.

The names are not lightly invoked. Carey Clarke was conditioned in his training as an artist to understand the qualities which these painters mastered, and make fruitful use of them. His teachers in the College of Art – Sean Keating and Maurice MacGonigal – were inspired by similar standards. They believed in a well-tested hierarchy of talent and achievement. The idea of greatness being related to the co-ordination of hand and eye, the understanding of

1. Carey CLARKE (b.1936): *Dublin Mountains from Ballycorus*, 1965. Oil on canvas, 56 x 81cm. (Private Collection). This early landscape was painted out of doors over about six sessions in the month of July. The picture won Third Prize in the Munster and Leinster Bank Calendar Competition the year after it was painted.

A MASTER CRAFTSMAN: CAREY CLARKE, PRHA

2. Carey CLARKE: *Self-portrait.* 1960. Oil on canvas, 46 x 35.5cm. (The Artist's Collection). After receiving his Diploma from the College of Art in 1959, Clarke taught part-time there. But with no plans for a career as a painter he went to England in April 1960 and took a job in Wall's ice-cream factory, living in Acton. This picture was painted there before his return to Dublin in June.

example was far from perfect, the truths expounded were well-worn.

What is disparagingly called the 'academic' in painting prevailed, as it always must, because continuity is the great survivor, not revolution. If you paint, day after day, never letting up, always trying to capture the impossible, the magical, no matter how simple and direct the subject may be, then issues of colour and pigment, of properties in paint, the weave of a canvas, the effect of different glazes, dominate your life. And bit by bit, arduously, with a mixture of good luck and good judgment, memory, experiment and inspiration, the longed-for result becomes something that can be more or less predicted.

Carey Clarke comes from a Protestant, middle-class background. Class standards, real or residual, do not greatly matter. But his Protestantism – as much for identity as for belief – is real. He is an only child. His father was an engineer. His mother, who lived to be ninety-four, inspired at least one fine portrait. He grew up in Donegal, but went to an awful, Dotheboys Hall of a school in Dublin, run by an eccentric tyrant called Commiskey. There was talk of Portora, which Carey's mother favoured as a school but when his parents moved to Dublin he left Morgan School in Castleknock and studied for a short time at St Andrew's College, in Clyde Road, before entering the National College of Art in 1954.

Like William Orpen, he was totally happy as an art student. He had shown indifferent abilities at

pigment and contrast, was not strange to them. And it inspired in them those standards which they tried to teach their students.

Light suffused their thought. Where did it come from? What colour was it? How is it made? Composition was the embodiment of style, with the mind reaching out to apply such ancient orders of design as the Golden Section, believing that they prevailed in a world of change and challenge. They did, of course. But fewer and fewer people were noticing. How unfashionable they were! That was the judgment. They were also not very good; the

school in virtually every discipline. Art was his best subject, but his art teacher at St Andrew's, a sculptor, Chris Ryan, did not think he had much visual imagination, and told him so, only to be surprised by the success of his former pupil. Carey Clarke won prizes. In portrait painting, life studies, landscape, his work was admired and rewarded. These were quiet triumphs. The inner confidence was built by them. But the outer expression remained cautious, correct, 'academic'. He obeyed the rules. He completed the course, taking his diploma five years later, in 1959.

A Master Craftsman: Carey Clarke, PRHA

Like so many other students before him, he then spent a short time teaching in his own college, before taking up an outside job, in the then fledgling world of advertising. It did not last. In 1963 he was appointed as a part-time teacher in the School of Painting, and since then, with minor breaks for foreign study, he has been part of the staff of the National College of Art and Design. It is his Rome.

It could be said that the Royal Hibernian Academy – at least, high office in that Academy (President since 1992, and earlier Treasurer, for a period of four years) – represents his court experience. Election as an associate, in 1967, hardly ruffled the waters at all. This was a low period in the Academy's rocky existence, at least in the second half of the twentieth century, a high period for the Irish Exhibition of Living Art (Clarke, in fact, had exhibited with the Living Art in 1956, a year previous to his first showing at the Academy). It was the year of the first Rosc exhibition. New modernism was all the rage. Serious academic painting was under suspicion. It was even under threat. A collective sentence of death had been passed by its opponents, and they were seeking, with growing success, an endorsement from the public of their judgment.

Could it be said that Clarke's painting, at the time, reflected the time? Sensitive, withdrawn, carefully composed, restrained in colour, and pervaded by stillness: these are the essential thoughts provoked by *Canal Scene* and *Ringsend under Snow*. Clarke simply painted his way through the confrontations, exhibiting mainly still life and landscape works, and teaching the principles which he himself had acquired as if this represented an acceptable norm for the artist, an antidote to the turmoil, which gathered as a storm at the end of the 1960s, and really broke over the world of art in a way that has shattered most of the standards by which Clarke and his generation had been educated.

He was a contemporary of James Nolan, Ruth Brandt and Brett McEntaggart. And he would have seen himself as of their company. All three followed Clarke into full-time teaching in the College. He had a joint show with Nolan in 1971. But

3. Carey CLARKE: *Near Carraroe, Evening*, 1970. Oil on canvas, 35.5 x 38cm. (Private Collection). Staying in Carraroe, Co Galway, for about a month, the artist painted a number of oils and watercolours of the neighbouring landscape. This small canvas was painted in one evening.

4. ON THE GRAND CANAL, Dublin: . A photograph of Carey Clarke at work *en plein air* in 1964

A MASTER CRAFTSMAN: CAREY CLARKE, PRHA

5. Carey CLARKE: *Evening Light: Notre Dame des Ardilliers Saumur.* 1985. Watercolour, 72.5 x 102cm. (Private Collection). Entering the church late in the evening, the artist was impressed by the effect of the light and immediately took photographs and made sketches which he later used in painting this picture in the studio. The actual painting of the picture was an unusually long process.

6. Carey CLARKE: *Candes sur Loire,* 1984. Oil on canvas, 66 x 81cm. (Private Collection). In 1984, the artist travelled in France and painted in Brittany, the Loire and Provence. Fascinated by the colour of the stone, the architecture, and the reflection of the scene in the river, he committed them to canvas.

stylistically they were quite different. Almost without realising the significance of his own responses, Carey Clarke would look at quite different painters, of a slightly earlier generation, and see in them the kind of technical qualities, as well as the visionary dimension, which he wanted to achieve in his own work. He admired greatly the work of Patrick Hennessy. He still gasps at the impact of some of his canvases. He never met him, but he recalls saying about one exhibition: 'God! I wish I could paint like that!' He admired also the work of Patrick Swift, another he never met, and also Edward Maguire. He saw something of John Ryan at this time, whose work he also liked, and he painted theatre scenes for him, including backdrops for James McKenna's *The Scattering*, and Mervyn Wall's *Fursey*.

Full academician status was achieved in 1980. By then, the battle, seemingly lost in the mid-1960s, had been rejoined. Academic painting, which had never fought back in any conscious way – indeed, how could it? – had simply fought on. As a label it is misleading. Even the invoking of the two names – MacGonigal and Keating – is misleading. Keating, essentially a linear painter, created a following different from that of Maurice MacGonigal, who spent the best part of his life trying to escape the linear discipline in favour of impressionistic techniques. These suited his vision of the West of Ireland, his loose and imaginative mixing together of figures and landscape through a well-organised palette, but without great compositional constraint.

Carey Clarke was somehow stretched between the two artists, and their differences allowed him to find his own line, which in every sense – the conceptual, the range of colour, the compositional standards – was more disciplined. Discipline is a high priority. It is also productive of something infinitely more valuable: self confidence. Behind the uncertainty and evident shyness in Carey Clarke as a person, there is an aggressive sense of his own worth, as an artist, his own absolute certainty about what he does, his own supreme realisation of each individual work. The very nature of his work, and in

A Master Craftsman: Carey Clarke, PRHA

7. Carey CLARKE: *The Tobacco Barn.* 1980-82. Tempera on panel, 70 x 91.5cm. (Private Collection). Located in the Lot area of France where the artist had visited the painter Brett McEntaggart in 1979, the effect of light entering through the slatted walls of the barn made an immediate impact on Clarke who later painted this picture in the studio from references taken on the spot.

particular his still life paintings, inspires comment on an item by item basis. It is like looking at Vermeer and considering the falling stream of milk from the spout of the jug, or the texture of a patterned carpet. Carey Clarke will place a small dish, a silver bowl, a kettle in sunlight with a distorted, elongated shadow; and this will invite comment and examination.

He admired MacGonigal's colour, Keating's line. Liking the idea of discipline, he found it more easily appreciated in line than it is in colour. Yet the more appealing figure as a teacher was almost certainly MacGonigal. Neither, should be underrated. Yet neither did more than designate a general course of development in his art.

Anyone who goes today to the Academy, and absorbs that general atmosphere or style which a school derives from the past, must read in the works, not just of Carey Clarke, but of Brett McEntaggart, James Nolan, the hands of their teachers.

And the prevailing messages are about light and colour. This would once have been a platitude, not worth putting on paper. But such have been the changes, the eccentricities, the loss of direction, even the departure from basics, that concern over what were once essentials has become noteworthy as a means of defining a painter's style. And it must be said, Carey Clarke, perhaps above all others of his generation, has distilled extreme forms of colour discipline, of compositional rigour, and of line, which mark him off.

Contrary to expectation, this is emphasised, rather than lessened, by his range of subject-matter. To say he was indifferent about what he painted would be a presumption. Yet there is a certain truth in it. He always chooses the arrangement of subject-matter with care, and in the realisation of a canvas, the purpose behind his choice becomes quite clear. We understand why a church interior has imposed huge challenges, and what a joy it

8. Carey CLARKE: *A March Day from the Studio,* 1984-85. Oil on canvas, 68.5 x 87cm. (Private Collection). This is the garden outside the artist's Foxrock studio. The picture was painted at a time of year when plants and trees were bursting into bud.

has been overcoming them. We see the importance of a white table cloth, how difficult to realise, how magical the texture can be, so that the smell of the linen, its faintly rasping surface, its warmth, its absorbency, are all there in the oil paint. But they do not dominate. They did not choose him. His rational mind, not unlike that of Poussin, wandering along the banks of the River Tiber, and picking up small stones which would be turned into great massy boulders in his classical subject-paintings, has picked a way through the confusion of objects towards the calm resolution of light and purpose on the surface of the canvas.

This can be demonstrated in different ways. His painting, for example, from the river bank, of Candes-sur-Loire (Fig. 6), a truly wonderful work, was done over a period of three weeks in high summer. It was terribly hot. When the heat made it impossible to go on, Clarke would go into the cool church. There he found an interior and painted that; splendid also, totally different,

an accident of climate forcing a choice which became magical in its realisation. Still life is approached in the same way, the objects manoeuvred to suit such accidental reference-points as grey, distorted shadow on white wall.

He came to portrait painting with a similar indifference. He won an early prize for portrait painting, while still a student. It was a modest event, a Royal Dublin Society award, followed by a prize in the Taylor, the following year. But it did not designate a purpose or a direction. He did not, as a result, become a portrait painter. Nor is he now a portrait painter. He paints portraits.

It was no longer possible, anyway, at that time, to choose such a path with any confidence. He did paint portraits, including one of his mother (Fig. 12), which was much admired by the then Director of the National Gallery of Ireland, Homan Potterton. Potterton asked why he did not paint more of them. His reply: no one asked him. And this, in turn, led to a commission, and then

A MASTER CRAFTSMAN: CAREY CLARKE, PRHA

to further portraits. His painting of Potterton (Fig. 15) is exemplary of classicism in all its detail. Three times, the artist consciously applied the principle of the Golden Section, so that its line designates the position of the figure, the position of the eyes, the arrangement of the background. These are carefully thought-through components. They are, in painting, the injection of life through visual vibrancy learned over centuries.

Portrait commissions did not really change him from being just a painter. He defies any confining description because he has a questing spirit, and because he is free. It seems an odd word to use. All his life he has been part of the national school in art. His life is bounded by timetables and administrative obligations, which he affects to despise, and from which he imagines Time will release him. He is a creature of the system; he has grown up always aware of a wider authority governing his life. Yet within that set of constraints he has organised a life as a painter which glows with its own authority, independence and freshness of vision and attack. In a way that would not have been possible in any other generation, he has managed to turn to his own advantage the very constraints which both

9. CAREY CLARKE: *Still-life with Madonna & Child after Desiderio da Settignano.* 1985. Oil on canvas, 81 x 91.5cm. (Private Collection). On a visit to Florence in 1977 Clarke was fascinated by the delicacy of Renaissance bas-reliefs and commissioned this copy of a relief in the Bargello Museum which he has since used in several paintings.

MacGonigal and Keating, and many others before them, saw as prison bars. Those prison bars – the grinding duties of teacher, week in, week out, to process a never-ending file of young men and women – have protected Carey Clarke and liberated him inwards, into his own vision, his own soul, his own perception of the intrusiveness of light and colour and design.

Choosing his work in order to demonstrate his life, is like writing a catalogue not entirely dissimilar from Poussin's. We do not necessarily recognise, or admire, because of the subject. The fact that Godfrey of Bouillon is winning a victory, or the infant Pyrrhus is being saved, is a key with which the intensity of colour and the elegance of composition are justified. So, too, with a kettle on a shelf in a Carey Clarke still life, or the light on snow through a window emphasising the pale rose madder of a cyclamen on the studio shelf, or sunlight through the slatted walls of a tobacco shed in southern France.

Exact design has gone into the white bowl of overblown roses, against a white wall, standing on a slightly crumpled white cloth, and with a silver bowl to the left. The embroidery in the cloth is lovingly picked out. The shadows thrown by the folds in the

10. Carey CLARKE: *Night Reflections in the Studio with a Self-portrait.* 1982-85. Oil on canvas, 61 x 122cm. (Private Collection). Initially attracted by the effect of the black reflections, the artist started this picture at Christmas 1982 and left it unfinished: more than one poinsettia plant died during the painting. The picture was then completed in July 1985 for exhibition in Edinburgh that year and at the RHA in 1986.

11. Carey CLARKE: *Lough Reelan, Co Donegal.* 1990. Oil on canvas, 102 x 102cm. (Private Collection). Inspired by a moment in Donegal when travelling there with students in 1987, this picture was painted in the studio from references taken on the spot. The sky was repainted several times before the eventual solution of the cloud reflected in the water was reached.

texture are a faint interjection in the otherwise smooth study of white planes. And the vivid, but entirely balanced, shades of red and pink and yellow from the rose petals, some on the flowers still, some fallen on the flat white surface, are the only splash of carefully co-ordinated colour. The limited depth in the canvas, a deliberate foreshortening of our perspective, verges on the claustrophobic; we are being told exactly the confines of what we may

see. It is an imaginative realisation of the visual prison which an authoritative painter will impose upon his public. Thus far, he says; and within the material scope of a largish canvas —- this one is 23 inches by 29 inches – he offers a small, still, yet complete world.

BRUCE ARNOLD has written biographies of William Orpen and Mainie Jellett and has just completed a new Life of Jack B Yeats.

12. Carey CLARKE: *Portrait of the Artist's Mother.* 1980-86. Tempera and mixed media on gesso panel, 91.5 x 76cm. (The Artist's Collection). The artist had seen a portrait of Lady Playfair by Sargent and was attracted by that artist's combination of yellows and browns and decided to attempt a similar combination in this portrait where the glittering effect of the costume is also Sargent-like. Her left hand is painted in acrylic.

13. Carey CLARKE: *Still-life*. 1995 (Unfinished). Oil on canvas 46 x 66cm. (The Artist's Collection). In this unfinished canvas it is possible to study the artist's working methods. The prevailing brown of the background still requires further layers of paint before it is finished; the tangerines are almost complete but other areas such as the jug and nut-crackers still lack precision while areas of white have been left for a napkin to be painted in later.

14. Carey CLARKE: *Connemara: summer landscape*. 1989. Oil on canvas, 102 x 102cm. (Private Collection). This picture was painted in the studio based on references taken on the spot when the artist accompanied his students on a painting trip to Connemara. He was attracted by the possibilities of the high viewpoint.

15. Carey CLARKE: *Portrait of Homan Potterton*, 1988. Oil on canvas, 102 x 117cm. (The Artist's Collection). Exemplary of the artist's classicism in all its detail, the principle of the Golden Section has been applied three times in creating this composition .

16. Carey CLARKE: *Still-life: Summer Roses.* 1987. Oil on canvas, 58 x 76cm. (Private Collection). The bowl, which belonged to the artist's mother, is depicted also in Fig. 9. The yellow reflections of the rose petals did not fully satisfy the artist.

17. Carey CLARKE: *Substance and Shadow: Still-life with a Shelf.* 1978. Tempera on panel, 76 x 91.5cm. (Private Collection). Preoccupied by the effects of illumination of shape and pattern, Clarke has painted at least four pictures of similar subject matter.

DANIEL MACLISE AND A BANKRUPT PATRON

Philip McEvansoneya

explains the disappearance of the background in a painting by the Irish Victorian artist

At various points throughout his career, the Irish artist Daniel Maclise (1806-70) painted subjects drawn from literary sources, notably from the plays of Shakespeare. One of these, showing the wrestling scene from *As You Like It* (Act 1, Scene 2), was exhibited at the Royal Academy Summer Exhibition in 1855. On that occasion a woodcut of the painting was reproduced in the *Illustrated London News* under the title 'Scene – lawn before the Duke's Palace: Orlando about to engage with Charles, the Duke's wrestler' (Fig. 3).[1] A comparison of that reproduction with the painting itself (Fig. 4), reveals that it has been significantly altered: this article suggests why this might have been done.

Maclise had begun preparatory work on a painting from *As You Like It* in the winter of 1847-48, in response to an invitation from the great Victorian engineer Isambard Kingdom Brunel (1805-59) to contribute a work to the gallery of Shakespearean subjects by the most prominent artists of the day he was then planning. After reading through some plays, Maclise decided on the subject he wished to tackle, the very last scene in *As You Like It* (Act 5, Scene 4), where, as he wrote to Brunel in January 1847, 'most of the characters are brought together picturesquely in a woody landscape'. Maclise pointed out another attraction of his proposed subject, that 'Rosalind, Celia, Phoebe and Audrey would afford various agreeable phases of feminine beauty'.[2] With the letter Maclise sent a very rough sketch of the composition he was considering, and he later elaborated this initial idea into a preliminary drawing now in the Victoria and Albert Museum.[3] However, Maclise withdrew from Brunel's project soon after and this scene was never painted.

Maclise's interest in the play itself endured and when he was approached a short while later by another patron he turned to Act 1 Scene 2, the wrestling match between Charles and Orlando. This patron, a wealthy railway contractor called Edward Ladd Betts (1815-72), had a similar objective to Brunel, that of building up a collection of especially commissioned paintings by the best artists of the day, although the works he amassed were not thematically linked. Betts

invited some of the artists he employed to stay at his newly-built mansion, Preston Hall in Kent (Fig. 1), and it was in the dining room of that house that Betts's principal paintings by Maclise, Sir Edwin Landseer, Charles West Cope, Clarkson Stanfield and Thomas Creswick were displayed as part of a coordinated decorative ensemble. When these works were eventually sold they were specified as being 'from the Dining Hall, all painted for Mr Betts'.[4]

Old photographs of the room show the works *in situ* (Fig. 2). Maclise's work was hung next to Stanfield's *The Port of La Rochelle* (Walker Art Gallery, Liverpool) and next to that came Cope's *Marriage of Griselda*.[5] In a prominent place above the doors was Landseer's *Braemar*.[6] The other side of the room was dominated by the chimney piece containing a low relief sculpture by John Thomas (the architect of the house) of *Hengist entertaining Vortigern* (untraced). It was flanked on the left by an untraced sketch by Maclise and Lance showing a group in an interior around a table and *A Roadside Inn* by Creswick and J W Bottomley (untraced) on the right. These five works were all of the same dimensions, 130 x 180cm, give or take a centimetre or two, and were all framed in the same manner, indicating that the paintings were conceived of as a group. The subject pictures were complemented by a group of portraits on the upper level.[7]

Betts did not simply want a collection of works by eminent artists: from Maclise and from George Lance he commissioned works which specifically and directly referred to himself. He requested Maclise to paint his scene as if it were occurring in the grounds of Preston Hall which is clearly seen in the original background (Fig. 3). Betts was clearly proud of his house, hence Lance's work, *The Uninvited Guest: a Peacock among Flowers and Fruit, with a View of Preston Hall in the background* (untraced).[8]

Among the reviewers who commented on Maclise's painting, some were aware of the identity of the house, which was found to be thematically appropriate and a justifiable anachronism because the Elizabethan style of the architecture, as well as being fashionable, was congruent with Shakespeare's own life time. Modern elements

1. (*Above*) PRESTON HALL. Photograph taken about 1900. (Royal Commission on the Historical Monuments of England). The house, which still stands, was built about 1850: its Elizabethan style was congruent with Shakespeare's own lifetime and therefore appropriate as a backdrop to a scene from one of the bard's plays.

2. (*Opposite*) PRESTON HALL: *The Dining Room*. Photograph taken before May 1868 showing Maclise's *Wrestling Scene from 'As You Like It'*, bottom left. At the time this photograph was taken, the background of Maclise's picture had already been altered.

such as the large, domed conservatory at the left-hand end of the range of buildings were considered to be out of place.[9] It may have been Betts's desire to have his house included in a painting that led Maclise to choose the subject. Maclise depicts the action not just as if it is taking place 'before the new Duke' as the text mentions (Act 1, Scene 1), but on a lawn in front of the palace – Preston Hall. That Betts might therefore be associated with the

3. W J LINTON (1812-98): *The Wrestling Scene from 'As You Like It'.* Wood engraving, 23.2 x 32.7cm of a redrawing by Morin after Daniel Maclise. From *The Illustrated London News,* 9 June 1855. The print shows the picture as originally painted for Edward Ladd Betts with a view of the latter's home, Preston Hall (See Fig. 1), in the background.

character of the usurping Duke, the seated figure on the left of centre, seems not to have mattered.

Why should the detailed and seemingly accurate view of the house have been painted out? The answer seems to lie partly in events in Betts's own life and partly in artistic considerations. Betts's business activities, mainly railway building, had suddenly collapsed in the spring of 1866.[10] To help discharge his bankruptcy Betts decided in 1867 to sell off virtually everything he owned including his country estate and art collection, but the sales were postponed until 1868.[11] Since Betts would have needed to realise as good a sum as possible for each item, then it may be that an artist, perhaps Maclise, was employed to repaint the background, eliminating all personal (and possibly embarrassing) reference to its original owner. The *pentimenti* of the over-painted house in the background are clearly visible in the painting.[12] Professor John Turpin says that when he saw the painting twenty-odd years ago the alteration was evident, but that he put the *pentimenti* (which Maclise was not in the habit of making) down to the interests of the subject.[13] The repainting did not remove all reference to the original country house setting since certain details like the step and flagstone path in the foreground, and the celestial globe on a plinth on the right were left behind.[14]

Moreover, the alteration improved the picture: the removal of the architectural background means the viewer is no longer distracted from concentrating on the figures, and the painting is made more in keeping with the rustic context of Shakespeare's play. The minutely studied dead leaves and other foliage in the foreground, almost Pre-Raphaelite in their detail, contrast well with the more summarily painted background, and the characteristic staginess of Maclise's multi-figure works is, for once, highly appropriate. Regarding the figures, which are completely unaltered, Maclise was interested in the depiction of easily recognisable types appropriate to each of the roles: thus we find an effete-looking Orlando, a bold and aggressive Charles (the contrast between whom led the *Illustrated London News* to compare them to David and Goliath), a demure Rosalind, a proud and haughty Duke and so on. Maclise's concentration, however, is on the highly dramatic moment just before the wrestling begins, with everyone expecting Orlando to be humiliated, whereas he is the eventual victor.

The alteration must have been made at some time in 1866-67, because the painting in its new form was engraved in the January 1868 number of the *Art Journal.*[15] The painting would then still have been Betts's property, but the need to sell it already evident. Indeed the publication of the engraving may be considered an advertisement. When the painting was auctioned with Betts's other works in May 1868 it fetched 588 guineas.[16] Mention of the alteration was made in neither the short descriptive text which accompanied the 1868 engraving nor in the reports of Betts's sale.[17]

Post-hoc alterations to paintings are common in many periods. In Maclise's time one thinks of the Pre-Raphaelite William Holman Hunt who retouched *The Awakening Conscience* (1853-54, Tate Gallery, London) on a number of occasions, and in 1856 completely repainted the face of the woman because its owner found her expression too painful to live with. In the case of Hunt, no evidence of the original appearance survives, but with Maclise we can identify precisely the painting's two states. Perhaps Betts saw the expected permanence of the painting as a kind of antidote to the brevity of life. Unfortunately for him, circumstances intervened to disrupt this hope and his indulgent commemoration of himself might be seen as an act of hubris.

DR PHILIP McEVANSONEYA is a Lecturer in the History of Art Department in Trinity College, Dublin

ACKNOWLEDGEMENT
I am very grateful to Professor John Turpin for information provided and invaluable suggestions made during the preparation of this article; to the Maas Gallery Ltd., London and to the Forbes Magazine Collection, New York for the provision of photographs; to the owner of Fig. 2 for permission to reproduce it here, and also to Adrian Le Harivel and Neil Wilson.

4. Daniel MACLISE (1806-70): *The Wrestling Scene from 'As You Like It'*. Oil on canvas, 127 x 177.8cm. Signed and dated 1854, altered c.1867. (The Forbes Magazine Collection, New York). Following his bankruptcy in 1866, Betts was forced to sell his collection and at that time had the representation of his house painted out of the background of the picture.

1. *Illustrated London News*, 9 June 1855, p.568.
2. Maclise to Brunel, 15 January 1848, Oxford, Bodleian Library, MS Autogr. c.6, fols.71r-72r. Brunel's Shakespearean paintings are the subject of an article by the present author and Hilarie Faberman, *The Burlington Magazine*, CXXXVII, February 1995.
3. See R Ormond and J Turpin, *Daniel Maclise 1806-1870*, exh. cat., National Portrait Gallery, London and National Gallery of Ireland, Dublin, 1972, pp.75-76, no.83.
4. C H Cope, *Reminiscences of C W Cope*, London, 1911, pp.195-96; Betts's sale, Christie's, London, 30 May 1868.
5. Cope's work appeared at Sotheby's, 26 November 1985, lot 42.
6. *Braemar* was sold at Christie's, 25 March 1994, lot 85.
7. In this article I have confined myself to a consideration of Maclise's painting. I hope to discuss the room as an ensemble on another occasion.

8. Betts's sale, lot 62; 173 x 132cm, more-or-less the same size as the dining room paintings, but in a vertical format. It was with the Owen Edgar Gallery, London in 1984. It was exhibited in 1855 at the same RA exhibition as Maclise's work, with a quotation from *Hamlet* as its title. Betts also owned a view by Philip Phillips of the previous house on the site *Preston Old Hall*, (Betts's sale, lot 58), which had been exhibited at the RA in 1846, and a *View of Preston Hall* by 'Pitts' (Betts's sale, lot 44).
9. 'The Royal Academy', *Illustrated London News*, 9 June 1855, p.562; 'Fine Arts: The Royal Academy', *Athenaeum*, 12 May 1855, p.558.
10. See the reports in *The Economist*, 16 June, 6, 13, 20 October 1866, 14 March, 22 August 1868.
11. Detailed particulars of the house and estate were published in 1867, copy in the Centre of Kentish Studies, Maidstone.
12. The *pentimenti* are especially evident in the colour reproduction of a detail in J B Priestley,

Victoria's Heyday, London, 1972, p.88.
13. J Turpin, 'The Life and Work of Daniel Maclise (1806-1870)', unpublished Ph.D. thesis, Courtauld Institute of Art, 1973, pp.225-26.
14. This globe actually existed, albeit in a different part of the grounds: see the volume of photographs of Preston Hall and the surrounding area, dated 1904, by Bedford Lemere & Co, Victoria and Albert Museum Print Room, X1003A, p.12.
15. 'Orlando and the Wrestler, – "As You Like It",' *Art Journal*, 1868, frontispiece.
16. Christie's, London, 30 May 1868, lot 66, bought by the dealer Vokins. It fetched 798 guineas at Christie's on 2 May 1874 but failed to sell there at 250 guineas on 16 May 1891.
17. 'Orlando and the Wrestlers' [sic], *Art Journal*, 1868, p.4; 'Picture Sales', *ibid*, p.136; 'Mr Betts's Collection of Pictures' *Times*, 1 June 1868, p.9.

THE TALENTED AND IDLE
MR WILLIAM GANDY IN IRELAND

Jane Fenlon *rescues from obscurity the life and work in Ireland of the seventeenth-century painter, William Gandy*

Owing to the accidental connection of these Gandys, father and son, with infinitely greater names, they have managed to keep their memory long enough above water, one might say, to be noticed and pulled ashore.

This amusing comment made by Charles H Collins Baker,[1] author of several books on seventeenth-century painting, aptly sums up the survival of two obscure names in the history of painting. They are the painters James (1619-1689) and his son William Gandy (c.1665-1729). James is said to have worked with Sir Anthony Van Dyck (1599-1641), while William is linked to Sir Joshua Reynolds (1723-92), two of the more famous names in art history.[2] This essay is concerned mainly with William Gandy and his work in Ireland.

Even today the Gandys cannot be said to have been wholly rescued from oblivion; some progress has been made with William although new information about him is still scarce. Most of the known biographical material comes from secondary sources, except for a brief sentence in George Vertue's notes, which tell something of William's early training. Vertue (1684-1756), a London-based engraver and antiquary, was an inveterate gossip who compiled informative notes on painters and collections during the eighteenth century.[3] He also engraved a portrait of *Rev. John Gilbert*, by William Gandy, (Fig. 1). James Northcote (1746-1831), a pupil of Reynolds, is the best source on William. Northcote wrote a biography of his master, in which he recounts his father's stories about Gandy's personality and adds his own insights and information about the painter's work in the Exeter area.[4] In 1770 when the Revd Matthew Pilkington,[5] who had lived in Dublin, compiled his dictionary of artists, he provided material about James Gandy but nothing about the son. All other writers on the Gandys, even Strickland, have based their biographical material on these three sources.[6]

A brief re-examination of the main sources yields some more useful scraps of information. For instance, in Vertue's notes he writes:

> Mr Maubert had his first instructions in drawing and painting from him [Gaspar Smitz] in Dublin ... Mr Gandy of Exeter had some instructions from him when in London. This Gandy did paint Shadwell- Poet.[7]

This connection between William Gandy and the painter Caspar (or Gaspar) Smitz (fl. 1662-88/1707), does not manifest itself in Gandy's known paintings which show no obvious signs of Smitz's influence.[8] In his note Vertue also places William in both London and Exeter. To date no works by him have been traced to a London-based patron. Only the Exeter connection produces useful material; in fact most of William's English portraits have been found in that area and these we will return to later. It also emerges that there was a family of Gandys prominent in the town during the seventeenth century, but no record of either a James or a William being born there has been traced and no family connection has been established. What can be confirmed is that William died in 1729 and was buried in St. Paul's Churchyard in Exeter.[9] Northcote, in his writing corroborates the Exeter/Devon connection but expresses his ignorance about Gandy's origins when he says:

> *William Gandy was an itinerant painter in the county of Devon where he lived and died, but it is uncertain whether he was a native of the county.*[100]

Northcote also places William in Plymouth in 1714 and gives his approximate age as sixty years at that time. This would suggest a birth date of around 1655, although there is no firm evidence to support it.[11] Perhaps Northcote's most useful contributions are his remarks on Gandy's personality and several detailed descriptions of portraits painted by Gandy in and around Somerset and Devon, all of which he dates to later than 1714.

There is insufficient evidence to substantiate a more recent claim that William Gandy was the author of a technical manuscript contained in the *Memorandum Book of Ozias Humphrey, 1777-1795* which is in the British Library.[12] These *Notes on Painting, 1673-1699*, as they are described, are attributed to Gandy on very thin grounds.[13] Lately some erroneous facts about William Gandy have also been published. These include the misattribution of a portrait of William Jane which is signed and

2. George VERTUE (1684-1756): *Rev. John Gilbert,* engraving after portrait by William Gandy (c.1655-1729).

IOHANNES GILBERT
Ecclesiæ Cathedralis Exon:
·Canonicus Residentiarius.

1. (*Opposite*) Willem WISSING (1656-87) and Jan VANDERVAART (1653-1727), *Master Montague Drake 1685-6.* Oil on canvas, 238.7 x 127 cm (Private collection). This portrait displays a similar range of colours and background to those in Gandy's portrait of *Master Willcocks* (Fig. 5). The pose and dog in this portrait are very close to those same features in Gandy's portrait of *Kendrick Fownes* (Fig. 7).

3. William GANDY (c.1655-1729): Portrait, said to be *Henry Stewart of Killymoon* (d.1717) c.1700, Oil on canvas 76 x 63.5cm. Signed *W. Gandy* and inscribed *AEt: 16.* (Private Collection). Gandy's latest known work in Ireland.

4. William GANDY: *James Butler, 2nd Duke of Ormonde when Lord Ossory, (1666-1745), c.1686.* Oil on canvas, 76 x 63.5 cm. (National Maritime Museum, Greenwich). This portrait was painted immediately following Ossory's return from France, hence the extremely fashionable arrangement of his neckcloth. There is another version of this portrait which is oval; it was sold at the Princess Royal Sale at Christie's in 1929. Both versions appear to be by the same hand.

dated 1706 by William, as being by his father James Gandy.[14] The same source also suggests that William was the brother of a Thomas Gandy of London when there is no evidence provided to confirm this.[15]

With regard to William Gandy's work in Ireland, none of the three principal sources make any reference to it. Northcote expresses the opinion that this painter had never achieved much outside Somerset. 'William's little fame has seldom passed the limits of the county [Somerset] in which he resided'.[16] Strickland, who seems to have used Pilkington as his source, never mentions William, although he does attribute several Irish portraits to James Gandy.[17] Crookshank and Glin are the first to suggest that William practised in Ireland and illustrate a signed portrait of *Henry Stewart of Killymoon* (d.1717) (Fig. 3) painted by him.[18]

This brief review of known sources provides very few biographical facts and just the bare bones of William Gandy's painting career spanning some seventy years from around 1655 until 1729. The only new documentary evidence found recently is in the shape of notes and receipts for payments to William Gandy which definitely place him in Dublin in December/January 1686-87.[19] To summarise, it has been suggested that this elusive painter was born around 1655, and was in London at the same time as Caspar Smitz, which would probably have been before 1681, the date when the latter registered for the first time with

the Dublin Company of Painter Stainers.[20] Documentary evidence definitely places Gandy in Dublin in 1686-87 and at least two portraits of Irish sitters painted by him can be dated to the 1690s. He seems to have gone to England around 1700, where he painted his finest known work, a signed portrait of *Master Willcocks* (Fig. 5), son of the Sheriff of Exeter of approximately the same date, which provides evidence of his presence there. It seems unlikely that he ever returned to Ireland. Indeed Northcote's comment on his little fame seldom passing outside the county, combined with the concentration of portraits painted by him still to be found in that area, would suggest that he remained in the locality of Exeter until his death in 1729.

Five of William Gandy's known portraits can be linked to Ireland. These are early works, painted between the years 1685 and 1700. All have an appealing freshness about them. They include the following portraits: two versions of *James Butler, 2nd Duke of Ormonde when Lord Ossory, (1666-1745)*[21] which can be dated to around 1686 (Fig. 4); one of *Henry Stewart of Killymoon, (d.1717),*[22] (Fig. 3) a signed work; a portrait of *Richard*

5. *(Opposite)* William GANDY: *Master Willcocks, son of Thomas Willcocks Esq., Sheriff of Exeter, c.1700.* Oil on canvas 96.5 x 86 cm Signed *W. Gandy fe.* (Private Collection). This is undoubtedly William Gandy's finest known work. The choice of palette, pose and background show close affinities to works emanating from the Willem Wissing (1656-87)/Jan Vandervaart (1653-1727) studio.

6. William GANDY: *Richard Parsons, 1st Earl of Rosse (1687-1741) c.1698*. Oil on canvas 76.2 x 63.5 cm. (Private Collection). It can be seen that the pinkish-red tones of this coat match those of the bows in the much more sombrely coloured portrait in Fig 4. This particular pinkish colour features in four of the five Irish portraits by this painter. There is a copy of this portrait painted in 1925 in the Masonic Hall in Molesworth Street Dublin.

7. William GANDY: *Kendrick Fownes (d.1717)*. Oil on canvas. 126 x 99.75 cm. (Private Collection). The only known Irish whole length portrait in this painter's oeuvre; the pose is after a portrait of *Lord Burleigh c.1685* by Willem Wissing, engraved 1685 by John Smith. Note the still life of two small gamebirds on the rocky ledge to the sitter's left.

Parsons, 1st Earl of Rosse (1687-1741) (Fig. 6)[23] and finally a handsome full-length of *Kendrick Fownes*, (d.1717) (Fig. 7). All of these sitters had family seats in Ireland and all were young men under twenty years of age. Youth may explain why a minor artist like William Gandy was allowed to paint a sitter of such high social standing as James Butler. One other portrait of an unknown lady signed 'WG: fe: 1688', may be considered with these Irish works.[24]

There are very definite links between the portraits of *Lord Ossory c.1685* (Fig. 4) and that of the *Earl of Rosse* (Fig. 6), where the age of the sitter would suggest that it was painted approximately ten years later. Both display a soft handling with delicate pencilled strokes in some of the highlights. The figures are set confidently in space, although there is an ambiguity about the positioning of the right arm and shoulder in Ossory's portrait which is not evident in the Rosse portrait. Colouring is in sub-

dued brownish tones because of the armour in the latter, with just the warm pinkish-red of the bow and the well painted fine lace relieving the overall dark palette. The hair is a rich brown with lighter highlights. By comparison, the Parsons' portrait has a more cheerful aspect. Again the warm pinkish-red is used, on this occasion for the coat, where it contrasts well with the crisply painted white linen and silver waistcoat. As in the Ossory portrait, the hair is a rich brown with lighter highlights. The dating of the Ossory portrait is based both on the receipts of payments and on the very fashionable arrangement of the sitter's neck-cloth.[25] (A similar but much more flamboyant arrangement of this feature, can be seen in Largillière's portrait of the *Duke of York*, painted in 1685, at the National Maritime Museum, Greenwich).[26] The only full-length in this group of Irish pictures, is a portrait of *Kendrick Fownes*. Here the pose used is derived from an engraving after Wissing's portrait of *Lord Burleigh* of

THE TALENTED AND IDLE MR WILLIAM GANDY IN IRELAND

around 1686. A date after 1692 can be suggested for the Fownes portrait based on the arrangement of the *steinkirk* neckcloth. In this work the painting of the head and wig is crisper than that used in either of the portraits previously discussed[27] and this in turn would seem to link it with the portrait of the unknown lady of 1688.[28] The facial features, particularly the mouths in both of these works are much tighter than the softer fuller lips present in the portraits of the Earls of Ossory and Rosse. Colour tones in the Fownes portrait are generally light; they range from pale pink through to dark reddish tones for the lavish drape on the figure, deep mustard yellow for the coat, which is richly embroidered on the hem. Typical scribbling touches of paint are used to highlight drapery folds in this picture. A delightful still life study of two small game birds lying on the rock in the background of the Fownes portrait is unique in Gandy's oeuvre. The portrait of *Henry Stewart*, (Fig. 3), painted around 1700, is the latest of the Irish pictures known to us. In this portrait the mustard/gold garment, with blue drapery, the open-necked shirt worn by the sitter and the styling of the hair can be related to those same features in the picture of *Master Willcocks* of approximately the same date. It is a signed work, however some injudicious cleaning has left the face scrubbed, lacking in modelling and subtlety.

As already mentioned, George Vertue supplies the only information that we have about William Gandy's artistic training, when he tells us that Caspar Smitz instructed Gandy in London. It has, however, proved difficult to trace any similarities to that master's style in the pupil's known works. Prior to his instruction by Smitz, which probably took place before 1681, when that artist is first recorded in Dublin, William Gandy would have been introduced to the techniques of painting by his father. Some similarities between the work of father and son can be seen when the handling of hair and lace in the portrait of *Charles Cutliffe* by James is compared with those features in William's portraits.[29] A certain wistful expression can be discerned on the faces of the sitters in some of William's pictures, particularly in those portraits of *Henry Stewart* and *Master Willcocks*, which are vaguely reminiscent of those beautiful youths painted by Van Dyck during the late 1630s. These portraits also have a measured and at the same time casual elegance about them. William's earlier works do not display this trait and it is totally lacking from his later portraits. Another Van Dyckian feature found throughout that artist's work, can be seen

8. William GANDY: *John Patch* Oil on canvas 125 x 100 cm. (Exeter County Hospital). One of Gandy's English portraits which displays his uneven talent. The influence of Kneller has been detected in this work.

9. William GANDY: *Sir Henry Langford Bt.*, (?-1725). Oil on canvas 125.3 x 100.7 cm. (The Royal Albert Memorial Museum and Art Gallery, Exeter). One of William Gandy's more accomplished English portraits. The patterned robe was probably painted by an assistant.

THE TALENTED AND IDLE MR WILLIAM GANDY IN IRELAND

10. William GANDY: *Elizabeth and Sarah Gould, daughters of George Gould*. Oil on canvas 108 x 106.5 cm. (Private collection). The poses in this portrait are taken from the engraving after Kneller, Fig. 11.

11. John SMITH (1652-1742): *'The Lord Churchill's two Daughters', Henrietta Churchill, Duchess of Marlborough and Anne (Churchill), Countess of Sunderland*. Engraving after portrait by Sir Godfrey Kneller (1646-172). The image is reversed, which is usual in engravings.

in William's painting of hands. It is in the mannered pose of the sharply dropped wrist, which is present in at least two of Gandy's English works, portraits of *John Patch* and *Henry Langford*. (Figs 8 & 9) This posed feature was often used by Sir Peter Lely (1618-80) and others but several of the hands painted by Gandy are impressively sensitive and would seem to owe more to Van Dyck. Did William Gandy absorb these influences directly from his father or was he influenced by the study of portraits such as that of *James Stuart, Duke of Lennox and Richmond*, by Sir Anthony Van Dyck, which he may have seen hanging in the long gallery at Kilkenny Castle?[30]

Other artistic influences can be discerned in William Gandy's earlier portraits which often display marked similarities to the works of Willem Wissing (1656-87) and are even closer in general feel to those of his assistant Jan Vandervaart (1653-1727), in particular, elements such as poses, backgrounds, botanical and costume details. Poses used by Gandy for the portraits of *Kendrick Fownes* and *Master Willcocks*, follow closely designs emanating from Wissing's studio. Also the landscape backgrounds in both of these portraits by Gandy, although more broadly handled, contain several features in common with those used in the portrait of *Master Montague Drake* (Fig. 1), a work attributed to both Wissing and Vandervaart.[31] This portrait also uses the same palette of dark slatish blue and golden brown as that found in the *Master Willcocks* portrait. In addition it has one of the plainest backgrounds found in a portrait painting from the Wissing studio, where it was more usual to have works which were positively cluttered with details. Several engravings after portraits by these two artists show giant weeds, parrots, bowls of fruit and various flowering shrubs in abundance (Figs 12 & 13). The only feasible explanation for the similarities in the landscape background and general handling of these two portraits would be that Gandy had a close familiarity with Wissing's/Vandervaart's working methods. But until further facts about this painter come to light there is no way to confirm such a link.

Because there are no commentators on William Gandy's Irish work, it is of interest to examine what Northcote and Collins Baker have to say about his English portraits. Both remark on the painter's ability to paint hands. Northcote in his description of Gandy's portraits specifically mentions the qualities of the head and hands:

> *His portraits (for I believe he never painted anything else) are slight and sketchy, and show more genius than labour; they indeed demonstrate facility, feeling, and nice observation, as far as concerns the head; but he was so idle and so unambitious that the remainder of the picture, except sometimes the hand, was commonly copied from some print after Sir Godfrey Kneller.[32]*

Both writers also remark on the influence of Sir Godfrey Kneller (1646-1723) when they talk about William Gandy's style. Indeed, after 1700, it is noticeable that Gandy's portraits are often based on poses found in works by Kneller which had been engraved. One such example of this practice is a double portrait of *Elizabeth and Sarah Gould*, obviously based on Kneller's portrait of *Henrietta Churchill, Duchess of Marlborough*

THE TALENTED AND IDLE MR WILLIAM GANDY IN IRELAND

12. Bernard LENS (1659-1725): *The Hon. Charles Cecil Esq.* Engraving after portrait by Jan Vandervaart, published by E. Cooper. Gandy's earliest portraits often display similarities to the work of Vandervaart and Wissing particularly in the poses.

13. John SMITH (1652-1742): *The Hon. William Cecil Esq.* Engraving after portrait by Willem Wissing, published by E. Cooper.

and *Anne (Churchill), Countess of Sunderland* painted in 1688, and engraved by John Smith (Figs 10 & 11). Northcote, when describing a portrait of his father's mother, says that it is 'extremely fine' and then goes on to repeat his comments about Kneller and the quality of Gandy's painting of the hand;

> ... *The drapery of this picture is painted in a slovenly manner from a print after Kneller; but there is a hand in it very finely executed.*[33]

Collins Baker also remarks that Kneller's influence is apparent in the portrait of *John Patch*, (Fig. 8), but then adds 'in no degree suppressing its individuality' and that the hands are 'not at all Knellerian'.[34] When discussing colour, Collins Baker, using his keen eye, comments on William Gandy's favoured use of yellow-brown, which features in many of his portraits throughout his career. Yellowish-gold tones can also be seen in his Irish work, both in the portraits of *Kendrick Fownes* and the later *Henry Stewart*.[35] This colour is repeated in a darker shade in the portrait of *Master Willcocks*, where it can be seen on the drapery and sleeve linings. Collins Baker tells us also, 'a mustardy green curtain hangs in the right background'[36] of the portrait of *Ralph Allen*, although this is a doubtful attribution.[37]

When commenting on William Gandy's paintings and personality, Northcote often contradicts himself, alternatively describing Gandy's pictures as both 'very fine, and many more good for

nothing'[38] Collins Baker on the other hand, simply dismisses the artist as 'a mediocre painter, whose chief interest is that his technique, in its crumbly scumbled texture and grayish-mauve bloom, incontestably appealed to Reynolds, when he was in Devonshire in the 1740s.[39] These remarks now seem overly harsh, when one considers the freshness and appeal of the Irish portraits. Although, when ghastly survivals such as the double portraits *Elizabeth and Sarah Gould* (Fig. 10) and that of *Masters Matthew and Phillip Pear*, are compared with the more accomplished works, one cannot but empathise with the earlier writers.[40] How can these poor works be explained? A bad day, inadequate assistants, damaged by shabby restoration procedures or perhaps as the products of William Gandy's own difficult personality?[41] Whatever the reason, there is no doubt that they are in sharp contrast to the fresh and lively works of his Irish period.

DR JANE FENLON is a consultant specialising in Irish art and architecture of the sixteenth and seventeenth centuries

ACKNOWLEDGEMENTS
To Miss Jane C Baker of Royal Albert Memorial Museum, Exeter for her generous assistance and to Mr. Clifford N Gandy and Mr Richard Gandy for help with Gandy family connections. Also to Robin Simon and David Moore-Gwyn for their assistance in tracing the portrait of Montague Drake.

1. Charles H. Collins Baker, *Lely and the Stuart Portrait Painters'* London 1912, p.56.
2. Neither of these links has yet been backed up by documentary evidence. For James Gandy's links with Van Dyck see Rev Matthew Pilkington *A Dictionary of Painters*, with New additions, an appendix and index by H Fuseli, London 1805 p.208, also the first edition of his work, *The Gentlemen's and Connoisseurs' Dictionary of Artists*, London 1770. For William Gandy and Reynolds, see William Jackson, *Essays*, 1789, p.173 and James Northcote, *The Life of Sir Joshua Reynolds*, 1813 also his *Supplement to the Memoirs of ... Sir Joshua Reynolds*, 1815, appendix p.xvii. The connections with Reynolds are extremely muddled with James and William interchangeable. Collins Baker, *op cit* pp.56-63 tries to clarify the matter and finally George Pycroft, *Art in Devonshire*, pp.4-6, and pp.46-50 in his discussion only adds to the confusion.
3. Vertue's notes were bought by Sir Horace Walpole and used as a basis for his *Anecdotes of Painting in England*, London, 4 vols 1765-71. Vertue's notes on William Gandy are in the British Library Add MS 23072 f 21 v. They are also published by the Walpole Society.
4. Northcote *op. cit.*, pp.338-343
5. Pilkington, *op. cit.*, 1805 edit., p.208
6. Walter G. Strickland *A Dictionary of Irish Artists*. 2 vols, Dublin 1913, vol I p.394-5.
7. British Museum (BM) Add MS 23072 f 21 verso. Collins Baker actually misquotes this as 'Maubert had first lessons from him, [Gaspar Smith(z)] and from Gandy of Exeter when in London. Collins Baker *op cit*. p.63. That this quotation concerns William and not James can be gathered from the inclusion of Smitz and Maubert who were known to be in Dublin in the 1680s.
8. For explanation of Smitz' dates see Jane Fenlon, 'The Painter Stainers Companies of Dublin and London, Craftsmen and Artists, 1670-1740 in *New Perspectives*, ed. J Fenlon N Figgis, C Marshall, Dublin, 1987, note 22 p.108 also Pilkington *op. cit.*, 1805 edit., p.507.
9. Collins Baker *op. cit.*, p.59.
10. Northcote *op. cit.*, p 338.
11. No evidence of William Gandy's place or date of birth has yet been found. It is unlikely that William Gandy was born in Kilkenny as suggested by Ulrich Thieme and Felix Becker in their *General Encyclopaedia of Painters*, vol 13, Leipzig 1920 p.157. This is repeated in the *DNB* and in an exhibition catalogue *Sir Joshua Reynolds*, 250th Anniversary Exhibition, City Art Gallery Plymouth, England 1973.
12. British Museum Add. MS 22950.
13. See Mansfield Kirby Talley, *Portrait Painting in England: Studies in the technical literature before 1700*. Published privately Guildford 1981, pp.306-358. The main grounds for Talley's attribution to Gandy would seem to be the link between the father of the 'notes' author and Van Dyck. James Gandy's own link with Van Dyck is, as yet, based entirely on Pilkington's dictionary entry with no documented evidence to back it up. More conclusive evidence is required before this can be fully accepted. Also it does not seem that Talley can have read Northcote's account of William Gandy's fickle character and his later slovenly painting methods which cast serious doubt on his being the author of such painstaking notes on technique. There is also the question of Gandy's actual style which closely resembles work coming from the Wissing/Vandervaart studio, especially so during the latter part of the period when these 'notes' were being taken. No reference is made to either of these artists in the notes. Finally it seems unlikely that a professional painter such as William Gandy would still be interested in taking 'notes' of the sort described in Talley's chapter when he was about forty years of age (the date of the last entry being 1699).
14. Ellis Waterhouse, *The Dictionary of 16th & 17th Century British Painters*, Suffolk 1988 p.96. For the correct attribution of this portrait see Collins Baker *op. cit.*, p.62.
15. Waterhouse, *Dictionary op. cit.*, p.96 also makes the suggestion that William Gandy was apprenticed to his brother Thomas, a member of the Painter-Stainers Company of London. A Mr.Thomas Gandy, is listed in the Court Minute Books of the Painter-Stainers Company in London during the years 1675/76, however, there is no evidence, other than the shared surname, to link him with William.
16. Northcote *op. cit.*, p.339.
17. Strickland *op. cit.*, p.394-5
18. Anne Crookshank and the Knight of Glin, *Painters of Ireland*, London 1978, p.21. .
19. Jane Fenlon, 'French Influence in late Seventeenth Century Portraits, *GPA Irish Arts Review Yearbook* 1989-90, note 19 p.168.
20. See Fenlon, 'Painter Stainers ...' *op. cit.*, p.108, note 22.
21. The version now in the Maritime Museum in Greenwich, came from the Dingwall Collection. The other version, an oval, was in the Princess Royal Sale, Lot 126, Christie's 18th December 1931. There is a very poor engraving of this portrait which was produced by R. Dunkarton, (1744-after 1811) published by Woodburn 1815 and attributed to ?D. Loggan.
22. Another portrait of the same sitter has been attributed to this artist by Crookshank. See Anne Crookshank, 'Irish artists and their portraiture', *The Connoisseur*, December, 1969, pp.235-43 etc. This picture has a rather dry surface and lacks the painterly modelling evident in William Gandy's portraits. It seems closer to the work of Jan Vandervaart.
23. A copy of this portrait was made in 1925 and now hangs in Masonic Hall in Molesworth Street, Dublin.
24. Photograph in National Portrait Gallery, Photographic Archive, Orange Street, London., coll: G. Grimes, Alabama, U.S.A. The initials on this picture compare with those on the receipts and with the signature used on later portraits by William Gandy.
25. See Fenlon, 'French Influence in Late Seventeenth Century Portraits' *op. cit.*, p.161.
26. *Concise Catalogue of Oil Paintings in the National Maritime Museum*, Suffolk 1988. Catalogue No. BHC 2798. This portrait was engraved by John Smith after Largillière in 1685.
27. It may be that the ends of this wig have been cleaned off; a similar style of wig, with ends intact can be seen in the portrait of Daniel Ivie by William Gandy (whereabouts unknown). Photograph available in Witt Library, Courtauld Institute of Art. London.
28. Difficult to judge this portrait of an unknown lady, not seen, known only from photograph.
29. Attributed to James Gandy in Dr. W. G. Hoskins, *A New Survey of England*, Devon, p.483. This portrait hangs in St. James' Church, Swimbridge. Not examined, known only from photograph.
30. A portrait of this sitter attributed to Sir Anthony Van Dyck was hanging in the long gallery at Kilkenny Castle in 1684. There is as yet no evidence that William Gandy was ever in Kilkenny; this suggestion is based on the established link with the Butler family through the portrait of the second Duke of Ormonde.
31. Robin Simon, *The Portrait in Britain and America*, p.100, illustrated plate 26..
32. Northcote *op. cit.*, p.341.
33. *ibid.*, p.343.
34. Collins Baker *op. cit*, pp.61-62.
35. One must remember, however, that this portrait has been over cleaned and so a darker glaze may have been removed. The principal garment worn by Kendrick Fownes, for instance, is of a richer colour, which suggests a measure of over cleaning in the Stewart portrait.
36. Collins Baker, *op. cit.*, p.62.
37. The portrait of Ralph Allen has been examined; this is a doubtful attribution, the face is very hard and lacks any of the typical pencilling touches.
38. Northcote, *op. cit.*, p.343.
39. Collins Baker, *op. cit.*, p.62.
40. *Masters Matthew and Phillip Pear*, no. 1893.6.11, p.62, *Catalogue of Oil Paintings Watercolours, Drawings and Sculpture in the Permanent Collection*, 1978, Royal Albert Memorial Museum, Exeter.
41. Northcote, *op. cit.*, p.343, for his remarks on William Gandy's personality.

OLIVER HILL IN KILLINEY
AN IRISH VICTORIAN HOUSE REMODELLED

1. STRATHMORE, KILLINEY: *The Entrance Hall.* The influence of Lutyens is apparent in the rusticated doorcases. Now the home of the Canadian Ambassador, Strathmore was originally built in the 1860s to the designs of Alfred Gresham Jones. The interior was extensively remodelled by the English architect, Oliver Hill, in the 1940s.

Overlooking Killiney bay is a fine Victorian house called Strathmore, now the home of the Canadian Ambassador. The house was designed in the mid-1860s for Mr William Henry at a cost of £3,500 by Alfred Gresham Jones (1822-1915),[1] best known as the architect of the National Concert Hall, Dublin. It was a three-bay two-storey (over basement) house with tripartite windows and central entrance porch, and a fine conservatory to the left of the entrance front. The interior consisted of a dining room and drawing room on the south side, a salon opening from the drawing room on the east side, and a library opening out of the conservatory – a satisfactory arrangement of rooms for a comfortable Victorian lifestyle.

Simon Lincoln

documents the imposing interiors created at Strathmore in the 1940s

In 1946 Strathmore came into the possession of Sir Richard Brooks, Bart., who wanted to use the site for another house. Due to the lack of raw materials available at that time, however, he was unable to do this and instead satisfied himself with a remodelling of the existing house. An English architect, Oliver Hill (1887-1968),[2] was commissioned to carry out the plans. Hill, who was influenced by the work of Sir Edwin Lutyens (1869-1944) and the International Modern Style, had built up a large practice in the inter-war years in both domestic and commercial architecture. As an interior designer he created sumptuous interiors using materials like onyx, marble, gold and silver.

Hill's plans for the exterior of Strathmore included moving

OLIVER HILL IN KILLINEY: AN IRISH VICTORIAN HOUSE REMODELLED

2. STRATHMORE, KILLINEY: *View towards the Entrance Hall*. Hill created this long corridor, which runs the length of the house. With a barrel-vaulted ceiling and the walls forming a subtle recession of planes, the corridor is one of the most striking features of the house.

stone floor and to the left and right a drawing-room and dining-room respectively. The doorcases to these rooms are carried out in reconstituted Portland stone and come from a design by Batty Langley; but the influence of Lutyens' rusticated doorcases in the hall at Little Thakeham, Sussex of 1902 is also noticeable. The skirting and string courses are also of Portland stone.

By taking in some of the stables, a new dining-room was created with a domed ceiling and a bow window. A wall of mirrors opposite the windows reflected extra light and a round white marble dining table with fluted legs completed the decoration.[3] Opposite the front door are two arches, one of which leads to the service quarters; the other to a corridor which runs the length of the south side of the house and leads to the main staircase. This corridor has a barrel-vaulted ceiling and a stone floor and the walls form a subtle recession of planes. Hill joined the former drawing-room, entrance hall, and dining-room were together to form one large reception room replacing the dividing walls by Tuscan columnar screens in Portland stone placed very close to the wall, and a new bolection moulded chimneypiece with a plaque. These elements were used later by Hill at the Pavilion Coombe near Kingston, Surrey. The wooden floor is surrounded by a stone border which matches that of the hall. The plain coved ceiling is in three sections following the original shapes of the rooms. Two former doorcases at the end of the room were converted into niches and a pedimented doorcase gives access to the corridor beyond the drawing room; the library was extended and has a bay window and a vaulted ceiling in the style of Lutyens. The main staircase is a grand affair running around three sides of the stair-hall with a decorative wrought iron balustrade.

Strathmore was Hill's only executed Irish work[4] and his interiors there are among the most important examples of the period in Ireland.

the entrance front from the south to the east, and adding a fine new rusticated doorcase and steps. The windows were to have been replaced by tall casement windows with louvered shutters. However, with the exception of the new windows in the hall and external shutters on the east front, these proposals were not carried out. Instead a screen wall and loggia were added to the end of the south front with a central niche surrounded by an architectural framework inspired by Lutyens' design at Hestercombe, Somerset.

Hill's interior alterations were, on the other hand, mostly completed. The salon became the new hall, with a fine Portland

SIMON LINCOLN is on the staff of the Irish Architectural Archive.

ACKNOWLEDGEMENTS
I would like to thank the Canadian Ambassador and his staff for their kindness in allowing the Irish Architectural Archive to photograph Strathmore.

1. Alfred Gresham Jones Album. National Library of Ireland MS. 2006 T X.
2. See Alan Powers, *Oliver Hill, Architect and Lover of Life 1887-1968*, London, 1989.

3. The dining table is still at Strathmore, though now outside.
4. Hill's other Irish commission was for the rebuilding of Costello, Co Galway for Bruce Ismay in1926 though this was never carried out.

TIMOTHY TURNER
AN EIGHTEENTH-CENTURY DUBLIN IRONSMITH

Miriam O'Connor *has identified the maker of some elegant eighteenth-century wrought iron work*

1. STAIRCASE BALUSTRADE. *No 9 Henrietta Street, Dublin.* The house was designed by Sir Edward Lovett Pearce c.1730 and the design of the ironwork is similar to Turner's later work for Trinity College.

Ironsmiths by the name of Turner are recorded in Dublin since the seventeenth century. A William Turner provided ironwork for the Hospital in Oxmantown Green (that is, the old Blue-Coat School) in the 1670s. In the nineteenth century, Richard Turner of the Hammersmith Ironworks in Dublin was responsible for the famous Palm House in the Botanic Gardens of Dublin, Belfast and Kew. Documented work by Timothy Turner in the eighteenth-century can still be seen in Trinity College, Dublin, where, in the middle of the century he is one of the three people of that surname to be employed by the College as ironmonger.[1]

Timothy Turner's most easily identifiable surviving work at Trinity is generally large and of a very decorative nature. It includes the staircase balustrades in the Regent House, the Provost's House and Dining Hall (Fig. 2), together with a top-floor gallery front in the Provost's

2. Timothy TURNER (fl. 1743-66): *Iron balustrades of the Dining Hall staircase, Trinity College, Dublin.* The balustrades were delivered on 2 December 1765. The College accounts show that over a period of more than twenty years Turner supplied substantial quantities of ironwork to be used in the building of the Provost's House, Regent House, and the Dining Hall.

House, and scrollwork over its entrance gate on Grafton Street. Turner's work is among the finest eighteenth-century wrought iron to survive in the city.

The payments made to Timothy Turner by the College cover the period 1743 to 1766. From these we learn that his forge was capable of producing not only large-scale decorative pieces but also the screws and nuts and bolts, that were needed both as fixings for his large pieces and also as routine building components. He provided cramps for the masonry (at three pence per pound of iron); he charged two shillings and two pence. 'To a new key & altring [sic] a large stock lock'; he charged one shilling for two large hooks for hinges for a gate.[2] By far the greater part of his accounts were concerned with such day-to-day items.

The large-scale pieces date from the late 1750s and early 1760s. His final account from 1766 summarised his charges for work on the recent major building projects in the College: £1,459 4s. 4d. on Parliament Square, £455-4s.-11d on the Provost's House and £381 1s 1¹/₄d. on the Dining hall and Kitchen.[3]

Turner's documented staircase and landing balustrades in Trinity are composed – with the exception of those of the back stairs in the Provost's House – of scrolled balusters and occasional square panels. The designs of these are closely related to those of the balustrades in Edward Lovett Pearce's house at 9 Henrietta Street, Dublin of c.1730, one of the few earlier examples in the city of such work (Fig. 1). Characteristically he charged eighteen shillings and six pence for each baluster and for fixing it. He provided '59 Panells of neat scrold work' for the Regent House on 14 October 1761 (perhaps the surviving fifty-five balusters and the four parts of the large panel on the upper landing) (Fig 4), and the panels for the Dining Hall on 2 December 1765.[4] His account for the main staircase in the Provost's House dates from June 1763; the same account covers the balustrade surrounding the gallery on the top floor charged for in April 1762. For the square panels here he charged £2 15s. 6d. each. His account for the large decorative external grille to the staircase window – if it is his – has not been traced, but we know that on 20 July 1764 he provided 'a piece of Very large & Very neat scrold Work … over the front Gate' of the Provost's House.[6]

The very beautiful balustrade for the back staircase is also by Timothy Turner. This rises through all storeys of the house, the

3. William HUTCHINS (f.1758): *Iron gallery-front in the Chapel of the Rotunda Hospital, Dublin.* Hutchins supplied this ironwork in 1758: its similarity in style to the work of Turner suggests the possibility of a shared apprenticeship.

4. Timothy TURNER (fl.1743-66): *Iron balustrades of the Regent House staircase, Trinity College, Dublin.* Turner provided '59 panells of neat scrold work' on 14 October 1761: it is in his characteristically robust and decorative style.

simple shapes of its bars superbly accommodating the curved geometry of the space. On 19 December 1761 he charged £57 13s. 11d. for '223 Bellied Banisters & handrails & fix(in)g to the Back stairs' and £14 3s. 6d. for '6 Large Pillars w(i)th scrole work to support d(itt)o stair Case'.[7]

These simple and elegant uprights appear elsewhere: as area railings for Dublin houses and in the east wing at Russborough House, Co Kildare. This might tempt us to suggest an extension of Turner's oeuvre, particularly when we see mid-eighteenth century ironwork in the Rotunda Hospital in Dublin which, in staircase balustrade and chapel gallery front, repeats the patterns of Turner's Trinity College work (Fig. 3).

Interestingly, however, the Rotunda balustrades are the documented work of a different smith, WIlliam Hutchins, who, in 1758, was paid £42 3s. 2d. for the staircase balustrade and £79 4s. 0d. for the gallery front.[8] Were Hutchins and Turner repeating designs recalled from a shared apprenticeship or were they using the same pattern books? Whatever the explanation, we are warned against making quick attributions on the basis of style alone. The attribution to Turner of work on the back gate at Carton, Co Kildare or in a garden gate in St Patrick's College, Maynooth, or flanking the entrance to Newbridge House in Donabate, Co Dublin had better await the discovery of the relevant accounts.

MIRIAM O'CONNOR is researching eighteenth-century decorative wrought-iron work at Trinity College, Dublin.

1. Turner's accounts are in the Library, Trinity College, Dublin Manuscript Department (17 May 1756), Rebecca Turner was paid for ironmongery in 1756 and an account c. 1764 records a sum of £1,756 12s. 11d. paid to Timothy Turner and brother, MUN/P2/97 (16) & MUN/P2/132.
2. *Ibid.* (Nov. 1757 – July 1758) 'Ironmongers work done & Delivered for the use of the new Building at Trinity College by Tim Turner',

MUN/P2/116(1).
3. *Ibid.* (24 May 1766). MUN/P2/144.
4. *Ibid.* (July 1757 – April 1762). Ironmongers work done & delivered for the use of New Buildings Trinity College', MUN/P2/116/3a). (Mar 1764 – Dec 1765), 'Ironmongers work Done & Delivered for the New Hall and Kitchen at Trinity College', MUN/P2/138(44).
5. *Ibid.* Turner's account, December 1763 to July 1765: 'Ironmongers work done & Delivered for

the Provosts New House by Tim Turner', MUN/P2/135(11)).
6. *Ibid.* (Dec 1763 – July 1765), 'Ironmongers work done & Delivered for the Provosts New House by Tim Turner,' MUN/P2/138(45).
7. *Ibid.* (Mar 1759– Dec 1763), 'Ironmongers work done & Delivered for the use of the Provosts new house by Tim Turner', MUN/P2/135(11).
8. C P Curran, *The Rotunda Hospital, its architects and craftsmen,* Dublin, 1945, p.42.

An Irish Genius: J H De W Waller 1884-1968

Jeremy Williams *is fascinated by the extraordinary building inventions of*
James Hardress de Warrenne Waller

The acceptance by the Irish Architectural Archive of a photographic album documenting about five hundred Ctesiphon structures invented by the ingenious and neglected Irish engineer, J H de W Waller, and built across the world in one decade, 1943 to 1953, marks the first step in this country's recognition of his memory. His contemporaries were prepared to accept his brilliance as an engineer, but they failed to understand his obsession with transport, communications, self-help, unemployment and famine. Only in the emergency conditions of the two World Wars were his abilities readily appreciated, and apart from a short memoir written in 1982 by his assistant, Andrew Ross, and published privately, the one book that has mentioned him since his death, Mulroy's *Architecture of Aggression* (1973) illustrates only a demountable concrete tent devised for desert warfare and known as a Portable Patrick. There is no reference to him in the *Dictionary of National Biography* or in recent studies of Irish architecture. Three years ago a history of Locke's Distillery in Kilbeggan (by Andy Bielenberg, 1993), credited Waller's Ctesiphon warehouse there to an unknown young Trinity graduate, Jackson Owens, who was in reality Waller's assistant and T Burroughs, the architect of Waller's Ctesiphon Church of Christ the King in King's Weston, Bristol (1950) omitted all reference to their church in a history of Bristol architecture which he wrote a decade after it was constructed.

James Hardress de Warrenne Waller was the eleventh and youngest child of George Arthur Waller and Sarah, née Atkinson. His father was born heir to the family home, Prior Park near Nenagh – an Irish Palladian cube like the demolished Bowenscourt – but had left Ireland and a job as a brewer in Guinness's (procured through the mother being Augusta, daughter of Hosea Guinness, Chancellor of St Patrick's Cathedral in Dublin) to set up as a farmer in Tasmania. Here James was born and brought up. He was sent to school in Hobart and worked as a sheep-farmer in Australia and then as a miner back in Tasmania. He studied engineering first in Galway and then in Cork, going also to New York to study reinforced concrete. His first commission was to build a bridge across the Lee as an approach to his alma mater, Cork. His first job was as resident engineer on the (partially surviving) concrete bridge in Waterford. He formed a partnership in Dublin with a contemporary, Alfred Delap. He enlisted with the Corps of Royal Engineers at the outbreak of the First World War and was awarded a DSO and OBE. It was in Salonika that he started to study tents: observing one after it had been camouflaged with a coating of cement slurry instead of mud, he startled the inmates by removing the central post. This was to form the basis of his first studies in light-weight concrete and the invention of his Nofrango system. In Salonika he also built a jetty out of baskets filled with rocks, a system he never patented but which has been used widely since. He returned to England to marry Beatrice Kinkead, the daughter of a Galway medical professor. On his honeymoon he had the idea of a concrete battleship and persuaded the Admiralty to realise his project in Poole. His thousand tonne barge (178' long) the *Cretarch,* was successfully launched, but just before the Armistice and it ended up on a French inland waterway. With no further demand for ships, he was commissioned to construct a small housing estate in Poole that survives to this day; but a company set up to build houses throughout England in 'The Waller System' went bankrupt in 1921, snuffed out by the brick companies.

Shortly after this first commercial disaster, Waller was sent by the British Government to Iraq. Here he discovered the major architectural influence of his life: the banqueting hall of the sixth-century palace at Ctesiphon, the first inverted catenary

1. THE GREAT ARCH OF CTESIPHON. The banqueting hall of the sixth century palace at Ctesiphon in Iraq is the first inverted catenary vault ever devised. Waller's discovery of the building in the 1920s led to his own invention of a building technique which he named 'Ctesiphon'.

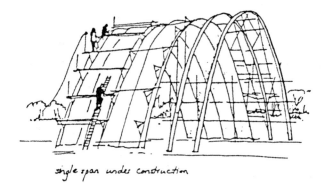

single span under construction

2. WALLER'S CTESIPHON BUILDING TECHNIQUE ILLUSTRATED. An inverted catenary arch (shaped on the basis of a curve formed by a chain hanging freely) was set up using temporary wooden ribs. This frame was then covered with hessian to which plaster or cement was applied to form the roofing. The technique permitted large areas to be covered without the inconvenience of supporting pillars.

AN IRISH GENIUS: J H DE W WALLER 1884-1968

vault ever devised (Fig. 1). Waller regarded its unknown constructor as his progenitor and named his system after the palace's unpronounceable name.

His next commission was to prove coincidentally logical: he was given the job of directing four thousand workmen building a railway across northern Spain linking the Bay of Biscay to the Mediterranean. Here he came into contact with the building tradition of the Sassanians, which, having been imported by the Moors, was still flourishing and inspiring, at that moment, Gaudi's final design for the Sagrida. At the same time he made friends that led to commissions forty years later from the Spanish company Iberlar – the only construction firm ever to perfectly execute his conceptions.

The money he made in Spain he promptly lost in Ireland on a bus company serving commuters from Clonmel to Dublin. This failure led him to concentrate on his engineering partnership based in Dublin and to codify his inventions, although he never lost his interest in transport: he published a study on the wear and tear of Asphalt. 'Coverbond', a new method of reinforcing concrete that he had devised in Salonika, was followed by a light-weight concrete system inspired by the slurry-covered tents

of Salonika that he christened 'Nofrango'. His initial experiment with this method was a chicken-house in his back garden; next was an entire street in Rialto commissioned by Dublin Corporation in 1928 of terraced two-storied housing that cost £330 per unit to build (Fig. 8). The street still exists in good condition, recognisable by the wide overhangs of their slightly sagging flat roofs. Like much of Waller's output the experiment was a success but was never repeated.

Only twice during Waller's professional practice in Ireland did he receive commissions that stretched his capabilities. The first was the pier at Foynes – he believed that the Shannon Estuary made the finest natural harbour in Western Europe – where he developed his experiment in constructing the pier at Stavros with hessian cylinders filled with concrete, extending his Nofrango techniques. The second commission, in Dublin, was the extension of Jacobs' factory as a multistoried Nofrango structure with wide spans and horizontal fenestration. The architect and builder of this project were brothers, George and Walter Beckett, who were part-time Methodist missionaries as well as being successful entrepreneurs and both neighbours in Foxrock (like their cousin Samuel). Walter became such an enthusiast

3. A CTESIPHON ROOF UNDER CONSTRUCTION. The workman is applying the liquid concrete or plaster to the hessian support which is draped betwen wooden arches. The weight of the concrete caused the hessian to sag which gave a corrugated appearance to the surface that was both pleasing and practical as it reinforced the strength of the shell.

for Nofrango that he commissioned a private house, presumably to his brother's design. This survives on Gordon Avenue but is now deprived of its Irish name *Teach Beag* (it is now known as *Balmoral*) and its concave Nofrango pitched roof. The Becketts were probably responsible for the staff quarters that Waller constructed at Rosapenna Hotel in North Donegal for the entrepreneurial Earl of Leitrim. This remains the core of the present hotel after its timber predecessor was destroyed by fire. The remainder of Waller's Irish works of this period were minor schemes for Manning Robertson, the most modest being a £225 house. The client was the writer C P Curran. Set on the mountains above Dublin at Ticknock, this survives along with two neighbours. Robertson also deployed Nofrango in two council estates: one in Carlow, the other in Wexford.

Waller's interest in cheap housing was linked to his concern for the unemployed, which at this time was increasing to crisis level. With Patrick Somerville-Large and Hugh Delap, his partner's son, he founded the Mount Street Club. Waller organised the renovation of a Georgian house, devised a currency known as a tally, acquired a farm to provide food and logs to provide fuel. But he was never able to weld the club into a building team. That had to await Waller's commissions in the Third World where survival was the crucial issue.

In 1939 survival was far more relevant in England than in Ireland. Waller tried to enlist at the declaration of war, was deemed too old, and instead decided to contribute to the war effort as an engineer working in London. Here, working in his Victoria Street offices disrupted by air raids, he was commissioned directly by his best clients, the War Office, to design portable huts, warehousing, and aircraft hangars. These did not have to be submitted to the scrutiny and scepticism of countless committees but instead had to be erected quickly by semi-skilled labour and had to be defensible and bomb resistant. In these conditions, using his Nofrango techniques, he reinterpreted the inverted catenary vaulting invented by the Sassanians which he had first encountered at Ctesiphon in Iraq.

His earliest non-military clients were farmers. The first was Alistair McGuckian who subsequently set up Masstock, the international company than has done so much to develop agriculture in the Middle East. A vaulted cattle shed, two hundred feet long, built without reinforcement in 1941 at Massarene, was demolished five years ago. His next Irish commission was an experimental farm east of Mallow for the Ballyclogh Cooperative. This survives but is much mutilated. The first sight of this cluster of parabolic vaulting set, not in the Arabian desert, but in the lush pastures of North Cork (the Irish counterpart to Hassan Fathy's contemporary village of Gourna in Karnak) must have been so startling that it had to be conventionalised; yet enough fragments remain to show how much we have lost.

This farm led to several untraced creameries and two garages in nearby Mallow for the Ford agent, William Thompson (Fig. 5). The earlier (1948) in Shortcastle was a single parabolic vault spanning sixty feet and springing from a concrete frame structure that served as a car showroom to the street. This was

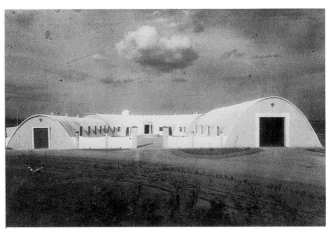

4. J H DE W WALLER (1884-1968): *Model farm Buildings, Spain.* Waller used the Nofrango principle in the construction of Ctesiphon buildings in many parts of Africa and Europe.

5. J H DE W WALLER: *Model of a garage building for W J Thompson in Mallow, Co Cork* (1948). The single parabolic vault had a span of sixty feet. Waller put the experience which he had gained in designing aircraft hangars and other military structures for the War Office during the Second World War to later use in industrial and commercial buildings such as this one.

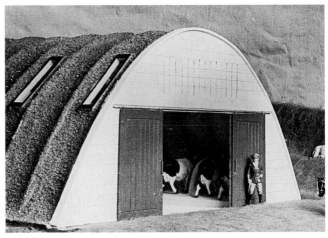

6. J H DE W WALLER: *Model for a Cow Shed.* This is probably one of the buildings for agriculture shown by Waller at the Spring Show. The model of the military-looking farmer at the entrance to the shed was probably one that had been used by Waller in the display of some of his military projects during the war.

topped in execution by a first floor administration block. The later garage (1951) on the Cork Road consisted of two adjoining parabolic vaults, one terminating in an apse. This has been demolished, a fate shared by many of his Irish commissions. The most ambitious of his agricultural structures of the time, built for Lord Dunraven at Adare Manor, partially collapsed during construction and was dismantled in secrecy. Also vanished are a precast concrete factory in Coleraine, warehousing in Waterford for Clover Meats and a golf club in Cootehill. This was for a chicken farmer, J P Gannon, who sponsored an exhibition of models at the RDS Spring Show of a Ctesiphon vault, summarily destroyed at the end of the show (Fig. 7). The models made by an assistant, A C Aston, no longer exist. The economy of Waller's system led to opposition from the building trade, spearheaded by the Plasterer's Union; and his next patrons were entrepreneurs taking advantage of the lack of organised labour on the African continent.

7. Display stand of Waller Buildings at the Royal Dublin Society's Spring Show. 1950s. The exhibition of Ctesiphon Buildings for Agriculture and Industry was sponsored by a Cavan chicken-farmer for whom Waller had designed a golf club.

Waller's surviving work in Ireland includes a modest apple store near Bray for his friend Patrick Somerville-Large, whose security was much tested by out of bound pupils of a local school – it was my own first experience of one of Waller's structures. Then there are several large agricultural structures built for Denis Baggaley at Grange near Trim and now owned by the state. His most significant commission, the Whiskey Bonded Warehouse for Locke's in Kilbeggan, is sited like a colossal congested black jelly fish on a small island. It still startles visitors who, emerging from a tour of Ireland's oldest distillery, come face to face with a possible Martian invasion. But after forty-five years it still performs its function.

The Seagram Chivas Distillery in Paisley was Waller's last Ctesiphon structure. Due to his fear that he would die and leave his wife penniless, he negotiated an agreement with Seagrams in Canada to sell the patent of his system for an annual pension transferable to his widow. This agreement was honoured by the company who used his system for their distillery but never deployed it again.

Waller retired to Devon where the album (now in the Irish Architectural Archive) was discovered twenty-five years after his death by his daughter, Beatrice Carfrae. The photographs record his Irish and English prototypes; the large factories built for Roberts in South Africa, for Taylor Woodrow in Nigeria, and Van den Bergh in Zimbabwe as well as further factories in Kenya and Tanganyika; village housing in the Belgian Congo, in Egypt and India (where Nehru is shown visiting the institute set up at Rorkree by Waller's erstwhile German partner, Dr Kurt Billig); models of accommodation for the Palestinian refugees presented to King Abdullah; experimental structures in Australia; and holiday villas, model farms and an airport designed by Julio Calderon de Guzman and Fernando Moreau Barbera in Spain. There are churches in Plymouth, Carmarthen, Bristol, Nigeria and Cyprus, where Waller also designed a grain store. Famine was his last great preoccupation and in his battle against hunger he transcended all divisions class, creed, race and state.

In 1993, a proposal for an exhibition devoted to Waller under the auspices of UNESCO failed to gain the necessary support of the Irish government and had to be abandoned; it is to be hoped that this decision will be reconsidered.

JEREMY WILLIAMS is author of A Companion Guide to Architecture in Ireland 1837-1921 *(Dublin 1994)*

8. J H De W Waller (1884-1968): *Housing scheme, Rialto, Dublin.* 1928. The scheme was part of an entire street, Loreto Avenue, which is still intact, commissioned by Dublin Corporation.

CHOOSING THE BATTLEGROUND
ROBERT BALLAGH'S PAINTINGS

Catherine Marshall *gives a critical account of the development of the career of the Dublin artist Robert Ballagh*

It's January 1995 and Robert Ballagh's studio is dominated by a large unfinished canvas temporarily placed in an arched frame (Fig. 17). Within this a painted stone archway, incised with the title *The Bogman*, reveals a full-length self-portrait of the artist digging a bank of turf. This is not the role we might expect for the Robert Ballagh who burst into the Irish art world in the late 1960s with the first pop art produced on this island and it is certainly not the picture of selfhood or Irishness which we might expect from someone who challenged the dominant image of Ireland as a country of thatched cottages, turf stacks and hungry-eyed, gaelic-speaking hurlers so familiar from the paintings of Paul Henry, Maurice McGonigal and Sean Keating.

Ballagh, born in Dublin in 1943 and educated there, was alienated by these images. 'I never had any access to the culture that many people think is the Irish culture, the rural Gaelic tradition. I can't paint Connemara fishermen … My experience of Ireland is an urban, Dublin one and I paint that. It would be dishonest of me to paint anything else. But being Dublin is being

Irish', he told John Stephenson in 1979.[1] Ballagh has had more reason than most people to define Irishness in visual terms. The Irish postage stamps he designed since the early 1970s (Fig. 15) provide an effective alternative picture of a more modern and pluralist society.

So why then the self-portrait as a bogman? This question is the first of many which arise out of the numerous paradoxes thrown up by Ballagh's art and the practice of it. When, in 1977 the Kilkenny Arts Festival Committee withdrew a piece of his work from a display of kites, Ballagh remarked, 'somehow you always get into these kinds of rows over works that are not all that important. The battleground is never of your own choosing'.[2]

Ballagh should know. In the almost thirty years since he started painting he has vigorously and consistently pursued a course which has brought him into conflict with those who favour traditional post-Renaissance approaches to art and art management.

Newcomers to a club usually show some deference to established members. Not so Robert Ballagh. His entry into Irish art

1. Robert BALLAGH (b. 1943): *The Third of May, after Goya.* 1969-70. Acrylic on canvas, 180 x 245cm. (Hugh Lane Municipal Gallery). Goya's picture commemorated the bloody massacre in Madrid by occupying French forces in 1808 and Ballagh intended that viewers would readily interpret his Pop version of Goya's original as a commentary on the Troubles in Ulster.

CHOOSING THE BATTLEGROUND: ROBERT BALLAGH'S PAINTINGS

2. Robert BALLAGH: *People and a Modern Painting.* 1975. Hand printed plastic laminate, 3 x 23m. (Clonmel Supermarket). Ballagh has always sought a wide audience for his work and, inspired by Marxist art theory, he has often chosen unconventional settings for his art as in the case of this mural in a supermarket.

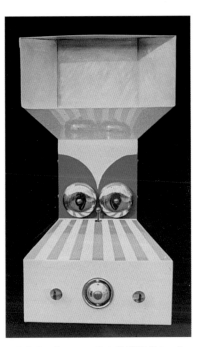

3. Robert BALLAGH: *Pinball.* 1967. Painted metal construction, 60 x 45cm. (The Artist's Collection). Shown at the Irish Exhibition of Living Art in 1967, this image demanded, and got, instant attention.

in 1967 with a *Pin Ball* (Fig. 3) machine and *Torso* made from aluminium at the Irish Exhibition of Living Art demanded, and got, instant attention. As clear Pop statements these works avoided both the academicism of the Royal Hibernian Academy and the abstract Cubist and Expressionist work of progressive artists like Micheal Farrell and Brian King. Within two years of this audacious beginning Ballagh abandoned Pop Art for directly political comments on emerging violence in Northern Ireland and socialist struggles in other parts of the world for which he felt a more realistic figurative style was appropriate. These works inevitably invited controversy as did his radical use of new materials and techniques.

One of his most earnestly pursued struggles has been to de-mystify art production. His paintings are the result of a disciplined work routine which would put a bank manager to shame. A visit to his studio reveals neat filing cabinets of research material for work in progress, photographs and sketches, an office desk and a squeaky swivel chair. The myth of the lonely genius, spattered

4. Robert BALLAGH: *Portrait of Gordon Lambert*, 1971. Acrylic and silkscreen on canvas, 180 x 90cm. (Gordon Lambert Collection, IMMA). Lambert, who was one of the artist's earliest and most important patrons, assembled a distinguished collection of Irish and international contemporary art that was to form the nucleus of the Irish Museum of Modern Art to which he presented it as a gift.

with paint and feverishly driven by his own angst, is not for him. Instead, Ballagh's model for himself is the journeyman artist of the medieval craft system who serves his community, as other craft workers do, in a variety of mutually agreed tasks. Just as Van Eyck and his contemporaries gilded religious statuary, designed jewellery, painted objects from pictures to furniture and horses' harness, so Robert Ballagh designs postage stamps, street tableaux, and fund-raising prints for the local national school in addition to more conventional easel paintings.

While most artists work within the gallery system, Ballagh seeks a wider audience. He takes his cue, not so much from established art practice as from Marxist art theory. In *The Work of Art in the Age of Mechanical Reproduction*, Walter Benjamin called on artists to become truly political and to use reproduction technology to create for a mass audience.' Ballagh set out to do this in a variety of ways, for a multiplicity of venues, painting conventionally 'unique' murals in unconventional settings such as those for a

CHOOSING THE BATTLEGROUND: ROBERT BALLAGH'S PAINTINGS

5. Robert BALLAGH: *Inside No 3.* 1979. Oil on canvas, 180 x 180cm. (Ulster Museum, Belfast). With a stated intention of reversing the usual model for male/female relationships, the artist has painted a beautiful female nude who is looking at her husband on television.

Clonmel supermarket (Fig. 2), a set of oil paintings to be projected on to a screen as a stage backdrop to Riverdance at the Point Theatre, posters for the Irish Ballet Company, portraits which are popularized as book-covers, and most widely known and used of all, the newest set of Irish banknotes (Fig. 16), several of which are already in use.

One of the most light-hearted and enjoyable expressions of his

ardent wish to bring art out of the gallery and into people's lives was his project for the Irish Architectural Archive. In this, a limited number of incompleted black and white prints by Ballagh were sent out to well-known people who were invited to construct their *Dream House* around Ballagh's partial drawing. The picture completed by them was then offered for sale on behalf of the Archive. The spectator is forced to interact with the artwork

CHOOSING THE BATTLEGROUND: ROBERT BALLAGH'S PAINTINGS

in another of Ballagh's prints, this time in a more unsettling manner – he made prints of prison windows seen from inside on mirror glass so that the viewer confronts her/his own reflection through the bars. The image thus created is both comic and disturbing, forcing the viewer to consider loss of freedom in a very personal way while at the same time becoming part of the art work, completing it for the artist. Ballagh's irreverence here embraces the world of art and that of the viewer; the material used is unusual in high art, reminiscent of bar-room mirrors, while the breakdown in the traditional artist/public relationship reasserts the artist's political aim.

The idea of usable art is very central to Robert Ballagh's aesthetic. For this reason he particularly likes to work to commissions. 'People need to realise that using art is not something esoteric or unusual. That's still a bridge we must cross in Ireland'.[4] While this does not pose problems for the general public it opens up a different and more insidious battleground for the artist and those purists who espouse an art for art's sake philosophy. Working to a client's specifications and for money is a denial of the Romantic image of the artist – a strong one in Ireland ever since James Barry renounced all payment in return for the honour of painting a scheme of his own devising for the Society of Arts in London. To those, and there are many, who accuse him of compromising too much for financial reward, Ballagh's response is that the alternative process – complete dependence on commercial galleries for sales – leads to elitism, and isolates the artist from the wider community.

Despite Ballagh's auspicious beginning as a pop artist at the IELA, Rosc and *The Irish Imagination* exhibitions, most people think of him as an academic

artist, inheriting the mantle of Orpen, Keating and Edward Maguire. This is at once both ironic and complimentary: ironic, because 'academic' implies adherence to a set of rules, yet the only rule Ballagh acknowledges is truth to Modernist design principles. It also presupposes a certain kind of training based on drawing from the model which Robert Ballagh did not have. It is complimentary because those who consider him academic do so on the grounds of his superlative technique. They are amazed that this was self-taught.

Ballagh never went to art school although he spent three years studying architecture in Bolton Street College of Technology. His teacher there, Robin Walker, who had recently returned from America, attached particular importance to the Miesian principles of good design based on a happy alliance of form and function; he also insisted on the integrity of the materials. Ballagh's subsequent career has been profoundly influenced by these two principles. 'I design a painting' the way an architect designs ... and then I build it up'.[5] The years in Bolton Street have been useful to Ballagh in another way. They encouraged his innate interest in problem solving, helping him to find solutions, in his early commissions, for the shortcomings in his art training. In 1967 he spent some weeks working with Micheal Farrell on Farrell's large abstract, hard-edge paintings for the National Bank (now the Bank of Ireland) in Suffolk Street in Dublin. This introduced him to masking tape and acrylic paints. It was from Farrell, too, that Ballagh learned to use a badger brush, invaluable for creating special decorative effects such as marble, wood grain or the channels between the sods of turf in *The Bogman*.

6. Robert BALLAGH: *Upstairs No 3*, 1982-83. Oil on canvas, 180 x 180cm. (The Artist's Collection). The semi-nude artist ascends to the bedroom where his wife awaits him but their intimacy is negated by such details as the surveillance helicopter, his awareness of the spectator, and above all, the circular format of the picture which suggests a voyeur's spyhole.

7. Robert BALLAGH: *Portrait of Dr Noel Browne*. 1985. Oil on canvas with stones and books, 180 x 137cm. (National Gallery of Ireland). Browne was an inspired and courageous Minister for Health (much admired by Ballagh) who fought for the eradication of TB and whose celebrated Mother and Child scheme led him into confrontation with the Catholic Church.

8. Robert BALLAGH: *Homage to Albrecht Dürer*. 1984. Oil on canvas, 60 x 120cm. (Albrecht Dürer House, Nuremberg). This picture was commissioned by the Dürer House in response to Ballagh's similarly inspired painting of Vermeer, called *The Conversation*.

9. Robert BALLAGH: *My Studio 1969* (Study for a larger painting). 1976. Oil and acrylic on canvas, 60 x 90cm. (Private Collection). When Ballagh's political paintings (see (Fig. 1) failed to make the impact he desired, the artist revived the theme in this canvas where his *Homage to Delacroix's Liberty Storming the Barricades* is shown in the background with a newspaper headline 'Derry' in the foreground.

CHOOSING THE BATTLEGROUND: ROBERT BALLAGH'S PAINTINGS

10. Robert BALLAGH: *In the heart of the Hibernian Metropolis.* 1988. Oil on canvas, 60 x 80cm. (Private Collection, Holland). Ballagh depicts himself as Stephen Dedalus strolling with James Joyce through an historic view of O'Connell Street, Dublin. 'My experience of Ireland is an urban, Dublin one, I paint that …' he is quoted as saying.

Something more fundamental, however, was needed to compensate for his lack of basic training.

Since the early 1970s Ballagh's work has been completely figurative, in keeping with his commitment to the Marxist aesthetic of involvement with the wider society and his desire to communicate with a mass audience. This posed particular problems for him as he had no training in anatomy or in painting from the live model. Initially Ballagh overcame this by using photographs silk-screened on to canvas, as in his *Marching Workers* series or his portrait of Gordon Lambert (Fig. 4) In this picture Ballagh, the pragmatist, breaks all the academic rules by combining three different methods of image-making: a silk-screened photographic portrait is teamed with a painted replica of an Albers painting which Lambert owns, held by hands which were

11. Robert BALLAGH: *The History Lesson.* 1989. Oil on canvas, 120 x 120 x 120cm. (The Artist's Collection). In an amusing self-portrait, the artist depicts himself as undecided between the teachings of Pearse and Connolly.

cast for Ballagh by Brian King. There is no frame and no background, instead the portrait has all the immediacy of an advertising cut-out, reminiscent of pop art. Ballagh's limitations as a painter of the human figure were speedily overcome by hard work, but his portrait practice remains heavily dependent on the camera. Clients are never asked to pose for long periods in his studio while he sketches as he feels that they will not be able to relax in this artificial environment. Instead Ballagh works from photographs of the sitter in his/her customary ambience, using these and basic information about the client's interests and life as a basis for a finished portrait. The variety of techniques and materials involved in the Gordon Lambert portrait is indicative of Ballagh's irreverent approach to traditional methods of picture making.

Ballagh received no formal instruction in the handling of paint

CHOOSING THE BATTLEGROUND: ROBERT BALLAGH'S PAINTINGS

12. Robert BALLAGH: *Portrait of Bernadette Greevy*. 1979. Oil on canvas with recorded sound, 120 x 120cm. (Gordon Lambert Collection, IMMA). In this portrait of one of the leading Irish singers of our time, he depicts her in a photograph surrounded by mementoes of her art. Incorporated in the portrait is a tape of the singer's voice which is triggered by any sound made by the viewer.

13. Robert Ballagh, Bernadette Greevy and David Hendriks with the portrait of Bernadette Greevy at the Hendriks Gallery, 20 September 1979. David Hendriks was an inspirational figure in the contemporary art world in Ireland for many decades and his Gallery, where Ballagh showed from the time he burst on the scene in the late 1960s, was the most important contemporary exhibition space in Ireland.

either. This, he feels is the most significant difference between his painting and those that he considers academic. Most other artists paint *alla prima*, that is, wet paint into wet paint, glorying as Patrick Graham and Mick Cullen do, in the sensuous qualities of the paint itself. When Ballagh switched from the use of acrylics to oil paint in the 1970s, he developed a method similar to that employed by Jan Van Eyck, applying paint slowly in thin layers interwoven with glazes to give the finished product a smooth and brilliant surface like polished glass. The integrity of this surface is never disturbed by obvious signs of brushwork, an obsessive attempt to remove evidence of a personal style. In this Ballagh resembles one of his heroes, Vermeer. Vermeer used a *camera obscura* in order to achieve greater fidelity to the retinal image and maximum objectivity. For similar reasons Ballagh enjoys using mechanically produced images, readily exposing himself to petty allegations that he is only painting by numbers.

14. Robert BALLAGH: *Portrait of Oscar Wilde*. 1990. Oil on canvas, 90 x 60cm. (The Gate Theatre, Dublin). In this recent portrait Ballagh moves away from the stereotyped images of Wilde although at the same time he uses a William Morris backdrop, the design of which is synonymous with the Aesthetic Movement of which Wilde was an exponent.

Ironically while Ballagh censors traces of his facture he paradoxically presents himself, his family, his house and his work as subject matter in his art. 'The artist is of necessity an exhibitionist', Gerry Dukes said in an essay on Ballagh's designs for the theatre.[6] Ballagh has always been a brilliant self-publicist. Nowhere was this more evident than in his gesture in response to the Bloody Sunday shootings in Derry in 1972. Unwilling to make money out of such a horrific event he made chalk outlines of bodies, smeared with blood, on the floor of Dublin's Project Arts Centre. The blood and chalk disappeared within a few hours, carried away on the feet of those who attended the opening but Ballagh got widespread publicity. His stand on Northern Ireland and republican nationalism has also received much media attention, largely because of his openly partisan approach. There is considerable naivety in the artist's disclaimer that he abhors all violence while sharing political platforms with those who condone it.

Ballagh admits that it was also naivety on his part which led him to expect that viewers would readily interpret his 'pop' versions of Goya's 'Third of May' (Fig. 1), David's 'Intervention of the Sabine Women'[7] and Delacroix's 'Liberty Storming the Barricades' (Fig. 9) as commentaries on the troubles in Ulster in 1969. When critics failed to make the connection, Ballagh issued a pamphlet clarifying his intention. He was forbidden to distribute these when the pictures were exhibited at the Hugh Lane Minicipal Gallery. In typical Ballagh fashion he refused to abandon the subject. Six years later he painted 'My Studio 1969', (Fig 9) in which he shows his workplace and the tools of his trade – immaculately clean brushes, masking tape and paint, but the claustrophobic space is dominated by his version of Delacroix's Liberty, while a picture of the original and a newspaper headline referring to Derry make its significance clear.

A similar charge of naivety can be levelled at Ballagh's handling of another of the hallowed genres of art history, the nude. As late as 1971 Brian O'Doherty remarked on the paucity of nudes in Irish art.[8] Ballagh may or may not have been responding to this when in 1976 he painted a screen for Gordon Lambert with a full-length female nude obligingly undressing for Lambert on the other side. Despite Ballagh's championship

of civil rights causes, there is no indication here that the artist was aware of growing feminist demands for equality.

More seriously, in 1979 and 1981, following a reading of John Berger's Ways of Seeing,[9] he painted two pictures Inside No.3 (Fig 5) and Upstairs, No.3 (Fig 6) respectively, in which his stated intention was to reverse the usual model for male/female relationships in western art. However, far from challenging the stereotype of woman as property, Inside No. 3 presents a beautiful but faceless nude, her body available but her face turned away from the viewer. We see her through his eyes as she looks towards her husband's face on the television screen in a room filled with objects associated with his life, his guitar case, his 'Liberty' on the wall. In 'Upstairs, No. 3' the roles appear to be reversed but with important modifications. The semi-nude artist ascends the stairs to the bedroom where his wife awaits him but their intimacy, suggested by her erotic book, is negated by the surveillance helicopter seen through the open curtains on the window, by his anxious gaze towards the viewer and by the circular format of the picture which suggests a voyeur's spyhole.

Ballagh's Homage to Albrecht Dürer, (Fig 8) a reiteration of western art's traditional manipulation of the female body, casts

15. Robert BALLAGH: *Irish Postage Stamps.* The artist is recognised as particularly gifted in the small scale design required for postage stamps and since the 1970's has produced many successful and renowned designs that have been used by the Irish Post Office.

16. Robert BALLAGH: *Irish Bank Notes.* 1993. Ballagh won the commission for the design of a new £20 note (to feature a portrait of Daniel O'Connell) in competition with other designers and has since designed the series of Irish banknotes that are currently in use.

CHOOSING THE BATTLEGROUND: ROBERT BALLAGH'S PAINTINGS

doubts on the sincerity of his political stance or at least intimates that a re-reading of John Berger might be in order.

Ballagh's work is altogether more successful in the public domain. His portraits of politicians can be double-edged; watch out for the ironic difference between the constructed media image and the 'real' man. Among well-known public figures painted by him, those of Bernadette Greevy (Fig. 12) and Hugh Leonard are marvellous examples of Ballagh's commissioned work. In keeping with his regular practice, he sought them out in their natural environment instead of in his studio, adding taped music which comes into play when the spectator approaches in the Greevy portrait and representing her public persona through a variety of media images including record sleeves and cassette covers rather than a conventional portrait.

The *Portrait of Dr. Noel Browne* (Fig 7) was uncommissioned and is one of Robert Ballagh's personal favourites. Painted in 1985, it shows Ballagh at his best; his style has matured but his principles have not changed. The unusual but symbolic cruciform format is reminiscent of his early portrait of Gordon Lambert in which the traditional frame has been cut away, while the little heap of stones and books which spill onto the floor continue to stress the connection between art and life which Ballagh has always advocated.

In 1995 Ballagh remains the creature of paradoxes he was at the outset, the rebel who takes awkward stands on political issues has become the 'official' artist of the state, designing stamps and currency, the untrained pragmatist who uses new technology and new methods is seen by many as the most academic, the rebel of the 1960s has become an establishment figure without relinquishing, to any degree, his independence.

With his *Self-portrait as The Bogman* one of his initial conflicts has been resolved. An Irish proverb, carved into the simulated stone archway reads 'Briseann an duchas tri shuile an chait'. A

17. The Artist in his studio at work on *The Bogman*, 1995. The picture is a self-portrait cutting turf. 'A visit to his studio reveals neat filing cabinets of research material for work in progress, photographs and sketches: the myth of the lonely genius is not for him'.

less poetic but more graphic equivalent of this in English is 'You can take the man out of the bog but you can't take the bog out of the man'. Ballagh, the city man, the Stephen Dedaelus to Joyce's Bloom in *In the Heart of the Hibernian Metropolis* (Fig. 10) has been reconciled to his ancestral roots, but the spade he digs with is pristinely new and the sods of turf he cuts are architecturally precise.

CATHERINE MARSHALL is Curator of Collections at the Irish Museum of Modern Art.

ACKNOWLEDGMENTS

I would like to thank Robert Ballagh for the patience and humour with which he replied to my many questions.

1. John Stephenson, *A Sense of Ireland*, 1979, p.50.
2. Ciaran Carty, *Robert Ballagh; A Biography*, Magill, 1986, p.134.
3. Walter Benjamin, 'The work of Art in the Age of Mechanical Reproduction', in *Illuminations*, 1977.
4. Carty, *op cit*, p.120.
5. Brian O'Doherty, *The Irish Imagination*, Exhibition Cat., Dublin, 1971, Cat. entry by

Hayden Murphy, p.36.
6. Gerry Dukes, *From Page to Stage; The Set Design of Robert Ballagh*. Cat. of Retrospective Exhibition of Robert Ballagh, Arnott's Henry St. Dublin, 1992.
7. David's *The Intervention of the Sabine Women*, first exhibited in the artist's studio in 1799 has been incorrectly entitled *The Rape of the Sabines* in Ballagh's version of it. See *The Rape of the*

Sabines after David, by Robert Ballagh, Crawford Municipal Gallery, Cork, also Cat. of Robert Ballagh, exhibition at Lunds 1883, Carty, *op cit* p.218.
8. Brian O'Doherty, *The Irish Imagination*, 1971, Introduction.
9. John Berger, *Ways of Seeing*, London, 1972.

Couture for a Countess
Lady Rosse's Wardrobe

The Irish fashion industry benefited from the late Countess of Rosse's unique sense of style, writes **Robert O'Byrne**

It is indicative of both the relative novelty and modest scale of the Irish fashion industry that few efforts have been made to investigate its history or even to develop any substantial collection of twentieth-century costume in this country. Indeed, outside the Ulster Museum's impressive assemblage of clothing – the result of a twenty-year-old policy initiated by the institution's Elizabeth McCrum – probably the most important single collection in Ireland is the legacy of one woman, the late Anne, Countess of Rosse who died in 1992.

Anne Rosse's highly-refined visual sense, as expressed through her interest in fashion along with a number of other fields such as interior decoration and garden design, must be considered at least in part an inherited family trait. Born in 1902, she was the middle child and only daughter of Maud and Lieutenant Colonel Leonard Messel. Her paternal forebears were Jewish bankers from Darmstadt in Germany who had acted as advisors to the Grand Dukes of Hesse. The London stockbroking firm of L Messel & Co was founded by her grandfather, Ludwig Messel, following his move to England.

At his country home, Nymans in Staplefield, Sussex, he created a series of outstanding gardens. Subsequently bequeathed by Leonard Messel to the National Trust which maintains them still, these presumably helped inspire Anne Rosse's own enthusiasm for gardening, the results of which can be seen in the demesne of her home, Birr Castle, Co Offaly.

Maud Messel was a talented draughtswoman who began contributing sketches to *Punch* at the age of fifteen. Her father, Edward Linley Sambourne, one of the best-known artists and illustrators of his generation, had taken over from Tenniel as political cartoonist in *Punch*. He also created the famous series of illustrations for Charles Kingsley's *The Water Babies*. The Linley Sambourne home in London's Stafford Terrace – a perfectly-preserved example of late-nineteenth-century interior design now in the care of the Victorian Society and much used for films such as Merchant-Ivory's *A Room with a View* – is filled with pictures and

2. Anne ARMSTRONG-JONES, later Lady ROSSE. Photographed by Cecil Beaton in 1933. She is wearing a bias-cut dress made by Charles James.

china from the period. Maud and Leonard Messel were, in turn, friendly with many artists, most notably the English portraitist, Glyn Philpot, who painted their daughter's picture in 1913.

Given such antecedents, it is hardly surprising that, from her earliest years, Anne Rosse displayed creative skills which were encouraged by her family. Contributing to a posthumous biography of her younger brother, theatre designer Oliver Messel, she wrote that 'there were months when we had to be in bed. We both had a bit of tuberculosis ... and that was when we made so much with our hands. We'd sit up in bed making things: little maquettes, perhaps a chapel, little candlesticks, altars and satiny bishop, all dressed up, because we both loved sewing.'

Anne Rosse never lost her passion for sewing. Among the collection of dresses now in Birr Castle is a yellow taffeta ballgown she made for her daughter Susan Armstrong-Jones (subsequently Viscountess de Vesci) to wear at Buckingham Palace in the 1950s. The present Earl of Rosse recalls that even in her later years when his mother retired to her bedroom every afternoon, ostensibly to rest, 'she'd actually be spending the time sewing something.' Such was her ability as a needlewoman that when Oliver Messel was beginning his career in the 1920s she often worked closely with him. All the costumes he designed for the successful 1929 Charles B Cochran revue *Wake Up and Dream*, for example, were made by his sister.

This understanding of how clothes are constructed clearly informed Anne Rosse's own personal taste. In an interview from 1963, the Irish designer Irene Gilbert commented that, of all her clients, the Countess of Rosse demonstrated the best imagination for clothes. 'She is never slow to disagree with me, but I always welcome it because she is a woman of exceptional talent with a needle. When I make something for her, it combines the best of our ideas.'

Anne Rosse's intense interest in her clothes is also noted by her son from her first marriage, the Earl of Snowdon, who says that 'unlike nowadays when people just go off and buy clothes from a particular designer, she was *totally* involved in anything made for her. She could – and did – add a lot.'

It helped, of course, that Anne Rosse was a woman of

1. *(Opposite)* BALL GOWN. Designed by Irene Gilbert in 1948. Scarlet taffeta. Following her marriage to the Earl of Rosse in 1935, Anne Rosse began to patronise Irish designers favouring particularly Irene GIlbert from whom she bought most of her clothes in the post-war years.

3. EVENING DRESS. Made by Irene Gilbert in 1969. Flesh coloured silk embroidered with sequins. This is the last Irene Gilbert commission and is exceptional in that Lady Rosse generally favoured bright, positive colours.

4. BALL GOWN. Made by Irene Gilbert, probably late 1950s. Black net over-sewn with bands of blue daisies. Lady Rosse liked to emphasise her figure with clothes that were closely fitted.

exceptional good looks – both Evelyn Waugh and James Lees-Milne in their respective published diaries commented on her extraordinary resemblance to the late Vivien Leigh – whose figure never changed from a size ten. 'She never lost her very good figure, don't forget,' points out Lord Snowdon. 'And being Oliver Messel's sister, she'd been used to standing as a model.' However, regardless of circumstances, she made a point of taking immense trouble over her appearance at all times. 'It was an art form for her,' believes her daughter-in-law Alison, the present Countess of Rosse. 'Everything had to be just perfect.'

This is borne out by Margaret Shortt who first came to work at Birr Castle in 1945, eventually becoming Anne Rosse's lady's maid. 'She was very, very particular,' explains Mrs Shortt, who estimates that dressing for the day took on average two hours because 'everything had to be right.' Although 'she really loved dressing up for evenings and special occasions,' there was never a time when standards were allowed to drop. She would, says Lord Snowdon, 'always dress for the occasion, even if it were just going to church. She'd always dress up like mad, because she thought she should. She did take tremendous trouble and make an effort to look nice.' His half-brother Lord Rosse points out that even when gardening, she would still be immaculately dressed, often wearing jewellery such as her five favourite diamond brooches

5. DRESS AND COAT. Designed by Victor Stiebel in 1960; the hat by Simone Mirman. White silk brocade. This is the outfit worn by Lady Rosse to the wedding of her son, Anthony Armstrong-Jones, to Princess Margaret. 'The coat had a beautiful black mink collar which I could not afford to buy,' she recalled.

6. *(Opposite)*. EVENING DRESS. Designed by Irene Gilbert, date unknown. Printed brown silk. Lady Rosse was herself a gifted needlewoman and Irene Gilbert recalled that 'she was never slow to disagree with me, but I always welcome it as she is a woman of exceptional talent with a needle'.

made in the shape of stars. Lord Snowdon recalls that on one occasion in London she pinned these to the back of her coat with the comment that 'it'll be rather nice for other people to see them when I'm talking to someone else.' This reminiscence highlights Anne Rosse's disregard for strict conformity in matters of dress. Confident of her own judgement, 'she had no great reverence for fashion,' insists Lord Snowdon. Similarly, the present Earl of Rosse believes that 'a lot of her things were incredibly daring for the time – no one else would have worn them.' Certainly she was exceptionally prescient in her taste, patronising designers before they became well-known, such as Anglo-American Charles James whose clothes she bought in the 1930s when he worked in London. It has been reported that, James's dresses being notoriously difficult to wear, she would on occasion allow herself to be sewn into one of his designs and then unstitched again at the end of the day.

For a 1982 exhibition catalogue dedicated to Charles James's work, Anne Rosse contributed a short essay in which she wrote that 'the wearer, if she wanted to enjoy his creations, had sometimes to be sacrificed for the designs. To begin with there could be a mystery as to how to get into the clothes when they arrived!' This is borne out by a note in her hand-writing pinned to a dark green evening dress now at Birr. 'Always hell to wear,' this says, adding 'never sure which way to swing it. Typical Charlie James – but when right looked too chic.'

Following her marriage to Michael, sixth Earl of Rosse in 1935, Anne Rosse began to patronise Irish designers, in particular

9. BALL GOWN. Made by Anne Rosse for her daughter Susan Armstrong-Jones. Presumed to date from 1948. Yellow taffeta. Lady Rosse's love of sewing derived from a childhood when she and her brother Oliver Messel (who shared her passion for sewing) spent months in bed as both suffered delicate health.

10. FANCY-DRESS COSTUME. Made by Anne Rosse and presumed to date from the 1930s. In the 1920s and 1930s Lady Rosse and her brother Oliver Messel were famous for the elaborate costumes they made and wore to fancy dress parties.

8. COCKTAIL ENSEMBLE. Designed by Irene Gilbert in the early 1960s. Dress of purple satin covered in black net, with black and purple net hat, and purple satin double-breasted swing coat. Lady Rosse's favourite jewels, visible in almost all photographs of her, were five diamond star brooches.

7. (*Opposite*) EVENING DRESS. Designed by Charles James in 1939. Pink organdie and multi-coloured ribbon. Anne Rosse patronised the Anglo-American designer Charles James, whose clothes were notoriously difficult to wear, before he became well-known. 'To begin with there could be a mystery as to how to get into them when they arrived,' she commented.

11. SUIT. Made in the 1950s and probably designed by Anne Rosse. Red Wool. This is the suit made from wool which Lady Rosse saw drying on the rocks of Connemara. She had it dyed red and wore the suit with red laced shoes and red ribbed stockings.

12. DAY DRESS. Made by Ib Jorgensen, date unknown. Taupe-coloured silk chiffon. Apart from Irene Gilbert, Lady Rosse also patronised other Irish designers such as Sybil Connolly and Ib Jorgensen.

Irene Gilbert from whom she bought the great majority of her clothes in the post-war decades. 'She was always especially pleased with the work of Irene Gilbert,' confirms Lord Rosse. Her interest in promoting Irish fashion is confirmed by designer Pat Crowley who began her career in the late 1950s working for Gilbert. Ms Crowley agrees that Anne Rosse was 'totally involved' in everything she ordered, adding that 'she was always trying to help fashion in this fashion.' Similarly Sybil Connolly, who made one of her famous pleated linen dresses for the Countess, recalls, not just that she was 'terribly fussy about details' but also 'very keen that her clothes be made here.' Sybil Connolly describes Anne Rosse as 'ultra-feminine at all times; she had a touch of the theatrical about her.' It's undeniable that, like her brother Oliver Messel, she loved making the grand dramatic statement. In the 1920s and 30s they were both famous for the elaborate costumes they made and wore to fancy-dress parties. 'She loved being noticed,' confirms the Earl of Snowdon. 'She'd have been furious if people hadn't seen what she was wearing – and they always did.'

One way of ensuring that she would make an impact was to dress in bright tones. 'I don't think she'd have been very good in anaemic colours,' says Lord Snowdon. Equally she liked to emphasise her good figure by wearing clothes which were closely-fitted. 'If a thing wasn't properly fitting everywhere,' remembers Margaret Shortt, 'she'd just chuck it aside and say "that's no good." She had a most wonderful figure and had her clothes made to show it off.' Pat Crowley, who travelled to Birr on behalf of Irene Gilbert, confirms that 'the fittings were important for her. She always had fitted bodices and dresses built close to the body.'

Despite her fondness for grand evening dress, Anne Rosse did not constantly feel obliged to spend large sums of money on clothing. 'She'd shop at C&A on Kensington High Street, buy some quite ordinary cheap suit and then add an extraordinary fringe which completely transformed it,' explained Lord Snowdon. 'She tested what she called "good taste" all the time.' Obviously her talent with the needle and her experience of making

13. DAY DRESS. Designed by Charles James in 1938. Silk with Snow-White print. Lady Rosse, who loved dressing up, even for the simplest occasions, took immense trouble over her appearance at all times.

COUTURE FOR A COUNTESS: LADY ROSSE'S WARDROBE

14. *A collage of press photographs of Lady Rosse taken in the 1960s and 70s.*

theatrical costumes greatly helped, but in addition, Anne Rosse could see the potential in items which might have been overlooked by others.

On one occasion, for example, while motoring through Connemara; she saw woven wool drying on the rocks of the seashore, according to Margaret Shortt, 'she stopped the car and went to speak to the man in charge and said she would like to buy it. She bought the wool and had it dyed red. She had it made up into very smart suit which she used to wear with lovely red laced shoes, red silk head scarf, red blouse and red ribbed stockings.'

Mrs Shortt says that a 1948 Irene Gilbert-designed scarlet taffeta evening dress with cross-laced bodice was made 'so that she would wear and show off her lovely rubies.' Nothing was left to chance. As Lord Rosse explains, 'my mother always thought of what she wore as an ensemble – not just a dress but equally the hat, shoes and jewellery. That's really what she was so good at.'

The care Anne Rosse took over her appearance is evident in the careful preservation of her clothes over more than five decades. 'She was very particular, even with little things like gloves.' Many of the clothes now conserved at Birr carry hand-written notes recording their provenance. Others are tagged with personal reminiscences, one box being captioned with the description 'madly pretty.' 'Darling Michael loved me in this dress,' says the sheet attached to a cream and blue Schiaparelli dress from 1935, 'when I wore it mostly on my honeymoon.' Similarly, a Charles James dress carries the message 'had a *wonderful* time in this I'm ashamed to say – 1941!!'

Most detailed of all is the information attached to the ensemble Anne Rosse had made by Victor Stiebel for the marriage of her son, the Earl of Snowdon, to Princess Margaret in May 1960. 'This coat had a beautiful black mink collar,' she notes poignantly, 'which I could not afford to buy.' There was consolation to be found in the matching Simone Mirman hat which 'has been acclaimed by the world as the smartest – all press cuttings talked about it.' Thanks to Anne Rosse's diligence, it is possible to talk of this hat still – as well as many of her other extant pieces from her wardrobe.

ROBERT O'BYRNE is an Irish Times columnist.

ALL THE COSTUMES ILLUSTRATED ARE AT BIRR CASTLE.

IRISH SILVER SPOONS

The earliest identifiable Irish silver spoons date from about 1630.
Douglas Bennett *provides a guide to the variety of designs which developed over succeeding centuries*

Spoons must be the oldest of all table utensils. As far back as the neolithic period primitive people were making scoops of bone, horn and clay shaped to hold liquids and to eat from; wooden spoons dating from 3000 BC have been found in Europe and the British Isles; and from the time of the Bronze Age metal spoons have been in common usage and have been manufactured in various shapes and forms to the present day.[1]

Excavations of tombs of the Egyptians prove that they had a variety of spoons made of metal, slate, ivory and wood, while both the Greeks and Romans had spoons that were used for many purposes including eating from table – some of these being silver.[2] The Old Testament description of the furniture in the Ark of the Covenant mentions gold spoons[3] and again when the princes are giving offerings for the dedication of the tabernacle, gold spoons form part of the gift.[4]

In England it is possible to trace the history and evolution of the silver spoon from the fifteenth century to the present day. In Ireland the earliest identifiable spoons are seventeenth century. At Trinity College Dublin a practice was established whereby certain students on entering college were required to make a presentation of a silver spoon or twelve shillings in lieu of it. The earliest record of this is an entry written by Provost Alvey in 1605-06.[5] No examples of the spoons given to the College in this way have survived: in fact no Irish examples predating the 1630s are extant.

The earliest Irish spoons, dating from the 1630s, have ovoid shape bowls which are termed fig-shaped bowls. The stems are straight and have six or eight sides (Fig. 1). This type of spoon, known as a slip top, was fashionable in mainland Europe and Britain for two centuries before this time. The stem of the spoon was lengthened at the end of the sixteenth century because the introduction of the large ruff collars worn by both sexes rendered the shorter handle impractical when taking liquids. Before the introduction of the ruffle collar, soups, caudles[6] and possets[7] were drunk straight from pots. The new fashion in clothing created an increase in the number of silver spoons used at table and replaced the custom of drinking straight from a porringer.[8]

In the 1640s a new breakthrough in design in the form of the 'puritan' spoon replaced the slip top. It had a heavy, flat, hammered stem or handle and the shape of the bowl was more elliptical than the narrowing, rather pointed, end of the fig-shaped slip top spoon (Fig. 2). This modification was an important step in the evolution of the spoon. The flat hammered handle of the puritan spoon was much easier and firmer to hold in the hand; and with a more practical shape to the bowl, the forerunner of the modern spoon had arrived.[9]

An improvement in the design of the puritan spoon, originating in France in the reign of Louis XIV, reached Ireland in the 1660s. The flat stem widened towards the end with a trifid terminal (Fig. 3). In France these were known as 'pied de

1. SLIP TOP SPOON. Dublin silver of the 1630s. (National Museum of Ireland). This is the earliest known type of Irish spoon. Its design, with fig-shaped bowl and straight stem, was fashionable in Europe from the fifteenth century.

2. PURITAN SPOON. Dublin silver of the 1640s. (National Museum of Ireland). This design, with a flat hammered handle that was easier to hold and a more elliptical bowl, succeeded the slip top design in the 1640s.

3. TRIFID TERMINAL SPOON. Dublin silver of the 1660s. (National Museum of Ireland). This shape, with a flat handle that widened towards the end to a trifid terminal, originated in France where it was referred to as a 'pied-de-biche' (hind's foot).

5. HANOVERIAN SPOON. Dublin silver, post 1710. This style, with the handle slightly turned up at the end and a ridge down the centre, was introduced about 1710 and after the accession of George I in 1714 became known as 'Hanoverian'.

4. DOG NOSE SPOON. Dublin silver of the 1690s. (National Museum of Ireland). Essentially a variant of the trifid, this form of handle, so called because the lobed end resembled the profile of a dog's head, was introduced about 1690.

IRISH SILVER SPOONS

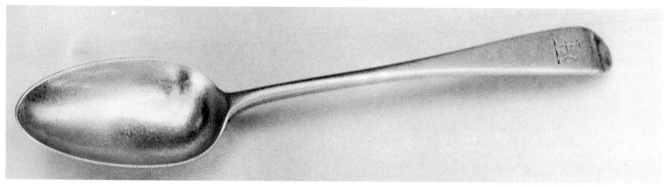

6. OLD ENGLISH SPOON. Dublin silver, post 1745. This design, with the end of the handle turned down, superseded the 'Hanoverian' about 1745 and became known as 'Old English'.

biche' (hind's foot), and very often they had a rat-tail back to the bowl. There is a very rare gold trifid spoon made in Dublin in the collection of the Worshipful Company of Goldsmiths, London. In approximately 1690 a variation on the shape of trifid was introduced, known as the dog nose pattern (Fig. 4). This lobed end resembled the profile of a dog's head and, like the trifid-shaped spoon, it was made until about 1715.[10]

By the eighteenth century spoons were commonplace and as a result it is much easier for the collector to pick up a variety of eighteenth-century spoons in second hand or antique shops, whereas seventeenth-century Irish spoons are rare and become museum pieces. An English design, referred to after the accession of George I in 1714 as the 'Hanoverian' pattern, was known in Ireland from 1710. On Hanoverian spoons, the end of the handle was slightly turned up with a ridge in the centre while the rat-tail on the back of the bowl was eventually replaced with a drop (Fig. 5). A variation on this design came into vogue about 1745 when the end of the handle was turned down and the term 'Hanoverian' appears to have been dropped in favour of 'English' or 'Old English' (Fig. 6).

The rococo period is regarded as an aberration interposed between the plain designs of the first quarter of the eighteenth century and the calm restraint of neo-classical influence after 1770. The rococo period in Irish silver dates from about 1740; it came incontestably from France where Juste-Aurèle Meissonnier had introduced the rocaille style in the early 1720s. A pair of spoons in this style are illustrated with attractive shells on

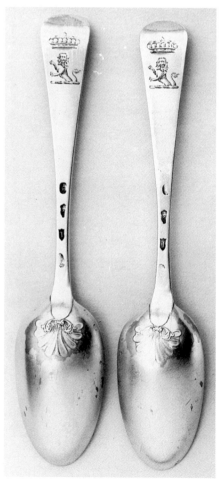

7. ROCOCO SPOONS. Dublin silver, post 1740. The simple design of these spoons is enhanced by the addition to the back of the bowls of attractive shell motifs, typical of the period.

the back of the bowls (Fig. 7). Asymmetrical designs in ornamentation based on nature become evident at this time on the handles of some flatware as may be seen on the ladle (Fig. 8).

By 1770 a new generation of patrons with fashionable town houses were demanding something different from the highly decorated styles of the rococo and in its place came the restrained neo-classical influence. The formal charm of this period was most successfully interpreted with the engraver's tool. Engraving is decoration by removing tiny slivers of metal with steel implements whose points are sharpened to suit a specific cut. Feather-edge design was introduced about this time (Fig. 9). This was immediately followed by bright-cut engraving, and an enormous number of these delicately engraved patterns were made in Ireland up to about 1810; the popularity of the design continued to a lesser extent throughout the nineteenth century (Fig. 10).

One of the most interesting studies in Irish silver is to see how the rural makers outside the city of Dublin did their work. Cork was the second silversmithing city in Ireland, Limerick was the third. The quality of the wares made in both these places was remarkably good. In general the silversmiths who worked in the south of Ireland from the seventeenth century to the famine period knew their business very well.[11] By charter of Charles I in 1631 the mayor of Cork had been empowered to appoint a clerk of assay but after 22 December 1637 the assaying and hall-marking of all silver wares in Ireland was controlled by the Company of Goldsmiths of Dublin. All silverwares, no matter where they are made, must according to law, be sent to Dublin to be tested and the fineness mark, a harp crowned, together with the maker's mark, stamped thereon. However, in the seventeenth and eighteenth centuries, a geographical problem arose and the distance, together with the likelihood of highwaymen seizing parcels of silver at gunpoint, resulted in very little of that metal ever finding its way to Dublin for examination.

During the seventeenth and early eighteenth centuries, the Cork manufacturers used the emblems of a ship between two castles and after about 1714 the craftsmen of that city seem to have agreed among themselves on the use of a punch with the word 'sterling' and the maker's initials or name for identification (Fig. 11).

It is impossible to say when the working of precious metals first took place in county Limerick, but from archeological evidence we know that goldsmiths certainly plied their trade there from about 700BC. A fair quality of silver was manufactured in Limerick from the mid-seventeenth century until about 1820 by which time the Act of Union had dealt a hard blow to craftsmen generally in Ireland.[12] During the seventeenth century, marks on Limerick silver consisted of the maker's mark, a castle gate and a star. Like those of Cork, the Limerick silversmiths seem to have adopted the sterling mark about 1710 and for most of the eighteenth and nineteenth centuries their products bear the word 'sterling' and a maker's mark often struck twice (Fig. 12). The designs of the provincial spoon makers followed closely the patterns executed by the Dublin makers, sometimes with interesting variations. During the period of bright-cut engraving, many Limerick spoons bore the motif of a fleur-de-lys or of Prince of Wales feathers, these not being in general use elsewhere (Fig. 13).

The most common of all the

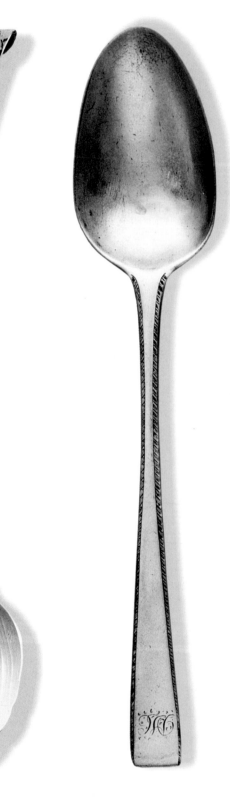

8. LADLE with flat-chased asymmetrical decoration. Dublin silver, post 1740. This type of ornamentation, derived from nature, became popular in the rococo period.

9. FEATHER EDGE SPOON. Dublin silver, c.1770. Engraved design on silver became the norm in the second half of the eighteenth-century and the feather-edge design, where the edges of the handle were engraved was introduced about 1770.

10. BRIGHT-CUT SPOON. Dublin silver, c.1770 Bright-cut patterns, of which this example is typical, were particularly popular in Ireland in the neo-classical period of the late eighteenth century.

designs in the nineteenth century must be the fiddle pattern spoon (Fig. 14). This shape arrived in Ireland about 1800 and continued to be made by hand in Dublin until about forty years ago. In the British Museum there are very early Christian spoons made of silver with handles resembling fiddle pattern and early in the eighteenth century the French developed the *forme violon*. This was in the true shape of a fiddle or violin as the name infers; it came into fashion after the dog nose lost its popularity. Variations of this are found throughout Europe in the second half of the eighteenth century but the stilted form that we know as 'fiddle pattern' came from England in the late eighteenth century and arrived in Ireland at the turn of the century.

One of the advantages of assembling a collection of spoons is that there are so many types and variations readily available at reasonable prices. It must be realised that this article is only a guide to dates. It takes time for new designs and shapes to emerge and very often patterns overlap for a few years. Spoon makers did not suddenly decide one day to stop making Old English pattern and only concentrate on the Rococo. As the whims of fashion dictated change so did the spoon maker slowly adapt to the demands from the public for something different.

DOUGLAS BENNETT'S books include Irish Georgian Silver *(1972),* Collecting Irish Silver *(1984) and* The Silver Collection: Trinity College Dublin *(1988).*

ACKNOWLEDGEMENTS
I am grateful to the director of the National Museum of Ireland for granting permission to reproduce spoons Figs 1-4 and to Mrs L Wyse Jackson for permission to quote from her late husband, Robert Wyse Jackson's book Irish Silver. *My thanks also go to the Board of Trinity College Dublin for allowing me to quote from records in their Manuscripts Department.*

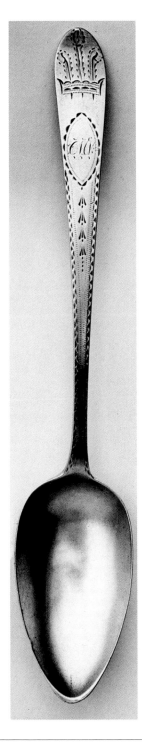

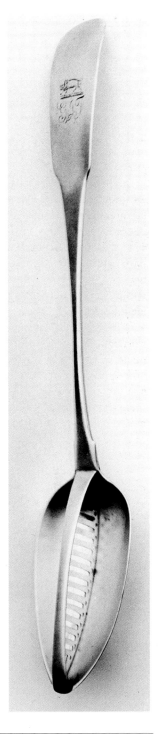

11. *(Above left)* CORK SILVER MARK. The maker is John Toleken. After 1714 Cork silversmiths used the word 'sterling' together with a punch of their own name or initials.

12. *(Above right)* LIMERICK SILVER MARK. The maker is Maurice Fitzgerald. Limerick silversmiths also used the sterling stamp and the maker's mark, often struck twice.

13. *(Right)* LIMERICK SPOON. Post 1770. The bright-cut pattern was popular with Limerick silversmiths who often incorporated in the design a fleur-de-lys or Prince of Wales feathers motif that was not generally used elsewhere.

14. *(Far right)* FIDDLE-PATTERN STRAINER SPOON. Dublin silver, 1800. The fiddle pattern became the most common of all nineteenth century designs. In this spoon the divider in the bowl was used to strain gravy.

1. Society of Antiquaries. *Archaeologia*, Vol LIII, 1892.
2. *Ibid.*
3. *Exodus*, 25 v 29, 'and thou shalt make the dishes thereof, and spoons thereof and covers thereof, and bowls thereof to cover withal; of pure gold shalt thou make them.'
4. *Numbers* 7, v. 84 and 86. 'This was the dedication of the altar, in the day when it was anointed, by the princes of Israel: twelve chargers of silver, twelve silver bowls, twelve spoons of gold: The golden spoons were twelve, full of incense weighting ten shekels apiece.' Gold spoons are also mentioned in *1 Kings* 7, v 50 and in *2 Chronicles* 24, v 14.
5. Manuscripts Department Trinity College Dublin '1605 paid for a dozen silver spoons 4L-05'. A 1609 entry includes 'silver spoons a dozen and a half'.
6. Caudle was a warm drink of wine and eggs for an invalid or a woman in childbed.
7. Posset was a pick me up of hot milk curdled with ale or wine flavoured with spices and sugar.
8. Victor Houart, *Antique Spoons*, Souvenir Press 1982.
9. Douglas Bennett, *Collecting Irish Silver*, Souvenir Press 1984.
10. *Ibid.*
11. Robert Wyse Jackson, *Irish Silver*, Cork, 1972.
12. Douglas Bennett and Rosemary ffolliott, *Irish Ancestor*, No. 2. 1978.

THE ADARE BUREAU-CABINET AND ITS ORIGINS

John Hardy *discusses an exceptional example of the Irish cabinet-maker's craft*

The bureau-cabinet was a greatly esteemed item of furniture in the eighteenth century and served a variety of purposes. It functioned in the bedroom apartment as clothes-chest, writing-bureau, dressing-table and cabinet for books and documents. And, when equipped with mirrored doors and sliding candlestick-trays, it could also take the place of the window-pier furnishings, comprising mirror, table and pair of *torchères*. Since the fashionable lady's dressing-room then served for a morning reception-room as well as a dressing-room and study, the bureau was often richly ornamented with carving, inlay or gilding to harmonise with the room's architecture and decoration. Particularly exotic examples, imported from India and China, were embellished with ivory or lacquered with glossy flower-filled landscapes, while others were brightly painted in the Oriental manner such as Messrs. Stalker and Parker had described in A *Treatise of Japanning and Varnishing,* 1688 which provided patterns for 'Japan-work, in imitation of the Indians (ie Chinese)' for tables, stands and frames as well as cabinets.

However those provided for the gentlemen's libraries or studies were generally more sombre and architectonic, especially during George II's reign, when the enthusiasm for 'Roman' architecture was combined with the fashion for mahogany. Indeed it was the abolition of the American timber tax in 1721 that encouraged the importation of West Indian mahogany and contributed to the production of a group of cabinets, which are masterpieces of the Irish cabinet-makers' craft. Amongst them is a bureau-cabinet (Fig. 1), which was discovered in the attics of Adare Manor, Co Limerick in 1960, and acquired by the Victoria & Albert Museum, London. Its scroll-pediment typifies the antique or 'Palladian' style promoted by connoisseurs in the art of architecture such as Richard Boyle, 3rd Earl of Burlington and 4th Earl of Cork (d.1753), who served as George II's Lord Lieutenant and Treasurer of Ireland.

1. BUREAU-CABINET. Mahogany with fitted writing-drawer and bookshelves. Irish, c.1730s. (Victoria & Albert Museum, London). The cabinet was probably commissioned by Valentine Quin (d.1744) for the house which he had built at Adare about 1730.

THE ADARE BUREAU-CABINET AND ITS ORIGINS

Burlington's admiration for the work of the Italian architect Andrea Palladio (d.1580) as a follower of the style elucidated in the Roman architectural treatise written by Vitruvius, was to result in his sponsorship of *Fabbriche Antiche disegnate da Andrea Palladio*, 1730, as well as the translation of Palladio's *Quattro Libri dell'Architettura*, issued by Isaac Ware in 1738. In addition, he recognised Inigo Jones (d.1652) as having introduced this 'true' antique style to British court architecture; and it was his encouragement of William Kent (d.1748), King George II's 'Master Carpenter', in the imitation of the work of Palladio and Jones that resulted in a 'Palladian' pattern-book, *Some Designs of Mr. Inigo Jones and Mr William Kent*, which was published by John Vardy in 1744. One of the designs in this book illustrated Kent's pattern for a seat surmounted by a scroll-pediment (Vardy *op cit*, Plate 42), echoing some pedimented chairs that had been conceived in the 1720s for the banqueting-hall of Burlington's Chiswick villa in Middlesex.

A London pattern, also of the 1720s,[1] displays a bureau which sports a pediment that is triumphal-arched and hollowed for the display of a sacred urn (Fig.2). This Palladian feature is applied to an earlier form of cabinet with slope-fronted bureau, and doors that are headed by indented arches, after the French fashion popularised by Daniel Marot (d.1752), 'Architect' to King William III. The varied shapes of pediments on Georgian furniture are derived largely from engravings of overmantel-frames, such as those illustrated in James Gibbs' *Book of Architecture*, 1728 or Isaac Ware's *Designs of Inigo Jones and others*, 1773. The taste for the 'antique' in Ireland was fostered by those publications as well as by architects such as Richard Castle (d.1751) and Sir Edward

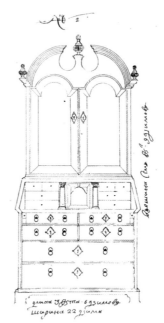

2. PATTERN FOR A BUREAU by a London designer. 1720s. (State Hermitage Museum, St Petersburg). The pattern was obtained by the St Petersburg craftsman, Fedor Martynov, during his London apprenticeship in the 1720s.

3. BUREAU-CABINET. Mahogany with mirrored doors. Irish, c.1740s. (Newbridge House, Co Dublin). Although previously linked with a payment made by Thomas Cobbe for a bureau in 1764, the style of the piece suggests a date of about twenty years earlier.

Lovett Pearce (d.1733). The latter, before his appointment as Surveyor of King George II's Works and Fortifications in Ireland, had been encouraged by Burlington to survey Jigginstown, Co Kildare in search of the influence of Inigo Jones.

The pediment of the Adare cabinet displays an eagle, which is emblematic of Jupiter, father of the Gods, to whom it also served as messenger. The noble bird[2] is perched in triumph within the festive-flowered volutes of the scrolled and serpentined pediment, whose form can probably be traced to a chimneypiece pattern from the Burlington collection, which featured in Vardy's 1744 publication. The same Jones design may also have provided the inspiration for the 'Walpole' overmantel-frame that was designed by Kent for Houghton Hall, Norfolk in the 1720s and later published by E Hoppus in his *Gentleman and Builder's Repository*, 1737 (Plate LV).

The bureau-cabinet is likely to have been commissioned by Valentine Quin (d.1744) for the Palladian villa at Adare, which he had built around 1730. Its architecture can also be compared to that of a pair of elegantly carved pier-glasses, which may have furnished his wife's apartments and bear her 'Wyndham' family crest displayed in the pediments.[3] Amongst a number of very closely related cabinets, there is one at Newbridge, Co Dublin (Fig. 3), which appears to have been manufactured in the same workshops, but is further embellished with mirrored doors.[4] The robust 'antique' character of this George II furniture recalls the Augustan age, and owes a debt to Lord Burlington, who was recognised by his contemporaries as an 'Apollo of the Arts'.

JOHN HARDY, a professional valuer specialising in furniture of the eighteenth century, was formerly in the Department of Furniture and Woodwork at the Victoria & Albert Museum.

1. N. Iurevna Guseva, 'Fedor Martynov, Russian Master Cabinet Maker', *Furniture History*, 1994, pp.92-99.
2. The eagle is a modern replacement copied from that on a related cabinet.
3. Christie's Adare Manor sale on the premises, 9 June, 1982, Lot 305.
4. Desmond Fitz-Gerald kindly drew my attention to the 'Newbridge' bureau-cabinet, which has been linked with a 1764 payment for a bureau made by Thomas Cobbe (d.1781). However on stylistic grounds it would appear to have been made at an earlier date. If so, it might have been commissioned by Charles Cobbe (d.1752) around the time of his appointment as Archbishop of Dublin in 1742. Illustrated J Cornforth, 'Newbridge, Co Dublin', *Country Life*, 20 June, 1985, p.1810, Fig. 7.

'RECREATING THE WORLD'
RECENT IRISH ARCHITECTURE

Frank McDonald *describes the Good, the Bad and the Ugly of Contemporary Irish Architecture*

In a country where anyone can claim to be an architect, simply by calling himself such, it is probably inevitable that Ireland's contemporary architecture would be characterised by an almost overwelming mediocrity. Indeed, even to use the word 'architecture' in this context is to invest the recent building boom with a dignity it does not deserve. The ruling thesis of urban renewal, Irish-style, seems to be 'Never mind the quality, feel the width.' There is such a desperate urge to put cranes on the skyline that hardly anybody questions the appalling quality of so much of what is being built – the 'heritage' we are leaving for future generations. All that matters is that the gaps are filled with *something*. The faceless planners who preside over this travesty are mainly engineers, geographers and sociologists rather than architects, so the last thing they want is to be challenged by thoughtful contemporary architecture. They are the bland leading the bland, and so long as new buildings are mocked up in Georgian pastiche style, however illiterate, planning permission is assured.

As elsewhere in this increasingly homogenised world, junk has inevitably become part of our popular culture, and this is reflected in our buildings just as it is in our food, fashion or jewellery. And those involved in producing junk architecture – whether as designers, developers or town planners – do not seem even remotely *angst*-ridden about their dubious legacy.

Ten years ago, in an inspiring address to the annual conference of the Royal Institute of the Architects of Ireland (RIAI), Seamus Heaney reminded its members that every time they designed or built a new building they were 'in a profound metaphorical sense, recreating the world.' It is an awesome responsibility which far too often is not considered, let alone fulfilled. How many times has Heaney's lofty phrase occurred to the creators of the Bungalow Blitz, which has made such an indelible mark on relatively unspoilt rural landscapes? Architects are often blamed for the *palazzi gombeeni*, but the truth is that most of these houses are copied from mass-produced pattern books, without any reference to site or orientation.

Good buildings are the exception rather than the rule in urban areas, too. It is surely extraordinary that the biggest single developer of city centre flats in Dublin, Zoe Developments, has built well over a thousand 'units' without employing any architectural advice – and just as extraordinary that its drearily predictable schemes of kennel-sized apartments were entertained by the city's planners.

Bachelors Walk, the most important site on the Liffey Quays, ended up being squandered for yet another scheme by Zoe Developments, and all that seemed to concern the planners was that it would be cloaked by a fake-Georgian facade. Lurking

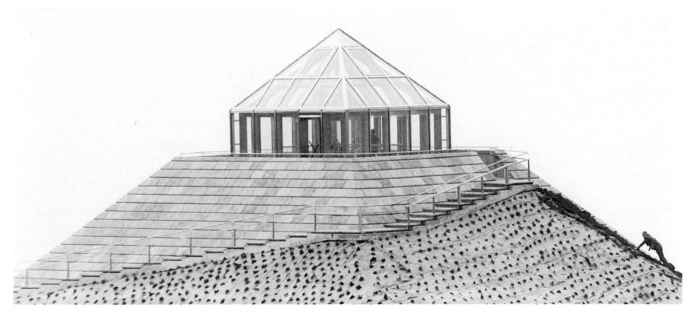

1. (*Above*) OFFICE OF PUBLIC WORKS (MARY McKENNA): *Visitor Centre at Ceide Fields, North Mayo.* Like other thoughtful architecture of the 1990s, this extraordinary pyramidical structure suggests that there is a younger generation of architects to whom the task of building for the future can be entrusted with confidence.

2. (*Opposite*) SCOTT TALLON WALKER: *Civic Offices at Wood Quay, Dublin.* The idea of holding an architectural competition has been vindicated and this splendid building serves as a mask to Sam Stephenson's 'bunkers' and, inevitably, Christ Church Cathedral.

'Recreating the World': Recent Irish Architecture

behind this, however, are 335 "apartments", of which a staggering 293 are single-bedroom units. Never has Bachelors Walk been more aptly named.

Nearly every provincial town has acquired a new shopping centre, usually a box-like structure with a neo-vernacular veneer of brick-cladding on the main 'facade' (Fig. 3). Indeed, such was the proliferation of illiterate pastiche that even Padraig Flynn, as Minister for the Environment, complained about the 'Noddy in Toyland' clocktowers which seemed to be popping up almost everywhere.

Galway, it seemed, had devised a relatively fresh neo-vernacular style for new infill buildings in its urban renewal zone, but it was repeated so often that it became formulaic. Only in Limerick, under the direction of its former city architect, Jim Barrett, was

3. The AMBROSE KELLY PARTNERSHIP: *Longford Shopping Centre*. Developed by Tiernan Properties of Limerick. Urban renewal tax incentives have encouraged developments like this in most provincial towns.

architecture placed in the context of the vision which he enunciated – to turn the city around to face the Shannon. This is now well on the way to being realised – a considerable achievement in a city which for many years had lost any sense of itself. Two of the best schemes, both by architects Murray O'Laoire, are the civic park and tourist information office (Fig. 13) at Arthur's Quay and the container-like visitor centre at King John's Castle – a prime example of gutsy contemporary architecture.

The Government's urban renewal package, with its lucrative tax incentives, could have been used as a creative opportunity to 're-invent' Ireland's principal cities and towns. But instead of aiming for excellence, like other European capitals with a real sense of their place in the world, Dublin led the way by lazily

4. The AMBROSE KELLY PARTNERSHIP: *Ha'penny Bridge House, Dublin*. Developed by Cosgrave Bros, this block of flats – an example of the new architectural dross which blights the quays – has a frontage mocked up to resemble three Georgian houses. The quays ought to have been recognised as the essential Dublin.

settling for the lowest common denominator. 'Development', in the crudely generic scense, was the over-riding objective, even along the Liffey Quays (Fig.4). The Quays ought to have been recognised as the essential Dublin, as the *Architectural Review* argued in 1974, but there was little hope when even the culturally-minded former Taoiseach, Charles Haughey, could say at late as 1990 that they were 'full of ramshackle old buildings'. Apologists for the new architectural dross which blights the quays maintain that schemes such as Arran Square (Fig. 8) are preferable to the derelict sites they replaced; anything, in other words, is better than nothing. But these sites could quite tolerably have been left derelict for another year or two if there was a reasonable chance of filling them with good quality buildings.

5. The AMBROSE KELLY PARTNERSHIP: *Ha'penny Bridge House, Dublin* (overdoor). The entrance to the block of sixty-four flats is surmounted by kitsch references to Dublin's most famous bridge.

Nothing can be done to dislodge mindless apartment 'architecture' once it is built. Unlike Lower Mount Street, where the tawdry collection of 1970s office blocks can all be replaced over time, there is no second chance to get it right for apartment buildings precisely because they end up in multiple ownership. Thus, their design requires a quite exceptional level of consideration.

Instead of learning from cities like Barcelona, with its highly-developed urban culture, we seem intent on continuing to make our own mistakes without any reference to what happens elsewhere. Thus, the model of urban living being offered to the public is essentially *suburban*, with show flats furnished as if they were in Templeogue rather than in the heart of the city.

There are notable exceptions. In Temple Bar, the only urban

6. GILROY MCMAHON: *Essex Street, Temple Bar.* The facadist nature of some of the new developments in Temple Bar has been rightly criticised: here the gable-front of a nineteenth century schoolhouse has been retained while a new Viking Museum is being constructed at the rear for Dublin Tourism.

area in the State with its own architectural framework plan, the drive to develop it as Dublin's 'cultural quarter' has produced such inspiringly imaginative schemes as The Printworks (Fig. 14), on Essex Street and Temple Lane, for which Derek Tynan deservedly won the 1995 Downes Medal of the Architectural Association of Ireland.

Temple Bar has become a sort of laboratory for innovative contemporary architecture. This is reflected in McCullough and Mulvin's quite stunning transformation of the Temple Bar Gallery and Studios (Fig. 16) into a superb working space for some thirty artists – though it will be lost on the seagulls that the roofscape is based on a Juan Gris picture in the National Gallery!

7. CARR, SWEENEY AND O'FARRELL: *Lower Bridge Street and Merchant's Quay.* This extension to O'Shea's Merchant pub is one of the most prominently located buildings on the quays. Sites like this should have been left derelict for another year or two if there was a chance of filling them with good quality buildings.

O'Donnell and Tuomey won much applause for their imaginative adaption of the Quaker meeting house in Eustace Street (Fig. 17) to house the Irish Film Centre, brilliantly blending old and new. The glazed courtyard in the middle, paved to recall a reel of film, is the most admired element of the scheme; not so successful are the restaurant, bar, toilets and the long, narrow entrance.

Murray O'Laoire's Green Building, between Crow Street and Temple Lane, created quite a stir when its quirky artist-designed doors were opened to the public in 1994. But despite such trappings as wind turbines and solar panels on the roof, columns clad in copper from recycled hot water cylinders and balconies with bicycle frames (Fig. 11), it was rated as 'pale green' by the seriously green purists.

8. ARRAN SQUARE, ARRAN QUAY, DUBLIN. This Zoe Developments scheme was designed by an in-house team of architectural technicians with some guidance from Dublin Corporation planners. Over 240 flats are laid out on long corridors behind a Georgian-style elevation.

9. Dermot HEALY: *Interior of the Black Church, Dublin.* The parabolic vaulted interior of John Semple's 1830 church has been sensitively converted for office use.

'RECREATING THE WORLD': RECENT IRISH ARCHITECTURE

10. FITZGERALD REDDY & ASSOCIATES: *Dean Court, Patrick Street, Dublin.* These apartment buildings are an example of well-mannered contemporary architecture and thoughtful urban design.

Of equal importance to buildings is the creation of public spaces and, here again, Temple Bar scores. The curved street linking Temple Lane and Eustace Street as well as two new squares – one off Sycamore Street, and the other between Crown Alley and Fownes Street – indicate a commitment to the concept that creating public spaces in the city is a public responsibility.

Where Temple Bar has fallen down is in the field of conservation. The 'facadist' nature of some of the new developments (Fig. 6) which supposedly retain pre-existing buildings has been rightly criticised, no less than the destruction of a terrace of five eighteenth-century houses on Essex Quay and the shameful gutting of SS Michael and John's Church to make it fit

11. MURRAY O'LAOIRE ASSOCIATES: *The Green Building, Temple Bar, Dublin* (detail). Designed as a European prototype energy-efficient building, the quirky and amusing building created quite a stir when it was erected in 1994: it takes recycling to the literal extreme by incorporating bicycle frames in the balconies.

a 'black box' Viking adventure. So many churches have become redundant that we are bound to see many more conversions. But few will be carried out with such sensitivity as the conversion of the Black Church, off Dorset Street (Fig. 9), with its vast parabolic vault, where Dermot Healy, the architect who had been commissioned to re-make it as offices, says he sat for three days before deciding what to do.

Elsewhere, the opportunity to remake city streets devastated by ill-conceived road plans has been realised, notably by Fitzgerald Reddy's well-mannered – but modern – apartment buildings opposite St Patrick's Cathedral (Fig. 10). Few architects get an opportunity to rebuild whole streets, but in this case it has been done in

12. *(Opposite)* BURKE-KENNEDY DOYLE & PARTNERS: *DIT College, Dublin.* Built on the site of the long-derelict Jacob's Biscuit Factory, the building is successful even if the corner entrance is somewhat overblown.

'RECREATING THE WORLD': RECENT IRISH ARCHITECTURE

13. MURRAY O'LAOIRE ASSOCIATES: *Tourist Information Office, Limerick*. This is one of the visionary schemes which has helped to focus the city of Limerick on one of its greatest assets – the River Shannon.

14. Derek TYNAN: *The Printworks, Temple Bar, Dublin.* Ten apartments and four studio/retail units were constructed on a L-shaped site with frontage onto two streets. The raised interior residential courtyard offers a solution to the problem of re-inhabiting the upper floors of city buildings. An inspirational example of imaginative urban renewal.

a way that complements, rather than mocks, the 1901 Iveagh Trust complex. The long-derelict Jacob's biscuit factory off Aungier Street has also been reclaimed by Burke-Kennedy Doyle's new DIT college (Fig. 12), even if the corner entrance is somewhat overblown. A much smaller, but no less remarkable, building is the nearby Accountancy and Business College, by Henry J Lyons and Partners, which shows how contemporary architecture can be slotted into a historic street. Meanwhile, the idea of holding an architectural competition – too rarely used in this country as a means of finding the best design – has certainly been vindicated in the case of Wood Quay, where Scott Tallon Walker have produced a splendid new building on the quayfront which serves to mask Sam Stephenson's 'bunkers' and also, inevitably, the Victorianised Christ Church Cathedral (Fig. 1).

But architecture isn't just about new buildings. The urgent need to conserve Ireland's built heritage has also been engaging the interest of a growing number of architects in recent years. Sheehan and Barry's glorious restoration of Newman House must surely be the flagship, alongside the Office of Public Works' sensational reinstatement of Turner's curvilinear range of glasshouses in Glasnevin.

Trnity College has also played its part, not only by looking after the largest single complex of historic buildings in Dublin but also by ensuring (in the main) that any additions to the college are of the highest quality. These include de Blacam and Meagher's much-admired work on the Dining Hall and Atrium and the Beckett Theatre, with its intriguing tower clad in Donegal oak (Fig. 15).

But there is still a seemingly irresistible urge to consign poorly-maintained historic buildings to the scrap-heap – particularly if they happen to be in public ownership. The 'grim reaper' attitude of officialdom towards the once-fine courthouses in Longford and

15. (*Opposite*) DE BLACAM AND MEAGHER: *The Beckett Theatre, Trinity College, Dublin.* In recent years the College has ensured that any additions to its historic campus are of the highest architectural quality as in this intriguing tower clad in Donegal oak which provides a foyer and dance/rehearsal studio.

16. McCULLOUGH MULVIN: *Temple Bar Gallery and Studios, Dublin.* An early-twentieth century factory building has been refurbished and extended to provide artists' studios and gallery space. The finished building was applauded as a striking contemporary design that fitted well into an urban context: one of the projects which has turned Dublin's cultural quarter into an architectural laboratory.

17. O'DONNELL AND TUOMEY: *Irish Film Centre, Temple Bar, Dublin.* The project consisted of adapting a Quaker Meeting House to contemporary use and resulted in a brilliant blending of old and new.

Carrick-on-Shannon is documented. But it may also be found even in Birr, designated as a 'Georgian heritage town.' The Government, of course, has no policy on architecture; successive administrations have viewed it in a utilitarian way, merely as an adjunct of the construction industry. It doesn't even rate a mention in the three-year 'Plan for the Arts,' but then this is a society which is obsessed with words – spoken, written or performed – and has a low level of visual awareness. When it came to building a batch of 'decentralised' offices in provincial towns, the Government opted for private sector design-and-build packages, despite the fact that the Office of Public Works (OPW) employs the largest architectural establishment in the State. Here again, short-termism ruled, with quality sacrificed in the cause of supposedly economical procurement. And it is unlikely that the OPW would have become embroiled in such a bitter controversy over its visitor centres for sensitive sites such as Mullaghmore, in the Burren, if it wasn't for the fact that their genesis owed more to the availability of free money from Europe

for tourism projects than to any mission to 'interpret' the landscape for uninitiated day-trippers.

Public reaction to the OPW's efforts in this area have been mixed. Nuala O'Faolain, of *The Irish Times*, felt 'bullied' by the Blasket Islands visitor centre near Dunquin, Co Kerry. Probably the biggest single building on the Dingle peninsula, it is supposed to evoke an Ogham inscription (for the seagulls?) – though this hardly compensates for its breathtaking arrogance.

The centre which people find most heart-warming is Mary McKenna's extraordinary pyramid at the Ceide Fields, in the bleak and beautiful landscape of North Mayo (Fig. 1). Like other thoughtful works of architecture in the 1990s, it suggests that there is a younger generation of architects to whom the task of building for the future can be entrusted with more confidence.

FRANK McDONALD is Environmental Correspondent of the Irish Times *and author of* The Destruction of Dublin *(1985).*

THE CLADDAGH RING

Ida Delamer *unravels the doubtful origins of a popular Irish jewellery design*

The story of the Claddagh ring, which is made up of a plain hoop attached to a hammered or cast bezel designed as two hands clasping a crowned heart, has so much folklore and myth attached to it that it is difficult to know where legend ends and truth begins. The most fanciful account (see Appendix I) describes how the original was dropped by an eagle into the lap of Margaret Joyce in the sixteenth century, but greater credence is generally accorded to the belief that the design originated with an early-eighteenth century Galway goldsmith, Richard Joyce.[1]

The motif of clasped hands, which is generally referred to as a *fede* (in Italian '*mani in fede*') or 'hands in faith' has been in use on bezels of love rings since Roman times.[2] The heart, regarded by lovers as the seat of affection, made an appearance on rings at a later date[3] as did the crown which denotes perfection. An example of a sixteenth century gold *fede* ring is one that was recovered in 1972 from the large Spanish Armada galleass *Girona* which was wrecked in 1588 off Port na Spaniagh, North Antrim.[4] The bezel consists of a tiny hand holding a heart and the ring is inscribed *No tengo mas que dar te* (I have nothing more to give you). Oman illustrates many eighteenth and nineteenth century rings with hands holding a heart. These are love rings or rings that were given on the occasion of a marriage for, as he explains, the custom of a bride giving a ring informally to her husband just before or after their wedding ceremony goes back some centuries.[5]

An English ring dated 1706 in the Victoria and Albert Museum (Fig. 1) has all the characteristics of a Claddagh ring except that the bezel, instead of being plain gold, is set with a diamond heart crowned and held by two white enamelled gold

1. FEDE RING. Diamond with enamelled gold. English, 1706. Inscribed on the inside, *Dudley and Katherine united 26 March 1706.* (Victoria and Albert Museum, London). This early ring has all the characteristics of a Claddagh ring with a pair of hands clasping a crowned heart. The inscription indicates that it commemorates a marriage.

2. CLADDAGH RING. Gold. By Richard Joyce of Galway. c.1700. Inscribed on the inside with the initials NCM and MRC and the maker's mark. (Collection The Hon Garech Browne). Joyce is traditionally believed to have originated the design of the Claddagh ring although, as this article makes clear, this is extremely unlikely.

hands. The inscription on the inside, 'Dudley and Katherine united 26 Mar 1706' obviously denotes a marriage. In Ireland, the four earliest extant rings of the Claddagh type are datable to about 1700 and of these, one is by a Galway goldsmith, Richard Joyce[6] (Fig. 2); but the other three are attributed to Thomas Meade, a goldsmith who was admitted a Freeman of Kinsale Corporation in 1689.[7] Of the latter, one is marked 'T Meade', another 'T Meade TM' and the third has the punch 'T M' struck twice (see Appendix III). The design of hands supporting a crowned heart was, therefore, known in Galway and also Kinsale in the early years of the eighteenth century. Further evidence of this is a curious mid-eighteenth century Chippendale-style ladderback chair which was the Presidential Chair of the Kinsale Knot of the Friendly Brothers Society (Fig. 3).[8] During a recent restoration of the chair, when a later armorial canvas was removed from the back, the painted armorials of the Friendly Brothers were revealed with a device of two hands holding a crowned heart above the motto '*Quis Separbit*'.

The initials which are inscribed on the inside of many of the eighteenth and early-nineteenth century gold Claddagh rings (see table) also suggest a commemoration of marriage. In Ireland during the same period similarly inscribed flatware – with three initials rather than the family crest – was often presented on the occasion of wealthy marriages (Fig. 4). The initial indicating the surname was placed centrally above the bridegroom's initial (on the left) and the bride's initial (on the right).

Probably due to economic and social circumstances, there are very few surviving gold Claddagh rings from the period 1730-70;[9] but the punches of two Galway goldsmiths, George

Robinson and Austin French, appear on many rings which date from the last thirty years of the eighteenth century.[10] From the early 1800s to about 1850, the following jewellers and watchmakers all contributed to the growing Claddagh ring industry in Galway: Andrew Robinson, Nicholas Burgh, James Clinch, and James Sealy.

Although Claddagh rings were known and made in Galway (and in Kinsale) from at least the early years of the eighteenth century, it was not until the middle of the nineteenth century that rings of this type became known as 'Claddagh' and the origin of the name may be traced to Mr and Mrs Samuel Carter Hall's three-volume description of Ireland which was published in London between 1841-43.[11]

3. CHAIR. Irish, c.1760. (Collection The Friendly Brothers, Dublin). This is the Presidential Chair of the Kinsale Knot of the Friendly Brothers which was revived in 1754. The motif of hands clasping a crowned heart in the centre of the decorated panel is presumably intended as an emblem of friendship.

The Halls wrote of the inhabitants of the Claddagh, a fishing village adjoining the town of Galway as follows: 'They have many peculiar customs. One is worthy of special note. The wedding-ring is an heirloom in the family. It is regularly transferred (by a mother) to her daughter first married and so on to their descendants. These rings are largely of solid gold and not infrequently cost from two to three pounds each.' Accompanying ths account was an illustration of a *fede* ring (Fig. 5).

While working on their volumes, the Halls had advertised for 'communication from persons who may be strangers concerning matters of interest connected with Ireland to assist in giving completeness to their work'.[12] One of those who obliged with information was Thomas Crofton Croker (1798-1854), the pioneering collector of Irish folklore to whom many acknowledgements are made throughout the Hall volumes (Fig. 6). Croker, a native of Cork, who in 1818 secured a clerkship in the British Admiralty in London – where he served until retirement in 1850 – was interested from an early age in old Irish legends and stories and he toured throughout Ireland several

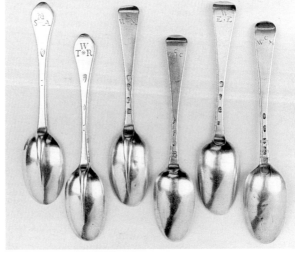

4. MARRIAGE SPOONS: Dublin silver, varying dates between 1701 and 1760. (National Museum of Ireland). The initials on the spoons are the bridegroom's surname above his Christian name (left) with the bride's Christian initial on the right. Similarly inscribed initials are found on the inside of Claddagh rings indicating that they, like marriage spoons, could have been given in commemoration of marriage.

times to sketch and study local traditions.[13] It is most likely that Crofton Croker was author of the legend of the Claddagh ring as recounted by the Halls as well as its illustration as a large part, if not all, of the folklore content of their work has been attributed to him. Croker's own work, *Irish Fairy Legends,* published in 1825, was the 'outcome of tales and conversations with peasantry he knew well, then elaborated over the midnight oil with great skill and delicacy of touch in order to give a saleable book, thus spiced, to the English public'.[14] Recently, however, Croker has been discredited as a reliable source: he 'could not contain his literary sub-editorial instincts which often overcame whatever regard he may have had for historical authenticity'.[15] His account of the origin of the Claddagh ring may also be questioned.

According to Hardiman's *History of Galway* (1820), the Gaelic-speaking people of the Claddagh were 'an extremely poor and unlettered race. They were living in thatched houses or cabins. Fishing was their sole occupation.' While the women of the Claddagh certainly wore wedding rings of the Claddagh type, these were often made of various alloys of gold, silver, brass, bronze, and guinea coins and were far from being the large solid gold ring romantically described by the Halls as passing from mother to daughter.[16]

The Halls' account may also be discounted on the basis of other evidence. In the first instance, with a few exceptions, all extant gold Claddagh rings made prior to 1840 are male rings.[17] This can be deduced from the internal diameter measurements of the extant rings. Secondly, the cost of a solid gold ring would have been beyond the means of the majority of the inhabitants of the Claddagh. Thirdly, the letters inscribed on the insides of the early rings are not Gaelic which was the language of the Claddagh people. One might also add that the use of three inscribed initials to commemorate a marriage was (as has been demonstrated) a practice of the wealthy upper classes and furthermore, for practical reasons, a fisherman was unlikely to have worn a ring with as large a bezel as a Claddagh.

Mr and Mrs Hall's account of the Claddagh ring is reiterated almost verbatim in a London publication of 1863, *Chambers Book of Days,* which includes an exact replica of the *fede* ring as illustrated by them; and the same illustration was used in another London publication, *Finger Ring Lore* by William Jones (1877) where it is captioned 'The Claddagh Ring'.

In 1906 a Galway jeweller, William Dillon, published on article in the *Galway Archaeological and Historical Journal* entitled 'The Claddagh Ring'.[18] Part of this paper was contributed by the journal's editor, part by Mr Dillon. An editorial note stated, 'It will be seen that this subject requires further investigation and this (paper) must be considered as a preliminary treatment of it'. The paper limited the district in which the Claddagh ring was worn 'roughly from the Aran Isles on the West, all through Connemara and Joyce's Country and then eastwards and southwards for not more than 12 miles.' Dillon concluded that while the ring was worn 'over a much wider district there is nevertheless some justification for its being designated the Claddagh ring. The objection to the title would be that the Claddagh people being, as is well known, in many respects a separate community with customs of their own, it might be inferred from the name that the use of this ring was among their peculiar customs, which of course would be a mistake'.

Mr Dillon, being a jeweller, naturally had a vested interest in the story of the Claddagh origin of the rings, and he mentions a pawn-

5. ILLUSTRATION OF A CLADDAGH RING. From Hall's *Ireland* (1841-43). Probably based on a drawing by Thomas Crofton Croker, the publication of this illustration in the mid-nineteenth century led to the proliferation and commercialisation of Claddagh rings.

6. Portrait of Thomas Crofton CROKER. Etching after Charles Grey from the *Dublin University Magazine,* August 1849. (National Gallery of Ireland). Croker was a pioneering collector of Irish folklore who supplied information, including the story of the Claddagh ring, to the Halls for their book on Ireland in the 1840s.

broker, Mr Kirwan, who 'after the famine of years of '46 and 47' had left on his hands Claddagh rings on which he advanced cash in his pawnbroking business to the extent of £500 and which he claimed were chiefly pawned by people of the Claddagh, who were even then emigrating in hundreds'.[19] This statement was committed to paper sixty years after the Famine and cannot possibly be correct. In 1846/47 five hundred pounds was a large fortune and the number of families living in the Claddagh prior to that period was merely four or five hundred. Furthermore, Slater's *Directory of Ireland* lists nine pawnbrokers trading in Galway in 1846 and Mr Kirwan's name is not among them.

The renowned antiquarian and scholar, Dudley Westropp (1868-1954), corresponded with William Dillon while researching, *inter alia,* Galway goldsmiths for Sir Charles Jackson's *English Goldsmiths and their Marks,* and a letter from Dillon to Westropp gives details of how his father, Thomas Dillon, came to Galway from Waterford in 1850.[20] The letter includes the information that Richard and Thomas Dillon, goldsmiths, Waterford, sons of Jonathan Dillon (watchmaker), Waterford[21] and grandsons of Joseph Dillon (goldsmith) Waterford,[22] after publication of the Halls' work manufactured Claddagh rings in Waterford. Especially noteworthy is a Claddagh ring made for Queen Victoria by Dillons of Waterford around 1849.[23] In 1850 Thomas Dillon moved to Galway and opened a shop in No 1 William Street, while his brother, Richard Dillon, remained in Waterford. Thus the manufacture of the Claddagh ring from 1843 onwards gradually became commercialised, the design being reproduced as far afield as Birmingham.

There is no doubt that the growing manufacturing activities of the jewellers and watchmakers of Galway between 1850 and 1900 added greatly to the increasing popularity of the Claddagh ring both here and abroad. Thomas Dillon, Roland Stephens, Louisa Burgh, Stephen Fallon, and Thomas Hartnell all made important contributions to the commercial success of these attractive love tokens for both men and women. By 1900 T Dillon and Sons were advertising in the *Galway Archaeological and Historical Society Journal* not only Claddagh rings but also 'Original Claddagh brooches, bangles and scarf pins'. Today every Irish jeweller displays a profusion of Claddagh rings, brooches, neck pendants, bracelets, ear rings, cuff links and other jewellery.

While we can be certain that the name Claddagh as applied to a gold ring with a motif of clasped hands holding a crowned heart goes back no further than the Halls' publication of the 1840s, the question of whether or not such rings actually originated in the Claddagh district of Galway remains problematic. In making rings, did eighteenth-century Galway silversmiths such as Richard Joyce, George Robinson, Austin French, and Andrew Robinson simply use a known motif symbolic of love and friendship and was it then copied in various metal alloys by the less wealthy such as the Claddagh women; or did they, as is less likely, take a motif already traditional to the rural community of Galway and surroundings and make it in turn fashionable for the wealthy?

APPENDIX I

James Hardiman in his *History of Galway* (1820) p.15 recounts a legend which at that time was still 'piously believed' by the Joyce family of Galway. The romantic story relates to Margaret Joyce, the wealthy widow of a Spanish merchant, who in 1596 married Oliver Oge Ffrench, Mayor of Galway. During the absence of her second husband this lady erected at her own expense most of the bridges of the province of Connaught and as 'she was one day sitting before the workmen an eagle flying over her head let fall into her bosom a gold ring adorned with a brilliant stone the nature of which no lapidary could ever discover'. Several authors have attempted to connect this ring with the origin of the Claddagh ring. It is difficult to see any connection between a ring with a large stone bezel and that of a cast metal crowned heart held by two hands. Furthermore the Blake family records of 1905 (Martin Blake, National Library Coll No. IR9292B6, p.239) note. 'A curious relic has been preserved in the senior line of the Joyces of Joyce Country for 300 years; it is a stone of the shape and size of an egg and of polished surface, possibly a species of crystal. According to the tradition of the family the stone was dropped by an eagle into the lap of Margaret, daughter of John Joyce and wife of Oliver Oge Ffrench who was Mayor of Galway 1596-1597. The relic is the possession of Martin B Joyce formally of Tinahille in Joyce Country by now, 1905, residing in the town of Galway'.

IDA DELAMER is a former Chairman of the Silver Society of Great Britain and a Member of the Antique Plate Committee of the Goldsmiths Company.

ACKNOWLEDGEMENTS
My sincere thanks to Mairead Dunlevy and Conor O'Brien for information on Thomas Crofton Croker. Also to Murough de Vere O'Brien for Robert Senuit's book on the Spanish Armada Treasures. My thanks to John Teahan, Dermot St. John and Valerie Dowling of the National Museum for their help with photographs. Many thanks to Anthony North of the V & A Museum and to Mary Boydell for photographs. Sincere thanks to Cathy Fitzgerald for typing this article.

APPENDIX II
Galway Goldsmiths, from 1500-1900

Silver wares stamped with local marks were made in Galway from about 1650 to 1750. These marks were:
(a) *The Maker's Mark*, the initial letters of the Christian name and surname of the maker.
(b) *The Town Marks*, a ship and an anchor struck singly or together on the one piece.

Maker's Marks		**Town Marks**	
	Bartholomew Fallon		Ship
	Richard Joyce		Anchor
	Mark Fallon		

Fineness marks were not used by the Galway goldsmiths. The use of the anchor as a town mark was not confined to Galway. It was used as a town mark by Goldsmiths of Birmingham, Greenock, Canongate, now part of Edinburgh, and possibly by goldsmiths of the smaller English towns in the west country area. For this reason the anchor mark has to be considered in relation to all other stamped marks found with it when identifying a piece of gold or silver. It is probable that silver chalices were made in Galway as early as 1600 as there are many extant of good quality, made during the the years 1600-1650 with engraved inscriptions associated with west of Ireland families.

ABBREVIATIONS: G.S.: Goldsmith; S.S.: Silversmith; J: Jeweller; C.+W.: Clock and Watchmaker.

Andrew FALLON. (G.S.) c.1500. Galway Council Book A. 390-91.
Donill Oge OVALLOGHAN. (G.S.) c.1500. Galway Council Book A. 390-91. (O'Nolan) Free of Galway 1500 for maintaining his father-in-law Andrew Fallon.
Thomas DAVIN. (G.S.) 1575. d.1579. Incription on tomb stone Francisican Abbey, Galway. Sketch of tomb Hardiman's p.316.
Bartholomew FALLON. (G.S.) Galway Corporation Book. 1679. d.1722.
Richard JOYCE. (S.S.) returned from Algiers 1690. Married 1709.

Last mentioned 1737 (Chalice N.M.).
Mark FALLON. (G.S.) Free 1696. Married 1722. Working c.1740.
Thomas LYNCH. (S.S.) Married 1706.
Robert ANDREWS. (J.) Mentioned 1740 (Hardimans). 1769 (Faulkner). d.1769.
John SHADWELL. (S.S.) Married 1757 Galway.
Elias TANKERVILLE. (C&W.M.) (1764 on Common Council of Galway, mentioned Hardiman's History of Galway, p.187).
Thomas Fitzfrancis LYNCH. (S.S.) d.1771.
George ROBINSON. (G.S.) Free 1772. Galway Corporation. Book K. Mentioned 1778 (Faulkner) Registered Dublin Goldsmiths Company 1784. d.1806.
Austin FRENCH. (G.S.) Perhaps working prior to 1771. Registered Dublin Goldsmiths Company. 1784.
Martin LAIN. (S.S.) Registered Dublin Goldsmiths Company. 1784.
Laurence COLEMAN. (S.S.) Registered Dublin Goldsmiths Company. 1784.
Francis DOWLING. (S.S.) Registered Dublin Goldsmiths Company. 1785.
Michael O'MARA. (S.S.) Registered Dublin Goldsmith Company. 1785.
William LEATHAM. (W.M.) Free 1775. Registered Dublin Goldsmiths Company. 1786.
James KELLY. (J.) Registered Dublin Goldsmiths Company. 1799. Pigots Director 1820.
Andrew ROBINSON. (J.&W.M.) Free 1813. Pigots Directory 1820-1824.
Nicholas BURGE. (J.&W.M.) Registered Dublin Goldsmiths Company. 1817. Pigots Directory 1820-24 and 1846.
James CLINCH. (J.&W.M.) Pigots Directory 1820.
Charles VERDON. (C.&W.M.) Pigots Directory 1820.
Roland STEPHEN'S (W.M.) Pigots Directory 1846.
Ed. O'FLAHERTY. (J.) Pigots Directory 1846.
James SEALY. (J.) Pigots Directory 1846.
Louisa BURGE (J.) Pigots Directory 1856.
Thomas DILLON. (J.&W.M.) Waterford 1842-50. Galway. 1850-c.1900.
Philip ROCHE (C.&W.M.) Pigots Directory 1881.
Chas. Shiffield (C.&W.M.) Pigots Directory 1881.
Luke STEPHENS (C.&W.M.) Pigots Directory 1881.
Stephen FALLON. (C.&W.M.) Pigots Directory 1894.
Thomas HARTNESS. (J.) 1900.
William DILLON. (J.&W.M.) 1900.

6. CLADDAGH RINGS: *The Hon. Garech Browne's Collection.* This collection which was originally made between c. 1910 and 1940 by John Costelloe of Tuam includes the earliest known Claddagh ring (top left) which was made by Richard Joyce of Galway (see Fig. 2).

1. For a recent survey that includes a bibliography see C Joyce, *Claddagh Ring Story* (Galway, 1990).

2. Charles Oman, *British Rings (800-1914),* London, 1972, p.38 (p.45 footnote 18. 'The name *fede* appears to have been introduced by the nineteenth century ring collectors'.).

3. *Ibid.,* p.39.

4. This ring is illustrated in exh. cat., *Treasures of the Armada,* Ulster Museum 1972, pp.156, 264 and is now in the possession of the Ulster Museum, Belfast.

5. *Ibid.,* p.35.

6. Richard Joyce, silversmith (Galway), fl. 1690-1737. Joyce, a native of Galway, as a young man in 1679 was captured on his passage to the West Indies by an Algerian corsair. On arrival in Algiers he was purchased as a slave by a wealthy Turkish goldsmith who instructed him in his trade. After William III's accession to the throne of England he demanded the immediate release of all British subjects detained in Algerian slavery. In 1690 Joyce returned to Galway, married in 1707 and had three daughters, two who married, one to Andrew Roe French, the other to a Lynch. It would come as no surprise if Austin French (G.S.) 1770-1810, proved to be related to Joyce.

7. Thomas Meade, silversmith (Kinsale), 1689-1730. Free Kinsale Corp., 1689. Married 1691. A reliquary cross in the National Museum of Ireland has Meade's punch struck four times.

8. Written records of the revitalised Ancient and Most Benevolent Order of the Friendly Brothers of St Patrick start in 1750 and record that 'an ancient order of the Friendly Brothers was in existence and had been dormant for about thirty years'. The order was established not in the capital of the country but in a small town in Co Galway with the professed objects of 'promoting friendship and benevolence among all men and with that view, inculcating religious and political tolerance, putting a stop to duelling and encouraging loyalty between man and man'. The Assemblies of the Brethren are known as Knots, signifying the indissoluble 'Tie of Love and Friendship,' The Galway Knot was revived in 1750, the Kinsale Knot in 1754. T Percy Kirkpatrick, *The Ancient and Most Benevolent Order of the Friendly Brothers of St Patrick. 'A Suggested Origin',* Dublin, 1943.

9. M S Dudley Westropp records (personal file on Irish silver viewed with Mrs E P How's kind permission) 'a ring marked E.T. incuse and a small + cross on the back of the bezel'. Westropp suggests Edward Topham, W.M., Castlebar (Pigot *Directory,* 1824), as the maker. The author suggests it could be Elias Tankerville C.M.&W.M., Galway, c.1764 (James Hardiman, *History of the Town of Galway,* Dublin, 1820, pp.183,187). It should be noted the Corporation records of Galway, Books G H and I, c.1732-c.1771 are missing (*Galway Archaeological & Historical Society Journal,* Vol. 1, 1900, p.132).

10. George Robinson of Galway, goldsmith. Admitted freeman on 29 October 1772, (*Liber K. Corporation of Galway.* Noted by M S D Westropp). Registered Dublin Goldsmith Company, 1784. Address given as High Street, Galway. Died 1806.

11. Mr and Mrs S C Hall, *Ireland its Scenery and Character,* 3 vols, (London, 1841-43).

12. *Ibid.* vol. 1, *The Authors' Advertisement.*

13. James Coleman, 'Thomas Crofton Croker as an Irish folklorist,' *Cork Historical and Archaeological Society Journal,* Vol. III, 1894, p.130.

14. 'The Gallery of Illustrious Literary Characters, No. IX, Crofton Croker,' *Fraser's Magazine,* London, 1831, p.67.

15. Ruan O'Donnell and Bob Rice, 'A Clean Breast – Crofton Croker's Fairy Tale of General Holt,' *Eighteenth-Century Ireland,* Vol. 7, Dublin, 1992.

16. See William Dillon, *Galway Archaeological & Historical Journal,* 1905-06, Vol V, pp.13, 14. The author has in her possession a letter written in 1906 by Robert Day F.S.A., an avid collector of Irish silver and a well known antiquarian from Cork, which reaffirms William Dillon's assertion that Claddagh rings were also made in brass, bronze, silver and guinea coins. In the letter he advises a friend on the acquisition of a Claddagh ring: 'You are doubtless aware that there are varieties of the so-called Claddagh to be met with in the country town pawn offices – the majority of which bear the Birmingham anchor mark. The gold in your ring has a large alloy of copper, it is well worn from age and time and altho' without a maker's mark of any kind, is in my opinion a genuine Claddagh. There is a variety of the Claddagh from which the crown is absent – these are known as Munster rings. I have met with them in Cork and Limerick.' 'Among my Claddaghs are representations in silver, brass and gold. Guineas were melted down for use in Claddaghs, one of the latter dated 1796, another with the posey *Yours in Hart'.*

17. The largest female wedding rings' internal diameter is usually regarded as 1.75cm (size T) and anything above 1.9cm (size W) as male.

18. William Dillon, *Galway Archaeological and Historical Society Journal,* 1905-06, Vol. IV, p.11.

19. *Ibid.,* p.13. Mr John Kirwan, Pawnbroker, is mentioned as one of the pawnbrokers of Galway in Sleaters *Directory, 1870 and 1881.* His name is not listed in the 1894 Directory.

20. Letter from Wm. Dillon to Dudley Westropp, (M S Dudley Westropp personal file on Irish Silver reviewed with Mrs E P How's kind permission).

21. Jonathan Dillon, watch maker, Waterford, 1820-1842 mentioned in Pigot & Co., *Commercial Directory,* 1820-1924.

22. Joseph Dillon, goldsmith, Waterford, 1750-1806. Regd. in Goldsmiths' Hall, Dublin, 1784.

23. Unfortunately this ring cannot now be identified. It was made perhaps for Queen Victoria's marriage to Albert in February 1840 or as a presentation piece during her visit to Ireland, August 1849. (Information in letter from Wm Dillon to Westropp with Mrs E P How's kind permission).

THE CLADDAGH RING

APPENDIX III
TABLE OF SOME GOLD 'CLADDAGH' RINGS EXTANT FROM 1700-1900

Most of the rings in this table have been assayed. Notes:
(a) The gold content varies between 7 carats and 18 carats per ring.
(b) All rings made prior to 1820 have the hoop soldered to each side of the bezel.
(c) The first and second ring on the table by R Joyce and T Meade respectively have a hammered bezel. All the other rings have a cast bezel.
(d) All rings with the internal diameter measuring ovr 1.9cm (Size W) are considered to be male rings.
(e) All rings from Austin French's workshop have a rudimentary crown over the heart.

Photographs and information on the rings are from the following sources:

The Hon Garech Browne	G.B.
National Museum of Ireland	N.M
A private collection	R.W.
The British Museum	B.M.
The Victoria & Albert Museum	V&A
James Weldon	J.W.
Some rings noted by Dudley Westropp	D.W.

Unless otherwise stated the maker is from Galway.

Circa Date	Ring	Internal Diameter cms	Internal Initials	Maker's Mark	Maker's Name (For details see Appendix II)
1700		2.2	N^{C}M M^{R}C	RI RI	(G.B. No. 1) Richard Joyce (G.S.) 1690-1737
1700		2.0	+ Cross on back of bezel	T·MEADE T·M	(R.W.) Thomas Meade (G.S.) Kinsale 1689-1730.
1700		1.95	A^{C}M	T·MEADE	(G.B. No.8) Thomas Meade (G.S.) Kinsale 1689-1730
1700		2.0	P^{S}F	T·M	(G.B. No.13) Thomas Meade (G.S.) Kinsale 1689-1730
1765 or 1824	Noted by Dudley Westropp		+ Cross on back to bezel	E*T	Pos. Elias Tankerville (C.M.) c.1765 or Edward Topham (W.M.) Tuam. c.1824
1784		1.95	M^{R}M	F	(G.B. No. 15) Austin French (J).
1784		1.7	P^{P}J	F	(J.W.) Austin French (J).
1784		2.0	T^{C}R	F (incuse)	(G.B. No. 2) Austin French (J).
1784		2.0	R^{D}M	F (incuse)	(G.B. No. 18) Austin French (J)
1784		2.0	I^{P}M	F (incuse)	(N.M. 1954-62) Austin French (J)
1784		2.0	P^{D}F	None	(N.M. 114 Cat. No.) Rudimentary Crown is similar to other AustinFrench (J)
1784		2.25			(G.B. No. 3)George Robinson (J) 1772-1806
1784		2.0	P^{C}H	GR	(G.B. No. 17) (George Robinson (J) 1772-1806
1784		2.0		GR	(G.B. No. 24) George Robinson (J)1772-1806
1784		2.2		GR	(B.M. Love & Marriage Rings No. 1105) George Robinson (J) 1772-1806
1800		2.25		R (incuse)	(B.M. Love & Marriage Rings No. 1104) Possibly G. Robinson. c.1800
1800		2.2		I.J.K	(R.W.)James Kelly (J) 1799
1800		2.2		I.J.K	(G.B. No. 14) James Kelly (J) 1799

Circa Date	Ring	Internal Diameter cms	Internal Initials	Maker's Mark	Maker's Name (For details see Appendix II)
1813		2.0		AR	(G.B. No. 4)Andrew Robinson (J. & W.M.) 1813-1824
1813		2.0		AR	(N.M. Cat. No. 1932.85) Andrew Robinson (J.&W.M.) 1813-1824
1813		2.1	J^{M}M	AR (incuse)	(V&A M12-1961) Andrew Robinson (J.&W.M.) 1813-1824
1813		2.1		AK (incuse)	(G.B. No.6)
1813		2.2	N^{Mc}N	NB	(G.B. No.12) Nicholas Burge. (J.&W.M.) 1817-1846
1813		2.3	I^{M}M	NB	(G.B. No. 19) Nicholas Burge (J.&W.M.)
1813		2.0		NB	(G.B. No. 23) Nicholas Burge
1820		1.9		IC IC IC	(G.B. No. 21) James Clinch (J.&W.M.) 1820-1824
1824	Noted by Dudley Westropp No photograph or measurement			JD	Jonathan Dillon (J) 1824. Waterford.
1824	Noted by Dudley Westropp No photograph or measurement			J·M	James Manion (J) c.1824. Tuam.
1846	Noted by Dudley Westropp No photograph or measurement			RS	Roland Stephens (W.M.) c.1846
1846		2.2		RD	(R.W.) Richard Dillon (J) 1846-c.1900 Waterford
1846		2.0	J^{M}C	JS	(G.B. No. 20) James Sealy (J)
1846		2.0		JS	(N.M. Cat. No. F1932.86) James Sealy (J)
1846		1.5		TD	(N.M. Cat. No. 1922.1) Thomad Dillon (J) 1842-50 Waterford 1850-90 Galway
1846		1.7		TD	(N.M. Cat. No. 1932.88) Thomas Dillon (J) 1842-50 Waterford 1850-90 Galway
1856	Noted by Dudley Westropp No photograph or measurement			LB	Louisa Burge (J) c.1856
1890		2.2		SF	(G.B. No. 11) Stephen Fallon (J) 1880 onwards
1900		1.9		TH	(N.M. 1913-8) Thomas Hartnell (J) 1900 onwards
1900	Noted by Dudley Westropp No photograph or measurement			WD	William Dillon (J) 1900 onwards

Book Reviews

Past Perceptions: The Prehistoric Archaeology of South West Ireland
EDITED BY ELIZABETH SHEE TWOHIG AND
MARGARET RONAYNE
Cork University Press, 1993.
183pp. 56 b/w ills. £17.95(p/b) 0-902561-89-8

Building on the Past – Urban Change and Archaeology
BY DOUGLAS HYDE
Environmental Institute, University College Dublin,
125pp, no ills. £18(h/b), £12(p/b) 1-898473-02-1

Irish Archaeology Illustrated
EDITED BY MICHAEL RYAN
Country House, Dublin, 1994 (paperback edition of the 1991 hardback).
224pp., 174 col., 88 b&w ills. £11.95(p/b)
0-946172-33-1

Ancient Ireland – The User's Guide
BY GERALD CONAN KENNEDY
Morrigan Books, 1994,
112pp., no ills, £4.95(p/b) 0-907677-60-6

Lynda Mulvin

HERE ARE FOUR books about Ireland ancient and modern, presenting at various levels of detail new and reviewed evidence of different aspects of archaeology.

The first is a valuable overview of prehistoric archaeology in south-west Ireland. In a well-referenced and refreshingly informative manner, the book sets out the contributions of expert participants in a conference held at University College Cork in February 1992. Sixteen narratives are accompanied by a rich assortment of maps, charts and drawings. Among the contributions are details of the exciting discovery of the Mesolithic period in Munster. Traces of post-glacial human activity are also recorded. These corroborating results, obtained by environmental research, demonstrate the merit of this painstaking science, often excluded from archaeological surveys on the grounds of cost. The discovery of new and unique forms of the rock art motifs at the Iveragh Peninsula, consisting of 'equi-armed crosses with cup-mark or ringed terminals contained within penannular rings', is described in some detail, and this comparative discussion is also of interest to the art historian. In addition, a survey of the development of

IVERAGH PENINSULA, Co Kerry. Rock art, probably of the Neolithic Period. From *Past Perceptions* edited by Elizabeth Shee Twohig and Margaret Ronayne. 'The discovery of new and unique forms of rock art motifs at the Iveragh Peninsula is described and this comparative discussion is also of interest to the art historian'.

the Bronze Age periods in South-West Ireland is presented along with comparative examples. A final part provides new directions for the practice of archaeology and for the better dissemination of scientific information. More generally, *Past Perceptions* is a useful resource book both for this geographical area and, as the editors stress, for the comparative study of other regions in Ireland.

In the second book, Douglas Hyde provides an appraisal of the complex question of archaeology and policies of urban renewal in Ireland. The book has a basis in research, where it began as a master's thesis, and although it lacks a certain beauty of design, the author uses a sure hand with a thorough knowledge of the subject to guide the reader through the surrounding issues. A wealth of supporting technical information is provided in the references and appendices, with extracts, for example, from 'The Dublin City Development Plan 1991', and the laws which seek to safeguard the Irish Heritage in its various forms are explained. The book serves to encourage an approach which combines the concerns of the classically opposing forces of archaeologists and developers. Through a set of case studies, it is demonstrated that the developer should

not fear the archaeologist, and vice versa; instead, cooperation is the name of the game. The case studies include the Jury's Hotel site at Christchurch Place, the centre of Dublin's medieval city where the only surviving tower in the city walls was, after a dispute, protected. One criticism is that the comparative discussion does not extend beyond Britain. Otherwise, this is a solid and interesting treatment of a potentially dry subject from which passions, nonetheless, are apt to rise.

The third book, *Irish Archaeology Illustrated*, is a lavish perusal of the history of archaeology in Ireland from prehistory to the seventeenth century. It contains a finely documented account of the archaeology, ancient history, architecture, landscape, and literature in the subjects chosen by each of the thirty-seven expert contributors from North and South. Happily, the personal style of each contributor is retained. The addition of a glossary and bibliography makes this a valuable possession for the enthusiast and scholar alike.

The last of the above titles, *Ancient Ireland – The User's Guide*, attempts to introduce to the subject of Ancient Ireland a 'user-friendly' approach which seeks to make aspects of ancient Irish culture more accessible to popular readers. However, this is a book whose simple promise is frustrated by the intrusion of irrelevant digressions and by the omission of any references to support its meagre text. If its audience is the interested visitor, it contains inadequate directions to the monuments selected; if targeted at the mythology enthusiast, there is nothing new; and if, as I suspect, its real intention is to amuse, its glib attempts to be witty and modern fall flat.

LYNDA MULVIN is an archaeologist, stone conservator and art historian, currently teaching in the Department of the History of Art, University College, Dublin.

Ireland: Art into History
EDITED BY BRIAN P KENNEDY AND RAYMOND GILLESPIE
Town House, Dublin, 1994
240pp., 100 col. 50 b/w ills £29.95 (h/b)
0-948524-47-2

Visualising Ireland: National Identity and the Pictorial Tradition
EDITED BY ADELE M DALSIMER AND NANCY NETZER
Faber and Faber, Boston and London, 1993
230pp. 55 b/w ills, £10.99 ($16.95) 0-571-19813-9

John Turpin

IN RECENT YEARS Irish art history has begun to shift from a concentration on biography and style to social and historical context. This is in line with international developments in the discipline. It is a valuable corrective to a previous over-emphasis on formal analysis and stylistic influence. A symposium on image and cultural content was held at the National Gallery of Ireland in December 1990 and a subsequent exhibition from the Gallery was presented at the Boston College Museum of Art. It is out of those events that these two volumes materialised.

The Dublin volume contains thirteen essays and the Boston one, twelve essays. In the Dublin series, six narrowly focussed essays concentrate on Malton's idealisation of Dublin architecture; Waterford Street Life; folk life sources for F.W. Burton; the idealisation of Famine depictions in the *Illustrated*

London News; portrait self-images of Daniel O'Connell and Albert Power's expression of Irish-Ireland ideals. Other essays in thè series take a broader slice of Irish art history: the transformation of tomb sculpture in the sixteenth and seventeenth centuries in relation to Counter-Reformation spirituality and family pride; the political motivation behind Nationalist sculptural movements; the architectural stylistic expression of the beliefs of Catholics, Anglicans and Presbyterians; Irish landscape painting in relation to perspectives from historical geography; images of furniture and costume, and finally the visual productions of the Free State period (stamps, coins, books, painting and architecture) as an index of ideology. Cross-disciplinary methods produced some of the freshest ideas such as those of P J Duffy, the historical geographer, and of Alistair Rowan who made the case for the inter-relation of ideology

T A JONES (1823-93): *Molly Macree*. (National Gallery of Ireland). From *Visualising Ireland: National Identity and the Pictorial Tradition* edited by Adele M Dalsimer and Nancy Netzer. One of the themes of the book is the idealised image of the colleen Molly Macree as a reflection of the place of woman.

and nineteenth-century Irish church architecture. Most of the contributors to this beautifully produced and illustrated volume were art historians which accounts for the strongly visual flavour of the enterprise.

The volume from Boston, while it shares a multi-disciplinary approach, is rather different in character. Its format is modest, the illustrations fewer and in black and white. There is a far greater emphasis on social history and literary criticism than in the Dublin volume.

The themes dealt with are: the idealised image of the colleen Molly Macree as a reflection of the place of woman; watercolours of Mildred Anne Butler and Rose Barton in relation to literary and political parallels; ideology contained in depictions of Dublin streets; cultural nationalism as revealed in three medievalising images and in views of the Irish Exhibition of Art and Industry of 1853; urban development documented by Francis Place's watercolours; the role of the antiquarian topographic artists (an article by the late Maire de Paor which was a superb analysis of the relation of art to archaeology and the cultural ideals of the period); Du Noyer's work for the Geological Survey; Francis Wheatley's Irish painting – a fine investigation of the interaction between art and politics; the representation of the thatched house with its artistic and ideological connotations; the daily life of a professional miniaturist; and the realistic drawings of the west of Ireland by Jack Yeats for Synge. In all of these cases the visual material is related to ideological standpoints. This is sometimes forced and unconvincing. It is particularly strong in the essays on Irish archaeological water colours, Wheatley, the Irish cottage and Jack Yeats.

These are timely volumes, alerting historians and art historians to the value of an inter-disciplinary search for historical evidence and explanation. There are, however, different perspectives for art historians as for other historians and literary critics. The social historian sees material culture, including the visual arts, as a further source of information.

The literary critic sees it as a text for speculative deconstruction. The art historian must be aware of the issue of visual stylistic conventions (major influences on the forms that representation takes) as well as the issues of quality. The only criticism I would make of these volumes, especially the Boston one, it is that several contributors seem unaware of these complexities about visual form and the conventions of representation. The best essays were those which made convincing arguments that the visual results were the outcome of a demonstrable intersection of ideological positions and stylistic options. The least successful essays seemed to be those which simply used visual evidence to lend additional support to arguments fundamentally generated by non-visual evidence in any broadly historical enquiry and the art historians must give greater consideration to social content at both empirical and interpretative levels.

JOHN TURPIN has written extensively on Irish art education and is the author of John Hogan: Irish Neo-classical Sculptor in Rome *(1982).*

Trees of Ireland – Native and Naturalized

By Charles Nelson and Wendy Walsh

Lilliput Press, Dublin. First printed 1993; reprinted with corrections 1994
pp.256, 30 colour plates £35 (h/b), £17.99 (p/b)
1-874675-23-6 (limited edition); 1-874675-24-4 (h/b);
1-874675-25-2 (p/b)

Thomas Pakenham

In Irish botany the villain of the piece is not an invading people – Vikings, Normans, Cromwellians – but an invading ice-sheet. A million years ago, Ireland had no Irishmen, but was rich in flora beyond the dreams of avarice. There were hundreds of native tree species, including giant tree ferns and cycads, and exotics like the ginkgo and sequoia, now native only to China and America. But the ice-sheet cometh. After four separate ice-ages, the ice-sheet had scraped Ireland as clean as a bar of soap, giving us beautiful lakes and mountains, but leaving our soil as bare

and treeless as the North Pole.

In this scholarly and entertaining volume, elegantly illustrated, like its predecessors, by the paintings and vignettes of Wendy Walsh, Dr Charles Nelson gives a roll-call of the survivors from that massacre of our tree population. He lists a mere twenty-one native species. These were the trees that limped back to Ireland, when the ice had melted but before the rising sea level had swamped the land bridge with Europe, returning after 100,000 years exile in the safe havens of Bosnia (yes, Bosnia). To find even twenty-one tree species Dr Nelson has had to be exceptionally generous. Seven of his trees – holly, elder, hazel, hawthorn, spindle and two kinds of buckthorn – are better known as bushes. There are only five native species that can grow to giant size – common oak, sessile oak, ash, yew and elm. And now the elm seems doomed to succumb to a new invader, the elm bark beetle and its murderous virus from America. To these Dr Nelson throws in a makeweight of nine naturalised trees that could not apparently hop over from Calais and Holyhead without a helping hand from man. These are: beech, hornbeam, sweet chestnut, horse chestnut, wild pear, white willow, laburnum, walnut and sycamore (I would have added a tenth, with as good a claim to an Irish passport, the irrepressible common lime. Burn an old lime stump on a bonfire and a new tree, with three hundred years life ahead, springs up from the roots).

Such are the scraps left behind by the ice-sheet – a mere thirty species, compared to more than two hundred in one province of China. Yet what richness remains is amply demonstrated by Dr Nelson. The book has many virtues. You can treat it as a botanical primer, sorting out the puzzles that botanists inflict on laymen (which oak has the longer stalked leaves, the short stalked oak or the long stalked oak? Answer: the short stalked (sessile) oak, silly. The stalks in question are on the acorns. You can learn identification. You can teach your-

self tree propagation, grabbing the acorns or the beech mast before the squirrels get them, and growing them in jam-pots on your window sill. You can dig out the folk-lore attached to each species, and learn why the elder was an accursed tree, though protected by the Laws of the Neighbourhood, *Bretha Conraithchesa.*

Most important, this is a book to make us cherish our exceptional heritage of specimen trees. Poor in species, we are rich in gigantic individuals. Last year I made a plant-collecting trip to China, and drove two thousand miles in Yunnan, botanically the richest of all Chinese provinces. Only once did we see a specimen tree of exceptional size. It was a ten-metre girthed hemlock spruce, *Tsuga dumosa,* the last of a great primeval forest that had once straddled the borders of China, Burma and Tibet. Somehow it had escaped the axes of the loggers, who had scoured this part of Yunnan with the zeal of an ice-sheet. Yet even that mighty hemlock, towering over the smashed scrubland of maple and bamboo, was nothing compared to an ordinary beech in an Irish demesne.

This is not just pub patriotism. As Dr Nelson documents, Ireland has some of the largest beech trees in the world at Birr, for example, and (if I say it myself) at our own house in the bog, Tullynally. Come and see a beech tree's natural engineering – thirty tons of it, with twenty-five miles of trunks, branches and twigs, with a quarter of a million leaves, annually renewed, and all built to the blueprint of an eighteenth century beech nut the size of a postage stamp.

Or why not a trip to Tullamore to see the 'King Oak'. It may be a relic of the wildwood of Ely O'Carroll. Or it may have been planted six hundred years ago by king or peasant. In age or bulk it is one of the champion oaks of Europe. Come and pay homage. When Tullamore is brought to dust, the King Oak could be still crawling out of the bog like a great green lobster.

THOMAS PAKENHAM, whose latest book is The Scramble for Africa, *is now writing a book on exceptional trees in Britain and Ireland.*

BOOK REVIEWS

The Watercolours of Ireland: works on
paper in pencil, pastel and paint,
c.1600-1914
BY ANNE CROOKSHANK AND THE KNIGHT OF GLIN
Barrie and Jenkins, London, 1994
329pp. 200 col. 200 b/w ills. £45 (h/b)
0-09-178369-0

Bruce Arnold

WATERCOLOUR PAINTING is a pure art
form, with rigorous conditions governing
its materials and its practice. Pigment,
mixed with water, and placed on paper,
is the essential ingredient. Pigment on its
own would fall off the paper, once the
water dried, and the artist would be back
where he started, so an adhering agent is
also required. This crucial ingredient –
gum, albumen, size – is minute in comparison with the water, and invisible
where the pigment is gloriously evident
in every square inch. Together with
brushes, paper, and other more periph-
al equipment, this is the defined centre
of the watercolourist's art and craft,
together with the actual palette of individual painters. How these developed,
how they made possible different
approaches to the actual painting of
watercolours, is central to any study; and
the absence of serious discussion, in this
book, must raise fundamental questions
at the outset of one's survey.

Should the focus be on the historical
narrative, or on those practitioners who
developed, changed, widened and
expanded the practice of watercolour
painting? And if the second, then does
the genre really exist, in Irish terms, to
justify a non-historical survey?

After more than thirty years collecting
watercolours, and almost ten years trying
to paint in watercolour, I think I would
have taken the same course as the one
adopted by the distinguished authors of
this book, which is the former, rather
than the latter. It would have been taken
with regret; but also with the clear
acknowledgement that the tradition of
watercolour painting, in Ireland, in the
purest sense, is marginal, and derivative.
And it is necessary to deal with the tradition primarily as an historical narrative,
and to throw the net as widely as possible,

Hugh Douglas HAMILTON (1740-1808): *Canova in his studio with Henry Tresham* (Private Collection, England).
From *The Watercolours of Ireland* by Anne Crookshank and The Knight of Glin. 'The book is comprehensive,
adopting a broad and catholic view, in which the authors embrace drawing, in crayon, pencil, pastel, as well as
true watercolour painting.'

in order to compensate for the short supply of major artists in the genre, and for
the limited respect the genre had. It is no
reflection on Irish artistic enterprise and
skill, and the judgment should not inspire
chauvinistic anger. The simple truth is
this: a small country, overshadowed, gov-
erned and taught by a larger neighbour,
produced a respectable number of practitioners in watercolour painting but less
than a handful in the first rank, and that
handful spread across two centuries.

As one would expect, from these two
distinguished scholars of Irish art, the
book, then, is a rich and detailed study,
from the late sixteenth century to the
twentieth-century work of Jack Yeats and
William Orpen (neither of whom, incidentally, were painters in watercolour in
the true sense, but used it, en passant, as
it were, and in Yeats's case in a qualified
way, primarily for illustration).

The book is comprehensive, adopting
a broad and catholic view, in which the
authors embrace drawing, in crayon,
pencil, pastel, pen, work in gouache and
body-colour, as well as true watercolour
painting; and it is historical, not in the
obvious sense only, of presenting us with

an historical narrative of periods and
developments, but in placing greater
emphasis on what artists did than on
how they did it. In summary, this
embraces the book's single most telling
defect: there is virtually no exploration
of the palette and practical technique of
individual artists, and no explanation of
the impact of technical change and
development on an artist such as
Mildred Anne Butler, who benefited
enormously from late nineteenth-century improvements in the handling of
paper, and in the transportation of paint.

We do have, in the book, the full
atmosphere of social and political events,
dominating in particular the early chapters, and in the later ones an enormously
rich examination of the lives of artists.
Indeed, the first hundred years or so are
marked by close and practical relationships between art and events.

The more settled, if patrician, life of
the eighteenth century inspired a different range of subject-matter. Views were
important. People wanted to be told what
they were looking at in a more pleasing,
and less cartographic way. They wanted
their houses, their cities, their antiquities,

Book Reviews

and examples of the picturesque placed clearly before them, and wrought in skilful and commanding styles.

The full flowering of this history is in the nineteenth century. It reflects the real life of the country then in work of great diversity and lasting accomplishment. Inevitably, the comparisons and linkages with English watercolour painting – probably that country's proudest and most lasting artistic tradition – are evident in stylistic terms and in subject matter. It is instructive, for example, when one is confronted with a clear example of a watercolour artist who stuck with the medium virtually throughout his life, John Henry Campbell, and who understood it within his limitations, displays little of the development to be found in his greater English contemporaries, and is marked out as a talent by his isolation, rather than by any school or fraternity within which he would have shone, had he painted in England.

There is a valuable examination of specialist artists. The chapter on still life and flower painting is good, that on subject painting opens many doors for future scholars, and reminds us of the parallel tradition of topographical printmaking, of which the country boasts a remarkable range.

In the 1830s, watercolour painting in Ireland extricated itself from the pencil, from gouache and body-colour, from line and dim shadow, from pastel, and from the tyranny of topography. In the works of Edward Hayes, George Petrie, Henry O'Neill, Francis Danby, we see the growth of well-reasoned technique and inventiveness, the inspired uses of colour and of pure washes, and the mastery of invention over labour. And this is carefully and thoroughly narrated, though the serious practitioner will crave details on colours used, and types of paint preferred.

It opened the way for an outstanding artist, Frederick William Burton, for the really grand manner of John Faulkner, applied in so honest and straightforward a way, and for artists such as Henry Newton, Samuel McCloy and William Henry Stopford, all new to me, and most impressive.

There is perhaps some awkwardness in the introduction of a chapter on primitive artists, and also one on colonial practitioners. Given the broad approach, and wide range of media, the absence, beside the illustrations, of any detail on this, and of the dimensions, is a serious shortcoming. But there is historic justification for the emphasis on women, towards the end of the century, with Rose Barton, Mildred Anne Butler, Helen O'Hara and others receiving justified attention.

The end is perhaps a disappointment. To rely on Jack Yeats, William Orpen, Patrick Tuohy, William Leech, Mainie Jellett and Margaret Clarke, all painters to whom watercolour painting was secondary, is to point up the marginal status, in Ireland, of the genre. The medium was exceptionally well used by these and other figures, and is infinitely revealing over more than three centuries, in its subtle and intimate expression of ordinary life. In the end it is chamber music we hear, not the beating of the big bass drum. The book, nevertheless, is a considerable achievement, and what magic and genius has come down to us, is fully extracted in these worthwhile pages.

BRUCE ARNOLD has written on Carey Clarke in this issue (pp. 115-122)

Illustrated Incumbered Estates – Ireland 1850-1905
BY MARY CECELIA LYONS. FOREWORD BY THE HON DESMOND GUINNESS
Ballinakella Press, Whitegate, County Clare, 1994, 304pp, 150 b&w ills. £38(h/b). 0-946538-16-6

Mark Bence-Jones

THE INCUMBERED ESTATES Commission, set up in 1849 after the Great Famine, and its successors, the Landed Estates' Court and the Land Judges' Court, facilitated the sale of landed property, urban as well as rural, that was heavily in debt. The records of properties sold by order of these bodies, or offered for sale by them but not actually sold, include descriptions illustrated with contemporary lithographs. In *Illustrated Incumbered Estates*, Dr Mary Cecelia Lyons has made a book of these descriptions, with their lithographs; and from the records she also gives the names of subsequent owners or occupiers of each property and its rateable valuation, which serves as a clue to its condition at various dates.

Though most of the charming and evocative lithographs are of country houses, some are of town houses in Dublin and elsewhere and of other property such as Carlow Quay, Deanough

CARHOO HOUSE, Co Cork. From *Illustrated Incumbered Estates* by Mary Cecelia Lyons. The value of the book lies in the lithographs of lesser country-houses and in the case of Carhoo (which collapsed under suspicious circumstances in 1896) they may be the only pictorial records in existence.

Mill in County Kerry and the Cork Atheneum. The country houses include some famous ones, such as Emo, Eyrecourt and Summerhill – which were, incidentally, among those offered for sale but not actually sold – but the chief value of the book lies in the lithographs of lesser country houses, particularly of houses that have been demolished. The lithographs of Drumrora Lodge, County Cavan, Skahard House, County Galway and Carhoo House, County Cork (which 'collapsed under rather suspicious circumstances in 1896') may well be the only existing pictorial record of these three houses, which appear neither in the present reviewer's *Guide to Irish Country Houses,* nor in *Vanishing Country Houses of Ireland* by the Knight of Glin, David Griffin and Nicholas Robinson.

As well as being an architectural record, the book makes fascinating reading. There are the contemporary descriptions, which take the reader into what Dr Lyons calls 'a Jane Austenish never-never land'; they also tell us the size of the rooms of certain houses and whether or not they possessed bathrooms and water closets. The lists of subsequent owners and occupiers are no less fascinating reading. One wonders whether Baron Henri D'Ivoley, who bought Clifden Castle in 1898, enjoyed living in Connemara. And what brought Vincento Bartelucci to Borrmount House in County Wexford in 1856? One also longs to know more about Harmonia Harding who lived at Carrigboy House in County Cork from 1893 to 1910. The book also contains a wide-ranging introduction in which Dr Lyons treats of her sources and the artists of the lithographs as well as of the circumstances which caused the estates to be sold up; in this respect she rightly points out that many Irish landlords came to grief, not through gambling and high living, as is popularly supposed, but through spending too much money on improving their estates and giving over-generous annuities to relations.

In her introduction, Dr Lyons rather unnecessarily speaks of Debrett and Burke as 'flawed sources', but had she made more use of these volumes she would have avoided a number of mistakes which take away from the book's value as a work of genealogy as well as of architectural history. For example, Lord Greville, who lived at Clonyn Castle in County Westmeath and bought the neighbouring estate of Rosmead in 1879, is rendered as 'Lord Greville Colyn of Colyn Castle'. And in her reverence for the late Professor Jocelyn Otway-Ruthven, to whose memory the book is dedicated, Dr Lyons states that she was 'the last direct descendant of the Otway family'; whereas a glance at Burke would have told her that there are other direct descendants who are alive and, one hopes, well.

MARK BENCE-JONES is the author of Burke's Guide to Country Houses: Ireland *(1978)*

CALLINAFERCY HOUSE, Co Kerry. From *The Houses of Kerry* by Valerie Bary with line drawings by Stephanie Walsh. The house, which was built in 1861 by Richard Leeson who was great-grandson of the Earl of Milltown of Russborough, is one of five hundred and forty Kerry houses described and illustrated.

The Houses of Kerry: Historical, Genealogical, Architectural Notes

BY VALERIE BARY WITH LINE DRAWINGS BY STEPHANIE WALSH

Ballinakella Press, Whitegate, Co Clare, 1994

280pp. 339 b&w ills. £38(h/b). 0-946538-08-5

Jeremy Williams

WHEN MY PARENTS retired to Kerry, my mother was persuaded to collect for the Distressed Irish Gentlewomen's Fund. So, armed with a list of subscribers, I would open rusty gates and immerse myself in avenues winding through sodden rhododendrons to emerge before unknown houses where the front door bell resounded into the silence of its nether regions. The longest and most impenetrable avenue led to Callinafercy which I knew to be the home of the Leeson-Marshalls who should have inherited Russborough from the last Earl of Milltown: he left his treasures instead to Dublin's National Gallery. But the elderly gumbooted chatelaine who opened the door immediately sensed that I had subverted my mother's good works to indulge my aesthetic curiosity. All I succeeded in glimpsing of the inner hall was a bucket collecting leaks from the much gabled roof – for how long I wondered. But miracles still occur: her cousin Valerie Bary has not only restored the house but has written this book which considers Callinafercy among five hundred and forty others. While the most intrepid patrons of architecture responded to the dramatic landscape with mock Gothic castles, the majority chose Elizabethan as more historically plausible and also more adaptable to greater comfort. The most assured neo-Elizabethan country house still survives, Muckrus Abbey, built on the estate that a Herbert grandfather had inherited from the last McCarthy More, his grandson. Death duties do not permit such paradoxes today. Beneath the deceptive charm of Kerry lurks an untamed ferocity. The Reeks, the ancestral seat of the McGillicuddys, has a bland Neo-Georgian facade due to its reconstruction after an explosion caused by a neighbourly dispute denounced by de Valera. This allowed the family to insert into their dining room a magnificent sixteenth-century carved stone fireplace depicting the wedding of an O'Sullivan ancestor.

The most serious defect of this volume is the shortage of architectural credits. J F Fuller appears as one of Kerry's characters, but his two largest country houses remain anonymous, Cahirnane and Dromquinna. William Atkins is not mentioned although all his Kerry commissions are illustrated, the subtly eclectic villas of Aghadoe and Southhill, and the exquisitely Venetian Oak Park. Architects this century get short shrift. Morley Horder, who designed Ard-na-Side for Lady Gordon (who described herself as the ninth demented member of her family to build in Kerry), is not mentioned, nor Henry Hill who worked for the McGillicuddys, nor Francis Pollen who designed two post-modern Georgian retreats for his cousin, Mrs Grosvenor, the niece of the last Lord Kenmare, in her retrenchment.

The illustrations are effective in showing the smaller houses but for the monumental it would have been better to have relied on the works of Neale and other typographers of that time, even if they exaggerate the picturesque. The scenery of Kerry is the missing element: for example the elegant Georgian casino of Foildarrig acquired by the Catholic Diocese as a summer retreat for its bishops with such momentous consequences a century later, is perfectly conveyed by a line drawing, but not its site high over Dingle Bay receding towards the setting sun. But what artist could do justice to that setting apart from Wagner?

JEREMY WILLIAMS' book A Companion Guide to Architecture in Ireland 1837-1921 *was published in 1994.*

Gothic Revival
BY MEGAN ALDRICH

Phaidon, 1994, 240pp, 236 colour, 44b &w ills.
£34.99 (h/b) 0-714828-8-66

Alistair Rowan

ONE OF THE minor genres of English literature is the 'Gothick' novel, usually a rudely predictable tale of innocent heroines, honourable yet unacknowledged heirs, voracious upstarts and ancient – preferably haunted – buildings, filled with echoing vaults and terrifying gloom. This volume entitled *Gothic Revival* and contrived by Megan Aldrich (who has studied art history in America and Canada and is a senior tutor at Sotheby's Educational Studies in London) is very much a modern equivalent for it tells in its style and conception

DROMOLAND CASTLE, Co Clare. Although Megan Aldrich in *Gothic Revival* writes about Ireland, she hardly mentions John Nash whose influence was enormous and she completely ignores the work of his pupils, the Pain brothers, whose Dromoland is a notable example of Picturesque Gothic Revival architecture.

something of the contemporary horror story of rapacious and ugly arts publishing. Why, one wonders, was this book written or commissioned? Dr Aldrich has done excellent work on the Craces, the Early Victorian father and son partnership which with A W N Pugin was to contribute many sumptuous Gothic interiors around the middle of the nineteenth century. She likes this work and she obviously enjoys the prettiness of the earlier eighteenth-century neo-Gothic designs, the Batty Langley era and particularly its fan-vaulted interiors, but – and it is a very big but – she is unfamiliar with the mainstream examples of British neo-Gothic architecture and is woefully at sea on the topic she has chosen for this book.

What the reader is offered is a lopsided survey of the Gothic Revival domestic building from about 1720 to 1900, arranged as six chapters. None of the material which is covered is new and the text rushes through its examples at such speed, and with such little discussion of the issues involved – dashing across the Atlantic in part of chapter

four – that the principal impression which it creates is that of a jolly adult-education lecturer, full of enthusiasm but with no real grasp, tossing off examples of glossy illustrations that appeal to his or her taste. I really suspect that this may be how this book began and it would have been much better had it never passed beyond that stage.

'This book', the publishers proclaim, 'is a visual delight and essential reading for all those interested in architecture and design,' yet its text is full of inaccuracies and its pages are fussy and over-designed, bedevilled by heavy-handed patterning, gratuitous Gothic script, a bewildering range of font sizes and a perverse determination in the arrangement of the plates to illustrate whole buildings at almost postage-stamp size and details as lumpy close-ups, Pugin wallpapers far bigger than they need to be, and details which, as they lack any context – like the part of a chimney-piece and tracery of Carriglas Manor, Co Longford on p.117 – are almost unintelligible. There is, as well, a remarkable lack of connection between the text and what the publishers have chosen to illustrate and we are given lengthy descriptions of buildings which the reader is not shown. For High Victorian architecture most books deal with churches and that is what Dr Aldrich has to make do with, or else with the Houses of Parliament, museums or the London Law Courts. And this in a book which claims to 'concentrate on the domestic forms of the style'. For in *Gothic Revival* Ettington Park does not exist, nor any of the Irish Victorian houses like Humewood, Co Wicklow, or Deane and Woodward's assertive medievalism at Kilkenny. In Ireland, J J McCarthy and E W Godwin are all good architects of Gothic revised houses and are all ignored.

Dr Aldrich has given in this survey rather more Irish Georgian material than is usual in books of this sort but, like so much of the rest of her information, it is disorganised, is presented without any clear chronology and is frequently wrong. Thus we are told that James Wyatt 'had a number of commissions for Gothic houses and castles in Ireland' and 'is often credited with having inspired the Morrisons' work in the style'. Wyatt built, or made proposals for, eight Irish houses but only one of these, Slane Castle in Co Meath, is neo-medieval and the others are all classical designs. Nor is Wyatt known to have exercised any influence on Sir Richard or William Vitruvius Morrison's style. The younger Morrison travelled in England and abroad and was a noted antiquarian in his own right and needed no hints from Wyatt. On the other hand, John Nash, the favourite architect of the Prince Regent, built many spectacular neo-Gothic castles in England and at least six in Ireland of which Killymoon, Co Tyrone and Loughcutra Castle, Co Galway both survive. John Nash had a huge influence in Ireland through his pupils the Pain brothers and Thomas and Kearns Dean who copied their style, yet he is hardly mentioned in this volume and the Pains, the Deans and all their Picturesque houses in Ireland, including Dromoland Castle, Co Clare, Mitchelstown, Co Cork and Dromore,

Co Kerry, are completely ignored. So why are bits of Irish architectural history stitched into this book? Either the story should be told properly or not attempted and surely the great Museum Building in Trinity College, Dublin (see *Irish Arts Review Yearbook 1995*, pp.149-54) deserves a mention in any book on this topic? It was a building that really broke the mould of nineteenth-century revivalism.

This book tackles too much, too quickly and in a disarmingly careless way. Dr Aldrich has an undoubted enthusiasm for showy architecture and opulent interiors but she is undisciplined as a historian and is here neither a reliable guide nor a dependable scholar.

ALISTAIR ROWAN'S books include The Buildings of Ireland: North West Ulster *(1979)*

A Companion Guide to Architecture in Ireland 1837-1921

By JEREMY WILLIAMS
Irish Academic Press, Dublin, 1994,
424pp. 200 b&w ills. £35(h/b). 0-7165-2513-5

Paul Larmour

THE ARCHITECTURE of the Medieval and Georgian periods in Ireland has been long and justly celebrated but the

achievements of the Victorian period and after are much less generally known or appreciated. This new gazetteer, the first of its kind, should do much to change that situation. Mainly by dint of his own research, much of it in the pages of *Irish Builder and Engineer*, Jeremy Williams has managed to cover the architecture of the whole island of Ireland from the start of the Victorian era up to 1921. This he has done in one manageable yet comprehensive volume.

The author is an architect based in Dublin and is described on the flap as having 'a special interest in architectural history', which does not quite do justice to his pioneering role for over twenty years in trying to safeguard the most notable nineteenth and twentieth century buildings threatened in the Republic of Ireland. On the purely scholarly side he was joint author of an important but unfortunately all-too-short publication on the career of Benjamin Woodward, the great Irish-born favourite of John Ruskin.

This new book is essentially an alphabetical gazetteer, arranged county by county with special 'chapters' for the three principal cities of Belfast, Cork and Dublin. There are simplified maps of each county to head the chapters and

HUMEWOOD CASTLE, Co Wicklow. From *A Companion Guide to Architecture in Ireland, 1837-1921* by Jeremy Williams. The most spectacular High Victorian castle to survive in Ireland, it was designed in 1866 by the English architect, William White. Williams's book is enhanced by the author's brilliant facility in pen-and-ink sketching.

these should prove a handy guide for both the traveller and the armchair reader alike, and a useful index of architects and craftsmen, giving their dates, is also provided. Apart from the unfortunate inclusion of a few buildings in the north-eastern area which have in fact disappeared, the book is a reliable guide to the existing work of not only the principal Irish architects of their time, but also of the various English and Scottish architects who received commissions here. The author has a good eye for High Victorian inventiveness and a sure feel for the plastic and spatial qualities of our best buildings, which are not always the large showpieces of the main towns or cities. Those who have known, for instance, the great English architect G E Street in Ireland, only by his large cathedral rebuildings at Kildare and Dublin can see how good he really was at Ardamine Church of Ireland, an interesting polychromatic exercise on a diminutive scale on an isolated coastal site in Co Wexford. Indeed much of the best High Victorian work in Ireland is to be found in out-of-the-way places and Williams' welcome gazetteer now directs attention to such hidden gems.

Names and dates are provided for a whole host of buildings, in many cases publicised for the first time since they were originally commissioned and opened. The descriptions of them show that not only is the author well steeped in the subject of architecture and can pronounce on the quality and importance of the buildings with authority, but also that he has clearly enjoyed finding out about people as well. Many of the entries are enhanced by their stories of human interest.

Apart from a few inexplicably wrong dates and some inconsistencies in the spelling of architects' names (not a reflection of the author's knowledge one would hasten to add), the book is well written with frequent brilliant patches where the author clearly bubbles with excitement at what he has found. His enthusiasm for the subject should prove infectious while his analytical powers make for a most illuminating read. His

brilliant facility in pen-and-ink sketching is well represented in the generous amount of black and white line illustrations which adds to one's enjoyment of the book. It is not only an easy-to-use guide for the prospective traveller but is also likely to prove a valuable reference work, and should become a force for conservation in the Republic of Ireland where statutory listing of buildings on the model of the rest of the British Isles is badly needed and long overdue.

PAUL LARMOUR'S book The Arts and Crafts Movement in Ireland *was published in 1992.*

Pugin: A Gothic Passion

EDITED BY PAUL ATTERBURY AND CLIVE WAINWRIGHT

Yale University Press, 1994
320pp. 300 colour, 215 b&w ills. £45stg(h/b),
£19.95stg(p/b) 0-300-060122 (h/b), 0 300 060149(p/b)

Anthony Symondson SJ

'I REGRET TO SAY that there seems little or no appreciation of ecclesiastical architecture among the clergy. The cathedral I built, at Enniscorthy, has been completely ruined. The new bishop has blocked up the choir, stuck the altar under the tower!! and the whole building is in a most painful state of filth; the sacrarium is full of rubbish, and it could hardly have been worse treated if it had fallen into the hands of Hottentots. I see no progress of ecclesiastical architecture in Ireland. I think if possible they get worse. It is quite useless to attempt to build true churches, for the clergy have not the least idea of using them properly.'

A W N Pugin (1812-52), the Catholic convert and church architect, experienced great frustration in his attempt to bring the true principles of Gothic, or Christian, architecture to Ireland. Neo-Classicism had gained firm ground among the urban middle class expressed in the fine Dublin churches built after Catholic Emancipation in 1829. Pugin regarded them as little more than bedizened paganism. His mission was to rescue architecture from the

LISMORE CASTLE, Co Waterford. *Wallpaper designed by AWN Pugin for the Duke of Devonshire, c.1850. From* Pugin: A Gothic Passion *edited by Paul Atterbury and Clive Wainwright. 'In 1850, shortly before his death from overwork and insanity, Pugin was brought in by Sir Joseph Paxton to work on the interiors of Lismore.'*

Renaissance and restore it to its Gothic integrity formed during an age of unquestioning faith. For Pugin Catholicism and Gothic were one; he believed that Catholics had a religious obligation to encourage Gothic architecture and no other.

Ireland, with its enormous Catholic population, seemed to present an ideal opportunity for Pugin. Dr Roderick O'Donnell, in this sumptuous volume of essays published to coincide with the exhibition of the same name at the Victoria & Albert Museum, London, last year, describes how his work is almost entirely confined to the South where the few Catholic gentry and aristocrats such as the Earl of Kenmare at Killarney Cathedral (1842-1912) were unusual among the almost exclusively Protestant land-owners. Wexford has the main concentration of Pugin's Irish work, of which the chapels of St Peter's College (1838-41) and, in a neighbouring county, the Presentation Convent, Waterford, are the most completely furnished. The enormous extensions to St Patrick's College, Maynooth, in 1845 gave Pugin one of his major commissions, even though he was disappointed in his ambition to concentrate his genius in the chapel.

It was not only the incomprehension of Irish bishops and clergy which foiled Pugin's schemes. His Irish churches were delayed by the Great Famine and completed by others, notably by J J McCarthy who was described as a 'friend and fellow labourer' of Pugin, 'his great master'. Despite Pugin's rueful feelings and the many drawbacks, the Pugin style was eventually received enthusiastically and came to fulfilment not only in the work of McCarthy but also in Pugin's son, Edward, and his partner George Ashlin. Their matchless mid-Victorian church of St Augustine and St John, Thomas Street, Dublin (1860-95), and the soaring Gothic steeples that punctuate the Irish landscape, culminating in William Hague's sublime spire at Maynooth, are a legacy of Pugin's innovations. And so too, dispersed throughout Ireland in a commercial form, are the elaborate marble altars and reredoses with engraved brass tabernacles, set with carbuncles, and twisted brass candlesticks standing before opaque windows of Munich glass. None of this would have come into being without Pugin.

In 1850, shortly before his death from overwork and insanity, Pugin was brought in by Sir Joseph Paxton to work on the interiors of the bachelor Duke of Devonshire's 'quasi-feudal and ultra-regal fortress', Lismore Castle, Co Waterford. This job included heraldic wallpaper and painted decoration, furniture, inlaid encaustic tiles, stained glass and a fireplace of carved stone which had been exhibited in the Medieval Court of the Great Exhibition of 1851. These were assembled in the banqueting hall by Pugin and his trained artificers Crace, Minton, Hardman and Myers. Lismore embodies Pugin's domestic style at its most exuberant, showing what he could achieve on a generous scale. Splendidly restored, it has no parallel in any house in Ireland.

Pugin: A Gothic Passion is an indispensable volume in Victorian studies. Seventeen experts have assembled twenty-four essays on aspects of Pugin's

life and work, illustrated by 515 plates (many in colour); but there is no bibliography. Pugin's architecture is well described by Alexandra Wedgwood and Roderick O'Donnell, the leading English Pugin scholars; his writing by Margaret Belcher; jewellery (but not, alas, plate) by Shirley Bury; furniture, book design and his antiquarian interests by Clive Wainwright; wallpaper and ceramics by Joanna Banham and Paul Atterbury; his work in Australia by Brian Andrews; monuments and brasses by David Meara. Other essays wearisomely take the form of slabs of undigested and clumsily written research, frequently lacking contextual analysis, of greater value as work in progress rather than considered conclusions. The result is uneven, repetitious and lacks an integrating philosophy which precisely defines Pugin and his achievement.

Two contributions illustrate the problem. Wainwright's opening essay on Pugin and his influence had to be written quickly due to a defaulting contributor. Excellent work is often done under duress, focussing an author's grasp of his subject in clear and distinct terms. Not here. Wainwright has assembled a mosaic composed of odds and ends of correspondence from enthusiasts lying about on his desk, or notes arbitrarily taken from files, or memories half-remembered of lectures heard thirty years ago, strung together in a careless narrative. There is much about Pugin's sailing activities and furniture but no clear presentation of the architectural implications of his work for contemporaries and successors. Pugin's intense Catholicism, which formed the determining force of his convictions and was the source of his passion, is dismissed in nugatory terms. There are no footnotes.

In contrast, placed at the end of the book is Andrew Saint's essay 'The Fate of Pugin's *True Principles*'. This is by far the most illuminating, and one of the most lucidly written, contributions. On its own it justifies the purchase of the volume. Saint should have been placed first. His is the only essay which successfully attempts to relate Pugin to a wider

context and the ideas that motivated him and led to the dissemination of his influence on the course of the Gothic Revival in the British Isles and the Continent. Saint does not subscribe to a Hegelian line of progress to the Modern Movement but demonstrates the unconscious way Pugin's moral purpose expressed in structural truth was applied by theorists of the Movement such as Le Corbusier and Nervi. He is generous in his recognition of pioneers in Pugin studies, notably Michael Trappes-Lomax (whose biography, *Pugin: A Medieval Victorian,* published in 1932, remains of permanent value) and Phoebe Stanton, the *doyenne* of Pugin scholars, both of whom are studiedly ignored by Wainwright.

Pugin: A Gothic Passion indicates the fragmented state of Pugin studies but is valuable for ventilating a crucial subject. A proper assessment remains to be published. There are indications that Phoebe Stanton's definitive study of Pugin's stylistic development as an architect, based on primary source material (notably letters and diaries) is imminent. Her work is unlikely ever to be emended except in minor points of detail. Until then this will have to do.

ANTHONY SYMONDSON SJ is an authority on the work of Sir Ninian Comper and has written on Irish art needlework and stained glass

A Dublin Anthology
By Douglas Bennett
Gill and Macmillan, 1994
288pp. no ills. £9.99(p/b). 0-7171-2122-4

Dublin's Eye and Ear: The Making of a Monument
By Gearoid Crookes
Town House, 1993,
211pp. 10 col, 52 b&w ills. £15.95(h/b).
0-948524-57-x

John Maiben Gilmartin

LIKE A VICTORIAN patchwork quilt Douglas Bennett's *A Dublin Anthology* covers almost every aspect of life in that city. His anthology is a mosaic richly inlaid with fascinating snippets culled

BOOK REVIEWS

BEWLEY'S ORIENTAL CAFE, Grafton Street, Dublin. Douglas Bennett's *A Dublin Anthology* includes a section on social and cultural conditions where 'the legendary Bewley's' is written about by Tony Farmar.

from the writings of authors, and they are many, who have written something about Dublin.

Bennett's encyclopedic gallery is well constructed and divided into five parts. Firstly there is a section on fiction relating to Dublin, with such favourites as Brendan Behan, Terence De Vere White and James Joyce. The next section deals with social and cultural conditions, where we have less well known writers, but equally rewarding in their observations. Here we find amongst the throng Thomas Bodkin on 'Hugh Lane and his Pictures', Tony Farmar on 'the legendary Bewley's Cafe', and Constantia Maxwell with a portion of her *Dublin under the Georges*.

Scholarship may have become more finely honed since Constantia wrote on Dublin, but no one has surpassed her in her sympathetic and discerning account of the City. As Elizabeth Bowen once remarked to me about our mutual friend 'Constantia loved every s-s-stone in the city'. It is indeed a surprise to find that Elizabeth Bowen writing on Dublin is omitted.

The biography section follows with some choice pieces by writers as different as Brian Behan with his 'The Mother of all the Behans', Louis Hyman on the 'Jews of Ireland' and Winston S Churchill's 'My Early Life'. Churchill's earliest years were spent in Dublin, and one of the incidents he recounts tells of

how he was looking forward to visiting The Old Music Hall, which preceded the present Olympia, for a pantomime. He was disappointed, however, as the place burned down.

The Royal Victoria Eye & Ear Hospital (or R.V.E.E.) is one of the great institutions of Dublin. Its splendid red and grey granite profile dominates the Adelaide Road area of the city. In Dr Crookes' book, *Dublin's Eye and Ear, The Making of a Monument,* we learn that the Hospital's tutelary deities are the presiding figures of Sir William Wilde and Sir Henry Swanzy. Wilde comes to us as a caring compassionate figure who did much to alleviate the awful eye afflictions so prevalent in nineteenth-century Dublin. Unkind reports said, that he once treated George Bernard Shaw's mother for a squint, when he was finished she had two squints!

Sir Henry Swanzy dominated 'The Eye and Ear' at the end of the nineteenth century and start of the twentieth century when the present hospital building arose. How interesting to learn that the design of the R.V.E.E. is ultimately derived from the Rijksmuseum in Amsterdam. This is appropriate, for Sir Henry was the father of the notable artist Mary Swanzy.

We learn of the pivotal role which the 'Eye and Ear' played in many areas of science, for instance in the development of the Department of Anaesthesia. Here the pioneering efforts of Dr Beckett (uncle of Samuel) led on to the great achievements of Dr Deane Oliver and Dr Sheila Kenny. The latter was a larger-than-life personality whose feminine allurement may have been unsettling for some but who was unusually well disciplined by her devotion to the science of anaesthesia.

This is a well produced book; my one quibble is that some of the fascinating illustrations are too small. Otherwise it is informative for all and most evocative for those who know or who knew the Hospital and its staff.

JOHN MAIBEN GILMARTIN is a lecturer in History of Art in the Dublin Institute of Technology School of Art and Design.

BOOK REVIEWS

Treasures from the National Library of Ireland

EDITED BY NOEL KISSANE

Boyne Valley Honey Company, 1994

243pp. 140 col. 50 b&w ills. £25(h/b), £9.95(p/b)

095-1782-347

L M Cullen

THE NATIONAL LIBRARY is a pigmy among Europe's national libraries: with a book stock of one million volumes, it stands at the level of large municipal libraries in British or European cities. What gives it its standing, international as well as national, is its specialist book collections and its manuscripts (Gaelic and non-Gaelic), maps, newspapers, corpus of photographs and prints, and genealogical material. They ensure that the Library is an essential resource for all areas of Irish study, and the main one for many; and some of its possessions are remarkable.

The useful short accounts in this volume of the various resource centres of the Library are not always as incisive or as authoritative as they might be. The account of the growth of the Library is also unduly short – even allowing for the fact that the emphasis of the book is on its treasures and not on the Library itself – and could have been more comprehensive. One of its most famous librarians, Best, is not mentioned, and the most eminent of its post-war librarians, R J Hayes, while at least mentioned (twice), earns no recognition in his own right. The income of the institution or its very modest staffing base are not discussed.

While a book of this sort could not properly be critical of the State (whose indifference to the point of hostility under the palsied hand of the Department of Education was for decades the Library's main problem) or detail its own misguided and persistent ambition for almost three decades to become the national archives (which would have carried it far beyond its competence and resources), some forthright recognition of its limitations – its exiguous purchase funds, the want of a repair service, the limited cataloguing of many of the non-book collections, especially

the manuscripts and the extent to which collections (notably maps) have been out of commission for long periods – would have been welcome in place of the few coy words that feature in the text.

However, the Library itself seems happily to have turned the corner, a tone of confidence is a novelty, and the book's purpose is the positive one of dwelling on the treasures of the library rather than on its travails, past and present. It does that well, even triumphantly. The Boyne Valley Honey Company's sponsorship of the volume is an enlightened and generous act, and its modest price should also ensure that it can circulate widely. In some respects it is a more effective appeal for the Library's collections and thus for the Library's best interests than words, and the variety and splendour of the illustrations will, for a small outlay, give pleasure to the casual reader as well.

LOUIS CULLEN is Professor of Modern History at Trinity College Dublin

Caring for Old Master Paintings

BY MATTHEW MOSS

Irish Academic Press, 1994

160pp. 14 col., 27 b&w ills., £24.95(h/b)

0-7165-2531-3

Alexander Antrim

WHEN I RETIRED from the Tate Gallery having been Keeper of Conservation for twenty years, I was asked at the farewell party by a previous Chairman if I would be writing a book of my experiences at the Tate and in particular the methods which had evolved over the last few years. My answer was an emphatic no, basically because it is extremely difficult to write in a general or popular way about an inevitably technical subject which requires skill as a communicator as well as a practitioner if the interested layman is to be enlightened.

So it was with interest that I picked up Matthew Moss's new publication, *Caring for Old Master Paintings*. In the past I used to meet Matthew Moss at Conservation Conferences when he was

Chief Restorer at the National Gallery of Ireland in the 1960s and 70s, and assisted in Dublin in the summer months by a considerable team of restorers from the Instituto Centrale de Restauro in Rome. The results of this programme were published in 1971 as a catalogue: *The Paintings Restored in the National Gallery of Ireland*, which listed 494 paintings treated since 1964. This was indeed an encyclopedic experience as the spread of the collection is from the fourteenth to the twentieth centuries. Subsequently, Moss moved on to Australia to set up a Conservation Centre in Victoria, and he has finally settled as a Conservation Consultant in Monaco, where this book was written. So his experience is extensive.

At the end of the introduction there is a statement as to the intent of the book: '*Caring For Old Master Paintings* is a guide to understanding paintings. It tells you how the artist painted them, how to care for them and how to uncover the secrets of their beauty.' This is quite a task, and is completed in eighty-nine pages of text and illustrations, supplemented by a further twenty-nine pages of 'Conservation Terminology' included in the final chapter. The limitation of the length of the text made me presuppose it would be highly structured and packed with information; this latter it is but, in presentation, the author flits about in time, technique and terminology. This lack of focus leaves one groping for authorative technical information and logical continuity.

What also disturbed me as I progressed through the book was a lack of clear information as to normal structures of panel and canvas paintings, and hence the causes of the problems which will evolve with the passage of time in a household or Gallery environment. I had to pursue my way until page 113 in the final chapter 'Terminology of Painting Conservation' until I got any reference to 'Sizing', where the following is written: 'The simplest way to prepare a support and make it less absorbent is to apply a thin layer of animal glue.' This, as is generally known, has been

BOOK REVIEWS

normal practice before the application of a ground or priming upon which the paint layers are superimposed. The characteristics of this layer are: it is strong, brittle and hydroscopic (it expands considerably with the absorption of moisture). It is an essential flaw in the structure of the painting yet it is this thin film which binds the paint or ground layer to the supporting fabric or panel. The majority of structural problems resulting from the degradation of the size layer originate from the undesirable history of changes in temperature, humidity and stress, which in turn, cause changes in dimension, the formation of crackle patterns, delamination between films and support and ultimately paint loss. All of these defects will require treatment by a conservator who, as the author implies and experience confirms, may cause as many future problems as they are intended to solve.

What this book lacks is advice as to the preventative conservation methods that have been developed over the past twenty years, based upon the premise that simple techniques of reducing the causes of deterioration, both on the wall and in transit are the best way of preserving paintings, be they painted today or six centuries ago. Protection by framing is the area that requires to be expanded: how the painting is fitted to the frame; the advisability of creating a microclimate by glazing and back boarding; the use of low reflective and laminated glass, acceptable light, temperature and relative humidity levels; the relation speed of environmental change as opposed to absolute limits and the use of storage transit frames for moving and storing particularly delicate paintings and frames.

All these topics and their possible solutions have been discussed at conferences and published in conservation journals over the years and it is sad that the author failed to emphasise this regime as part of the care that he set out to recommend, as these are the essential principles for preserving the works in our care. As a footnote I must say how much I appreciated the inclusion of a list of

LEO WHELAN, RHA (1892-1956): *The Kitchen Window* (Crawford Municipal Art Gallery, Cork). From *Irish Art 1830-1990* by Brian Fallon. 'It is difficult to retreat from this survey and feel that it has done its job responsibly.'

technical terms in seven languages, which will be an essential part of couriers' portfolios in future.

LORD ANTRIM (as Alexander Dunluce) was for many years Keeper of Conservation at the Tate Gallery, London.

Irish Art 1830-1990

BY BRIAN FALLON

Appletree Press, 1994.
208pp. 36 colour, 34b&w ills. £20(h/b)
0-86281-438-3

Kenneth McConkey

OSCAR WILDE declared that the critic was 'he who bears within himself the dreams, and ideas and feelings of myriad generations, and to whom no form of thought is alien, no emotional impulse obscure'. Wilde leads us to expect that

the critic will refuse to lard his text with irrelevant circumstantial detail, antiquarian annotation and needless casuistry. The critic is someone who, by virtue of first hand experience with works of art, can 'master the secrets of style and school and understands their meanings and listens to their voices ...'

It is important to set up these terms of reference before turning to Brian Fallon's short and selective survey of *Irish Art 1830-1990*. This is a far from exhaustive account of Irish art and design by someone who is billed as 'chief critic' of the *Irish Times*. It contains occasional inaccuracies of fact and interpretation, is, in sections, poorly proofed, and has been meanly illustrated. It is, nevertheless, a good read. We may be irritated by some of Fallon's phobias – the words 'English' and 'British' suddenly become pejoratives in his vocabulary. Painters from the north of Ireland, like John Luke, are omitted entirely, presumably because they are 'British', while Stanhope Forbes, whose claims to be Irish are tenuous in the extreme, is included. We may quibble with Fallon's failure to fully acknowledge the merit of a painter like Orpen. We may be amazed at his parsimony when it comes to Keating and Lamb – 'not actually bad painters' – but we cannot deny his right to his opinions. Sometimes they are stated in a language which has a freshness and vitality which aids rather than detracts from his synoptic overview. At his worst Fallon lapses into the idiom of Crookshank and Glin and merely stitches brief collectors' biographies together. But even here there are redeeming phrases and disarming elisions which lift the text. It is difficult, nevertheless, to retreat from this survey and feel that it has done its job responsibly.

The most disappointing aspect of Fallon's survey lies in its failure to come to terms with the recent exciting developments in Irish Art. Allegedly covering the period up to 1990, it fizzles out where it should become most interesting, around 1965, a time when there were extraordinary things happening in Dublin. Fallon mentions a couple of notable events – American Art being shown at the Irish Living Art Exhibition and the display of the Johnson Wax collection. These occurred at the time when James White was also staging retrospectives of Keating and Lamb, painters who had helped to forge a distinctive Irish identity in the visual arts in the Cosgrave and De Valera years. The gap between these and the modern Americans must have seemed enormous. Ironically this opens the period when Fallon started to write for the *Irish Times*, the period about which he knows most, and the period to which he ought to have devoted his considerable knowledge and experience.

KENNETH McCONKEY is Professor of Art History at the University of Northumbria at Newcastle and author of Sir John Lavery (1993).

Irish Furniture at Malahide Castle

By Gerald A Kenyon

Gerald A Kenyon, 1994,
144pp, 70b&w ills. £8.00(p/b) 0-9523665-0-9

Irish Furniture and Woodcraft

By John Teahan

Country House/National Museum of Ireland, 1994,
46pp. 18 colour, 28b&w ills. £4.95(p/b).
0-946172-39-0

Angela Alexander

It is encouraging to have two publications concerned with Irish furniture, a subject on which so little has heretofore appeared. In this respect Gerald Kenyon's decision to concentrate on a particular collection, that at Malahide Castle, seems both reasonable and sensible. He has been an antique dealer all his life, developing a special interest in Irish furniture which resulted in a move to Ireland in 1956. For anybody with a desire to learn about eighteenth-century Irish furniture, the collection at Malahide provides a good start, as it is both varied and of high quality. Gerald Kenyon's knowledge as a dealer gives the reader a good introduction to the materials used, details of construction and the stylistic and structural elements which indicate why he states it was made in Ireland. The book follows the collection room by room, so it would be most useful to have it in hand as one looks at the original piece of furniture. Using the book thus would also compensate for the poor quality of the illustrations.

Malahide Castle was offered to the State in its entirety in 1976. This proposal was, to our shame, turned down and an insistence on paying inheritance tax resulted in an auction of its contents at which some of the original furniture was acquired. The collection has continuously been augmented, in particular by a collection donated by Mr Ronald McDonnell. The author has made no pretence of this being an academic study but more an insight into how he personally looks at and considers Irish pieces and in this respect the book is of value to the collector, academic and anyone with an interest in Irish furniture.

On the other hand, John Teahan sets

himself the task of providing an insight into the development of wood-producing skills in Ireland from 700BC right up to the twentieth century. One might expect a rather hefty tome to cover this subject but *Irish Furniture and Woodcraft* is a surprisingly slim volume. The early periods of Irish prehistory, through to the medieval period have been previously well recorded and documented. The eighteenth and nineteenth centuries still await further research. In this book they cover a mere three pages of text. It is difficult to attribute furniture to makers in the eighteenth century but carvers and gilders have been well documented by the Knight of Glin. Surprisingly the book does not mention the work of the Booker family, the Jacksons or the cabinet-maker William Moore. In his survey of the nineteenth century the author does refer to various makers including the Del Vecchios, Mack, Williams and Gibton, Strahan and others, but unfortunately no trade labels or billheads are illustrated. Neither are any biographical details of the cabinet-makers given. There are some good colour illustrations but there is no piece from 1800-1830, when very stylish Regency furniture was produced in Dublin, in particular by Mack, Williams and Gibton (see *Irish Arts Review Yearbook 1995*, Vol 11, pp142-48). This book is very general in its approach and would best serve as an introductory guide for the Museum visitor. It is rather frustrating, therefore, that the Furniture Gallery at the National Museum is closed and has been for some time.

It has to be acknowledged that compiling information on Irish cabinet-makers is a slow and painstaking process, made even more difficult by the number of collections which have been dispersed and the scarcity of papers. Many cabinet-makers' trade labels were published by The Knight of Glin in his indispensable article 'Dublin Directories and Trade Labels', in *Furniture History*, Vol. XXI, (1985). It is important to record labelled and stamped pieces, to collect bills and to compile biographical material in order to complete a clearer picture of the furniture trade in Dublin. If the

Jack B YEATS (1871-1957): *The Liffey Swim*, (National Gallery of Ireland). From *A Vision of Ireland: Jack B Yeats* by John Booth. Taking as his theme Yeats's passion for Ireland, the author has soaked up everything possible that has been written about Yeats without adding anything of any substance of his own.

publication of these two books leads to more people looking under or behind furniture or to buying because a piece is by an Irish maker, that is indeed a step forward.

ANGELA ALEXANDER *is researching Irish cabinet makers of the nineteenth century.*

A Vision of Ireland: Jack B Yeats

BY JOHN BOOTH

Thomas & Lochar, 1993.

128pp. 58col., 25 b&w ills. £35(h/b). 0-946537-90-9

Hilary Pyle

A VISION OF IRELAND is a book that comes from an admirer of Jack B Yeats, who is already author of books on Vivaldi and Fabergé. Yeats's passion for Ireland is the theme he chooses. The fire set alight the minds and inspiration of painters and writers, including Yeats's brother and sisters, not to mention the many intellectuals and ordinary men and women of that period in Ireland, a time recognised, even willed, as a Renaissance. Taking the form of a loose biographical narrative in chapters, Booth's book is full of quotable and apposite sayings, which give a flavour of the painter's life and way of painting. It is illustrated by photographs (including

one of MacQuitty's studies of the artist in his studio), of more than sixty of Yeats's paintings, as well as pen and ink drawings, and some work by his father.

Enticing to handle, nevertheless, this attractive volume has the inescapable quality of a sponge. Having soaked up everything possible that has been written about Yeats, it has only to be squeezed to find how little of real substance has been added by the author. Jack Yeats has, as the author comments, been obscured by the 'long shadow' of his brother for too long, one explanation being that people tend to have strong emotions about his paintings, often against them. He himself was bowled over by them. He has read everything he can find about them. But does he really want to explore them in depth? In fact he disavows the need to do so. He is of the group of romantics who uphold the painter's view that his work speaks for itself (it must be admitted, though, that most artists have said this same thing). At the same time, though he is critical of the scholars, he uses the biographical frame established by these same scholars, and much else besides.

He includes passages from Kenneth Clark and John Berger, and other writers with whom the artist was happy to discuss his work. He quotes from all the

established critics, and bases quite a bit of his own narrative on William Murphy's *Prodigal Father*, that admirable biography of Yeats's father, John Butler Yeats. But, while acknowledging a general debt to the various sources, Booth never gives exact origins, and so is the author of some puzzling conclusions. In addition, he is sympathetic with, but misunderstands, Yeats's embargo on reproductions of his work. Yeats was all for the student, and many of his works were reproduced in journals and newspapers during his lifetime. It was the abuse of the paintings by the marketing of reproductions – which is rife at the present, alas – that he abhorred.

The book is undoubtedly designed by writer and publisher for dipping into, a place in which to savour 'bites' of visual and verbal pleasures, but it is sadly lacking the freshness of thought that such a presentation deserves. With the number of publications about Jack B Yeats increasing during the past few years, this volume gives pause for thought, for the opening up of Yeats scholarship has inevitably laid the ground for a Jack Yeats industry, albeit only in its infancy compared with that of his poet brother.

HILARY PYLE, *art historian and critic, is author of the definitive catalogues raisonnés of the works of Jack B Yeats.*

The Different Worlds of Jack B Yeats, His Cartoons and Illustrations

BY HILARY PYLE

Irish Academic Press, 1994

343pp., 30 col., 511 b&w, ills. £37.50(h/b)

0-7165-2521-6

Ciarán MacGonigal

FOLLOWING ON THE catalogues raisonnés of the works by Jack B Yeats by the same author, this volume is intended to fill out the remainder of the map of Yeats and his total oeuvre.

Yeats began work at a period when artists were the illustrators of popular imagery in and for the printed medium. The early Yeats illustrations (under the name W Bird) were always claimed by

Kenneth Clark as being an informing and illuminating visual experience for him. This reviewer just regards that early commercial work as the precursor of photography in magazines and journals, some of it is quite amusing, it is of its period and humour.

The watercolours by Yeats which form the basis of his early art, as opposed to the artisan work he undertook, are in many instances pure magic, and after his tour with John Millington Synge through South Connemara where he did so much to record the look of the man-made landscape all around Mweenish and Gorumna, his work took on a new strength and determination. In much of the work of this period he set down for all time the physiognomy of the people of the Western sea board and the landscape that they inhabited. A memorial for all time. So too are his works in and around the Erris Peninsula, particularly around Belmullet and Geesala.

His early Devon watercolours and his series of Irish characters are wonderfully evocative and works of art that exist in a double helix of developing intent. The great spiralling of ideas towards that which was to be his ultimate achievement of sensibility of line and pigment in such great works as *Grief, There is No Night, The Basin in which Pilate washed his Hands, Queen Maeve Walked upon this strand* and many others of the historically tempered works, and others such as *Harvest Moon, The Map, About To Write a Letter*, all are marked by the excitement of the paint, the impastoed surfaces like great mounds of coagulated blood. And, indeed in a way it was blood; it was Yeats's life blood which he poured out onto the immemorial canvases.

In the gallery of which I am director, we recently had a most splendid exhibition of works by Jack Yeats, and the sheer excitement of the visitors to this splendid show gave the galleries a crackle of excitement. Even for the very grand and the very rich there is that curious sensation of being in the presence of genius when they contemplate the works by this gentle painter.

Hilary Pyle's book is a once and for all audit of the cartoons and illustrations by Yeats and contains much useful information. It is very densely laid out and not always very easy to follow, at least I found myself puzzled by the page layout relative to the sequencing of the numbers and titles, but that aside, this is a really important book for the Yeats scholar and aficionado.

CIARÁN MacGONIGAL is Director of the RHA Gallagher Gallery.

The Yeats Sisters and the Cuala

BY GIFFORD LEWIS

Irish Academic Press, 1994

200pp. 17 b&w ills. £24.95. 0-7165-2525-9

Anne Crookshank

THIS IS ONE of those rare books which you put down wishing there was more to read. It deals with two aspects of art rarely considered, the hand printing of books by Elizabeth (Lolly) Yeats and the embroidery of her elder sister, Susan (always called Lily). It opens up areas of Irish life never closely considered before such as the impossibility of making enough money to live even when you are producing works of art of international fame as are the publications of the Cuala Press.

The extraordinary selflessness of the Yeats sisters is exhibited throughout their lives and meant that they were prepared to return to Ireland when it suited their father, not necessarily when it suited them, even though it meant giving up the reasonably paid careers they had achieved in London. Their salaries had of course not been spent on themselves but to support their family, notably their hopeless and irresponsible father and their selfish brother, W B Yeats. Jack B Yeats, their younger brother, comes over as charming and kindly but this book for once sees the father and the brothers as subsidiary figures so one can for a moment forget their genius. The drop in earnings this move involved for the girls was incredible. Elizabeth actually earned £300 a year in the late 1890s as a Froebel teacher but never achieved anything like this again in Ireland, indeed 7/- per week was often her fate while Lily earned £78 a year in London and fifteen years later in Ireland only about £26. They lived in such penury that they saved crumbs as a topping for vegetables. Meat was a rare luxury, usually purchased only when brothers or other visitors were expected. However they did employ servants and heaven alone knows how they paid them.

As this book is about women it is an account of every day life and society as well as careers. Given their incomes, they led quite active social lives. They were fine conversationists and their work brought them into contact with many notable people. It is also a book which shows from a new perspective, Protestant, female and impoverished, the changing attitudes to politics and the generosity of women, which helped them to overcome and to go on being friends throughout the Civil War with people of different political opinions.

The importance of Elizabeth's teaching of painting, her pupils included Mainie Jellett and Louis Le Brocquy, and her early and successful publications on teaching painting to children are little known and how many of us knew that when we look at the Dun Emer embroideries in Loughrea we are looking in the more complex sections at Lily's embroidery or that she embroidered the curtains for William Morris's famous four poster bed.

I suppose all books have faults and this one is at times repetitive and I found it irritating that the family tree of the Pollexfens did not include uncles, nieces etc who are important in the text and only earlier members of the family. It would be useful, too, to have had a Yeats pedigree.

Gifford Lewis has become an authority on Anglo-Irish women in the twentieth century with her work on Edith Somerville and now on the Yeats girls. She has opened a new and important vein of research and she does it so well that I want more. I cannot wait for her next book.

ANNE CROOKSHANK, formerly Professor of History of Art in Trinity College, Dublin is co-author of The Watercolours of Ireland (London 1994)

Nano Reid

BY DECLAN MALLON

*Sunnyside Publications, Drogheda, 1994, 144pp, 24 col
and 32 b&w ills, £13.99 (p/b). 0-9524792-0-6*

Rosemarie Mulcahy

NANO REID (1900-81) was one of the
most original and talented Irish painters
of her generation. During a long and
productive life she followed her own
intensely personal vision of landscape
and the everyday scenes of her own
environment. Born in Drogheda, she
loved the Boyne Valley and its archaeology, the sense of the past. She was equally attracted to less obviously appealing
subject matter, neglected back yards,
run-down farm houses, men at work.
This personal universe was represented
in her unconventional, earthy style with
what appears like a child-like
spontaneity.

Her expressionistic brushwork shares
qualities with Jack Yeats, of whom she
could not have failed to be aware of. As
a watercolourist she is in a class of her
own. Seán O'Faoláin wrote of her as 'a
poetic visionary, writing in code about
things behind the seen surface.'

In my opinion, she is the equal of
Patrick Collins, and a more original and
gifted painter than either of her exact
contemporaries, Maurice McGonigal
and Norah McGuinness. Although she
represented Ireland in the Venice
Biennale in 1950 and was honoured by
the Arts Council, north and south, with
a retrospective exhibition in 1974-5, her
work has not received the wider recognition that it deserves.

Nano Reid has always had the admiration of the discerning few, and now she
has found an effective champion in
Declan Mallon. Mallon mounted an
impressive retrospective exhibition in
1991 at the Droichead Arts Centre
which regrettably did not travel elsewhere. Now he has published a handsome, well illustrated and interesting
biography, which brings the shy, eccentric, and fiercely independent artist to
life. He traces her origins as a publican's
daughter in Drogheda, and follows her
career from its beginnings at the

NANO REID in the 1920s. Mallon's book 'brings the
shy, eccentric and fiercely independent artist to life'.

Metropolitan School of Art in the early
1920s, to Paris and London – which do
not appear to have made much of an
impression – her life in Dublin, the
founding of The Irish Exhibition of
Living Art, her struggle for recognition,
and her return to live with her sisters
above the family pub in 1962.

The artists who influenced her most
were three northern painters, Dan
O'Neill, Gerald Dillon and George
Campbell – Dillon was also probably her
closest friend. Their personal reminiscences of shared outings with Nano
reveal her sense of fun and her caustic
wit. Mallon's very readable text is
enriched by the recollections of her
friends – Hilda van Stockum, Robert
Greacen, Patricia Hutchins, Sam
Harrison, Pearse Hutchinson, and others. He achieves a good balance between
anecdotes of the artist's life and analysis
of her work. This biography is a work of
independent scholarship – Mallon is
both author and publisher – and makes a
valuable contribution towards the literature of modern Irish painting.

ROSEMARIE MULCAHY'S latest publication is
The Decoration of the Royal Basilica of El
Escorial *(1994).*

Irish Country Houses

BY TERENCE REEVES-SMYTH

96pp. 21 col. ills. 0-86281-373-5

Irish Gardens

BY TERENCE REEVES-SMYTH

96pp. 27 col. ills. 0-86281-374-3

Irish Trees and Shrubs

BY PETER WYSE-JACKSON

72pp. 32 col. ills. 0-86281-420-0

Appletree Press, 1994. All £3.99(p/b)

Ann Reihill

THESE APPLETREE guides, being very
compact in size, are definitely of the
pocket variety. Heading off criticism, Mr
Reeves-Smyth sàys in his introduction to
Irish Country Houses: 'Every effort has
been made to provide a representative
selection of houses, though inevitably
the choice reflects both a personal taste
and the constraints of this book'. My initial reaction was one of irritation at the
omissions but, on second thoughts, a lot
of information has been packed in about
those country houses open to the public
on a regular basis or by appointment.
The history of the houses has been well
researched, there is a good geographical
spread and some good colour photographs of interiors and exteriors.

In Northern Ireland, Castle Coole is
included in County Fermanagh and also
Florence Court. Castle Ward and Mount
Stewart represent Co Down; Ardress
and The Argory, Co Armagh; and also
featured is Springhill in Co L'Derry
(what tactful spelling).

Mr Reeves-Smyth also includes a list
of other country houses (and ruins) that
are accessible to the public. These
include the Victorian castle Blarney
House in Co Cork, and Glenveagh
Castle in Co Donegal, once the home of
the late Henry McIlhenny.

Irish Gardens by the same author lists
information about gardens open to the
public on a regular basis. The gardens
are mainly in the north, east and south
of the country and there is a strange
absence of gardens in the west and north
west. Perhaps the author considers the
coastlne too wild and windswept for serious gardeners.

There is some overlap with the guide

to *Irish Country Houses* – Glenveagh and Castle Ward are included in both as are Mount Stewart (wonderful garden) and Florence Court. Butterstream in Co Meath, Jim Reynolds's garden, visited in May by the Prince of Wales at his request, is there. In Co Wicklow Kilruddery, Mount Usher and Powerscourt are described but the beautiful Charleville House next door to Powerscourt which is open to the public for several months of the year and by appointment, gets no mention in either guide. Never mind, there are limitations to pocket guides.

Irish Trees and Shrubs by Peter Wyse-Jackson makes a good companion to *Irish Gardens*. It describes and illustrates sixty-four of the common species found in the countryside and also provides some hints on identifying a further thirty or forty other closely related species which are rarer.

For the serious gardener (as with the amateur) who wants to get down to identifying the finer points of Irish flora on garden tours, this is the answer.

ANN REIHILL is a publisher and gardener.

Joyce Images

CONCEIVED AND DESIGNED BY BOB CATE. EDITED BY GREG VITIELLO. INTRODUCTION BY ANTHONY BURGESS

W W Norton & Company, New York, London, 1994, 112pp. $40

Michael Patrick Gillespie

FOR ANYONE SEEKING an additional fixture for the coffee table and a bluffer's guide to the life and works of James Joyce, *Joyce Images* may seem to be a tempting choice. Its printed portion can be digested in less than twenty minutes, and so will not exhaust those who move their lips when they read. Its photographs consist, for the most part, of the straightforward amateur efforts that have become the familiar staple of any family album. And Anthony Burgess' brief introduction has enough generalities (with only a few really significant blunders) to give one the key phrases needed

to give the impression of having actually read Joyce's work.

If these features do not seem to offer sufficient value for the investment, I have an alternative suggestion. Use half of the forty dollars to buy the paperback edition of Richard Ellmann's biography, *James Joyce*. Look at the fifty-four pictures that appear as illustrations, and read the book's index (compiled by Mary Reynolds and one of the best sources around for a condensed view of Joyce's life and works). The book might even do well on the coffee table, offering implicit but not overly assertive testimony of its owner's intellectual curiosity.

If that ploy does not present a satisfactory fiscal alternative, I have one more suggestion. Go to a used book store and buy a copy of *Finnegans Wake*. I assure you that you will find scores on display, and, with luck, at least one will have received such rough treatment as to give the impression of arduous perusal. Put it on the coffee table with the title prominently displayed. No one will ever question you about its contents.

For those who have doggedly persisted reading this review in search of a more detailed response to *Joyce Images* let me at least offer my reasons for not presenting one. I do not know what the men who conceived, designed, and edited this book meant to suggest by its title, but I am quite sure that no sense of *double entendre* influenced its choice or shaped the selection of material found in the volume. *Joyce Images* does not set out to be a witty book. Nor does one describe it as avant garde.

One can best sum up *Joyce Images* as a *Reader's Digest* version of a Joyce pictography: bland, comprehensible, and truncated. It contains little that Joyce scholars have not already seen, and not much to interest those coming to Joyce for the first time. It is neither a bad book nor a good book. In fact, it is only its constitution of wood pulp, printers ink, and glue that makes it a book at all, for it lacks the metaphysical cohesion that could hold it together on aesthetic grounds.

What then is the point of *Joyce*

Images? I honestly cannot say, but I do feel from the depths of my *petit bourgeois* soul (or perhaps, given my grandparent's roots in rural Ireland, peasant is the better designation) that it is not worth the forty dollars that W W Norton & Company have not been embarrassed to ask readers to pay for a copy.

MICHAEL PATRICK GILLESPIE is a Professor of English at Marquette University, Milwalkee, USA and author of books on Wilde and Joyce.

Jonathan's Travels: Swift and Ireland

BY JOSEPH MCMINN

Appletree Press, Belfast, and St. Martin's Press, New York, 1994

160pp. 50b&w ills. £15.99 (h/b)

0-86281-453-7 (Brit Lib) and 0-312-12354 x (NY).

A Literary Tour of Ireland

BY ELIZABETH HEALY

Wolfhound Press, 1995

270pp., 56 col., 221 b&w ills. £24.99(h/b)

A Literary Guide to Dublin

BY VIVIEN IGOE

Methuen, 1994

362pp. 76b&w ills £14.99(h/b), £9.99(p/b)

0-413-67420-7 (h/b) 0-413-69120-9(p/b)

Valerie Pakenham

THE YEAR 1995 may prove a vintage one for literary travellers in Ireland. Here are three splendid books, admirably researched and illustrated, and worth a dozen 'Interpretation Centres' between them.

For a stimulating aperitif take Joseph McMinn's *Jonathan's Travels*, born from 'a fascination with the footnotes of Swift's life in Ireland.' (The author has already written a literary biography of the Dean). Swift was a compulsive traveller, partly from temperament, partly for reasons of health (he saw horseriding as a cure for all ills), partly from thrift. As he wrote without shame in 1718:

'In weather fine, I nothing spend
But often sponge upon a friend'
His visits to long-suffering country squires like Knightley Chetwode at Portarlington, or the Rochforts on Lough Ennell, or the schoolteacher, Thomas Sheridan, in Cavan could run to months.

As McMinn points out, Swift's career

predates the golden age of Irish land-scaping. The countryside was still littered with the ruins of the Williamite and civil wars, and Protestant Ascendancy had barely made its mark. His first parish at Kilroot in Co Antrim (which he fled after a year) had no rectory, no glebe, not even a church; his second at Laracor outside Trim, a church but no house. Much of Swift's energies, even after he came Dean of St Patrick's, went into hedging and draining his glebe there, and exhorting his friends to do the same and create orderly English landscapes.

Yet in 1725, aged fifty-three, he set out on a five hundred mile foray into wildest Munster and Connaught, probably to find material for *Gulliver's Travels*. His journey left much folklore as well, including an encounter with the great Kerry poet, Aoghan O Rathaille. Aoghan, primed by the locals, had dressed himself as a ragged cowherd with two mangy dogs. As Swift came within earshot, he began to speak Latin to one cow, Greek to another, rhetorical Irish to a third. As he proceeded to more cows and more languages, Swift turned to his servant in amazement, 'If the cowherds in Kerry speak seven languages, what then must the scholars be like?' and headed back in dismay in Dublin.

Elizabeth Healy in her *Literary Tour of Ireland* weaves her way as effortlessly as O'Rathaille from Gaelic scholars to Anglo-Irish novelists, from ribald ballads (there is a splendid one about a Dublin girl's attempted seduction of St Kevin in his Bed at Glendalough) to sinewy late twentieth century poets. The breadth of her reading is breathtaking, helped no doubt by her twenty or so years as editor of that excellent magazine, *Ireland of the Welcomes*. The book's layout allows her long and satisfying quotations and digressions, yet all bound firmly together by her own brisk humorous brand of prose. I can think of no better literary companion, except, perhaps, Patrick Kavanagh's *Voices in Ireland*, which has just come out in paperback.

Her illustrations are stunning too; many of the colour photographs taken by

OLIVER ST JOHN GOGARTY releasing a pair of swans into the Liffey at Islandbridge in 1924. From *A Literary Guide to Dublin* by Vivien Igoe. Accompanied by W T Cosgrave, Mrs Gogarty, W B Yeats and Cosgrave's ADC, Gogarty presented the swans to the goddess of the river in thanksgiving for escaping from kidnappers.

herself, or the book's designer, Jan de Fouw. And picture research has unearthed some treasures; for instance the ravishing photograph from Sligo Library of the two Gore-Booth sisters in fancy dress or two women sitting smoking their pipes on the Giant's Causeway a century ago.

After this deeply satisfying main meal, turn to Vivien Igoe's *Literary Guide to Dublin* for some exercise. She has carefully plotted five walking tours through Dublin, packed with literary encounters, and another two to salute the dead in Mount Jerome and Glasnevin. There is also an excellent guide to Dublin's literary and historical pubs, almost all of which seem to have been frequented by Brendan Behan.

The main bulk of the book is a biographical dictionary of writers, who lived or worked in Dublin, including some famous blow-ins: Shelley, Thackeray, Sir Walter Scott, John Betjeman. Sometimes I felt that Vivien Igoe had cast her net too far: Kipling's dull as ditchwater description of Dublin on a short visit in 1911 hardly merits a four-page potted biography. Still Kipling leads to Lord

Roberts and Lord Roberts to his warhorse, Vonolel, who is buried in the Master's Garden in Kilmainham. Literary guides can lead us to all sorts of odd discoveries.

VALERIE PAKENHAM is the author of The Noonday Sun *(1985) and (with Thomas Pakenham)* Dublin: A Travellers' Companion *(1989).*

The Book of Kells. Proceedings of a Conference at Trinity College, Dublin,
EDITED BY FELICITY O'MAHONY
Scolar Press, 1994 617pp, 45 col. 146 b/w ills £75
0-85967-967-5

The Book of Kells. An illustrated introduction to the Manuscript in Trinity College Dublin.
BY BERNARD MEEHAN
Thames and Hudson, 1995
95pp,117 col. 6b/w ills. £8.95(p/b)
0 500 27707

Jonathan Alexander

READING THE SIX hundred dense pages of scholarly articles which make up the Proceedings of the conference held at Trinity College, Dublin, as part of the celebrations of the quatercentenary of the College's foundation, one can only marvel at the amount of study that has now been devoted to this single manuscript. Of course it is no ordinary manuscript. Extraordinary as it is as an artefact, its fame has come above all from its being considered the *ne plus ultra* of Celtic art. It has received its special place because of the political history of Ireland, and it has become an icon of national culture, part of the Heritage Industry, reproduced on travel posters and postage stamps.

Bernard Meehan's much shorter book is aimed at a different, non-academic audience. Its good quality plates, all in colour, contrast with the other volume's mainly murky black-and-white and frankly awful colour plates. Meehan, who is Keeper of Manuscripts at Trinity, sums up in clear simple prose the directions which scholarly research has taken over the past one hundred years. He knows the whole enormous literature and has even been able to take into account the Conference Proceedings, since he was its convenor. From his position he has a first-hand familiarity with the manuscript, which shows in his text, for though there is now a fine facsimile available, even that is no substitute for constant and close examination of the original. His book is now the best reasonably priced introduction available.

As to the Conference papers, they range from, at the one pole, empirical research into the materials used to, at the other pole, speculative theories on the meaning of images and decoration. The Conference drew, greatly to its benefit, on international scholarship so that, for example the pigments are discussed by Robert Fuchs and Doris Oltrugge from Cologne, the parchment by Anthony Cains, conservator at Trinity, and the techniques of laying out the patterns by Mark van Stone, a designer and calligrapher with wide experience of Insular palaeography, from Portland, Oregon. All commentators on Insular art, beginning with Gerald of Wales in the twelfth century, have been fascinated by the intricacy of the patternwork.

The number of modern manuals on how to lay out 'Celtic' patterns are proof of the current fascination with this aspect. Van Stone's account is the easiest to follow and the most convincing I know as to how this was done.

Valuable papers by leading authorities, Donncadh O Corráin, Ian Fisher, D L Swan and Máire Herbert deal with the historical situation in Ireland and more specifically in Iona and Kells in the seventh and eighth centuries. Lisa Bitel's recent fine book *Isle of the Saints* is a fuller account, which gives a vivid picture of the monasteries at this time and the society within which they functioned. The complex problems of Insular palaeography are discussed in five papers including one by William O'Sullivan, former Keeper of Manuscripts, and another by Bernard Meehan. Another group of papers discuss parallels and comparisons with other artistic media, for example on the metal-work, Michael Ryan of the National Museum of Ireland, and on the High Crosses, Peter Harbison (whose recent book provides for the first time proper descriptions and illustrations of all the Crosses), and Roger Stalley, Professor of History of Art at Trinity. All these papers, though some are less directly concerned with the Book of Kells itself, give the reader an idea of recent discoveries and of a multiplicity of views on problems of origins and dating. If firm conclusions remain largely elusive, at least a huge amount of intense and valuable research is being done.

A final group of papers discuss the meaning of the imagery in the manuscript. Going beyond older types of iconographical study which concentrated on sources, written or visual, the papers particularly of Jennifer O'Reilly of University College, Cork and of Carol A Farr of the University of Alabama, raise questions about audience, demonstrating the importance of 'Reception theory' in recent art historical studies. Both O'Reilly and Farr and also Eamonn O Carragáin, in his paper on the ways in which Gospel Books were used in processions, emphasize the

catholic liturgy as a context for the manuscript's function and meaning. The assumption is that the Book of Kells was made by and for the use of literate monks who had a deep familiarity with scripture and the commentaries on it. Study was reinforced by the repetitions of the texts read at the Mass and Office. Analysis of the images therefore proceeds from the basis that this is a learned, allusive art full of complex theological reference. We may not be certain of the artists' intentions, but a contextual reading will yield a richer understanding.

Many of the papers inevitably raise the question of the origin of the Book of Kells. To me Iona still seems the most likely place, and the whole importance of this moment of extraordinary creative power is that it was achieved as a result of a meeting of different socio-cultural and artistic practices. I should like to end this review with the fine words of Professor O Corráin on the first page of the Conference Proceedings: 'I have no wish to join in the controversy about origins … The delusions of modern nationalism have done, and continue to do, enough damage in these islands, and even what may appear to be soberer feelings of national pride should have no place in our proceedings.' This is a strong warning. So long as it is heeded, we can welcome the present volumes which demonstrate the internationalism of the study and enjoyment of this particular master piece.

JONATHAN ALEXANDER is Professor of Fine Arts in the Institute of Fine Arts, New York University.

Dublin: A Grand Tour

BY JACQUELINE O'BRIEN AND DESMOND GUINNESS
Weidenfeld and Nicolson, 1994. 256pp., 292 col. ills.
£30stg h/b, 0-297-83224-7

George Mott

THIS IS A sumptuous book about the buildings of central Dublin. A guide for the peripatetic visitor, it is not. Being large and heavy, it is designed for reading at desk, table or lectern rather than in

No 38 NORTH GREAT GEORGE STREET, Dublin. From *Dublin: A Grand Tour* by Desmond Guinness with photographs by Jacqueline O'Brien. 'At the risk of sounding condescending, the author notes that several houses in this street were saved by idealists while the wretched inhabitants were housed elsewhere.': when the owner of No 38, Miss Desiree Shortt, rescued her house there were twenty-seven people living there in crowded conditions.

bed. The copious photographs and text are clear and packed with information. There are close to three hundred illustrations reproduced in colour on fine quality paper; its moderate price is commendable.

The buildings included are in the heart of Dublin, an area bounded by the two canals and Phoenix Park, though there are some exceptions farther afield. The layout is roughly chronological beginning with early buildings such as Christ Church Cathedral and St Audoen's and ending with the likes of Pearse Street Garda Barracks and the Garden of Remembrance at Islandbridge. There is a map showing building location, two interesting eighteenth-century maps, a biographical list of architects, artists and craftsmen, a bibliography and a good index.

Jacqueline O'Brien's photographs are technically superb and give much pleasure. The enormous interior spaces of churches, ballrooms and banking halls are lit with great skill. The overuse of certain points of view can be tiring, however, and the temptation to show too much in one shot might have been resisted. Repeatedly shooting into the corners of rooms gives the impression of a series of spread-eagled specimens ready for dissection, like T.S.Eliot's 'patient etherised upon a table'.

I have to admit to some surprise at the name of this book. Grand is not a word I would normally associate with Dublin. In fact, 'Grand' used in conjunction with Ireland evokes its more popular meaning as merely good, like the North American 'nice'. Dublin is not, nor was it ever, a Grand City in the manner, say, of Edinburgh, Paris or Vienna.

Dublin: A Grand Tour gives a striking impression of Ireland's architectural conservatism. The authors end their 'tour' in 1920, 'just as the last wave of Classicism petered out, giving way to the international modern style of architecture which makes one capital so like another.' (This is certainly not true of European capitals.) From the evidence of one's eyes, however, Classicism has not so much petered out as metastasized. Ireland is dotted with 'Georgian' bungalows and the newly-rich aspire to the porticoed mansions of the past. As with the Colonial style in the United States or Nuremberg 'Gothic' in Germany, 'Georgian' in Ireland still signifies prestige and respectability, instant architectural 'roots'. Even so, it comes as a shock not to find any examples of modern architecture in this book.

Far more than its content, though, it is the manner of this 'tour' that is Grand. As a speaker Desmond Guinness is a master of ironic pomposity. While this is delightful *a viva voce*, it can be irritating in print. What is more, it risks sounding condescending, especially when the inhabitants of Dublin and their relation to its buildings is at issue. According to Mr Guinness, several houses in North Great George's Street were saved by 'idealists' while the wretched inhabitants were housed elsewhere. Of No 71 Merrion Square we are told twice on the same page that it was the birthplace of Princess Margaret of Hesse and the Rhine. Had I not remembered playing charades with this delightful lady in Rome years ago I might have been forgiven for saying: 'Who?' Comments like these, however, are probably lapses of taste in an otherwise engrossing text. Desmond Guinness's heroic commitment to the preservation and restoration of Georgian buildings is a great and lasting achievement. But in order to truly save and protect the beautiful buildings of the Ascendancy in Ireland, they must be reinscribed in a context free of the least trace of that flip snobbery that so often adheres to them.

GEORGE MOTT is a photographer and writer who has worked extensively in Ireland. His books (with Brian de Breffny) include The Houses of Ireland, The Churches and Abbeys of Ireland, The Land of Ireland *and* Castles of Ireland.

Auction Records for Irish Painters

A TABLE OF THE HIGHEST PRICES EVER PAID AT AUCTION FOR THE WORK OF A SELECTION OF IRISH PAINTERS.

(Prices, in sterling and Irish pounds, are hammer prices and do not include auctioneers' fees).

S = Signed, D = Dated.

William ASHFORD
£120,000
Punt on the River Clodiagh, Charleville (ill. IAR vol.9, p.256)
39 x 50 ins. S & D 1801
Christie's, 12 July 1991, lot 67

George BARRET Senior
£154,362
The Dukes of Cumberland & York driving a Landau in Windsor Great Park
41 x 54 ins. S in monogram
Sotheby's (New York),
14 Jany 1994, lot 85

Rose BARTON
IR£25,000
The Custom House, Dublin before the Rebellion
W/c, 10 x 14 ins S.
Mealy's (Brooke Sale, Knoctoran),
30 June 1987, lot 301

Mildred Anne BUTLER
IR£26,000
Dry Morsel and Quietness Therewith
25 x 38 ins S.
James Adam, 14 Dec 1989, lot 110

George CAMPBELL
IR£17,000
Mozart Quartet
30 x 36 ins. S.
James Adam, 14 Dec 1989, lot 69

Robert CARVER
£15,972
Pastoral landscape
47 x 61 ins. S & D 1754
Goteborg's (Goteborg, Sweden),
11 May 1993, lot 135

Harry CLARKE
IR£14,000
The Countess Cathleen
17 x 11 ins. WIC
Christie's (Dublin),
29 June 1994, lot 135

Sarah Cecilia HARRISON *Carlos* £15,500

J Humbert CRAIG *Sorting the Catch* IR£13,000

Mildred Anne BUTLER
Dry Morsel and Quietness Therewith IR£26,000

George BARRET Senior *The Dukes of Cumberland & York driving a Landau in Windsor Great Park*
£154,362

Lilian DAVIDSON *Boats at Wicklow, Dusk*
IR£10,000

Francis DANBY *Winter Sunset* £35,000

Nathaniel HONE the Younger *Fishing Boats in Dublin Bay* IR£38,000

John LAVERY *On the Loing* £160,000

Evie HONE *Composition* IR£9,500

Gerard DILLON *Dun Aengus, Aran Boat* IR£12,000

Harry KERNOFF *A Country Circus*
£19,800

Paul HENRY *Mountain and Lake, Connemara*
£58,000

William CONOR
£26,000
The Lost Child
36 x 28 ins. S.
Christie's, 27 October 1989, lot 281

J Humbert CRAIG
IR£13,000
Sorting the Catch
16 x 20 ins. S.
James Adam, 1 June 1989, lot 121

Francis DANBY
£35,000
Winter Sunset
27 x 41 ins. S & D 1850
Sotheby's, 14 July 1993, lot 93

Lilian DAVIDSON
IR£10,000
Boats at Wicklow, Dusk
36 x 28 ins. S.
James Adam, 5 Oct 1993, lot 60

Gerard DILLON
IR£23,000
Aran Islanders in their Sunday Best
22.5 x 30.5 ins. S.
Sotheby's, 2 June 1995, lot 329

Norman GARSTIN
£11,500
What's New ?
14 x 20 ins/ S.
Phillips, 4 May 1990, lot 81

Beatrice GLENAVY
IR£7,800
World War. I (Ill. IAR, vol 11, p.173)
20 x 14 ins. S.
Christie's (Dublin), 6 June 1990, lot 112

May GUINNESS
IR£13,000
Portrait: Two Irish Girls
51 x 40 ins.
Christie's (Dublin), 24 Oct 1988, lot 87

Eva HAMILTON
IR£7,500
*Dray Carts on city quays opposite the
Custom House*
5 x7 ins.
Christie's (Dublin),
6 June 1990, lot 167

Letitia HAMILTON
IR£30,000
The Harbour, Roundstone
20 x 24 ins. S.
James Adam, 28 Sept 1989, lot 58

Sarah Cecilia HARRISON
£15,500
Carlos
152 x 76 cm. S & D 1891
Sotheby's, 14 Oct 1987, lot 65

Edwin HAYES
£14,000
Holy Island, Isle of Arran
15 x 54 ins. S & D 1862
Christie's (South Kensington),
13 April 1989, lot 160

Patrick HENNESSY
IR£7,000
Courvoisier Bottle, Books and Print
24 x 35 ins. S.
James Adam, 28 Feb 1989, lot 111

Grace HENRY
IR£19,000
Boats, Chioggia
32 x 24 ins. S.
James Adam, 1 June 1989, lot 196

Paul HENRY
£58,000
Mountain and Lake, Connemara
27 x 31 ins. S.
Christie's, 9 March 1990, lot 258

Thomas HICKEY
£70,000
The MacGregor Family Group
78 x 99 ins.
Sotheby's, 9 March 1988, lot 49

Evie HONE
IR£9,500
Composition
25 x 36 ins.
James Adam, 28 September 1989, lot 70

Nathaniel HONE the Elder
£65,000
Jason, a Racehorse belonging to Sir Nathaniel Curzon, Bt
40 x 50 ins. S & D 1755.
Christie's, 14 July 1994, lot 58

Nathaniel HONE the Younger
IR£38,000
Fishing Boats in Dublin Bay
26 x 38 ins. Initialled.
James Adam, 17 May 1990, lot 81A

Mainie JELLETT
IR£28,000
Composition with three elements
29 x 35 ins. James Adam,
28 Sept 1989, lot 71

Charles JERVAS
£17,000
Portrait of Charles I and his page, Lord Hamilton
87 x 75 ins.
Sotheby's, 8 April 1992, lot 18

Sean KEATING
IR£65,000
Quayside with fishermen mooring, Galway Harbour
35 x 32 ins. S & D.
James Adam, 1 June 1989, lot 162

Harry KERNOFF
£18,000
Country Circus
48 x 60 ins. S.
Sotheby's, 4 Nov 1992, lot 50

Charles LAMB
IR£18,000
Fisherman with Pollan
20 x 24 ins. S & D 1926.
James Adam, 28 Sept 1989, lot 170

John LAVERY
£160,000
On the Loing
31 x 30 ins. S & D 1884
Christie's, 22 Nov 1994, lot 10

William John LEECH
£37,000
The Blue Shop, Quimper
24 x 16 ins. S.
Christie's, 30 May 1990, lot 525

James LE JEUNE
IR£23,000
Grafton Street
20 x 24 ins. S
Christie's (Dublin), 6 June 1990, lot 99

John LUKE
IR£70,000
Landscape Composition
17 x 23 ins. S & D
James Adam, 30 March 1994, lot 39

Maurice MacGONIGAL
IR£24,500
Gardens: a Summer's Day, Booterstown
28 x 36 ins. S.
Adams Blackrock, 28 May 1990, lot 43

Norah McGUINNESS
IR£17,000
St Declan's on Sunday
24 x 30 ins. S.
Christie's (Dublin), 6 June 1990, lot 133

Charles LAMB *Fisherman with Pollan* IR£18,000

Sean KEATING *Quayside with fishermen mooring, Galway Harbour* IR£65,000

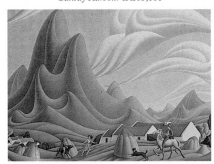

John LUKE *Landscape Composition* IR£70,000

Daniel MACLISE *The Choice of Hercules* £42,000

Letitia HAMILTON *The Harbour, Roundstone* IR£30,000

William ORPEN *Early Morning* £290,000

Mainie JELLETT *Composition with three elements*
IR£28,000

Andrew NICHOLL *Ferrycarrig Castle, co. Wexford
seen through a bank of flowers* £11,000

Maurice MacGONIGAL *Gardens: a Summer's Day,
Booterstown* IR£24,500

Frank McKELVEY
IR£42,000
Swans on the Lagan
20 x 26 ins. S.
James Adam, 1 June 1989, lot 119

Daniel MACLISE
£42,000
The Choice of Hercules
41 x 51 ins. S
Christie's, 5 November 1993, lot 171

Colin MIDDLETON
£20,000
Requiem for Dan O'Neill
26 x 30 ins. S & D 1974
Christie's, 27 Oct 1989, lot 351

Richard MOYNAN
£86,000
Ball in the Cap
24 x 40 ins. S & D 1893
James Adam, 14 Dec 1994, lot 41

Andrew NICHOLL
£11,000
*Ferrycarrig Castle, Co. Wexford seen
through a bank of flowers*
14 x 20 ins. W/C S.
Christie's, 19 Dec 1989, lot 137

James Arthur O'CONNOR
IR£27,000
*Extensive Wooded Mountain Landscape
with Figures*
24 x 29 ins. S & D
James Adam, 5 Oct 1993, lot 22

Roderic O'CONOR
£140,000
The Bridge at Grez sur Loing
29 x 36 ins.
Phillip's, 12 June 1990, lot 146

Aloysius O'KELLY
IR£14,000
Breton Woman Cleaning Pans (ill. p.82)
25 x 21 ins. S & D 1909
James Adam, 11 Dec 1991, lot 75

Daniel O'NEILL
IR£19,000
Picnic
14 x 21 ins. S.
James Adam, 1 June 1989, lot 137

William ORPEN
£290,000
Early Morning
35 x 33 ins. S.
Sotheby's, 2 May 1990, lot 54

AUCTION RECORDS FOR IRISH PAINTERS

Walter OSBORNE
IR£271,000
Spoilt Pets
24 x 18 ins. S.
Sotheby's, 2 June 1995, lot 267

William OSBORNE
£16,000
Portrait of Mrs Thomas Conolly seated on a Chestnut Hunter
44 x 52 ins.
Christie's,
14 April 1992, lot 82

Thomas ROBERTS
£129,944
Wooden Landscape with Stags and Doe
44 x 60 ins. S & D 1774
Christie's (New York),
15 Jany 1988, lot 46

George RUSSELL (AE)
IR£9,200
The Big Oak, Raheen, Co Galway
29 x 40 ins
Christie's (Dublin),
12 Dec 1990, lot 168

William SADLER
IR£25,000
Donnybrook Fair
21 x 35 ins.
Christie's (Dublin),
24 Oct 1988, lot 25

Stephen SLAUGHTER
£42,000
Ladies Gathering Fruit
48 x 39 ins
Sotheby's, 19 Nov 1986, lot 46

James SLEATOR
IR£18,000
A Dublin Interior
23 x 12 ins.
Christie's (Dublin),
12 Dec 1990, lot 185

Mary SWANZY
IR£22,000
La Maison Blanche, Samoa
22 x 30 ins. S.
James Adam, 14 Dec 1989, lot 74

Jack B YEATS
IR£505,000
Tinkers' Encampment: The Blood of Abel
36 x 48 ins. S.
Taylor de Vere,
11 Oct 1994, lot 79

Frank McKELVEY *Swans on the Lagan* IR£42,000

Grace HENRY *Boats, Chioggia* IR£19,000

Mary SWANZY *La Maison Blanche, Samoa*
IR£22,000

Daniel O'NEILL *Picnic* IR£19,000

James Arthur O'CONNOR *Extensive Wooded
Mountain Landscape with Figures* IR£27,000

Jack B YEATS *Tinkers' Encampment: The Blood of Abel* IR£505,000

PRICE GUIDE TO IRISH ART

An Index of Prices paid for Irish Pictures at Auctions between June 1994 and June 1995.

The artist's name and date is followed by the painting's title. Next is the medium, referred to by a single letter symbol (as indicated below) followed by the measurements of the work. The letters 'S', 'D', or 'I' indicate where the painting is signed, dated, or inscribed. The letter in parentheses refers to the sale and is followed by the lot number. Prices are quoted in local currencies. In the case of James Adam, Taylor de Veres and other Irish sale-rooms, the prices are hammer prices and do not include the buyer's premium; (on average, 15%). Unsold pictures are not included.

A: Acrylic; C: Collage; D: Drawing; O: Oil; M: Mixed media; P: Pastel; Pr: Print; T: Tempera; W: Watercolour/Gouache/Wash. The following sale catalogues, referred to in the Guide by a single letter symbol, have been indexed:

A: Sotheby's – 22 June 1994;
B: Christie's – (The Mill House Sonning Berkshire) – 20, 21, 22 June 1994
C: Christie's – 23 June 1994
D: Christie's – 12 July 1994
E: Christie's – 14 July 1994
F: Christie's (South Kensington) – 12 May 1994
G: Christie's – 15 September 1994
H: Christie's – 13 May 1994
I: Christie's – (Mere Hall, Knutsford, Cheshire) – 23 May 1994
J: Sotheby's – 28 September 1994
K: Christie's, Dublin – 29 June 1994
L: James Adam – 5 October 1994
M: James Adam – 14 December 1994
N: James Adam 15 June 1994
O: James Adam – 29 March 1995
P: Taylor de Veres – 11 October 1994
Q: Taylor de Veres – 14 March 1995
R: James Adam – 8 November 1994
S: Taylor de Veres – 31 May 1994
T: Taylor de Veres – 13 December 1994
U: James Adam – (The Wicklow Collection) – 16 November 1994
V: Mealy's – (The Ronald McDonnell Collection Part II), – 15, 16 June 1994

W: Mealy's – (Cregg House, Carrick-on-Suir) – 5 July 1994
X: Mealy's – (Lisdonagh House, Caherlistrane) – 19 July 1994
Y: Mealy's – (Thornfield, Adare – 3 October 1994)
Z: Mealy's – (Moyne Park) – 25 October 1994;
AI: Mealy's – 6 December 1994
BI: Mealy's – (The Old Vicarage, Swords) – 3 April 1995
CI: Hamilton Osborne King –15 June 1994
DI: Hamilton Osborne King – (Windrush, Shankill)– 26 July 1994
EI: Hamilton Osborne King – (Woodbrook, Co Wexford) – 4 October 1994
FI: Hamilton Osborne King – (Mike McGlynn, Bunratty) – 15 November 1994
GI: Hamilton Osborne King – (Ballycarberry, Killiney) – 25 January 1995
HI: Hamilton Osborne King – (Airfield, Dundrum) – 28 March 1995
II: Christie's (South Kensington) – 22 September 1994
JI: Christie's – (South Kensington) – 3 November 1994
KI: Christie's – 8 November 1994

LI: Christie's – 11 November 1994
MI: Christie's – 22 November 1994
NI: Christie's, Glasgow – 1 December 1994
OI: Christie's (South Kensington) – 15 December 1994
PI: Christie's (South Kensington) – 2 March 1995
QI: Christie's – 10 March 1995
RI: Christie's – 23 March 1995
SI: Christie's – 25 April 1995
TI: Sotheby's – 23 November 1994
UI: Sotheby's – 8 March 1995
VI: Sotheby's – 12 April 1995
WI: Christie's (South Kensington) – 27 April 1995
XI: Adams, Blackrock – 7 November 1994
YI: Adams, Blackrock – 2 May 1995;
ZI: Phillips – 10 May 1994
AII: Phillips – 7 June 1994
BII: Phillips – 4 October 1994
CII: Philips – 22 November 1994
DII: Lynes & Lynes,Cork – 21 February 1994.
EII: Sotheby's – The Irish Sale, London – 2 June 1995
KII: Christie's – 28 June, 1995
GII: Taylor de Veres – 13 June 1995

ALLEN, Harry Epworth (1894-1958)
The Holy Well
T 14.5 x 21" S, (Q: 27) — £3,000
View from Keel, Achill Island, Co Mayo
T 14 x 20" S (EII: 332) — £4,450
ARMSTRONG, Arthur (b. 1924)
Boats
O 24 x 18" S, (K: 296) — £880
A Peninsula of Fields
P 20.5 x 15" S, (K: 118) — £385
Before Sundown
O 30 x 35" S, I, (T: 82) — £1,100
Deserted Cottages
O 24 x 30" S, I, (K: 243) — £660
Green Landscape (The Twin Beaches)
O 36 x 42" S, (T: 35) — £1,400
Landscape near Ballyconnelly
O 30 x 36" S, (O: 105) — £1,800
Shore Series I
O 6 x 8" S, (O: 89) — £300
View towards the Sea
O 7.75 x 9.5" S, (P: 132) — £380
Western Seascape
O 7.5 x 8.5" S, (N: 137) — £300
Donegal Landscape
W 11.5 x 9.75 S (GII: 119D) — £420
Early Morning Shave
O 29 x 22.5" S, (GII: 142) — £770
ASHFORD, William (c.1746-1824)
A still life of flowers in a vase on a stone ledge with fruit and a butterfly
O 25.25 x 30" (HI: 276) — £8,000
Orpheus and Eurydice in a classical river landscape
O 31.25 x 41.5" (EI: 303) — £4,000
Opening of the Ringsend Docks, 23 April, 1796, with Lord Camden Conferring Knighthood

on Sir John MacArtney
O 0.29.25 x 38.25" S, D (EII: 220) — £73,000
ATKINSON, George Mouncey Wheatley (c.1806-1884)
Moonlit Coastal Scene with Shipping in Cork Harbour with Blackrock Castle
O 23.25 x 34.25" (EII: 231) — £7,475
BAKER, Henry A. (18th Century)
Perspective view of the New Four Courts, Dublin
W 19 x 24" S, (U: 19) — £1,500
BALLARD, Brian (b. 1943)
Dark Fields, Mourne
O 18 x 21.5" S, (M: 11) — £520
Freesias in a bottle
O 11.5 x 10" S, D, (N: 126) — £380
Kneeling Model
O 19 x 15.5" S, D, (Q: 43) — £1,300
Rocks, Howth
O 9.5 x 11" S, D, I, (S: 33) — £360
White Vase
O 12 x 9" S, D, (N: 111) — £340
BARRET Jnr., George (1767-1842)
Lovers by Moonlight
W 10.25 x 8.5" S, D, (D: 54) — £920
Windsor Castle from the Great Park
W 9.75 x 14.5" S, D, (D: 51) — £2,415
BARRET, George (1734-1784)
Landscape with Classical Ruins and Shepherds
O 23 x 37" (EII: 234) — £20,700
A View in the Dargle called The Dahool
O 38 x 48" (O: 46) — £67000
Horses in a wooded Landacape
W 9.875 x 12.5" (D: 52) — £1,035
BARRY, Moyra (1886-1960)
Bowl of Flowers
O 24 x 30" S, (S: 91) — £800

Daffodils & Hyacinths
O 14 x 21" (S: 2) — £620
Primroses
O 10 x 13" S, (P: 133) — £400
Summer Blossoms
O 12 x 17.5" S, I, (S: 27) — £420
BARTON, Rose (1856-1929)
A quiet harbour
W 7 x 10" S, (L: 105) — £700
Children on a beach
W 5.25 x 8.5" S, (L: 79) — £650
On the Thames
W 10 x 14" S, D, (V: 1135) — £1,700
On the Thames
W 10.25 x 14" S, D, (V: 1137) — £1,600
The School Yard – Eton
W 14 x 20" S, (V: 1150) — £3,200
Kensington
W 14.4 x 9.75" S, D (EII: 264) — £3,680
At the Garden Gate
W 10 x 7.25" S, D (EII: 265) — £8,625
Dublin Castle
W 6.75 x 6" S, (EII: 266) — £4,370
BENSON, Mary Kate (d. 1921)
Coastal Landscape
O 8.5 x 11" S, (P: 143) — £80
BEWICK, Pauline (b. 1935)
Horse asleep
W 19 x 24" S, D, (O: 25) — £700
BLACKHAM, Dorothy (1896-1975)
Achill Views & 3 others
Pr 12 x 11" (4) (S: 117) — £160
Amoreiro, Portugal
O 20 x 30" S, I, (P: 56) — £620
Siamese
W 9.75 x 14" S, (Q: 2) — £180

St. Stephen's Green in the Summer
O 26.5 x 20.5" (P: 55) £700
BLACKSHAW, Basil (b. 1932)
Landscape
O 16 x 23" S, (T: 66) £700
BOURKE, Brian (b. 1936)
Dublin Garden
M 30 x 34" S, D, (Q: 85) £620
Landscape
M 24 x 17.5" S, D, (P: 26) £510
Mare & Stallion
M 22.5 x 14.5" (2) S, D, I, (P: 166) £900
BRADLEY, Basil (1842-1904)
Irish Cabin - flax spinning
O 19 x 23.5" S, (O: 78) £3,000
BRADY, Charles (b. 1926)
Italian Pear
O 10 x 17" S,m (P: 130) £500
Japanese Pear
O 7.25 x 10.25" S, (S: 109a) £420
Pencil Standing
O 15.5 x 11.5" S, D, I, (T: 170) £280
BRANDT, Muriel (1882-1978)
Michael MacLiammoir
D 19.5 x 16" S, (S: 96) £100
Coppermines Junk VI
W 9.5 x 9.5" S, D, (P: 120) £100
BRANNON, Philip (1817-1890)
The Salmon Leap at Leixlip, Co Dublin
W 17.5 x 27" (KII: 47) £1,000
BROCAS, William (c.1794-1868)
A View of Bray, County Wicklow
O 14.5 x 18.5" (E: 104) £5,175
Cattle and Pigs in a wooded River Landscape,
a bridge beyond
O 28.25 x 36.25" S, D, (LI: 108) £1,610
Dandy, a Bay Hunter in the Grounds of
Sheephill Castleknock, County Dublin
O 25 x 30" (EII: 235) £6,900
Roller, a Bay Hunter with Hounds Jolty Boy
and Jackey Boy in a Stable
O 25 x 30" (EII: 236) £5,750
A Grey Hack, Yarcoute, with a Groom
beside a Gate
O 25 x 30" (EII: 237) £5,520
A Bay Stallion with a Spanial in a Landscape
O 25 x 30" (EII: 238) £4,370
BEHAN, John
Standing Farm
Bronze 15.5" high S, (GII: 85) £400
BROWN, Christie (1932-1981)
Sailboats on a River
W 15.25 x 31.25" S, (KII: 81) £900
BUCK, Frederick (1771-c.1839-40)
A Gentleman in a Grey Coat
E 2.5" ht. oval S, (K: 149) £330
BUCK, Frederick (1771-c.1839-40) Circle of
Miniature Portrait of an Officer
W 2.75 x 2.5" (GI: 147) £180
BURKE, Augustus (1838-1891)
The Old Street Vendor, with wooden leg
O 17 x 13" (V: 1131) £725
On the Apple Tree, Brittany
O 17 x 25.5" S, (EII: 268) £16,100
BURTON, Sir Frederick William (1816-1900)
The Blind Girl at the Holy Well -Scene in the
West of Ireland
W 34.75 x 28.5" (QI: 148a) £5,750
BUTLER, Mildred Anne (1858-1941)
A Cottage Scene
W 10 x 14" S, D, (P: 16) £3,600
Cattle Grazing by the River, Kilmurry
W 10 x 14" S, I, (K: 71) £1,320
A Pair of Peacocks Grazing
W 3.75 x 7.25 & 4.75 x 7.25" S, (YI: 10) £2,900
Figures in an Arcade, Paris, 1894
W 7 x 5.25" (K: 68) £715
Figures in an Interior, Face and Leg Studies of Man
D 5.5 x 8.5" (Y: 295) £130
Picnic in Kerry
W 5 x 7" S, (O: 74) £950
Rhododendrons in a wooded landscape
W 10.5 x 7" S, D, (K: 143a) £2,750
Sweet Contentment
W 5 x 6.5" S, (N: 22) £2,000
Three Kittens
W 6.5 x 9" S, (T: 140) £800

Trees in blossom at Kilmurry
W 5 x 7" (K: 70) £440
Peacocks
W 9.75 x 13.75" S, (EII: 261) £7,475
Nice Dark Balmy Warm Day – Kilmurray
Diary, 9 May 1915
W 7 x 10.5" S, D, (EII: 262) £977
BYRNE, Patrick (18th/19th Century)
A Prospect of the Customs House
W 21 x 31.5" S, D, (U: 65) £2,300
CAMPBELL, Cecilia Margaret (1791-1857)
An Album of drawings of Ruins and Landscapes
D 9 x 13" S, D, I, (K: 12) £605
CAMPBELL, George F. (1917-1979)
Abstract
M 10.5 x 14" S, (Q: 119) £350
Bog & Rock
O 20 x 30" S, I, (P: 33) £1,100
Cattle Winter, Co. Cavan
O 20 x 16" S, (L: 99) £1,600
Coastal Landscape
M 9.75 x 13" S, (P: 40) £160
Malaga from the Hill (The Bull Ring)
W 18 x 23" S, (L: 116) £1,400
Near Marbella, Spain
W 18 x 14" I, (P: 18) £600
Spanish Town
O 13.5 x 17.5" S, (S: 11) £1,000
Still life
O 13.5 x 18.5" S, (K: 245) £528
Still Life with Candle
O 30 x 40" S, (T: 78) £2,200
Still Life with Radishes and Things
M 14 x 19" S, I, (K: 142) £440
The Artist's Wife
O 23 x 19" S, (Q: 24) £1,700
The Musicians
O 20 x 30" S, (EII: 351) £8,050
Bog and Rock
O 20 x 30" S, (KII: 223) £1,100
Abstract
W 22 x 28" S, (KII: 224) £300
Woman in a Hat, and Profile of a Woman
W 12.25 x 9", (KII: 225) £750
A Goat Herder in a Coastal Landscape, Malaga
W 9.5 x 11.5" (KII: 205) £450
Spanish Town in Winter
O 30 x 25" S, (KII: 184) £4,000
Coastal View with Figures and Boats
W 9 x 12" S, (GII: 6) £500
The Bell Boy
W 28 x 20" S, (GII: 24) £770
Cork Mountains
O 13.5 x 17.5 S, (GII: 144) £750
CAMPBELL, John Henry (1755-1828)
A Figure by a ruined Castle and a Bridge, Killarney
W 10.25 x 16.75" I, (K: 10) £935
A Figure resting by a Waterfall, Killarney
W 11.75 x 16.75" (K: 9) £1,045
Dunluce Castle, Co. Antrim
W 8 x 11.25" (K: 6) £1,430
Entrance of the Dargle, Co. Wicklow
from Fassero Bridge
W 20 x 26" S, I, D, (M: 33) £935
Figures by a Bridge, Killarney
W 10.75 x 15.75" (K: 8) £935
Polaphouca, Co. Wicklow
W 8 x 11" S, (K: 5) £770
CARACCIOLO, Niccolo d'Ardia (1941-1989)
Houses in Fiesole
W 8.5 x 11" S, (T: 108) £600
Montaren Uzes (Gard) South of France
W 10.5 x 15" S, (P: 129) £700
Reclining Nude
W 14 x 19.5" S, (S: 74) £850
Still Life with Bottle, Bowl &
Silver Vase
O 9 x 11.5" S, (XI: 27) £1,500
Tunnell Under Finchley Road
O 9.75 x 16" S (GII: 149) £1,300
CARR, Tom (b.1909)
A Story by the Stove
Pr 16.5 x 26" S, (P: 47) £100
Liffey Night
O 19.5 x 15.5" S, I, (T: 67) £3,500
Swans
W 20 x 30" S, (T: 127) £420

CARRICK, Desmond (b.1930)
Figures on a beach
O 16 x 20" S, (K: 293) £825
Whit Weekend at Ballysmutten
O 16 x 19" S, (N: 15) £450
CARSON, Robert Taylor (b. 1919)
A Fisherman
O 15 x 13" S, (K: 216) £286
Atlantic Drive Co. Donegal
O 17 x 29" S, I, (T: 174) £480
Coast near Rosapenna, Co. Donegal
O 14 x 20" S, I, (OI: 34) £440
Fair Head, Co. Antrim
O 12 x 15.5" S, (O: 58) £300
Sheephaven Bay, Co. Donegal
O 18 x 24" S, I, (K: 214) £660
A Coastal Village
W 10.5 x 14.5" S, (KII: 222) £200
CLARKE, Harry (1889-1931)
The Countess Cathleen
W 16.75 x 11.25" (K: 135) £15,400
COLLINS, Patrick (1911-1994)
Cows Sheltering
O 9 x 10" S, I, (YI: 32) £1,000
Flowers in a Vase
O 9.75 x 6.75" S, D, (T: 65) £870
Nymph & Fawn
O 12.5 x 10.5" S, I, (S: 63) £3,200
Portrait Study of a Girl
O 13.5 x 10" S, (P: 20) £1,600
Swallows under the Roof
O 21 x 26" S, I, (P: 148) £2,000
Achill Coast
O 15 x 19" S, (GII: 73) £2,700
COLLIS, Peter (b. 1929)
Ballinteskin Gully
O 11 x 13" S, (Q: 97) £260
Buttermilk Mountain
O 7 x 8" S, (Q: 139) £180
Early morning near Laragh 1975
O 10 x 12" S, (O: 5) £350
Garden and trees
O 12 x 14" S, (L: 25) £250
Killiney
O 8 x 10" S, (P: 67) £320
Path Through Ballycoyle Forest
O 4.5 x 6.5" S, (P: 59) £150
Snowfall Glencree
O 7 x 7" S, (R: 77a) £280
Still Life with Pots and Fruit
O 32 x 36" S, (S: 30) £570
Still Life with vase of Flowers
O 16 x 12" S, (L: 53a) £570
Sunset in the Dublin Mountains
O 22 x 24" S, (S: 115) £720
The Obelisk, Killiney III
O 12 x 13" S, (M: 60) £340
The West Road to Glencree
O 12.5 x 16" S, (L: 140) £320
The Wicklow Road
O 11.5 x 12" S, (L: 38) £300
Winter Evening Near Roundwood
O 9.5 x 11" S, (P: 60) £300
Glenasmole
O 34 x 34" S, (GII: 79) £2,900
Road to Powerscourt Waterfall
O 6 x 7" S, (KII: 138) £400
COLVILL, Helen (d. 1953)
A March morning
W 15 x 22.5"7.5 x S, (O: 55) £600
The Top of the Hill
W 11 x 15" S, (BII: 163) £600
CONOR, William (1884-1968)
Barges on the River Lagan
W 10.75 x 14.75" S, (N: 66) £500
Coortin
P 10 x 8" S, (XI: 34) £2,700
Study of a child
D 17 x 13" S, (L: 48) £1,400
Study of a Young Girl
P 20 x 16" S, (Q: 48) £1,000
The Accordion-player
O 10.5 x 14" S, I, (J: 115) £5,520
The Fiddler
P 14.25 x 11.5" S, (T: 71) £900
The Flautist
P 6 x 5" S, (O: 9) £750

PRICE GUIDE TO IRISH ART

The Gossips		
P 20 x 15" S, (P: 11)	£5,500	
The Hunt		
O 14 x 17.5" S, (O: 49)	£750	
Donegal Woman and Child		
P 18 x 15" S, (KII: 122)	£4,200	
Join in the Chorus		
D 14.25 x 12" S, (KII: 182)	£3,200	
A Girl in a Book Shop		
D 9.5 x 7.5" S, (KII: 183)	£1,400	
The Cellist		
O 14.25 x 12.25" S, (KII:229)	£4,300	
Bridal Morning		
O 16 x 22" (KII: 86)	£12,500	
COOKE, Barrie (b. 1931)		
Nude		
W 19 x 17.5" S, (S: 64)	£380	
River Current 4		
M 28 x 24" S, I, D, (T: 141)	£300	
Waterfall (2)		
W 14 x 21" S, D, (YI: 46)	£760	
COTTON, William (1880-1958)		
A.E. hob-nobbing with one of those Irish Gods		
P 12.25 x 9" S, I, (K: 128)	£220	
CRAIG, Henry Robertson (1916-1984)		
Florians, Venice		
O 10 x 14" S, (U: 14)	£800	
Seascape		
O 25 x 34" S, (T: 115)	£900	
Sunday Morning in the Park		
O 30 x 40" S, I, (K: 236)	£1,980	
CRAIG, James Humbert (1878-1944)		
A Bogland Scene – Near Burtonport		
O 14 x 18.5" S, (YI: 75)	£1,250	
A Summers Day on the River		
O 8.75 x 11.75" S, (Q: 18)	£3,100	
Bloody Foreland (1939)		
O 12 x 17" S, (P: 136)	£1,500	
Cattle by a Cottage in a sunlit Landscape		
O 15 x 20.25" S, (K: 250)	£2,200	
Country Road in Achill with figures		
O 16 x 20" S, (L: 102)	£2,600	
Cushendun, Co. Antrim		
O 12 x 17" S, (UI: 199)	£1,725	
Donegal landscape with figures		
O 9 x 12" S, (L: 77)	£1,000	
Evening in the Garden		
O 9.5 x 13" S, (S: 53)	£900	
Going Home		
O 14.5 x 18.75" S, (YI: 70)	£1,800	
Horn Head, Dunfanaghy		
O 12 x 17" S, I, (K: 189)	£880	
Mid-Summer in the Rosses		
O 15 x 20" S, (M: 64)	£1,900	
Potato Pickers in a Coastal Landscape		
O 15 x 20" S, (K: 251)	£1,760	
Sessiagh Lake		
O 10 x 14" S, (K: 249)	£1,100	
Sheep in a Landscape		
O 9 x 13" S, (P: 52)	£1,200	
Sheephaven, Co. Donegal		
O 15 x 20" S, I, (K: 190)	£880	
Sheephaven, Co. Donegal		
O 20 x 24" S, I, (T: 17)	£3,600	
Solitude		
O 15 x 20" S, (M: 49)	£1,300	
The Cabbage Pickers		
O 14.5 x 19" S, (S: 70)	£3,000	
The Tullabeglly River, Co. Donegal		
O 28 x 36" S, (T: 40)	£4,800	
The Tullabeglly River, Co. Donegal		
O 28 x 36" S, (BII: 9)	£2,800	
Wooded river landscape		
O 10.5 x 13" S, (O: 7)	£1,200	
Getting Ready for the Herrings		
O 15 x 20" (KII: 68)	£7,000	
A Rocky Coastline near Fair Head		
W 13.5 x 16.25" (KII: 197)	£400	
Figures by a Loch		
O 22 x 26" S, (EII: 339)	£3,450	
Cottages by the Coast		
O 20 x 15" S, (EII: 343)	£1,610	
Glenveigh Bog		
O 15 x 20" S, I, (EII: 214)	£2,530	
CREGAN, Martin (1788-1870)		
Portrait of Louisa Broughtan, later		
Mrs James		

McAlpine		
O 35.5 x 27.25" S, D (EII: 214)	£1,955	
CREGAN, Martin (1788-1870) Attrib.		
Portrait of Miss Pakenham		
O 29 x 25" I (EII: 213)	£1,265	
CROZIER, William (b. 1930)		
Abstract		
O 60 x 48" S, I, (F: 286)	£1,320	
Burnt Out Lot		
O 30.5 x 36" S, I, D, (PI: 195)	£650	
Harbour Scene, Granton		
W 11 x 11" S, (P: 39)	£220	
Junction Hill		
O 36.25 x 30" S, I, D, (J: 236)	£1,552	
North Shore, Ayrshire		
W 20 x 16" S, (OI: 350)	£176	
DAVIDSON, Lilian Lucy (d. 1954)		
Donegal Lough Scene		
W 8.5 x 11.5" S, (R: 121)	£140	
Fishing Boats at Anchor		
O 30 x 26" S, (ZI: 87)	£2,000	
The Road Through the Rosses, Co. Donegal		
O 11 x 15" S, (N: 104)	£770	
Winter Gardens		
O 19.5 x 15.5" S, (N: 10)	£2,400	
The Black House, Victoria		
W 12.25 x 9.25" S, (KII: 214)	£280	
DE GENNARO, Gaetano (b. 1890)		
Female Portrait Study		
D 17 x 15" S, D, (P: 171)	£80	
A Man from Aran		
O 23 x 18.25" S, (KII: 210)	£1,700	
DILLON, Gerard (1916-1971)		
A Grey Day		
W 14.5 x 22" S, (Q: 81)	£800	
A Kitchen Table		
C 10.25 x 14" S, (K: 137)	£770	
A View of Drogheda		
O 11 x 14.5" S, D, (Q: 36)	£2,800	
Bedhead		
M 35 x 34" S, (P: 13)	£800	
Birds		
M 11.5 x 18" S, (P: 34)	£950	
Christmas Themes		
D 25 x 19" S, (T: 59)	£480	
Dreamer (Pierrots & Cats)		
W 15 x 22" S, (Q: 41)	£1,000	
Islanders		
W 7.5 x 12.5" S, (K: 141a)	£770	
Landscape		
O 9 x 11" S, (Q: 115)	£650	
Night Falling		
Pr 6.75 x 7" S, (K: 138)	£308	
Old Owl		
M 13 x 17" S, I, (T: 144)	£300	
Reflections		
M 14 x 22" S, (S: 140)	£500	
Sea Drift		
M 16 x 24" S, (L: 132)	£200	
Sorrowful Head		
P/C 11.5 x 6" S, (Q: 80)	£400	
The Playground		
W 10.5 x 15" S, (J: 111)	£805	
Well Bottom		
M 12 x 16" S, (T: 5)	£400	
Wren Boys in the Snow		
O 16 x 18" S, I, (P: 32)	£9,200	
The Procession		
O 14 x 18" S, (KII: 89)	£3,800	
Shy Visitors		
O 16 x 20" S, (KII: 89)	£3,800	
Inishmore Lads		
O 15.75 x 13" S, (KII: 90)	£4,000	
Sunday Afternoon, the Aran Islands		
O 20 x 24" S, (EII: 325)	£19,550	
Mellifont Abbey, Co Louth		
O 30 x 31.5" S, I, (EII: 325)	£9,775	
Aran Islanders in their Sunday Best		
O 22.5 x 30.5" S (EII: 329)	£23,000	
The Moon-Worshippers		
O 13.75 x 19.75" S, (EII: 330)	£4,025	
Donkey on the Stones		
O 14 x 18" S, I, (EII: 336)	£4,025	
Dreamer in a Landscape		
O 25 x 30" S, I, (EII: 360)	£10,350	
Floating Forms		
P 15 x 22" S, (GII: 54)	£600	

Children at the Door		
O 7.5 x 8.5" S, (GII: 25)	£1,500	
DIXON, James (20th century)		
The Famous Schooner Hesperus		
O 22.5 x 30.5" S, (KII: 13)	£1,200	
Tory Island		
O 22 x 30" S, I, (EII: 364A)	£920	
DIXON, Samuel (fl. 1748-1769) Follower of		
A Basso Relievo Picture - Birds and Flowers		
W 12.5 x 16.25" (Z: 419)	£625	
DOBBIN, Lady Kate (1868-1948)		
Japonica		
W 12 x 16" S, (Q: 17)	£600	
DOYLE, John (1797-1868)		
A Celebrated Stag Hunt: Turning Out		
O 16.75 x 35.5" (EII: 232)	£12,650	
DUFFY, Patrick V (1836-1909)		
Glendalough, Co Wicklow		
O 14 x 24" S, (KII: 23)	£600	
EDOUART, August (1789-1861)		
Silhouette of the Hon. George William Massy/		
Silhouette of the Hon. Major John Massy		
S 12 x 8.5" (2) S, D, (K: 148)	£1,430	
EGAN, Felim (b. 1952)		
Grey Diptych with Four Lines		
A 31.5 x 15.75" S, (P: 65)	£370	
EGGINTON, Frank, J. (1908-1990)		
A Connemara Cottage		
O 24 x 36" S, D, (K: 188)	£3,850	
A Cottage Interior		
W 10 x 14" S, D, (Z: 297)	£850	
A Cottage near Belmullet, Co. Mayo		
W 10 x 14" S, I, (K: 116)	£660	
A country road, Autumn		
W 21 x 30" S, (M: 20)	£1,600	
A View in Connemara		
W 15 x 21" S, (P: 61)	£850	
Autumn landscape with caravan on a road		
W 21 x 30" S, (L: 51)	£2,200	
Ballinskelligs Castle, Co. Kerry		
W 21 x 30" S, (L: 53)	£1,500	
Ben Ola, Sessiagh, Co. Donegal & In the Gap of		
Dunloe, Killarney		
W 10 x 14" (2) S, I, (K: 112)	£1,100	
Bringing home the turf		
W 21 x 30" S, (M: 46)	£1,500	
Collecting the turf, Connemara		
W 21 x 30" S, (N: 69)	£1,700	
Currach in a quiet cove		
W 21 x 30" S, (M: 59)	£1,500	
Killarney Harbour at Aasleagh, Connemara		
O 24 x 36" S, (L: 23)	£2,000	
Lough Currane, Co. Kerry		
W 20.5 x 29.5" S, I, (K: 111)	£1,100	
Near Bantyr. West Cork		
W 15 x 21" S, D, (M: 9)	£950	
The Crully River, Co. Donegal		
W 21 x 30" S, (L: 12)	£2,000	
The Hungry Place Tomhaela, Clifden Road		
W 14.5 x 20.75" S, I, (K: 145)	£660	
West of Ireland, Coastal Scene		
W 18 x 21" S, (AI: 553)	£750	
A Wintery Day, Donegal		
W 14.5 x 21" S, (KII: 57)	£1,200	
The Glencoaghan River, Connemara		
W 14.5 x 21" S, (KII: 58)	£600	
Evening, Clare Island, Co Mayo		
W 9.5 x 13.5" S, (KII: 59)	£750	
Owenduff Bridge, Connemara		
W 14.5 x 20" S, (KII: 146)	£600	
The Ox Mountains, Co Sligo		
W 14 x 20.5" S, (KII: 147)	£520	
Snow Scene, Ballynagilly, Co Tyrone		
W 14.5 x 20.5" S, (KII: 148)	£800	
Ringhaddy, Strangford Lough		
W 15 x 21" S, (KII: 219)	£650	
The Hungry Place, Tomhaela, Clifden Road		
W 14.5 x 20.75" S, (KII: 220)	£1,200	
St Finan's Bay and the Skelligs, Co Kerry		
W 14.5 x 21" S, (KII: 149)	£700	
The Road from Comber, Co Down		
W 15 x 21" S, (KII: 150)	£950	
Lake Scene, Co Galway		
W 21 x 30" S, (EII: 338)	£1,495	
EGGINTON, Wycliffe (1875-1951)		
Bringing Home the Sheep		
W 21 x 28" S, (Z: 299)	£1,250	

Grey Sea, Iona
W 14.5 x 21" S, I, (K: 133) — £385
Lough Crosach, near Tongue
W 14 x 20.5" S, I, (K: 134) — £495
The Quiet of Lough na Naugh
W 14 .25 x 21.25" S, (KII: 43) — £450
A Moorland Road
W 14 x 19" S, (KII: 55) — £500
Dark at Dartmoor
W 14 x 20.25" S, (KII: 56) — £600
A Cloudy Evening, Lough Laggan
W 14.25 x 20.75" S, (KII: 60) — £600
North Strand, Iona
W 14.5 x 21" S, (KII: 61) — £600
Old Cottages, South Devon
W 10.25 x 14" S, (KII: 62) — £380
Rainbow over a Castle on a Hill
W 6.5 x 14" S, (KII: 103) — £280
Driving Cattle on a Moorland Road, North Wales
W12 x 16.5" S, (KII: 104) — £480
Coombe-in-Teighnhead, Northern Village,
South Devon
W 10.25 x 14.25" S, (KII: 105) — £280

FARRELL, Michael (b. 1945)
Presse Series
Pr 23 x 23" S, D, (T: 176) — £100
Red Hand of Ulster
Pr 26 x 25" S, I, (P: 149) — £140
Study for Miss Murphy's Bedroom
D 22 x 29" S, I, D, (T: 85) — £260
Study with Piece Cut Out
M 31 x 31" S, I, D, (Q: 170) — £640

FAULKNER, John (1835-1894)
A Breezy Morning
W 22.5 x 39.5" S, I, (K: 17) — £1,210
Boatmen on a quiet lake
W 12 x 20.5" S, D, (M: 32) — £1,500
Cliff at Achill Island, Co. Mayo
W 40 x 25" S, I, (K: 28) — £1,980
Cromwell's Bridge
O 7.25 x 11" (K: 158) — £550
Landscape with Horse & Cart, Figures and Cattle
W 11.5 x 21.5" S, (T: 130) — £970
Lough Corrib, Co. Mayo
W 18.5 x 29" S, I, (T: 73) — £2,600
Ireland's Eye and Lambay, Bay of Dublin
W 26 x 45" S, (KII: 1) — £2,400
Malin Head Looking East
W 15.5 x 28.5" S, (KII: 2) — £900
A Fisherman and Cattle on the Bend of the River
W 13 x 22" S, (KII: 3) — £650
Malin Head, Donegal
W 15 x 25.5" S<, (KII: 4) — £550
A Beached Fishing Boat before a Hilly Coastline
W 21 x 38" S, (KII: 43) — £2,600
A Ballynahinch Lake, Co Galway
W 17.5 x 29.5" S, (KII: 45) — £1,350
Bealanabrack, Co May
W 27 x 47" S, (KII: 121) — £700
Fisherman on the Bank of a Lough,
Connemara
W13.25 x 22.5" S, (KII: 174) — £900
Sundown
W 17 x 30" S, (KII: 175) — £700

FLANAGAN, T.P. (b. 1929)
Autumn River
W 16 x 19" S, D, (Q: 9) — £450
Grey Shore
O 24 x 29" S, I, (P: 73) — £720

FRENCH, Robert (19th Century)
Four sketch books
D/W 5.5 x 9.75" S, D, I, (K: 13) — £660

FRENCH, William Percy (1854-1920)
A Bog at Sunset
W 8 x 11" (K: 66) — £550
A Garden Path
W 11 x 9.25" S, (O: 85) — £1,050
Alpine Chalets
W 10 x 7" S, D, (L: 59a) — £750
Among the Twelve Pins Connemara
W 6.5 x 9.5" S, I, (T: 32) — £970
Bluebells in Spring
W 10 x 14" S, D, (M: 40a) — £3,500
Bogland landscape
W 7.25 x 11" S, (R: 36) — £500
Coastal Landscape
W 6.75 x 10" S, D, (T: 18) — £700

Cottages in a rural landscape with geese
W 7 x 10" S, (M: 18) — £2,100
Evening on the Bog
W 6.25 x 9.25" S, (V: 1123) — £500
Moorland Scene & Country Road
W 4.5 x 6" (2) (V: 1124) — £1,100
Mountain scene with marsh
W 7 x 10" S, (M: 56) — £2,300
Near Falcarragh, Co. Donegal
W 4.5 x 6.5" S, (O: 79) — £1,150
Pastoral River Landscape
W 6 x 9" S, D, (L: 54) — £1,700
Peat Stacks by a flooded Bog
W 9.25 x 13" S, (K: 62) — £880
River in mountain landscape
W 7 x 10" S, (M: 36) — £2,200
River Landscape
W 9.5 x 13.5" S, I, D, (O: 24) — £1,700
River Landscape with Boat and Distant Town
W 5.5 x 9.5" S, (L: 10) — £1,500
Sailing on a Lough
W 5.5 x 9.25" S, (K: 63) — £880
Summer Days near Strokestown
W 6.75 x 9.5" S, I, (Q: 39) — £1,700
Sunset over a bog
W 7 x 10" S, (M: 65) — £2,800
The Bog Road
W 7 x 10" S, (L: 55) — £2,100
Tramore, Co. Waterford
W 7 x 9.5" S, I, (M: 4) — £920
In Ould Donegal
W 10 x 13.75" S, (KII: 9) — £1,700
Lake View
W 5.5 x 9.25" S, I, (EII: 290) — £1,092
Coastal landscape
W 5 x 6.5" S, (GII: 67) — £720

FRYE, Thomas (1710-62)
Young Man in Classical Landscape
O 44 x 56" S, (GII: 47) — £7,000

GALBALLY, Cecil (d. 1995)
Woman in a doorway
O 40 x 26" S, I, (M: 68) — £3,000

GALE, Martin (20th Century)
The Exterior of a House with a Car
& Cases
O 18 x 19" S, D, (P: 114) — £720

GANLY, Rose Brigid (b. 1909)
A Dark Day – Holmeston Avenue
O 15 x 20" S, (Q: 102) — £420

GARSTIN, Anthea (1894-1978)
Gymkhana
O 9.5 x 13" (EII: 301) — £2,070

GARSTIN, Norman (1847-1926)
A Street Market in Brittany
W 14.25 x 10" S, (K: 72) — £2,200
The Chalk Quarry
O 36 x 28" S, (EII: 288) — £4,370

GAVEN, George (fl 1760-1775)
Portrait of Speaker John Po nsonby
O 58.25 x 46" I, (EII: 205) — £10,350

GEOGHEGAN, Trevor (b. 1946)
High Plains Light No. IV
O 36 x 36" S, I, D, (P: 5) — £1,000

GIBNEY, Arthur (20th Century)
Roman buildings
M 33 x 55" S, (M: 72) — £300

GILLESPIE, George (b. 1924)
A Summers Day on the Hills
O 24 x 36" (Z: 301) — £1,050
Coastal Landscape with Boys Fishing
O 9 x 11" S, (S: 134) — £300
Donegal Coast near Gortahurk
O 30 x 40" S, (V: 1147) — £1,800
Harbour near Leenane, Co. Galway
O 18 x 24" S, (O: 108) — £1,000
On a Summers Day, River Landscape
O 20 x 30" S, (Z: 304) — £1,000
River Landscape
O 9.5 x 11.5" S, (S: 25) — £300
River Landscape with Children and Cattle
O 24 x 36" (V: 1138) — £1,400
Solitude in the Rosses, Co. Donegal
O 30 x 40" S, (Z: 307) — £1,500
Toombeola District, Co. Galway
O 20 x 30" S, (P: 78) — £500
Turf Gatherers Near Gort-a-Hurk
O 15 x 19" S, I, (S: 93) — £470

Evening Light, Strangford, Co Down
O 9.25 x 9.5" S, (GII: 3) — £500

GLEESON, Evelyn (1855-1944)
Study of a Girl
P 15.5 x 12" S, (Q: 95) — £460

GLENAVY, Lady Beatrice (1883-1968)
Madonna
O 14 x 11" S, (L: 78) — £1,150
Still Life with Madonna
O 16 x 18" (P: 145) — £160
Waiting
O 11.5 x 13" S, D, (P: 94) — £300

GRACEY, Theo J.(1903-1959)
River of the Mountain and Bringing
home the Turf
W 15 x 21" (2) S, (R: 117) — £285
Country Road, Co. Wicklow
W 10 x 14.5" S, (Y: 182) — £150

GRAHAM, Patrick (b. 1943)
Man & Child Study
D 16 x 23" S, D, (Q: 13) — £620
Station 1
M 32 x 44" I (P: 146) — £2,700
Swinging a Child
D 23 x 16" S, D, (Q: 12) — £400
The Philosophers
D 16 x 22" S, (P: 131) — £970
The Thinker
D 30 x 22" S, D, (Q: 11) — £400
Untitled
O 30 x 24 " (tryp (P: 99) — £480

GREENLANES, James (fl 1860-1884)
Lower Lake, Killarney
O 9.25 x 12.25" S, (KII: 193) — £500
Portrait of Speaker John Ponsonby
O 58.25 x 46" I, (EII: 205) — £10,350

GREY, Alfred (fl.1864-1924)
Cattle by a Stream - Grey Day
O 9 x 12.5" S, I, (V: 1141) — £600
Highland Cattle
W 5.75 x 8" S, (T: 158) — £260
Mother & Child with a Calf
O S, (YI: 65) — £1,500
The Hillside
O 22.25 x 29" S, D, (K: 171) — £2,860
Head of a Cow
O 6.75 x 8.25" S, EII: 252) — £1,092

GUINNESS, May (1863-1955)
At Sienna
P 12 x 8.5" (S: 35) — £320
The Little Stream
W 8 x 10.75" S, (P: 101) — £500
View from St. Thomas
O 29 x 21" S, (N: 125) — £950
Autumn Flowers
O 28 x 36" S, (EII: 298) — £16,100
Still Life with Flowers and Fruit
O 28 x 36" S, (EII: 322) — £10,350
Pump at Pont l'Abbe
O 7.5 x 9.5" S, (GII: 26) — £2,000

HALL, Kenneth (20th Century)
Mountain landscape with cottages
O 17 x 21" S, (N: 106) — £470
Western Village
O 12.5 x 16" S, (N: 35) — £350

HAMILTON, Gustavus (1739-1775)
Flower Studies
W 14.75 x 11" (2) S, D, (S: 31) — £4,200

HAMILTON, Hugh Douglas (1738-1808)
Portrait of Sir James Graham, 1st Bart.
in a wooded landscape
P 33.5 x 25.75" I, (I: 269) — £73,000
Portrait of a Lady
P 23 X 18" (V: 1037) — £150
Portrait of a Lady & Portrait of a Gent
W 9.5 x 7.5" (2) (V: 999) — £340
Portrait of Anne, Countess of Cork
P 9.5 x 7" (R: 104) — £110
Portrait of Miss Plunket of Rathmore,
Co Meath, Wife of Garrett Dease of
Turdotston, Co Westmeath
P 9 x 7.5" (KII: 176) — £420

HAMILTON, Letitia Marion (1878-1964)
A Breezy Day on Portmarnock Beach
O 26 x 36" S, (T: 61) — £2,200
A Cottage in the Mountains
O 21 x 25" S, (P: 15) — £950

A Currach full of people
O 7.5 x 9.5" S, I, (HI: 266) — £550
A Mountain Stream
O 15 x 19" (Q: 101) — £1,500
A View at Glengariff
O 20 x 24", S, (T: 81) — £2,000
A view from Akhista, West Cork
O 20 x 24" (K: 221) — £2,860
A View in Glengarriff
O 20 x 24" (T: 132) — £1,100
A Village Near Errigal
O 15 x 19" S, (YI: — £2,300
Beech Trees by a Lough
O 10 x 10.5", (K: 225) — £550
City Bridge (and landscape on verso)
O 12 x 16" (O: 6) — £1,250
Cropatrick, Connemara
O 12 x 16" S, (BII: 117) — £800
Dingle Bay
O 12 x 16.375" I, (K: 224) — £2,420
Dubrovnic
O 16 x 20" S, (L: 4) — £1,000
Glengariff, Co. Cork
O 20 x 26" S, I, (RI: 89) — £1,955
Glengarriff
O 20 x 24" S, (M: 41a) — £1,000
Huntsmen & Hounds of The Bray Hunt
O 8 x 10", S, (M: 87) — £700
Punchestown Races
O 22 x 26" S, (MI: 162) — £8,625
Roundstone Harbour
O 17 x 19" S, (K: 222) — £6,050
Roundstone
O 16 x 20" S, (BII: 116) — £2,600
St. Georgia, Venice
O 16 x 20" S, (T: 16) — £2,000
Sunlit trees in a hilly landscape
O 12 x 16" S, (K: 223) — £825
The Feeding Trough
O 18 x 23.5" S, (T: 39) — £3,600
The Kildare Hounds at Beggars End
O 8 x 10" S, (M: 93) — £670
The Market Place
O 26 x 22" S, (UI: 178) — £2,530
The Meath Hounds
O 7 x 10" S, (M: 25) — £700
The Square, Bruges
O 22 x 24.5" S, (P: 29) — £1,500
The Twelve Pins from Roundstone
O 16 x 20" S, (Q: 126) — £3,000
The Village Shop
O 20 x 16" S, (T: 84) — £3,000
Venetian Canal with Gondola
O 16 x 18" S, (L: 19) — £3,000
Western coastal mountain landscape
O 16 x 20" S, (O: 100) — £2,000
Window over the lake at Glengarriff
O 16 x 18" S, (P: 31) — £1,700
The Kildare Hounds at Castletown
O 8 x 10" S, (KII: 198) — £1,800
View Through the Trees of Cottage and Lake
O 20 x 24" S, (GII: 7) — £1,400
Kilkee
O 14 x 18" S, (GII: 43) — £1,800

HANLON, Jack P. (1913-1968)
A Farm House, Wexford
O 19 x 23" S, I, D, (P: 147) — £1,600
At the Seaside
W 11 x 15" S, (S: 109i) — £470
Into Limerick
W 10 x 14" (S: 109m) — £500
Jerpoint Abbey
W 13 x 20" S, I, (T: 88) — £420
Madonna and Child
O 18.5 x 13" (Q: 165) — £920
Maynooth Nocturne
W 17.25 x 13.5" (V: 1120) — £130
Mediterranean Village
W 11 x 16" (S: 109l) — £600
St. Brigid's - Anemones
W 12.5 x 18" S, D, (Q: 58) — £400
Sunlit Tree
W 15 x 11" S, (N: 18) — £300
The Golden Madonna
O 17 x 11.5" (P: 134) — £500
The Village Green
W 9 x 12" (T: 156) — £250

View from a Balcony
W 13 x 19" (P: 113) — £500
View from the Window
W 10.5 x 14.5" S, (S: 14) — £470

HARGREAVES, Lucy (19th Century)
A pony in a landscape
O 14.75 x 14.75" (EI: 305) — £240
A study of a Connemara pony in a landscape
O 14 x 12" (EI: 312) — £700
Portrait of a horse Dolly in a stable yard
O 14 x 16.5" S, D, (EI: 310) — £500
Study of a pony
O 11.25 x 15.5" S, (EI: 304) — £240

HARMAN, Ann S. King (20th Century)
Western cottages
W 11.5 x 20" S, (N: 34) — £300

HARTLAND, Henry Albert (1840-1893)
A Lough among Hills, Connemara
W 13 x 20.5" S, D, (K: 2) — £330
A Wooded Bank
W 24 x 32" (KII: 44) — £1,500
Corn Stooks in a Field with a Village Beyond
W 13.5 x 27.5" S, (KII: 69) — £550
Coastal Landscape
W 11.5 x 23.5" S, (S: 124) — £440
Mountain Landscape
W 9 x 17" S, (T: 92) — £380

HAYES, Claud (1852-1922)
Pastoral landscape
W 10 x 18" S, (L: 128) — £150
A portrait of a youn man, William Blacker
W 24 x 20" S, (EI: 266) — £450

HAYES, Edward (1797-1864)
A Young Lady Seated with a Harp
W 10.5 x 9.5" S, D, (P: 2) — £260

HAYES, Edwin (1820-1904)
A Seascape
O 5 x 5.5" S, D, (P: 9) — £720
Bamborough Castle
W 14 x 20.5" S, D, (K: 19) — £2,750
Dutch fishing boats at harbour mouth
O 9 x 12" S, (M: 30) — £2,600
Farmouth smack leaving Gorleston harbour
O 9 x 12" S, D, (M: 31) — £1,900
Shipwreck near Ryde
O 10.75 x 15.25" S, I, (K: 147a) — £440
Fisherman and Boats in a Coastal Landscape,
and Fishing Boats in a Choppy Sea
W 3.75 x 4.75" S, (both) (KII: 117) — £500
A Fishing Boat in Calk Sea, and Fishing
Boats offshore
W 11.75 x 18" S, (KII: 123) — £2,000
Fishing Smacks off the Coast
O 16.25 x 34.25" S, (EII: 233) — £6,325
Penzance from the Sea
O 6.75 x 9.25" S, I, D, (EII: 253) — £632

HEALY, Henry (1909-1982)
A View of Howth Harbour
O 13.5 x 17.5" S, (Q: 23) — £820
Howth Harbour
O 17 x 13" S, (Q: 111) — £720
Morning Tide
O 13 x 17" S, (Q: 1) — £650
Sundown
O 12 x 16" (ZI: 92) — £200
Donkey's Head
W 6 x 4" (O: 109) — £50
High Tide
O 16 x 20" S, (GII: 108) — £550
Over Dooagh, Achill
O 12 x 17" S, 9GII: 117) — £360
A Connemara Cottage
Overlooking a Lake
O 18 x 14" S, (GII: 95) — £300

HEALY, Michael
Dubliners
W 10 x 7.5 (GII: 138) — £150
Dubliners
W 10 x 7.5 (GII: 139) — £150
Dubliners
W 10 x 7.5 (GII: 140) — £150

HELMICK, Howard (1845-1905)
The Summons Server
O 20 x 16" S, (P: 14) — £3,200

HENNESSY, Patrick (1915-1980)
Horses on a strand 1969)
O 30 x 40" S, (L: 109) — £1,600

Midsummer
O 35 x 45" S, (T: 48) — £1,700
Rose Study, Speke's Yellow and
Madame Butterfly
O 8 x 10" S, (M: 21) — £1,200
Portrait of a Young Man in a Chinese Robe
O 51 x 61" (ZI: 57) — £550
Sea Wall
O 24 x 35" S, (K: 268) — £2,200
Self portrait
O 20.25 x 13.5" (K: 267) — £1,540
Still Life at a Window
O 20 x 14" S, D, (L: 56) — £3,400
Still life with playing cards, bank note and coin
O 7.75 x 11.5" S, (U: 23) — £2,200
The Enchanted Village - Kinsale 1941
O 24 x 16" S, D, I, (L: 100) — £6,600
The Moorings, County Cork
O 20 x 30" S, (O: 30) — £3,150
The Moorings, County Cork
O 20 x 30" S, (ZI: 120) — £2,100
Woman with a Rose
O 11 x 7" S, (T: 87) — £900
Dublin Docks, 1977
O 16.25 x 20" S, (EII: 352) — £3,450
Sunlight on the Floor
O 43 x 55" S, (EII: 365) — £6,900

HENRY, Grace (1868-1953)
An Irish Lough
O 15 x 18" S, (J: 186) — £2,415
Boats at Chioggia
O 9.5 x 12" (S: 62) — £800
Claddagh Village
O 9.5 x 13" S, (P: 22) — £2,000
Evening, Achill
O 23.5 x 19" S, (Q: 29) — £1,700
Feeding the Ducks
O 14 x 11" S, (L: 13) — £1,000
Fishing boats moored by a river mouth
O 10.75 x 13.25" S, (K: 194) — £1,045
Foynes-on-the-Shannon
O 12 x 16" S, (S: 60) — £1,900
Moon & Mountain Achill (Fields by the sea verso)
O 14 x 11" S, (S: 61) — £1,700
New Hat
O 12 x 15" S, (Q: 98) — £800
Still life – vase of flowers
O 18 x 21" S, (N: 119) — £2,000
The Dove
O 21 x 19" S, (N: 24) — £2,500
The Gardener, portrait of Paul Henry
O 20 x 24" S, (K: 192) — £6,050
The Red House at Mougins
O 10.5 x 13.5" S, (S: 58) — £7,200
The Stream Champlay
O 5.5 x 6.75" S, (Q: 7) — £1,400
Vase of Flowers
O 14 x 11" S, (S: 59) — £2,400
Woman Ironing
W 8.5 x 11" S, I, (P: 115) — £480
Greystones Harbour
O 11.5 x 16" S, (Q: 16) — £230
The Hills of Connemara
O 13 x 16" S, I, (EII: 345) — £2,450
The Storm
O 23.5 x 32" S, (KII: 14) — £2,800
Study of a Young Lady
O 11 x 9" S, (GII: 51) — £250
Orange Tree
O 13 x 9.5" S, (GII: 28) — £600
A Canal View in Venice
O 11 x 14" S, (GII: 27) — £1,100

HENRY, Paul (1876-1958)
A Lough in the West of Ireland
O 7.5 x 9.75" S, (J: 114) — £4,600
A Western Village
O 5 x 6" S, (O: 68) — £5,200
Bringing Home the Harvest
O 14 x 15.75" S, (CII: 33) — £3,500
Coomasaharn, Co. Kerry
O 12 x 14" S, (M: 24) — £13,500
Cottage in wooded mountain landscape
O 10.5 13.5" S, (O: 15) — £6,500
Cottages by the Lake, Connemara
O 14 x 16" S, (RI: 84) — £24,150
Cottages in Connemara
O 8.5 x 10.5" S, (M: 45) — £13,500

Dusk, West of Ireland
O 16 x 24" S, (UI: 173) £13,800
Evening on the Bog
O 14 x 16" S, (K: 260) £24,200
Glencar, Co. Kerry
O 11.5 x 13.5" S, I, (T: 95) £7,800
Road across the Bog
O 15 x 18" S, I, (K: 235) £8,800
Thatched Cottages
O 7.265 x 10.375" S, (K: 263) £5,500
The Blacksod Bay, Co. Mayo
O 12 x 14" S, (O: 50) £17,000
The Roadside Cottage, Killary Bay, below Mweelrea Mountain
O 14 x 16" S, (J: 141) £21,850
Misty Morning
O 10 x 12.5" S, (KII: 66) £4,200
Turf Stack by a Pool, Connemars
O 16.5 x 21.25" S, (KII: 67) £8,000
The Lobster Pots
O 20 x 24" S, (GII: 50) £28,000
HICKEY, Patrick (b. 1927)
Bogland, Wicklow
O 45 x 60" S, (T: 129) £700
In Glenmalure, Carraway Stick Night
Pr 19 x 23" S, I, (T: 6) £180
HICKEY, Thomas (1741-1824)
Portrait of Captain George Robertson
O 28.25 x 21.5" S, (JI: 7) £3,220
HILL, Derek (b. 1916)
Portrait of the Earl of Wicklow
O 20 x 24" U: 45) £950
HILL, Roland (1919-1979)
Apples and Chrysanthemums
O 25 x 18.5" S, (K: 147) £770
Cottages, Atlantic Drive, Co Donegal
O 20 x 26" S, (KII: 85) £100
HONE, David (20th Century)
Evening, Sandymount Strand
O 7.5 x 9" S, I, (P: 100) £540
Kerry landscape & Towards Dun Laoghaire
O 8 x 10" (2) S, (L: 28) £800
Merrion Strand
O 7.75 x 10" I, (T: 76) £700
HONE, Evie Sidney (1894-1955)
At Barmeath Castle
W 10.75 x 7.125" S, (CII: 96) £400
A carpet design
W 11.25 x 6.75" S, (GI: 126) £260
Composition
O 25 x 36" S, D, (P: 50) £3,500
Deposition
W 15 x 12" (U: 38) £920
Fireside
W 6.5 x 8" S, (P: 122) £520
Howth, Co. Dublin
W 9 x 10.5" S, (M: 90) £360
Marley
D 8 x 8.5" S, (S: 118) £160
Saint standing in landscape
W 22 x 9" (N: 139) £400
San Gimanano
W 14 x 10" S, (Q: 90) £660
Scenes from The Life of Christ
W 9 x 3.5" (2) (M: 71) £250
St. Catherine of Siena
W 12 x 3.375" (CII: 100) £320
St. Francis, A cartoon for a stained glass panel
W 20 x 6" (N: 37) £650
St. Joseph and The Blessed Virgin
W 39 x 14" (2) (L: 110) £1,900
The Bird Bath at Marley
W 13.5 x 11" (N: 134) £380
The Crucifixion
W 22.5 x 38.75" S, (K: 102) £1,100
The Old Church
W 15.5 x 13" (N: 138) £400
Three figures
W 12.5 x 11.5" (N: 140) £260
Winter Day, Marley
W 10 x 13.75" (P: 19) £500
Youghal
W 10 x 14.5" S, D, (M: 85) £670
View from a Window at Montparnasse
W 14 x 9" (KII: 650) £650
A Canal, France
W 14 x 9" (KII: 75) £650

The Eiffel Tower
W 14X 9.25" S, (KII: 76) £700
Dianthus painting
O 23.5 x 13" S, (KII: 154) £3,000
Still Life
P 10.25 x 14.5 S, (GII: 15) £670
Small Garden
W 13 x 9.75 (GII: 56) £450
Composition 1924
D 8 x 7.5" S, (GII: 57) £550
HONE, Horace (1756-1825)
Portrait of the Countess of Lanesborough
P 4 x 3.25" (HI: 315) £2,200
Portraits of Lord Edward Fitzgerald (two by Hone/ one by H. D. Hamilton/ one by Irish Sch.)
E 2.375" / 2.25" (K: 150) £4,400
HONE, Nathaniel (1718-1784)
Jason, a grey Racehorse of Sir N. Curzon
O 40 x 50" S, D, I, (E: 58) £73,000
Portrait of Miss Sunning, head and shoulders
O 25 x 19.75" (E: 24) £7,475
HONE, Nathaniel (1831-1917)
A Wooded Landscape at Sunset
O 13.25 x 20" (KII: 40) £400
A Beached Fishing Boat, Malahide
W 7.5 x 10.5" (KII: 120) £900
Gathering Seaweed on the Strand, Malahide
O 25 x 36" S, (KII: 215) £20,000
Stormy Coast, Clare
O 24.25 x 40.25" S, (KII: 216) £18,000
Portrait of a Lady with her Three Daughters
O 36 x 46" (EII: 203) £26,450
Portrait of a Gentleman
O 29.25 x 24.5" (EII: 215) £9,200
Cattle at Moldowney
O 24 x 39" S, (EII: 269) £8,625
Landscape
O 18 x 24" (EII: 270) £3,680
Vista Through Trees: Cows in Sunlight Approaching
O 39 x 32.5" (EII: 271) £12,650
The Crest of the Hill
O 20 x 30" (EII: 272) £4,830
Coastal Scene
O 24.5 x 43" (EII: 274) £17,250
Three Studies – Cattle in Sunlight under Trees; Haycocks; Landscape with Cattle and a Stream
O each 5 x 7" (EII: 275) £2,875
A Windy Day, Barbizon
O 17 x 24" S, I, (EII: 287) £5,520
Irish Landscapes
W 3.25 x 4.5"; 4.5 x 8.25" S, (EII: 289) £632
Windmill on dark green height, Feltrim Hill, North Co Dublin
W 5 x 7" (L: 118) £380
Estuary at Malahide
O 9.5 x12" (N: 56) £700
Fishing Boats returning Home
O 12 x 18" S, (K: 262) £3,850
Malahide, Co. Dublin
W 7.5 x 11" I, (T: 182) £600
Sea and Hill
W 6 x 9.5" (O: 1) £450
HUSON, Thomas (1844-1920)
Showery, Co Donegal
O 27.25 x 48" S, I, (EII: 255) £1,350
HUSSEY, Philip (1713-1783)
Portrait of Master Blacker
O 50.75 x 38.5" I, (EII: 202) £6,900
ITEN, Hans
An Irish Castle by the Sea
O 13 x 16" S, (KII: 114) £1,700
JELLETT, Mainie (1897-1944)
Abstract Composition
W 5 x 7.5" (ZI: 84) £500
Design for Safety Curtain
W 11 x 16.5" (T: 161) £600
Female Nude Study
D 14 x 10" (T: 163) £400
Harvest Time
W 7.75 x 12.5" (S: 34) £650
Life Study
W 12 x 17" S, D, (S: 47) £1,400
Nude Study
D 9 x 8" (S: 116) £240
Nude Study
D 12 x 8.5" S, (S: 67) £400
Abstract Study

W 8 x 10.5" (GII: 71) £1,700
JERVAS, Charles (1675-1739)
Portrait of Edward Wortley Montagu
O 48.75 x 39.75" (VI: 41) £7,500
Portrait of Lady Mary Wortley Montagu
O 29.75 x 24.75" I, (VI: 42) £10,000
Portrait of Sir Thomas Lowther
O 30 x 25" (G: 8) £550
JOHN, Augustus (1878-1961)
Portrait of William Butler Yeats
M 24 x 18" (EII: 304) £62,000
JOHNSON, Nevill (b. 1911)
Abstract Forms
O 14.5 x 11.5" (S: 17) £500
Dawlish 1978
C 7 x 9.25" (Q: 169) £130
Landscape
O 11 x 19" S, I, D, (P: 76) £280
Still Life - 3 Apples
O 13 x 14" S, D, (P: 35) £420
Surreal Landscape
O 16 x 21" S, (P: 173) £970
Pastoral Landscape
O 17 x 20" S, (GII: 39) £800
Interior with Nude After Picasso
D 5.5 x 10" S, (GII: 83) £70
JONES, Thomas Alfred (1823-1893) Attrib.
Hope – Mother and Child
D 13.5 x 10" S, D, (W: 345) £200
JONES, Henry Thaddeus (1859-1929)
A rocky Coastline
O 13.5 x 17.75" S, D, (K: 170) £880
KAVANAGH, Joseph Malachy (1856-1918)
Cockle Pickers
O 17 x 21" S, (O: 62) £32,000
The Salt Marsh, Portmarnock, Co. Dublin
O 17 x 21" S, (K: 182) £3,080
Tending the Flock
O 17 x 21" S, (KII: 84) £2,800
KEATING, Sean (1889-1977)
Men in a Curragh
D 22 x 29.5" S, (L: 117) £850
Nil Si Ag Eisteacht (She is not listening)
O 14 x 18" (O: 72) £7,500
Study of a Young Girl
P 17 x 15.5" S, (P: 42) £2,400
The Limerick Girl
O 36 x 30" S, (K: 240) £26,400
Young Lady, Connemara Seascape I
O 30 x 36" S, (L: 26) £5,000
Man of Aran
P 25 x 15" S, (KII: 228) £1,800
The Aran Island Turf Boat
O 25 x 30" S, (EII: 327) £13,800
The Playboy of the Western World
O 48 x 48" S, (EII: 344) £5,520
Head of a Man
D 12 x 14" S, (GII: 59) £670
Study of a Young Woman
D 16 x 13" S, (GII: 131) £550
KERNOFF, Harry Aaron (1900-1974)
Aran Fisherman
P 18 x 14.5" S, D, (S: 158) £770
Armoor
W 8.5 x 6" S, (S: 165) £170
Bacchante
O 63 x 48" S, (S: 189) £1,500
Beeches at Woodbrook, Co. Wicklow
O 27 x 37" S, (S: 152) £5,200
Captain Jack White
P 15 x 12" S, (Q: 56) £400
Christy Brown
P 15 x 11" S, D, (S: 161) £340
Cubist Study - Man & Apple
O 7.5 x 6" S, (S: 164) £380
Dance of Death
O 60 x 84" S, (S: 192) £2,800
Death
O 60 x 84" S, (S: 191) £3,200
Dublin Character
P 13.5 x 11" S, D, (S: 160) £450
Dunquinn, Co. Kerry
M 20 x 29" S, (S: 155) £750
Eros
D 9 x 8" S, D, (S: 163) £280
Female Study
O 11 x 17.5" S, (T: 10) £400

Figures on a beach
W 9 x 13" S, D, (L: 34) — £620

Girl Holding a Cigarette & 2 Others
D 18 x 14" (3) S, (S: 170) — £400

Head study - boy
D 12 x 9.5" S, D, (O: 53) — £100

Inchicore Railway Works
W 11 x 14" S, D, (S: 156) — £850

Jupiter and the Muses
O 48 x 60" S, (S: 190) — £4,800

Komnccap & Another
M 21 x 16" (2) S, D, (S: 174) — £600

Lake View
W 17.5 x 21" S, D, (S: 159) — £500

Man With a Purple Tie & 3 Others
P 15 x 112" (4) S, D, (S: 173) — £200

Man with Umbrella
W 9 x 7.5" (S: 168) — £500

Nurse with a Flower
O 34 x 26" S, (S: 153) — £2,000

Old House, Digges Street, Dublin
O 24 x 28" S, D, (S: 150) — £2,800

Portrait of a Young Girl
P 15 x 12" (V: 1089) — £450

Portrait of James Joyce
O 8 x 6" S, (L: 104) — £1,550

Portrait of Oliver St. John Gogarty
O 8.25 x 6.25" S, (L: 103) — £900

Portrait of William Butler Yeats
O 8 x 6" S, (L: 46) — £1,700

Portrait Study & 2 Others
O 7.5 x 6" (3) S, (S: 175) — £370

Portrait Study - A Sailor & 2 Others
P 13 x 11" (3) S, (S: 183) — £800

Portrait Study - Hugh Maguire & 3 Others
P 19 x 13" (4) S, D, (S: 178) — £540

Portrait Study - Kathleen Egan & 2 Others
D 19.5 x 14" (3) S, D, (S: 180) — £360

Portrait Study - Mdme.Kirwood Hackett &
2 Others
D 22.5 x 19" (3) S, (S: 179) — £470

Portrait Study - Young Man & 1 Other
O 7.75 x 5.75" (2 S, (S: 172) — £400

Portrait Study - Young Man at Work
O 19 x 14" S, D, (S: 157) — £850

Portrait Study Tom Casement & 2 Others
D 19 x 14" (3) S, D, (S: 177) — £320

Reclining female nude
O 38 x 26" S, D, (L: 122) — £1,900

Red and his bowler
O 8 x 5.5" S, (N: 7) — £320

Set of 6 woodcuts
Pr 5.5 x 3.5" (6) S, (S: 182) — £170

Set of 6 woodcuts
Pr 5.5 x 3.5" (6) S, (S: 181) — £160

Star of David
D 4.5 x 4.5" (6) (S: 185) — £240

Still Life Apples & Biros
W/P 8.5 x 11" S, (S: 154) — £370

Street Scene, Killarney
W 10.25 x 14.25" S, D, (T: 12) — £1,000

Study of a Child
P 7.75 x 6" S, D, (S: 167) — £180

Study of an Elderly Lady
P 21 x 16" S, D, (S: 169) — £520

Study of Michael Collins
P 14 x 11" S, (S: 162) — £220

Sunshine After Rain
W 8 x 11" S, I, (P: 21) — £450

Thatched Cottages, College Street from
Arbutus Hotel, Killarney
W 10 x 14" S, (P: 45) — £1,500

The Brazen Head & 6 Others
Pr 8 x 6" (7) S, (S: 184) — £170

The Nativity
O 60 x 84" S, (S: 188) — £2,000

The Toucher Willie Doyle & 2 Other
D 18 x 14" (3) S, D, (S: 171) — £420

The Warrior
O 50 x 42" S, (S: 193) — £1,500

There's only a Few of Us Left
O 20 x 27" S, (S: 151) — £3,200

Various unframed prints
Pr various S, (S: 186) — £700

Village View with 2 Children
W 18 x 20.5" S, (S: 174a) — £900

W. B. Yeats & Street Scene

Pr – (2) S, I, (P: 46) — £100

Wicklow Labourer & 2 Others
P 17.25 x 13.5" (S, D, (S: 176) — £400

Wind and Sun, near Bray
O 12 x 16" S, D, (K: 211) — £1,100

Young Girl Holding Flowers
W 20 x 16" S, (S: 166) — £360

Your Time Has Come - Faust
O 38 x 26" S, I, (L: 44) — £3,000

The Killarney Mountains
W 10.75 x 14.5" S, D, (EII: 355) — £805

The Brazen Head
O 8 x 6" S, (GII: 11) — £720

Caravans by the Canal
O 6 x 7" S, (GII: 12) — £800

The Elf
O 8 x 6" S, (GII: 13) — £350

KING, Cecil (1921-1985)
Berlin Series, 1970
P 13.5 x 10" S, (Q: 79) — £340

Illustration to Omar Khayyam
M 29.5 x 17.75" S, (K: 140) — £275

Illustration to Omar Khayyam
M 29.5 x 17.75" S, (K: 140a) — £330

KNUTTEL, Graham (20th Century)
Ace of Hearts
O 41 x 41" S, (N: 122) — £1,200

Vase in a Window
O 20 x 24" S, (Q: 142) — £360

KYLE, Georgina Moutray (1865-1950)
Fishing boats
O 10.5 x 13.5" S, (L: 14) — £600

LAMB, Charles Vincent (1893-1964)
Bog landscape, Connemara
O 20 x 24" S, (K: 206) — £1,760

Bringing Home the Kelp
O 21.5 x 16.5" (O: 16) — £1,100

Coastal Landscape
O 13 x 16" S, (T: 86) — £870

Coastal Landscape
O 10 x 13" S, (T: 96) — £600

Cottages
O 10.5 x 14" S, (V: 1130) — £1,200

Cottages before Dooega Head, Achill Island
O 12.75 x 16" S, (K: 205) — £1,650

Figure on a Hill
O 12.5 x 7.25" S, (K: 292) — £528

Galway Hookers
O 12.5 x 15" S, (P: 70) — £2,400

Head
O 16 x 12.25" S, I, (K: 146) — £1,760

Houses through trees
O 10.5 x 14" S, (O: 59) — £800

In the Village of Carraroe
O 10.5 x 14" S, (K: 207) — £990

Lake in Connemara 1929
O 10 x 13.5" S, (O: 99) — £1,300

Newport, Co. Mayo
O 9 x 12" S, (U: 25) — £1,050

Nude Study
O 14 x 8.5" S, (S: 9) — £650

Strutan Harbour, Carraroe, Co. Galway
O 10.5 x 14" S, (T: 134) — £1,200

The Cottage, Connemara
O 9.5 x 13.5" S, (Q: 148) — £1,200

West of Ireland Coastal View
O 10 x 14" S, (Q: 20) — £3,400

West of Ireland Cottage
O 10 x 14" S, (Q: 109) — £1,200

West of Ireland Harbour
O 13 x 16" S, (V: 1128) — £1,900

West of Ireland, Coastal View
O 13 x 16" S, (V: 1129) — £900

Winter lake and mountain landscape
O 12.5 x 15.5" S, (O: 95) — £1,000

A Connemara woman (1932)
O 24 x 20" S, (K: 62) — £4,000

Girl in a Red Shawl
O 25 x 19" S, (L: 60) — £5,000

The Maam Valley, Co Galway
O 13.25 x 16.25" S, (EII: 333) — £1,150

Connemara Landscape
O 18 x 22" S, (EII: 346) — £2,185

LATHAM, James (1696-1747)
Portrait of Edward Aston
O 29.5 x 24.75" S, (VI: 28) — £1,000

Portrait of Mary, Wife of Edward, 9th Duke of

Norfolk
O 75 x 53" (VI: 43) — £19,000

A portrait of Letitia Carey, of Milburn,
Mrs William Blacker of Carrickblacker, 1739
O 29.5 x 25" (EI: 263) — £2,800

Portrait of Richard Lambart, 4th Earl of Cavan
O 29 x 23.5" (EII: 200) — £3,220

Portrait of George Berkeley
O 27.5 x 22.5" (EII: 201) — £17,250

LAVERY, Sir John (1856-1941)
Bab Es Sek
O 14 x 10" S, D, (A: 25) — £10,350

Funeral of Michael Collins
O 30" x 25" (D II) — £120,000

Figures on the beach, St. Jean de Luz
O 10 x 14" S, (K: 238) — £11,000

Miss Idonea La Primaudaye
O 54 x 33" S, (MI: 137) — £29,900

Miss Lillian McCarthy as Lady Mary in the
Admirable Crichton
O 18 x 14" S, I, D, (RI: 83) — £1,840

Moonlight - The Bridge
O 25 x 30" S, (ZI: 36) — £20,000

On the Loing
O 31 x 30" S, D, I, (MI: 10) — £293,000

Portrait of a Gentleman
O 14 x 10" S, (PI: 63) — £800

Portrait of Dinkie Chisman
O 50 x 30" S, I, D, (CII: 63) — £4,500

Portrait of General Sir Henry Rawlinson
O 30 x 24.5" S, D, I, (RI: 81) — £6,325

Portrait of Pauline Chase as Joan of Arc
O 28 x 20.5" S, I, (K: 239) — £5,280

Portrait of the Artist's Daughter, Alice
O 14 10" I, (A: 38) — £17,250

Portrait of the Artist's Wife, Hazel
O 18.5 x 15.5" (A: 37) — £12,250

The Little White Boats
O 30 x 25" S, D, I, (J: 105) — £7,475

The Rising Moon, Tangier Bay (1912)
O 34 x 44" S, (L: 43) — £18,000

The Terrace - Hazel and Eileen in Tangier 1912
O 25 x 30" S, I, D, (ZI: 69) — £62,000

The Wreck of the SS Delhi, Sidi Cassim, Morocco
O 32.5 x 45.75" S,D,I, (A: 26) — £18,400

A Study of Miss Cynthia Weaver
O 18 x 16" S, (KII: 164) — £4,500

Kaid McLean's Camp, A Wet Day
O 21 x 17.75" S, (KII: 162) — £4,500

La Pecheuse, Grez-sur-Loing
O 29 x 38" S, D, (EII: 282) — £221,500

The Grey Drawing-Room, Tangier
O 14 x 10" S, (EII: 285) — £177,500

The Lakes of Killarney
O 25 x 30" S, D, (EII: 292) — £56,500

Les Orange du Beau Site de Cannes (Tennis
under the Orange Trees, Cannes)
O 18 x 24" S, I, D, (EII: 296) — £78,500

Portrait of Miss Hozier
O 13.5 x 19.5" S, D, (EII: 303) — £1,725

Twilight, Earl's Court
O 24 x 28.75" S, (EII: 315) — £73,000

A Study of Michael Collins
Pr 17 x 13.25" S, (GII: 159A) — £2,100

Study of Arthur Griffith
Pr 17 x 13.25" S, (GII: 159B) — £420

LAWRENSON, Edward Louis (1868-1934)
A Kerry Valley
O 18 x 24" S, I, (EII: 341) — £1,725

LE BROCQUY, Louis (b. 1916)
Ballyconneely Harbour, Low Tide
P 7 x 9" S, (P: 92) — £620

Carros Village
W 7.5 10.5" S, D, (L: 59) — £1,050

Francis Bacon
P/W 23.25 x 17.5" S, D, I, (K: 107) — £1,650

Francis Bacon, no. 458
O 31.5 x 31.5" S, D, (A: 147) — £5,750

Image of Francis Bacon 2
O 31.5 x 31.5" S, D, (K: 271) — £5,720

Image of Francis Bacon 5
O 31.25 x 31.25" S, D, (K: 275) — £5,720

In Fear of Kane & Irish Travellers
W 12 x 9.5" (2) S, D, (P: 23) — £4,800

James Joyce, Study no. 29, 1977
W 9 x 7.5" S, (A: 154) — £920

James Joyce, Study no. 588

W 23.5 x 18" S, D, (A: 155) £1,265
James Joyce, Study no. 61
O 27.5 x 27.5" S, D, (A: 153) £5,750
Naked Woman
Pr 21 x 15" S, D, (V: 1094) £425
Samuel Beckett
P/W 23.25 x 17.5" S, D, I, (K: 106) £1,650
Samuel Beckett
D 29.75 x 22" S, D, (A: 152) £575
Study of W. B. Yeats (Study 11)
D 8.75 x 7" S, D, (S: 5) £900
The lovely Child
W 7.25 x 9.5" S, D, (K: 109) £2,750
The Tain
Pr S, (N: 55) £250
Tone Study for Classic Theme 3
M 7.5 x 5" S, D, (O: 33) £570
Woman
O 30 x 25" S, D, (P: 24) £8,000
Wood, Tipperary
W 12 x 10" S, D, (T: 157) £1,500
Eden 1952
Tapestry 44.25 x 69" (KII: 156) £5,000
Study towards an Image of WB Yeats
W 8.75 x 7" S, (KII: 185) £1,400
August Strindberg
O 31.5 x 31.5" S, (KII: 186) £4,000
August Strindberg
M 23.25 x 17.5" S, (KII: 187) £650
Presence, 1957
O 10 x 7" S, I, D, (EII: 357) £4,600
Francis Bacon, no 460
O 31.5 x 31.5" S, D, (EII: 363) £12,075
Untitled
O 20 x 24" S, D, (EII: 366) £3,680
Harvest Mon
D 16 x 14" S, (GII: 117 £160
LE JEUNE, James (1910-1983)
Landscape near Mallow (1973)
O 11.5 x 16" S, (N: 41) £500
The Strand
O 30 x 25" S, (KII: 151) £10,000
The Market at Annecy
O 20 x 22" S, (KII: 168) £3,100
Frilly Dresses
O 7.7 x 16" S, (KII: 152) £1,000
LEECH, William John (1881-1968)
Coastal View (Possibly Dublin)
O 8.25 x 12" S, (T: 72) £1,800
Consultation of Fishermen
O 8.5 x 6" S, (O: 32) £2,400
La France, Brest
O 21.5 x 25.5" S, (M: 67) £20,000
Sailing Boats at the Quayside
W 13.5 x 10" S, (K: 55) £3,300
Spring Day, Grasse
O 7 x 9.25" S, I, (T: 31) £3,400
Spring in Sunningdale
O 18 x 14" S, (O: 41) £7,000
The Banks of the River Moreau
O 5.5 x 8" S, I, (T: 135) £2,200
The Urn, Maison Cabris, Grasse
O 13.5 x 10.5" S, (ZI: 123) £2,500
Untitled - A Quiet Harbour
O 9.5 x 12" S, (O: 94) £3,800
Towers, Grasse
O 9.5 x 7.5" S, (KII: 70) £1,800
LUKE, John (1906-1975)
Landscape
T 15.75 x 29.5" S, D, (TI: 30) £21,850
Portrait Study- Mrs. Busby
D 14 x 10.5" S, D, (Q: 118) £720
Pax
T 11.25 x 15.5" S, (KII: 106) £65,000
MacCABE, Gladys (b. 1918)
Still Life
O 24 x 31" S, (P: 71) £300
Clown
O 20 x 15" S, (CI: 35) £70
Flowers and Apples
O 26.5 x 22.5" (CI: 190) £60
Gallery Party
O 15.5 x 20" S, (S: 138) £470
Library Interior
O 15 x 19.5" S, (S: 101) £400
Market Day, Galway
O 16 x 32" S, (K: 146a) £715

MacGONIGAL, Maurice (1900-1979)
At the Corner
O 15 x 8" S, (O: 93) £1,600
Autumn Cattle Fair, Connemara
O 38 x 51" S, (P: 51) £16,000
Balscadden Bay, Howth, Co. Dublin
O 11 x 15" S, I, D, (Q: 37) £1,600
Cattle in the Park
W 13.5 x 22.5" S, (Q: 91) £800
Cloud Forms, Dunhallow, Connemara
O 20 x 30" S, I, D, (S: 16) £5,200
Connemara Coast
O 7 x 13" S, (P: 139) £1,400
Connemara Landscape
W 10 x 16" S, D, (T: 111) £420
Crucifixion - Sketch Desigh
W 6.75 x 8.5" (T: 80) £300
Currach Racing, Roundstone Regatta
W 10 x 13" (T: 83) £320
Harvest from the Sea
O 30 x 37" S, (O: 42) £10,000
Landscape and sea from The Sky Road, Connemara
O 18 x 24" S, (N: 49) £2,300
Michaelmas Daisies
O 13.5 x 13.5" S, (Q: 4) £920
On The Aran Islands
O 15.5 20.5" S, (N: 87) £3,200
Posting a Letter
O 12 x 14" S, (Q: 72) £900
The Old House, Connemara or the Blue Donkeys
O 18 x 24" S, (L: 95) £5,000
The Spinning Wheel
O 30 x 48" (P: 17) £2,400
Kerry Street
O 20 x 24" S, (KII: 12) £1,800
Fear an Iartair (Man from the West)
O 24 x 20" S, (KII: 35) £4,200
The Lovers
O 16 x 8" S, (GII: 10) £1,500
MACLISE, Daniel (1806-1870)
Portrait Studies of Thackeray, Byron and Charles Lamb
D (3) 12.5 x 8.25 S, D, I, (D: 94) £805
Portrait of Three Women
D 10.75 x 8.5" S, (EII: 241) £805
The Ballad-Seller
O 23.5 x 18" S, D, (EII: 256) £16,100
MAGUIRE, Cecil (20th Century)
Cattle in the Evening
O 23.5 x 19" S, D, I, (T: 22) £770
Winter Sun, White Rocks, Portrush
O 18 x 36" S, (N: 4) £950
Inishmaan
O 14 x 11" S, (GII: 145) £720
Twelve Bens from Monastery Pier in Roundstone
O 17.5 x 23.5" S, (GII: 94) £700
Goodman Joe, October Fair, Maam Cross
O 13 x 17" S, (GII: 87) £1,500
MAHONEY, James (1810-1879)
The Morning Wash
W 18 x 12.5" S, (M: 14) £800
MALTON, James (d.1803)
A picturesque and descriptive view of the City of Dublin
Pr - x - (25) (M: 34) £5,000
MALTON, James (d.1803) Attrib.
The Parliament Buildings and Trinity College with figures in the foreground
W 17 x 24" (U: 63) £3,000
McCAIG, Norman J. (b. 1929)
Boats at Cleggan
O 10 x 12" S, (M: 38) £240
Children Paddling at the Beach
O 11 x 11.5" S, (YI: 40) £540
Poppies
O 16 x 20" S, (M: 97) £500
Poppy Fields
O 16 x 20" S, (N: 120) £700
Trawlers, Burton Port
O 14 x 18" S, I, (YI: 39) £560
The Turf Cutters, Co Antrim
O 13.5 x 18.25" S, (KII: 142) £1,000
Glendun Parish Church, Co Antrim
W 8 x 10.4" S, (GII: 104) £150
McCLOY, Samuel (1831-1904)
Picnic in the Heather
W 9.5 x 13" S, (K: 57) £1,650

A Beauty Among Roses
W 22 x 17" S (KII: 17) £2,400
McEVOY, William (fl. 1858-1880)
Alpine Scene with figures and an animal near a Cascade, and a Bridge in foreground
O 24 x 30" S, D, (V: 1059) £70
McGUINNESS, Norah Allison (1903-1980)
A statue in a formal garden
W 10 x 14" S, (O: 51) £320
Brent Geese on the Salt Flats
O 20 x 36" S, (P: 95) £1,500
Child at Study
D 13 x 10" (T: 44) £200
Child with a Pot
D 13 x 10.5" (T: 45) £180
Enniskerry
W 14 x 18" S, (P: 116) £1,500
Estuary Waters
O 17.5 x 21.5" S, (CII: 98) £1,800
Gathering Fish
D 12 x 16" S, (Q: 134) £480
Harbour
W 15 x 22" S, (O: 18) £750
Italian Landscape
P 12 x 16" S, D, (T: 55) £650
Julian Trevelian & Companion Painter
P 7.75 x 9.5" (2) S, (S: 80) £1,500
Leixlip View
W 17 x 22" S, (K: 142a) £1,870
Marley
W 12 x 18.5" S, (Q: 70) £650
New York
W 15 x 20" S, D, (Q: 40) £1,500
Path to the Sun
O 20 x 28" S, D, I, (K: 284) £1,980
St. Francis Xavier Church, Temple St.
W 14 x 20" S, D, (Q: 73) £900
Still Life of Flowers in a Jug
O 18 x 14" S, (ZI: 88) £1,250
Still Life - Vase of Flowers
W 14.25 x 18" S, D, (PI: 123) £700
Street in Kinsale
W 8.5 x 11" S, (T: 117) £1,100
The Blue Pool
O 21.25 x 27.5" (P: 43) £1,700
The Custom House, Dublin
W 15 x 22" S, D, (K: 123) £4,180
The Jagged Rocks, Ballycotton
W 13 x 19" S, (M: 2) £620
The Little Cornfield
O 25 x 30" S, (N: 39) £11,200
Turf Stacks by a River
P 9.75 x 12" S, (T: 42) £310
Woman with Pot
D 13 x 10" (Q: 100) £240
Female Study
P 13 x 10" (GII: 124) £170
The Cockrel
W 8.75 x 14.5 (GII: 106) £240
A Mountainy Road, Donegal
O 16 x 22" S (GII: 42) £1,500
The Custom House and Liffey Bridge Heads
P 10 x 14" (GII: 110) £260
McGUINNESS, William Bingham (fl. 1874-1929)
Bringing Home the Turf
W 9.25 x 13.5" S, (K: 32) £440
Cahir Castle on the Suir, Co. Tipperary
W 14 x 20.5" S, I, (K: 58) £935
Carrig-a-tar
W 14.75 x 21.75" S, (K: 33) £550
Continental Street Scene
W 18 x 12.5" S, D, (M: 28a) £750
Cottages beside Lake
W 10 x 13.5" S, (S: 112) £240
Gondolas on a Canal, Venice
W 21.25 x 14.25" S, (K: 31) £880
Grannagh Castle, Waterford
W 15 x 21" S, (K: 30) £660
Kilvrock Castle, Morayshire
W 20.5 x 14" S, (K: 34) £242
Lochan Lahn, Inverness-shire
W 10.25 x 14.375" S, (K: 36) £55
On the Suir at Ballybrado
W 10 x 14" S, (K: 35) £110
Surrey Cottages
W 9.5 x 14" S, D, (V: 1093) £650
Venetian Street Scene

W 19.5 x 10" S, (V: 1091) £540
View of the Colosseum, Rome
W 19.5 x 10" S, (T: 75) £1,400
Wooded River Landscape
W 12 x 8" S, (R: 35) £130
Figures & Carts by a Lakeside Tower
W 20 x 13" S, (KII: 96) £600
Cahir Castle on the Suir, Co Tipperary
W 14 x 20.5" S, (KII: 98) £350
Breezsy Day, Donegal Coast
W 9.5 x 14.25" S, (KII: 99) £350
A Fisherman by a Cottage, Hornhead, Co Donegal
W 9 x 13.25" S, (KII: 100) £320

McGUIRE, Edward (1932-1986)
Barn Owl
O 24 x 18" S, D, (V: 1088) £6,000
Self-Portrait
D 8.5 x 6.75" (K: 103) £550

McKELVEY, Frank (1895-1974)
Cattle Resting by Trees with Lake Beyond
O 19 x 26" S, (T: 138) £4,200
Coastal landscape
W 10 x 14" S, (O: 60) £570
Collecting Turf, Co. Donegal
O 19.5 x 23" S, (S: 37) £3,400
Donegal Landscape
O 18 x 24" S, (CII: 56) £4,500
Evening Island Magee, Co. Antrim
O 10 x 14" S, (Q: 69) £820
Friary, Donegal
O 18 x 24" S, (O: 48) £7,000
Glen Gog, Co. Donegal
W 14.5 x 21" S, I, (K: 48) £1,210
Landscape with stone bridge and cottage
W 11 x 15" S, (O: 26) £850
Lough Annure, Co. Donegal
W 10 x 14" S, (P: 10) £670
Moyola River, Castle Dawson
O 13.5 x 16.5" S, (Q: 19) £2,300
Rosbeg, Co. Donegal
O 12 x 17.5" S, (P: 8) £2,200
Salisbury Cathedral
W 11 x 15" S, (K: 50) £935
The Road to Derrybeg, Co. Donegal
W 15 x 22" S, (K: 47) £1,320
In the Park, St Stephens Green, Dublin
O 18 x 27" S, (KII: 115) £7,500
The Park Pond
O 15 x 20.25" S, (KII: 116) £12,000
Sand Hills, Coast of Donegal
O 20 x 27" S, (KII: 125) £4,700
By the Millpond
W 14 x 19" S, (KII: 213) £3,800
Coastal Landscape
O 20.5 x 26.75" S, (EII: 273) £9,200

MacLIAMMOIR, Michael (1899-1978)
The Cauldron and the Pixies
W 11.25 x 9" S, (KII: 226) £1,100

MacMANUS, Henry (1810-1878)
Dalkey Newsboy
O 13.5 x 10" S, (KII: 127) £900

MIDDLETON, Colin (1910-1983)
Abstract form
O 16 x 16" S, D, (M: 47) £1,100
Barcelona
W 18 x 13" S, I, (T: 94) £1,600
Bonfire Lady
O 18 x 24" S, D, (J: 180) £7,475
Cloud Across the Moon
O 17 x 23" S, I, D, (Q: 64) £2,900
Composition
O 16 x 19" S, (O: 34) £1,800
Early Morning: Dundrum
O 23.5 x 23.5" S, I, D, (K: 252) £1,650
Emu Point
W 6 x 6" S, I, D, (Q: 67) £340
Enigma 1, Mary Queen of Scots
O 12 x 12" S, (Q: 60) £1,700
Fir Trees in a landscape
O 23 x 29" S, (Q: 65) £2,900
Legend
W 6.25 x 6.25" S, (Q: 66) £660
Seated Nude
O 24 x 24" S, (Q: 62) £1,800
Shipyard Family
O 12 x 12" S, (H: 89) £1,495
The Artist's Children: John and Jane,

Ballyholme Strand, Winter 1953
O 18 x 24" S, (ZI: 59) £3,600
Two Heads, Nendrum
O 9 x 9" S, (Q: 59) £700
Woman with Bird
O 24 x 24" S, I, D, (Q: 61) £1,800
The Sister Voice
O 24 x 42" S, I, D (EII: 359) £4,025
Northern Landscape
W 5.5 x 7.5" S, (GII: 93) £300
Bablyonian Dream, Meenabad
O 13 x 12" S, (GII: 86) £1,200
August, West Fermanagh
W 7 x 7" S, (GII: 88) £400
Mourne Elegy
O 24 x 24" S, (GII; 101) £1,350
The Garry Bog
O 24 x 30" S, (GII: 80) £2,900
Nude at Piano
O 18 x 9" S, (GII: 37) £820
The Garry Bog
O 17 x 23.5" S, (GII: 143) £2,000

MILES, Thomas Rose (fl 1869-1888)
Coastal Landscape with Lighthouse
O 7 x 19" S, (M: 67a) £380
Kelpweed Harvesters, Gorteen Bay, Connemara
O 24 x 42" S, I, (EII: 254) £3,450

MITCHELL, Flora H. (1890-1973)
Dublin Doorsteps
W 8.5 x 8" S, I, (M: 95) £480
Grafton Street, Dublin
W 9.75 x 13" S, I, (P: 159) £900
Hampreston Church
D 7.5 x 10" S, I, D, (M: 8) £270
Hoey's Court - Birthplace of Jonathan Swift, Dublin
W 12 x 9.5" S, I, (L: 9) £700
Sackville Street Bridge and Sackville Street, Dublin
W 4.25 x 8" (2) S, I, D, (N: 136) £420
The Last of Holles Street, Dublin
W 12.5 x 10" S, I, (N: 6) £700

MORPHEY, Garret (fl. 1680-1716)
A portrait of General Sir Frederick Hamilton
of Milburn,
O 30 x 24.5" (EI: 274) £4,000
Portrait of James Bryan of Jenkinstown Park,
Co Kilkenny
O 26 x 21" (EII: 204) £11,500

MOYNAN, Richard Thomas (1856-1906)
Ball in the cap
O 24 x 40" S, D, (M: 41) £86,000

MULCAHY, Jeremiah Hodges (d.1889)
Sheep on a wooded bank in a River Landscape
O 22 x 29" S, D, (K: 160) £2,970

MULREADY, William (1786-1862)
Figures outside cottages, by a mill stream
O 14 x 17.25" I, (EI: 347) £2,000
The Recruit
O 10 x 12" (M: 54) £2,100

NICHOLL, Andrew (1804-1886)
A Bank of Wild Flowers
W 12.5 x 19" S, (P: 44) £2,500
A Verge with Poppies, Cornflowers and
Daisies in a Coastal Landscape
W 10.25 x 19.25" S, (K: 41) £4,400
A British Man-of-War off the Isle of Gallelona
Morleianan
W 18 x 26" (KII: 6) £1,400
A Verge with Poppies, Daisies and other Summer
Flowers in a Coastal Landscape
W 12.5 x 19.25" S, (KII: 8) £3,200
A Riverbank with Poppies, Daisies and Thistles
W 12 x 18.5" S, (KII: 10) £4,500
A Heron alighting from a grassy bank with Cattle
in the distance
W 9.5 x 18.5" S, (KII: 83) £750
Steamboats in a Choppy Sea off St Helena
W 11.75 x 18.5" S, (KII: 172) £350
The Giant's Causeway, Co Antrim
M 13.75 x 20.25" S, (EII: 247) £2,185
The Nurse and Child, Pleaskin, Co Antrim
M 13.75 x 20.25" S, (EII: 247) £4,025
A Loughside Path
W 13.5 x 20" S, (EII: 248A) £1,265

NICOL, Erskine (1825-1904)
Interior Scene with old man pondering about
his change
O 18 x 14" S, (X: 489) £1,300

Study of a Flute Player
O 8 x 6.74" S, D, (EII: 257) £1,725
NISBET, Tom (b. 1909)
A View of Donnybrook Church
W 11 x 15" S, (M: 74) £200
Approaching Autumn, Elgin Road
W 10.5 x 14.5" S, (L: 71) £180
Cottage by a Stream
W 10.5 x 14.5" S, (T: 183) £240
Cottage in a wooded landscape
W 9 x 11" S, (R: 23) £60
Lord Edward Street, Dublin
W 11 x 15" S, I, (N: 5) £250
Mare and Foal
W 11.5 x 15.5" S, (Y: 180) £340
News Dartmouth Square, Dublin
W 11 x 15" S, (L: 131) £170
Sugar Loaf from Killiney
W 11 x 15" S, (L: 20) £200
View of a village church
W 11 x 15" S, (O: 110) £220
Wooded river landscape with bridge
W 14.5 x 10.5" S, (R: 13) £140
Landscape with Trees
W 10 x 14" S, (GII: 4) £190

O'BRIEN, Dermod (1865-1945)
Cap D'Ail
O 9.5 x 13.5" S, (O: 54) £1,000
Portrait of a Gentleman
O 24 x 20" S, D, (M: 53) £900

O'BRIEN, Kitty Wilmer (1910-1982)
Belcaire, Co. Mayo
W 13 x 16" S, (S: 36) £240
Connemara landscape
O 20 x 24" S, (L: 70) £750
Italian Maitre d'Hotel, reputed to be
Hilton Edwards
O 18 x 16" S, I, (BI: 446) £280

O'CONNOR, James Arthur (1792-1841)
A Shepherd with sheep crossing a bridge beneath
a ruined castle
O 10.75 x 13.25" (EI: 344) £4,000
Mother and Child in Woodland Path
O 10 x 12" (YI: 27) £560
Soldiers Bivouacking by a wooded stream
O 13.25 x 15.5" S, D, (EI: 346) £2,600
Figures on a Road, a Coastal Landscape Beyond
O 10 x 11.75" S, (KII: 7) £1,800
The Mountain RIver and the Ford
3.75 x 5" framed overall (KII: 178) £240
Stormy Landscape with Figures on a Path
O 24.5 x 29.25" S, (EII: 219) £10,925
A Deer Park
) 24.5 x 29.25" S, D, (EII: 221) £5,175
An Irish Glen
O 25.25 x 30" S, (EII: 222) £4,600
Landscape with Figures on a Path
O 10.5 x 14.75" (EII: 225) £3,680

O'CONOR, Roderic (1860-1940)
Jugs of Flowers and Fruit on a Table
O 25.5 x 21" S, (C: 163) £56,500
Nu Allongé
O 25.5 x 19.75" S, D, (ZI: 42) £32,000
Reclining Nude on a Chaise Longue
O 18 x 21.625" (CII: 26) £25,000
Study of a young girl
O 25.5 x 21" (O: 64) £3,900
Seated Nude, half length
O 25.5 x 21.5" (KII: 34) £23,000
Still Life with a Compier of Fruit
O 11.75 x 14.25" S, (KII: 31) £20,000
Maree Montante (Rising Tide)
O 25.75 x 21.75" S, I, (EII: 293) £111,500
Reclining Nude
O 10.5 x 14" (EII: 294) £11,500
French Lanscape (Landscape with Tree)
O 14 x 18" (GII: 90) £29,000

O'HARA, Helen (1881-1919)
Breakers on the rocks
W 14 x 20.5" S, (M: 91) £700
Hard Times
W 9.75 x 14" S, (K: 1) £1,320

O'KELLY, Aloysius (1851-1928)
Boats at Concarneau, Brittany
O 9 x 13" S, I, (Q: 38) £2,000
Coastal Landscape
O 12.5 x 9.75" S, (T: 136) £600

Figures on a sunlit Street, Cairo
O 20.25 x 13.75" S, I, (K: 202) £4,620
Mass in a Connemara Cabin, 1795
W 8 x 11" S, I, (OI: 181) £462
The Hareem Guard
O 28 x 36" S, (KII: 49) £24,000
A Fête, Concarneau
O 10 x 13" S, (KII: 200) £2,400
O'MALLEY, Tony (b.1913)
From Still Life
O 6 x 16" S, D, (S: 109b) £650
Homage to John McCormack
O 48 x 18" S, D, I, (P: 25) £2,000
Wexford Landscape with Horse & Cottage
W 21.5 x 30" S, (XI: 89) £980
Self Portrait
W 13.5 x 9.75" S, (GII: 9) £380
O'NEILL, Daniel (1920-1974)
Approaching Storm
O 18 x 24" S, (T: 25) £3,000
Bog of Allen
O 20 x 30" S, (L: 75) £750
Cold Spring Morning, Donegal
O 20 x 24" S, I, (Q: 42) £3,600
Figures in a Landscape
P 16 x 20" S, (Q: 136) £2,200
Girl's Head and The Bride
D 8 x 5" (2) S, (L: 21) £1,120
Head of a Girl
O 18 x 14" S, (T: 29) £1,300
My Country
O 27 x 40" S, (T:I: 29) £17,250
Night & Day, Still Waters
O 18 x 24" S, I, (Q: 28) £4,200
Reclining Figure
O 16 x 24" S, (S: 23) £4,500
Romantic landscape, Co. Down
O 12 x 16" S, (N: 62) £2,400
Singers
O 12.25 x 16" S, I, (K: 209) £3,850
Study of Sheilagh
O 7 x 5" S, I, D, (Q: 120) £400
The Proud Possessor
O 14 x 18" S, (Q: 25) £2,400
The Visitors
O 16 x 20" S, (ZI: 57) £4,200
Young Spanish Girl
O 23.5 x 20" S, (S: 68) £2,500
The Bath
O 20 x 16" S, (KII: 158) £3,200
Flowers in a Window
O 14 x 18" S, (KII: 27) £2,200
Figure on a Shore
O 16 x 24" S, I, (EII: 328) £6,325
Portrait of a Lady
O 24 x 20" S, (EII: 334) £11,500
Donegal Landscape
O 21 21.75 x 25.75" S, I (EII: 335) £2,990
Still Life with Fruit, Flowers and a Bottle
O 20 x 24" S, (EII: 337)
O'RYAN, Fergus (1911-1989)
An April Day
O 12 x 17" S, (T: 180) £400
Ballydonnell River, Co. Wicklow
O 15 x 20" S, (Q: 138) £670
Dublin Canal Views
W 11 x 15" (2) S, (L: 141) £450
Green Street Market
O 21 x 28" S, D, (M: 23) £950
On the Canal
O 16 x 19" S, (T: 179) £600
On the Seine
W 10.5 x 14.5" S, (L: 57a) £400
St. Patricks Park, Dublin
O 24 x 34" S, I, (V: 1110) £2,500
The Anglers, Newbridge
O 10 x 15" S, (L: 129) £570
The Kildare Street Club, Dublin
O 12 x 16" S, (O: 10) £750
The Metal Bridge, Dublin
O 23 x 13" S, (Q: 137) £700
O'SULLIVAN, Sean (1906-1964)
Western Village Landscape with
Girl on a Path
O 13 x 16" S, (L: 73) £1,000
Borthrin - The Lane
O 10 x 14.5" S, I, (V: 1132) £1,200

ORPEN, Bea (1913-1980)
A Lake among the Hills
W 5.75 x 9.125" S, (K: 29) £242
Dawros Bog, Rosbeg
W 13.5 x 19.5" S, (S: 84) £370
Mweenish, Carna, Co. Galway
W 14 x 19" S, (O: 2) £300
Old Currachs, Sheephaven
W 14.5 x 18.5" S, (Q: 159) £300
ORPEN, Richard Caulfeild (1863-1938)
Morning
W 3 x 5" S, I, D, (U: 67) £3,100
Shadow of a Gunman
W 8.5 x 12.5" S, D, (U: 3) £250
ORPEN, Sir William (1878-1931)
A seated Woman
D 9 x 8" (OI: 73) £770
Head of a man
D 10.75 x 8". S, D, I, (J: 59) £1,380
Hugh Lane reading
D 9 x 7" (H: 187) £1,092
Kit
D 13. 75 x 10.75" (J: 43) £10,350
Portrait after Ingres
D 11.75 x 8" S, D, I, (UI: 27) £1,380
Portrait of a Negro
O 30 x 22" S, D, (C: 164) £60,900
Portrait of Miss Jenny Simson
O 49.75 x 39.75" S, (ZI: 25) £30,000
Standing Nude
O 31 x 13.5" (CII: 106) £1,200
Self-portrait
O 20 x 16.5" (A: 39) £13,800
The Edge of the Cliff, Howth
O 19.75 x 24" S, (ZI: 26) £55,000
The End - A Glaze of Copal Varnish
W 9.75 x 8.5" (ZI: 97) £1,800
The Entertainer
D 7.5 x 5.75" (T: 160) £320
The Wandering Jew
W 10 x 6.5" S, D, I, (F: 215) £187
The Window : Night
O 42.5 x 31.25" S, (ZI: 68) £72,000
Howth Harbour
W 13.5 x 19.75" S, (KII: 161) £580
A Nude
D 18.5 x 12" S, (KII: 79) £1,900
Her First Holy Communion
O 24 x 20" S, (KII: 19) £4,500
Portrait of Miss Harmsworth in a landscape
O 36 x 28" (KII: 140) £40,000
A Nude
O 31.5 x 15" S, (KII: 157) £2,800
Portrait of Sir Robert WIlliams
O 40.25 x 34" S, (KII: 181) £2,600
The Fly Catcher
O 26 x 21" S, D, (EII: 278) £34,500
Lottie and her Child
M 12.5 x 10" S, D, (EII: 283) £14,950
The Reflection
O 30 x 25" S, (EII: 284) £40,000
OSBORNE, Walter Frederick (1859-1903)
At the Racecourse
W 13.25 x 20.25" S, (K: 53) £19,800
A Portrait - J. Marshall Murray
O 25 x 29" (YI: 52) £900
Boats in a Waterway
O 5.25 x 9" (S: 73) £4,200
Mermaid Street, Rye
O 20.25 x 5.75" S, D, I, (J: 79) £8,050
Near Didcot, Byberry clumps in the distance
O 5.75 x 8.5" (RI: 86) £6,325
Portrait of Annie Jane Osborne, the artist's mother
P 11 x 10.5" S, D, I, (K: 54) £6,050
Sheep in a field at dusk
O 20 x 27" S, (M: 28) £30,000
Sketch of a Boy
D 8 x 4.5" (L: 123) £770
Spoilt Pets
O 24 x 18" S, (EII: 267) £271,000
Primary Education
O 20 x 27.5" S, (EII: 279) £67,500
OSBORNE, William (1823-1901)
Comet - A Chestnut Hunter in a stable
O 19.5 x 25.5" S, I, (M: 39) £1,900
Ruby - A Chestnut Hunter in a stable
O 19.5 x 25.5" S, I, (M: 40) £1,700

PUGH, Herbert (fl circa 1758-88)
Lord Granard being Powdered
O 23.25 x 29.25" (EII: 218) £5,175
PURSER, Sarah (1848-1943)
Autumnal Landscape
O 9.75 x 10.75" (P: 121) £600
PYE, Patrick (b. 1929)
The Crucifixion
M 12 x 10" S, (P: 37) £800
Still life with teapot and chair
P 13 x 8.5" S, (R: 24) £170
REID, Nano (1905-1981)
Abstract Interior
D 9.75 x 8" S, (S: 119) £120
Country Pub
O 30 x 24" S, (M: 88) £2,200
Figures
O 10.5 x 14.5" S, (P: 93) £550
Fishermen
O 24 x 48" S, (O: 36) £4,800
Portrait of a Young Woman
O 19 x 15" S, (P: 96) £360
Rugged Country
O 19.5 x 23.5" S, (P: 28) £2,000
Seadrift & Figures
W 10.5 x 14" S, (T: 110) £450
The Struggle
O - S, I, (XI: 10) £110
Tinkers & Pony
O 29 x 15" S, (GII: 20) £1,900
ROBERTS, Thomas (1748-1778)
A View of Slane Castle, the Seat of Lord Conyngham
O 16 x 23.5" (EII: 223) £91,700
ROBINSON, John Markey (b.1918)
A Figure and Cottages
O 7 x 16" S, (K: 254) £385
A Musical Evening
O 24 x 19" (V: 1090) £550
Clown
W 23 x 13" S, (N: 16) £250
Departure of the Widow
W 12 x 20" S, (R: 108a) £220
Figures and Cottages on a Shore
O 8 x 16.5" S, (K: 253) £550
The Potato Harvest
O 14 x 24" S, (KII: 143) £600
Tall Ships in a Bay
W 14.25 x 21.25" S (KII: 212) £550
ROCHE, Sampson Towgood (1759-1847)
A miniature portrait of Daniel O'Connell,
as a young man
W - (HI: 314) £3,200
RUSSELL, George / AE (1867-1935)
A woman stnding beside trees in a landscape
O 16 x 21" S, (O: 88) £3,200
Figures on a Beach
O 15.5 x 20.5" (P: 57) £1,700
Mystical Figures in a Landscape
O 15 x 19" / 15 x (P: 164) £1,400
Returning from the Fields
O 18 x 24" S, (T: 109) £3,600
Riding the Waves
O 20 x 30" S, (K: 280) £1,100
The Silver Birches
O 18 x 22" S, (T: 30) £2,000
Two Girls on the Shore
O 16 x 18" S, (P: 30) £2,500
Wooded landscape with stone wall
O 15.5 x 21" S, (L: 49a) £1,800
Lead and Set Me Free
O 16 x 21" S, (EII: 300) £4,600
The Sultry Children of the Air
O 16 x 21" S, (EII: 302) £5,520
RYAN, Thomas (b. 1929)
Apples
O 14 x 18" S, (O: 91) £470
John Field
P 22 x 17 S, (L: 37) £550
SADLER II, William (c.1782-1839)
A View of Dublin
O 5 x 8" (Q: 68) £600
A View of Killua, Co. Westmeath/A View of the Lake
from Killua/The parkland of Killua
O 21 x 31" and smaller (K: 151) £26,400
Farmer Folk Outside an Inn, in Co. Wicklow &
Shelter from a Storm
O 6 x 9" (2) (Z: 425) £3,000

Horseman resting in a Valley
O 12 x 17.25" (K: 153) £935
Portrait of a Gentleman
O 8 x 6" (L: 106) £360
River Scene with Building and Figures
O 7.75 x 11.75" (P: 75) £900
View of St. Patrick's Cathedral
O 12.75 x 15" (S: 148) £4,000
River landscape with Fishermen
O 9.25 x 13.5" (EII: 227) £4,025
The VIllage Gossips
O 6 x 7.25" (EII: 229) £690
The Village Dance
O 8.75 x 13" (EII: 230) £1,265
SALKELD, Cecil Ffrench (1808-1968)
Lotus Land
O 15 x 19" S, D, (V: 1119) £160
The Ballerinas
O 20 x 24" S, D, (V: 1151) £1,200
The Lotus Eaters
O 14.5 x 19" S, D, (P: 69) £900
SCANLON, Robert R. (fr. 1826-64)
The Road to London
P 14 x 26" S, (GII: 32) £770
SCOTT, Patrick (b. 1921)
The Mountain
O 12 x 10" S, (S: 79) £620
Red Moon
O 12 x 18.5" S, (GII: 21) £850
Gold Painting '59
T 33 x 30" S, (GII: 133) £600
SCOTT, William (1913-1989)
Landscape with Houses
O 8.75 x 12.5" S, (Q: 105) £9,000
Ruabon, North Wales
D 3 x 6" S, (Q: 106) £220
SHAWCROSS, Neil (b. 1940)
Still Life with Whiskey Jar
O 12 x 14" S, D, (P: 157) £240
SHEE, Sir Martin Archer (1769-1850)
Portrait of a Gentleman, probably Colonel
William Bagwell M.P. of Marlfield,
Co Tipperary
O 50 x 39.75" (E: 82) £4,600
Portrait of a Gentleman, probably
John Bagwell M.P.
O 50 x 39.75" (E: 81) £3,450
SHEEHAN, William (1894-1923)
A Couple in A Restaurant
O 27 x 34" S, (Q: 31) £2,600
SLAUGHTER, Stephen (1697-1765)
Portrait of two Gentlemen, small full-length
O 13.875 x 11.875 I, (E: 19) £10,350
Portrait of two Gentlemen, small full-length
O 13.875 x 11.875 S, I, (E: 18) £14,375
Portraits of Charles Suft and his wife Patience
Bedwell.
O 29.5 x 24.25" (2) S, I, D, (N: 115) £2,000
SLEATOR, James Sinton (1889-1950)
A Still Life with a Bottle and pottery Jug
O 26.5 x 19.75" (K: 261) £825
The Dressing Table Mirror
O 18 x 21" (KII: 227) £3,500
SMITH, Daniel Albert Vere (1861-1932)
Sun Spots
O 20 x 24" S, D, I, (P: 158) £1,200
SMITH, Stephen Catterson (1806-1872)
Portrait of the Hon Richard Ponsonby, Bishop of
Derry and Raphoe
O 22.5 x 17.75" (EII: 207) £1,495
SOMERVILLE, Edith Oenone (1858-1949)
Upper Lake, Killarney
O 16 x 20" S, I, (K: 183) £880
SOUTER, Camille (b. 1929)
Landscape with cottages
O 22 x 31" S, D, (M: 48) £5,000
Pigalle
O 7.75 x 5.75" S, I, (P: 117) £1,000
Red Achill
O 13 x 16" S, (GII: 72) £900
STAPLES, Sir Robert Ponsonby (1853-1943)
Harland and Wolff's Yard
O 12 x 14" S, (K: 178) £3,300
Quite Friendly - after lunch
D 10 x 13.75" (2) S, D, I, (K: 46) £132
The Christmas Tree Dolls
W 17.5 x 13" S, (K: 26) £550

The Skater
W 24 x 21" S, (K: 25) £605
Picking Berries
O 45.5 x 37.75" S (KII: 107) £11,000
At the Seafront
P 10.5 x 8" S, (GII: 118) £150
STOKES, Margaret (b. 1916)
Still Life
O 13.5 x 17.5" S, (T: 27) £400
STOPFORD, R L (fl. 1857)
A Country Church with large Stalely Home beyond
W 20 x 29" S, D, (V: 1032) £500
SWANZY, Mary (1882-1972)
House in the Forest
O 16 x 22.5" S, (YI: 18) £2,100
Castle with Trees & Market Scene
P 6 x 3.5" (2) S, (Q: 129) £190
Continental Village
P 10 x 7" (T: 149) £210
Cubist Landscape
O 15.5 x 18" S, (P: 38) £2,600
Cubist Landscape
O 23 x 17" S, (T: 41) £1,900
Flowers on Window Ledge (Boats on Lake verso)
O 11 x 9" (P: 138) £1,200
Green Window - Sunlit Garden
O 13 x 17" S, (S: 28) £1,800
Harbour Scene
P 7 x 10" (T: 150) £360
Market Scene
P 6.75 x 3.75" (T: 186) £220
Pink Parasol, Czechoslovakia, 1917
P 7.5 x 10" (K: 198) £550
Snow Scene
O 10.75 x 15.5" S, (P: 142) £1,600
Street sellers, Czechoslovakia
P 7.5 x 10" (K: 199) £715
Street Singer
O 11.5 x 8.25" (O: 13) £2,200
Trio 1969
O 9.5 x 14" S, (KII: 110) £2,800
Grasses
O 22 x 21" (KII: 72) £5,500
Levanto on the Italian Riviera
O 22 x 30" S, I, D, (EII: 297) £10,350
Boarding the Boat
P 4.5 x 10" (GII: 107) £180
Sailing Boat
P 5.5 x 10" (GII: 84) £220
SWIFT, Patrick (1927-83)
The Fig Tree
O 66 x 58" (GII: 78A) £23,000
Pickers Among Almond and Fig Trees
M 18 x 24" (GII: 78B) £970
Trestle Studio Table
O 20 x 24" (GII: 78C) £3,000
The Italian Gardens, Hyde Park, No 4
O 47 x 47" (GII: 78D) £7,000
Verandah and Garden at Alfanzina
O 18.75 x 25.5" (GII: 78E) £6,000
THADDEUS, Henry J (1860-1929)
Portrait of a Young Lady, three-quarter length,
standing in al fur-lined coat
O 12 x 8" S, (KII: 82) £1,050
TOPHAM, Francis William (1807-1877)
Two children on a country road
W 19 x 14" S, D, (O: 44) £800
VAN STOCKUM, Hilda
Andre L'Hotel's Studio
W 8 x 8.5" S, (GII: 8) £320
WADE, Jonathan (1941-1973)
Chinese Warrior
W 13 x 7" S, (S: 125) £170
Device III
O 58 x 33" (S: 126) £400
District 3 (The Gasometer)
O 23 x 33" S, (GII: 111) £370
WARREN, Barbara (20th Century)
Evening, Lettermore
O 10 x 18" S, (O: 4) £700
Glendalough, Co. Wicklow
O 13.625 x 20.25" S, (K: 168) £4,400
The Ruins of Clonmacnoise
W 13.75 x 22.5" S, I, (K: 15) £2,750
WEBB, Kenneth (20th Century)
African Drummer
O 30 x 20" S, (Z: 308) £320

Farm buildings in landscape
O 20 x 24" S, (N: 132) £380
Kircubbin Harbour
O 15.5 x 18.5" S, (T: 137) £400
Portavogie harbour
O 15 x 36" S, (N: 130) £800
Still Life - Woodland
O 15 x 36" S, (V: 1087) £500
Sunset in Connemara
O 15 x 30" S, (V: 1086) £420
Village beneath a mountain
O 15 x 36" S, (O: 67) £600
White water, Donegal
O 14 x 36" S, (O: 20) £700
Seaweed Theme, Turquoise and Sienna
O 20.25 x 30" S, (KII: 29) £550
Blackthorn, Saintfield
O 20 x 24" S, (KII: 30) £500
WEST, Richard Whateley (1848-1905)
Alassio, Italy
O 8 x 12" S, I, D, (Q: 8) £570
WHEATLEY, Francis (1747-1801)
A Peasant Woman Carrying Wood
M 16.75 x 11.75" S, (EII: 248) £4,830
Domestic Happiness
O 14.25 x 12.25" (KII: 39) £4,000
WHELAN, Leo (1892-1956)
Portrait Study
O 13 x 10" S, (S: 7) £650
WILKS, Maurice Canning (1911-1984)
An Antrim Farm, Near Belfast
O 20 x 24" S, (YI: 31) £4,000
A Curragh off the Coast
O 20 x 24.5" S, (HI: 260) £4,500
Among the Connemara Mountains, near
Recess, Co. Galway
O 20 x 24" S, (OI: 25) £1,980
Among the Connemara mountains, Recess
O 17.5 x 23.5" S, (M: 63) £3,000
At Ards, near Creeslough, Co. Donegal
O 14 x 28" S, (M: 44) £1,100
At Ballintoy, Co. Antrim
O 20 x 26" S, I, (K: 228) £3,960
At Mahee Island, Strangford Lough
W 10.5 x 14" S, (T: 91) £340
At Recess, Connemara
O 20 x 24" S, D, (BII: 10) £1,200
At Toombeola, Connemara
O 11.5 x 15.5" S, (N: 108) £700
Daffodils
O 24 x 20" S, D, I, (K: 179) £495
Downings Pier, Rosapenna, Donegal
O 20 x 24.5" S, I, (H: 155) £1,840
Evening light, Roundstone, Co. Galway
O 16 x 20" S, I, (K: 227) £770
Figure in a Boat in Lake &
Mountain Landscape
O 11.5 x 16" S, (T: 89) £700
Garron Point, Antrim Coast
O 16 x 20" S, (BII: 34) £380
In The Maam Valley, Co. Galway
O 16 x 20" S, I, (K: 229) £990
Low Tide, Rockport, Cushendun, Co. Antrim
O 18 x 24" S, (YI: 37) £3,200
Lough Fee, Connemara
O 17 x 36", S, I, (P: 161) £920
Lough Inagh, Connemara
O 15 x 19" S, I, (Q: 124) £1,800
Mending the Boats
O 15 x 20" S, (XI: 19) £1,475
Muckish Mountain from Ards, Co. Donegal
O 12 x 16" S, I, (K: 231) £770
On the Antrim Uplands, above Cushendun
O 16 x 20" S, (M: 19) £1,750
Portrait
P 18 x 13" S, (P: 62) £160
Portrait of Nick McLaughlin of Cushendun
O 26 x 22" S, (K: 42) £550
Reflections, Roundstone, Connemara
O 18 x 36" S, I, (BII: 33) £1,250
Sandunes at Melmore, Co. Donegal
O 14 x 16" I, (Q: 114) £520
Silver Day, Dunfanaghy, Co. Donegal
O 20 x 26" S, (L: 96) £2,500
Sunlight and Shadow, Muckish Mountains,
Co. Donegal
O 15 x 18" S, (O: 22) £1,400

Tra-Na-Rossan, Co. Donegal
O 20 x 24" S, I, (CII: 105) £1,600
The Mourne Mountains from Minerstown, Co. Down
O 20 x 24" S, (XI: 29) £1,950
The Pool
O 18 x 14" S, I, (OI: 80) £1,430
Evening, Lough Ballinfad, Connemara
O 18 x 24" S, (KII: 130) £1,200
Reflections, Lough Derryclare, Connemara
O 18 x 24" S, (KII: 201) £800
Changing Weather, Larne, Co Antrim
O 16.75 x 20" S, (KII: 202) £450
Showery Day, Galway Coast
W 10 x 14.5" S, (KII: 203) £380
Roundstone Co Galway
W 10 x 14.25" S, (KII: 204) £320
Western Landscape, near Roundstone, Connemara
O 18 x 24" S, (KII: 132) £1,100
Donegal Cottage, Gortahork
O 17 x 20" S, (KII: 111) £4,200
Muckish Mountain, Co Donegal
O 20 x 27" S, (KII: 112) £3,000
The Rosses Country, Co Donegal
O 25 x 30.25" S, (KII: 109) £4,800
Among the Connemara Mountains near Recess,
Co Galway
O 20 x 24" S, I, (EII: 340) £3,450
West Coast Crofts
O 25 x 30" S, (EII: 342) £3,220
Killary Harbour, Leenane, Connemara
W 10 x 14.5" S, (GII: 1) £500
WILLIAMS, Alexander (1846-1930)
A Portrait of a Lady with Flowers
W 8 x 6" I, D, (Q: 52) £160
A Western lake scene
O 7.25 x 13.5" S, (HI: 252) £550
Diamond Mountain, Kylemore, Connemara
W 10.5 x 18.5" S, I, (S: 26) £300
Glen Granchan of the Northern Shore
O 14 x 24" (2) S, (N: 58) £1,050
Invery Bay, Donegal
W 8 x 15" S, I, (M: 16) £240
Kingston on Thames, River Scene & Coal Wharf
W 5.25 x 8.75" (2 I, (S: 110) £240
Lakeland scenes
O - (2) S, I, (HI: 253) £2,200
Landscape
O 7.25 x 10" S, (Q: 161) £300
Lough Conn, Co. Mayo
O 10.25 x 18.5" S, I, (HI: 254) £700
McCarthy's Castle, Killarney
W 7.5 x 14.125" S, I, (K: 4) £308
Misty Mountain Landscape with
Derelict Cottage
O 10 x 17.5" S, (T: 4) £500
Old Houses, Cork Street, Dublin
W 10.5 x 15" S, D, I, (P: 36) £340
Poolbeg, Dublin
D 4.5 x 7" (2) I, (Q: 113) £150
Poole Harbour Views
W 5.25 x 8.75" (2 I, D, (S: 111) £200
Rocky Coast, Brayhead, Co. Wicklow
O 17.5 x 9.75" S, (K: 176) £440
Rosapenna strand and the Ladies Cove
O 7 x 14" (2) S, (N: 53) £950
Seapoint & Sea Rescue, Dublin Bay
D 4.5 x 7" (2) S, I, (Q: 112) £150
Silent Evening
O 30 x 50" S, D, I, (K: 174) £5,500
The Glare of Summer
O 9.25 x 17.25" S, D, I, (BII: 35) £500
The Hour of Rest
O 7.75 x 14.5" S, I, (K: 175) £605
Views in Achill
O 6.75 x 14" S, (HI: 255) £1,600
Wooded river landscape
O 9.75 x 17.75" S, (N: 14) £650
A Most Distressful Country
O 9.75 x 15" S, I, (EII: 251) £977
WYNNE, Gladys (1878-1968)
River landscape
W 7.5 x 10.5" S, (R: 147) £85
YEATS, Jack Butler (1871-1957)
A carriage drawn by two horses
D 3.75 x 7" (L: 125) £250
A Dublin Newsboy (1912)
O 15 x 10.5" S, I, (O: 63) £36,000

A Full Tram
O 18 x 24" S, (O: 35) £56,000
A rustic cricketer; John Quinn & Peasant;
Self-portrait
W 11.5 x 8.75" S, D, I, (K: 74) £2,200
Addressed envelope with caricature figures
W 3.75 x 4.75" I, (K: 78) £2,750
Addressed envelope with Cowboy and Indians
& Autograph letter with sketches
W 9.75 x 7.25"/3. S, D, I, (K: 80) £4,950
Addressed envelope with ship and smugglers
W 5 x 8.75" I, (K: 82) £4,620
Addressed envelope with sketch of sailboat
W 4.5 x 3.75" I, (K: 79) £3,520
Alf Greer of St. Lukes and Young Cockney
Cowen of Leeds (1905)
D 5 x 3.5" I, (O: 86) £240
Allin Running
D 8.5 x 4.5" I, (K: 81) £880
Atlantic Coast
O 13.75 x 21" S, I, (TI: 62) £25,300
Autograph Letter and envelope with sketch
of Yeats and Synge
W 3.75 x 4.5" S, D, I, (K: 77) £6,600
Autograph letter with sketch of Robert Gregory
D 7 x 9" S, D, I, (K: 91) £572
Autograph letter with train 'Avoiding Athenryi'
W 7 x 4.5" S, D, I, (K: 87) £385
Christmas card with sketch of pirate
W 7 x 7.5" S, I, (K: 83) £1,540
Father Maurice
D 5 x 6" S, I, (N: 44) £600
George Robay
W 4.5 x 3.5" (2 I, (T: 100) £520
High Spring Tide, Rosses Point
O 18 x 24" S, (A: 79) £64,200
I'm Nobody in Particular
W 4.5 x 3.5" (2) I, (T: 97) £770
Looking Down on the Old Racecourse of Bowmore
O 8.75 x 13.75" S, (A: 93) £6,900
Looking Forwards, Looking Back
O 14 x 18" S, (TI: 32) £63,100
Man at a window and Ship in full sail
D 4 x 7.25" (L: 124) £210
Man with the Wrinkled Face
O 9 x 14" S, (XI: 89) £24,000
Music Hall Scene
W 3.5 x 4.5" I, (T: 102) £340
Music Hall Scene & On the Thames
(double sided)
W 3.5 x .4.5" I, (T: 103) £103
My Little Rose
W 4 x 5" S, (P: 119) £1,300
On the Thames
W 3.5 x 4.5" (T: 107) £400
Out
W 20 x 27" S, (L: 52) £2,600
Passing Barge
W 3.5 x 5" I, (P: 153) £480
Pirate with Crossbow & The Run Away Horse
W 5" ht cut-out (K: 97) £495
Portrait of a gentleman smoking a pipe
D 6.25 x 4.25" S, D, (O: 52) £720
Robert Gregory on Sarsfield, at the Gort Show
W 11.5 x 8.75" I, (K: 73) £4,400
Rockhill Dawn
O 14 x 21" S, I, (K: 258) £28,600
Sam Mayo
W 4.5 x3.5" (2) I, (T: 98) £580
Simon the Huntsman
D 5 x 6" S, I, (N: 47) £600
Simultaneous Dancers
W 4.5 x 3.5" (2) I, (T: 99) £520
Sligo
W 3.5 x 4.75" (5) (T: 69) £800
Stars
O 9 x 14" S, (O: 47) £29,000
Thames Hay Barge
W 3.5 x 4.5" I, (T: 104) £480
The Banquet Hall Deserted
O 24 x 36" S, I, (K: 185) £66,000
The Bather, 1918
O 18 x 24" S, (M: 27) £60,000
The Circus (1921)
O 14 x 18" S, (M: 42) £60,000
The Coal Boat
O 18 x 24" S, I, (C: 33) £45,500

The Dark Path
O 14 x 21" S, (B: 1316) £17,250
The Gay Moon
O 9 x 14" S, I, (K: 259) £28,600
The Haute Ecole Act
O 24 x 36" S, I, (K: 184) £220,000
The Kerry Mascot
O 13.75 x 8.75" S, I, (C: 30) £98,300
The Lesser Official (The Proprietor)
O 13.5 x 8.75" S, I, (C: 31) £84,000
The Morning Sea
O 24 x 36" S, (C: 32) £33,350
The Rag, 1945
O 18 x 24" S, (M: 57) £80,000
The Seafarer
W 6 x 4.5" S, (M: 26) £1,200
The Swan
O 10 x 14" S, (UI: 56) £19,550
The Thames
W 3.4 x 4.5" (T: 105) £300
The Vultures
W 4.5 x 3.5" I, (T: 101) £570
They are Far from the Land/ Me Dada/ Me
and Naree/ and sketch by A.E.
D 6.5 x 8.5" I, (K: 92) £715
Tinkers Encampment; The Blood of Abel (1940)
O 36 x 48" S, (P: 79) £505,000
Tunnel Pier
W 3.5 x4.5" (T: 106) £360
Two Characters from Oliver Twist
W 4.75" (double s I, D, (S: 136) £650
Two sets of twelve Broadsides
Pr (N: 54) £270
Waves at Bowmore (1936)
O 9 x 14" S, (S: 45) £15,000
Young Men
O 14 x 18" S, (TI: 31) £67,500
Archway in Galway
W 6.25 x 9.5" S, (KII: 78) £2,400
James Flaunty and the Scourge of the Gulph
hand coloured manuscripts and a black and white
bookplate, all in a morocco and gilt bound box
(KII: 194) £460
A Ship and a Horse
D 2.25 x 5.75" S, (KII: 171) £400
The Sea-Captain's Car
O 18 x 24" S, (EII: 305) £353,500
The Old Tar
M 6.75 x 3.75" S, (EII: 306) £3,680
A Bookmark for Ellen Terry
M 6.75 x 1.5" I, D, (EII: 308) £1,265
The Lighthouse Steamer, recto: Achill from
Geesala, verso
M3 x 4.75" I, (EII: 309) £977
Old Humbolt and the Missionary
D 6.74 x 6.75" S, I, (EII: 311) £575
An Illustrated Envelope
M 3.75 x 4.75" I, (EII: 313) £690
The Readers
O 10 x 14" S, (EII: 314) £73,000
The Atlantic
O 8.75 x 14" S, I, (EII: 316) £25,300
The Good Grey Morning
O 20 x 27" S, (EII: 317) £54,300
The Glutton of Evening
O 14 x 18" S, I, (EII: 319) £34,500
The Days of Heroes
O 9 x 14" S (EII: 320) £25,300
Singing 'The Dark Rosaleen', Croke Park
O 18 x 24" S, (EII: 321) £496,500
Dusty Lane, Co Kerry
O 9 x 14" S, (GII: 78) £21,000
The Tar Tar & Belmullet Bonfire
W each 5 x 3.5" S, (GII: 53) £600
YEATS, John (1839-1922)
Portrait of Sarah Allgood
D 8.75 x 7.5" S, (O: 96) £850
Portrait of Sarah Alice Lawson, bust-length, in
a lace trimmed pink dress
O 24.5 x 20.25" (KII: 20) £2,400
Self-Portrait
D 19.25 x 14.25" S, D, (EII: 307) £2,875
YOUNG, Mabel (1890-1973)
The Little Sugar Loaf in Wicklow
O 20 x 24" S, (P: 7) £970
Wicklow Landscape
O 15.5 x 21.5" S, (M: 51) £350

INDEX TO IRISH ARTS REVIEW YEARBOOK
VOL 12, 1996

INDEX OF ADVERTISERS IN IRISH ARTS REVIEW YEARBOOK 1996. VOL 12

PICTURE CREDITS FOR IRISH ARTS REVIEW YEARBOOK 1996

The numbers are those of the pages on which the photographs appear

Frontispiece Michael Warren; 1 Irish Times; 27, 31 (Fig 8) Maurice Craig: 28 (Fig. 3), 29 (Fig. 5), 30 The Conway Library, Courtauld Institute of Art; 28 (Fig. 2), 29 (Fig. 4), 31 (Fig 9), 32, 34 Irish Architectural Archive; 33, Alistair Rowan; 46 Christie's; 47 Sotheby's, Sussex; 48 Dan McMonagle; 49 Jonathan Hession; 50 (Fig. 9) Sotheby's, (Fig. 10) Christie's; 51 Peter Mooney; 53, 54 Christie's; 66 Irish Architectural Archive; 67, 68 Christie's; 72-79 Roy Hewson; 80, 82 James Adam & Son; 81 Gorry Gallery; 84 Witt Library; 98 Roy Hewson; 102 (Fig. 1) Irish Architectural Archive; 104, 107 National Library of Ireland; 111 Trustees of the Ulster Museum; 110, 113 (Figs 5 & 8); 114 (Fig. 9) National Museum of Ireland; 113 (Fig. 6) Board of Trinity College Dublin; 127 Phillips Fine Art Auctioneers; 128 Illustrated London News/Brendan Dempsey; 130 Sotheby's; 131 Courtauld Institute of Art; 132 Simon Dickinson Ltd., London; 133 National Portrait Gallery Archive, London; 134 (Fig. 6) Birr Scientific Heritage Foundation; 135 (Fig. 8) National Portrait Gallery Archive, London; 136 (Fig. 10) Exeter Museums, (Fig. 11) and 137 British Museum; 139, 140, 143-146 Irish Architectural Archive; 146 (Fig. 8) Alan Betson; 156, 158-162 Trevor Hart; 163, 170 Irish Times; 172-174 Alan Betson.

CUMULATIVE INDEX TO IRISH ARTS REVIEW, VOLS, 1-12 1984-1996

Every article published in *Irish Arts Review* (Vols 1-12) is listed in the
Author Index. The Subject Indices which follow are cross-referenced to the
Author Index.

AUTHOR INDEX

Named Artists & Craftsmen

Cumulative Index to Irish Arts Review, Vols, 1-12 1984-1996

SCULPTURE, CARVING, DECORATION

The Church and the Artist: Practice and Patronage 1922-45	Breathnach-Lynch, S
Ceramics as Sculpture	McCrum, S
Classical and Celtic Influences in the Figure-Styles of Early Irish Sculpture	McNab, S
Continental Influence in Eighteenth Century Ireland (Its Painting and Sculpture)	Turpin, J
Bronze by Gold, The Work of Irish Women Sculptors	Walker, D
Lively Irishmen: The Ruskinian Tradition in Ireland (Stone Carving in Ireland)	Sheehy, J
The Japanese Minor Arts of Netsuke and Imo	Hickey, P
The Acquisti Panels at Lyons House	Cashen, P
Eighteenth Century Papier-mache Ceiling Decoration	Griffin, D
Plasterwork Restoration at Birr Castle	Rosse, A

Parnell Monument: Ireland and American Beaux Arts	Rothery, S
The Politics of the Street Monument (Nineteenth Century Dublin monuments)	Murphy, P
A Monument by Grinling Gibbons in St Patrick's Cathedral, Dublin	McParland, E
Timothy Turner: An Eighteenth Century Dublin Ironsmith	O'Connor, M

STAINED GLASS

Wilhelmina Geddes' Ottawa Window	Brown, S, A
Michael Healy's Stained Glass Window of 'St Victor'	Caron, D
A New Setting for Evie Hone's Rahan Windows	Symondson, A
Richard King's Kevin Barry Memorial Window	Sheehy, R
An Túr Gloine Stained Glass in Arizona	Caron, D

BOOK REVIEWS